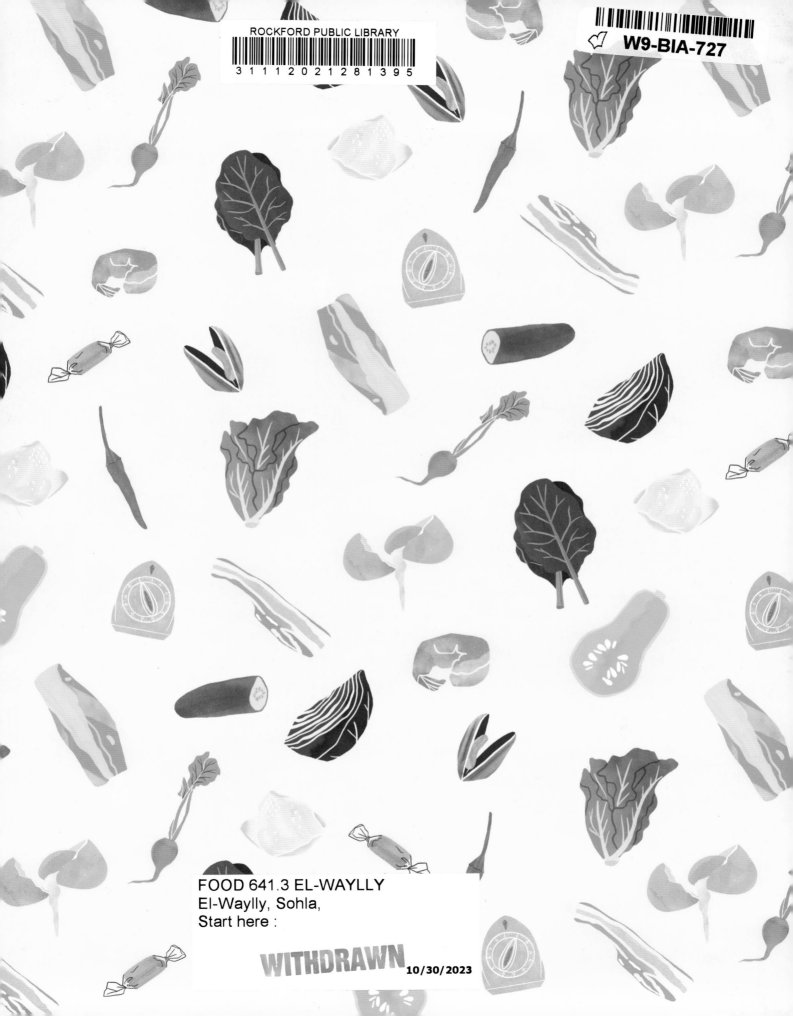

Start Here

Start Here

Instructions for Becoming a Better Cook

Sohla El-Waylly

Foreword by Samin Nosrat

Photographs by Laura Murray
Illustrations by Aly Miller
Design by Chris Cristiano

Alfred A. Knopf   New York   2023

To Ham,
I'm so lucky I get to spend my life messing up
in the kitchen with you.

Start Here ⬇

BAKING & PASTRY LESSONS

Contents

Recipe Index

Salads

Soups

Eggs

Vegetables

> In each category, recipes are listed from light to heavy.
> **E** = easy | **I** = intermediate | **A** = advanced | **V** = vegetarian (or can be with simple substitutions)
> **VV** = vegan (or can be with simple substitutions)
> **GF** = gluten-free (or can be with simple substitutions)

Rice

Pasta, Grains & Beans

Seafood

Meat

In each category, recipes are listed from light to heavy.
E = easy | **I** = intermediate | **A** = advanced | **V** = vegetarian (or can be with simple substitutions)
VV = vegan (or can be with simple substitutions)
GF = gluten-free (or can be with simple substitutions)

Cookies

In each category, recipes are listed from light to heavy.
E = easy | **I** = intermediate | **A** = advanced | **V** = vegetarian (or can be with simple substitutions)
VV = vegan (or can be with simple substitutions)
GF = gluten-free (or can be with simple substitutions)

Pies

Puddings

In each category, recipes are listed from light to heavy.
E = easy | **I** = intermediate | **A** = advanced | **V** = vegetarian (or can be with simple substitutions)
VV = vegan (or can be with simple substitutions)
GF = gluten-free (or can be with simple substitutions)

Pastries & Treats

Base Pastry Recipes

In each category, recipes are listed from light to heavy.
E = easy | **I** = intermediate | **A** = advanced | **V** = vegetarian (or can be with simple substitutions)
VV = vegan (or can be with simple substitutions)
GF = gluten-free (or can be with simple substitutions)

Foreword

By Samin Nosrat

Right now, you're holding the book I wish someone had handed me when I began my own journey as a cook. Instead, I was given a list, thirty titles long, of books filled with terms like *daube* and *brunoise,* with which to familiarize myself. It was unbelievably intimidating. I could hardly distinguish between parsley and cilantro, and suddenly I had to learn all the French names for everything in the kitchen, too. Not knowing what else to do, I began to cook.

It took me *years* of cooking from books and in a professional setting to really understand the hows and whys of the kitchen. Because there was no one to take me gently by the hand and teach me how to cook without judgment, with kindness, humor, and confidence. Because there was no Sohla yet.

Typically, the best we can hope for from a cookbook is clear enough instruction to guide us to our destination—a treasure map. But that doesn't really teach us to cook. It teaches us only to follow directions. The real challenge of a teacher, whether in person or on the page, is to empower students to think for themselves, to understand what is happening, and why, so that they can correct course when things go wrong—as they always do. Or so that they can fearlessly apply the lessons they've learned about cooking chicken on the stove to the campfire. Or so that they can look at a winter squash at the grocery store and see a perfectly suitable substitution for spring asparagus.

With this book, Sohla El-Waylly does all of that, and more. Whether you're a total novice or have your own chef's coat and knife roll, *Start Here* has something to teach you. We are the lucky beneficiaries of her decades of expertise, practice, and failure in the kitchen, of her boundless curiosity, and, of course, of her limitless generosity as a teacher. I, for one, have been bowled over by Sohla's extensive pastry know-how (I finally know why my chocolate pudding turns runny after it appears set! Hallelujah!). Sohla has improved my cooking, and I guarantee she will improve yours, too.

Start Here isn't a treasure map. Sohla isn't a cartographer. She is a master alchemist, and this is the manual that will teach you how to confidently craft your own treasure, each and every time you enter the kitchen.

Introduction

Introduction

I look like someone who would have done well in school. I don't know if it's the glasses, sharp bob haircut, model minority myth, or some combo of all the above, but people assume I was that girl in the front row with my hand always up. The truth is, I almost didn't graduate high school due to an excess of absences, I dropped out of college in my freshman year (don't worry, aunties, I eventually went back), and I nearly failed my final culinary school exam because I didn't know how to read an analog clock and thought I had an extra thirty minutes for the test.

I always struggled to learn the way I was *supposed* to learn, whether in the high school geography class I had to repeat or in a restaurant kitchen following a chef's blunt commands. Blindly memorizing state capitals or the steps to making rice pilaf doesn't work for me; it feels like trying to retain sentences in a language I don't speak. The teachers who taught me lessons that stuck were the ones who gave me context. Did you know that the capital of Alaska is named after Joseph Juneau, because he bribed some folks with booze to name it after him? Or that by toasting rice in fat before adding liquid (in a process called parching) you deactivate the surface starches, which ensures a clump-free, fluffy pilaf? But there's rarely time for that in a professional kitchen. When I first started cooking, I was taught to follow strict orders: laminate the pasta three times, bloom the gelatin in cold water, pat the steak dry before searing. But I don't know, maybe because I'm a naturally curious person or just have a problem with authority, I've never been satisfied with being told to just follow the rules. I needed to learn the whys, so I could confidently figure out the hows and whats. I mean, now I'll never forget the capital of Alaska or the most important step in making a pilaf, and you probably won't either.

Once I learned this fun fact about myself, I couldn't stop learning fun facts: You laminate pasta dough in order to weave the gluten network so that cooked noodles have a better chew. You bloom gelatin in cold water so it hydrates evenly and dissolves without any lumps. You pat a steak dry before searing because browning is slowed down in the presence of moisture. Digging a little deeper doesn't just make me the smartass everyone already assumed I was (although some of my former chefs might disagree), it allows me to understand bigger concepts that can be applied to countless dishes rather than trying to memorize a bunch of random commands for one recipe.

My stubborn way of thinking ended up being the superpower that's helped me teach and train countless cooks throughout my years as a professional chef, pastry chef, and recipe developer. In this book I'm here to teach you the way I've learned to cook, with nerdy deep dives and so much context behind the steps of every recipe. Think of this book as a one-stop culinary school in a book (without years of inescapable debt!). It will teach you foundational techniques and basic food science to hone your skills and intuition, whether you're a skilled culinary veteran who wants to look at things from another perspective or you've never even boiled an egg.

Each chapter in this book explores a topic that I believe is indispensable to any cook, with equal emphasis on savory and pastry—because a good cook shouldn't be afraid of anything in the kitchen. The lessons are divided into two parts, Culinary Lessons and Baking & Pastry Lessons. This is by no means an all-encompassing book about how to cook everything; that would be literally impossible. We're not grilling, there isn't much deep-frying, and I don't offer a single recipe with a wok. Instead, these core lessons are meant to offer a general grasp of vital culinary techniques to get you going on your journey. I'm offering you a place to start.

You can pick a few recipes at random and have a great meal. Or you can treat each chapter like a class: Read through the chapter to learn the concepts, then cook the recipes to gain practical knowledge of each technique. You'll learn all about braising in the Break It Down & Get Saucy chapter (page 155) and practice those skills by making Coconut Cauliflower Korma (page 182) and Stuffed Squid with Sofrito & Saffron (page 186). You'll become a gluten guru in the Getting to Know Dough chapter (page 475), then bake the fluffiest Parker House Rolls (page 516) and Perfectly Puffy Pitas (page 502). This book isn't just about the recipes (although there's a ton of them), it's also about the techniques. Once you learn how to sear a chicken thigh in a skillet so the skin gets crisp while the meat stays juicy, you can easily translate those skills to the open fire of a grill. Become an expert in basic egg cookery and simple sautés, and those temperature management chops will prime you for deep-frying and the fast action of wok stir-fries. Many recipes offer ways to "Get Loose!" so you can make it your own. Particularly hard recipes have a "What the Hell Happened?" guide so you can evaluate any issues and make the dish better the next time. The ultimate goal of this book is for you to gain a deep understanding of cooking so you can confidently try new cuisines, get creative in the kitchen, and, most important, make dinner.

You're Gonna Mess Up, but It's Gonna Be Okay

The first time I made a genoise was for Mother's Day when I was somewhere between eight and ten years old. A genoise is a delicate sponge cake enriched with butter and egg yolks. I had never eaten a genoise, I wasn't sure what a genoise was, and I definitely hadn't made one before. But after coming across the recipe in the pages of my first non–children's cookbook, *At Home with the French Classics* by Richard Grausman, I decided to go for it. What I ended up with was a flat, dense, sweet omelet. I didn't know how things were supposed to be whipped. I didn't know how things were supposed to be folded. Unfortunately, those happen to be the two most important steps to making a genoise.

So, there I was sitting on the floor crying (a lot of my early-cooking stories end up with me on the floor crying), holding this sweet omelet in my arms. My abu came home from work and asked me what was going on. He didn't say anything, turned around, and walked out the door. I assumed the worst, that my terrible baking had driven my family apart, but ten minutes later, he came back with a dozen eggs and I made the genoise again. It was only slightly better, but we stacked those two dense omelet cakes together with some pretty halfway decent frosting and celebrated Mother's Day. I'm never gonna forget it, because that's when I learned the most important cooking lesson: that you just have to keep trying. You're gonna mess up, but it's gonna be okay.

My confidence in the kitchen comes from failing. That might come as a surprise to those of you who now know me as the girl on your screen teaching you how to dauntlessly butcher a whole chicken, but in the beginning, I failed a lot, and it's nothing to be afraid of. Failing in the kitchen is an opportunity to zigzag, reassess, and think creatively to fix your failure into something delicious (or at least edible, because sometimes that's enough). The thing about failing is, the more you fail the less scary it'll feel. When I started cooking, every bump in the recipe road would send me into a tailspin. Stuck salmon fillets would lead me to the bathroom floor to cry, undercooked Thanksgiving turkeys would make me collapse on the kitchen floor and cry, broken gingerbread houses left me in the grocery store aisle clutching boxes of powdered sugar on the floor, yep, crying.

Now I welcome every mistake because it's just an opportunity to learn, get better, and discover something new. I seek out challenging situations or intentionally impose limitations on myself because that's when I think cooking is the most fun. Confidence isn't about always doing everything perfectly. It's about moving forward after you've messed up and believing in yourself enough to try again.

As you cook through this book you will make mistakes. There will undoubtedly be overcooked steaks, floppy green beans, and salty vinaigrettes in your future. I'm going to teach you how to assess your failures so you can fix them. I believe in you, because I've made all the same mistakes. And if you do end up on the floor clutching a pot of mushy rice and crying, that's okay, too. I'll help you turn it into rice porridge and top it with a crispy fried egg. So wipe your face, get up off the floor, and dig right in.

How to Use This Book

Each chapter in this book focuses on one fundamental technique. Before each group of recipes is a lesson in which I'll walk you through everything you need to know about that technique, while the recipes that follow offer a way to practice what you've learned. The chapters are organized in the order I believe they are best taught, while the recipes in each chapter are in order of difficulty. But I'm not you, so it might make more sense for you to do things your own way.

Easy recipes are fast, require few ingredients, and are a good way to get to know a new technique. **Intermediate recipes** require more time and skill, and **advanced recipes** are for when you've got a technique down and are ready to push yourself. Or course, you can jump around and make whatever you want without reading the lesson. The headnotes will have any special info you might need. Check out the Recipe Index (page viii) to peruse all the recipes in the book and the Putting It All Together section (page 549) at the end for menu ideas and game plans.

Cooking from Both Sides

In most cookbooks, dessert gets one puny chapter, unless it's a separate desserts-only book. This is the first cookbook to give savory and pastry equal billing. I believe that it's by learning how to cook everything—sweet, savory, and in-between—that I've become adept and creative in the kitchen. If you think you're a savory- or pastry-only person, join me and give the other side a try. Cooking savory food is all about touch, feel, and improvisation, while pastry requires precision and focus. Bring the two together and you'll start cooking the same way a skilled jazz musician riffs with their band, confidently weaving everything you know together. You'll become more patient and aware while cooking savory food, while relying more on your instincts when baking.

When I started working in restaurants, I kicked things off as a line cook working on savory stuff. The savory cooks I worked with took pride in how little they knew about dessert, bragging that they'd never even baked so much as a chocolate chip cookie. I worked for chefs who believed that pastry required no skills and was just about following a recipe—anyone who could read could do it. They thought pastry was a place for girls to follow the rules and stay in their lane, while cooking savory on the line was a masculine endeavor, a demanding art form requiring years to perfect. I don't think the cooks and chefs spewing this nonsense realized that these beliefs were actually just stunting their own development.

Over and over again, I found myself the only girl in the kitchen, so pastry kept trickling into my life. I would get hired as a line cook, but if the pastry team was swamped or someone didn't show, they'd throw me onto the other side. I learned how to prep and roast cases of whole chickens right alongside mixing and piping a thousand pâte à choux. I'd be cleaning chicken livers and beef tongue one minute, then tempering chocolate and rolling truffles the next. The men in the kitchen probably thought they were getting rid of me, but it actually gave me a leg up.

Savory and pastry seem to require opposing skill sets, temperaments, and equipment, but by learning how to do it all you'll develop a lifetime of unmatchable skills.

Tips for Cooking Through a Recipe

1. Read through the entire recipe before you get going—a couple of times if it's an unfamiliar or advanced technique. I recommend getting in there with a highlighter and pen and marking the whole thing up.

2. If you're cooking through more than one recipe, **make a game plan** (page xxxi).

3. Serving sizes are personal. My estimates are based on how my guests and I typically eat, but you might need more or less for you and your people. Keep in mind that **the more dishes you make per meal, the more servings you'll get from each item.**

4. I recommend you **measure by either volume or weight depending on the specific recipe.** For most savory cooking, extreme precision not only can slow you down, but also dampen your instincts, so in those cases I prefer volume and eyeballing certain ingredients. Pastry, on the other hand, requires precision, so I recommend you use a scale and measure in grams most of the time. I don't offer weights for pastry recipes in nonmetric units (like ounces and pounds) because decimal points are annoying and far too many folks confuse ounces with fluid ounces. For ingredients under 1 tablespoon, unless you have a microscale, volume is significantly more accurate. (Really! The average scale is accurate only to the nearest 2 grams, which is enough to throw off the leavening in cake.) I'll always list my preferred measurement first, with an alternative listed second if applicable.

5. Rely on sensory cues more than time cues. Your kitchen and equipment are different from mine, and every ingredient is unique. Use touch, smell, sight, and sound to determine doneness instead of just a timer.

6. Don't forget to **taste** early and often.

Want Extra Credit?

Evaluate your dishes after you cook them. Do you like the final taste, aroma, and texture? How could it be better? Leave yourself notes so the next time you make the recipe you've got all that knowledge to grow from. And do make a recipe more than once. Practice is the only way to get better.

Why I Love a Game Plan

As a professional cook, I was always late. I worked at a tasting-menu-only restaurant in Tribeca, where management had no patience for tardiness. We had to be in the kitchen, whites on and knives sharp, at 10 a.m., no exceptions. Service started at 6, but our stations needed to be set up and prepped by 4:30. The best cook would actually be ready at 4. (He liked to take 30 minutes to style his hair before service.) If you've ever worked in a restaurant, you know that this is not normal. What's normal is scrambling till the very last moment, cleaning vegetables and portioning meat, right until the first ticket prints—and sometimes even after things get cranking. Here, cooks had to be totally RTG (ready to go) by 4:30 so we could gather around the pass and take a minute to unwind before the long service ahead.

I never made it to the preservice matcha, instead rushing to churn ice cream at 4:15, pick herbs at the pass at 4:35, and get my plates lined up at 4:45. I didn't understand why being so ready so early was so important, but I was sick of being the only one who didn't make it on time. I wanted some damn matcha, too. I needed to prove to the rest of the cooks (and myself) that I could be set up on time. So every morning on the train to work, I'd break down my day into 15-minute increments (yes, including bathroom breaks). I'd start by writing a list of everything I needed to do before my 4:30 deadline and how long each task should take. Clean scallops—22 minutes. Portion beef tartar—15 minutes. Trim and blanch cabbage leaves—35 minutes. Next, I'd organize the list to make sure I was moving as efficiently as possible. Setting myself up to do all my veg prep at once, before moving on to sauces and vinaigrettes, and planning my blender tasks in one shot to minimize wasted movement.

I finally did get fast and organized enough to set up on time, and it made me more than just efficient. Now, cooking at home, by not wasting my thoughts on what I'm going to do next, I can target all my energy into what I'm doing *right now*. I can focus more intently, be deliberate and precise with my actions, and ultimately make better food. I no longer plan my day in 15-minute increments (most of the time), but I still make a game plan before cooking anything, whether it's a quick weekday breakfast or a multicourse dinner party. Taking even the briefest moment to figure out what I'm going to do makes all my cooking better.

How to Make a Game Plan

1. Zoom out and take an overhead view of all the steps in all the dishes you're making. Then break the recipes apart and weave them back together into one mega recipe. (For an example of this, check out the Fancy Weekend Scramble recipe on page 94.)

2. Think about how you can make your movements more efficient:

• What can you prep in advance?

• Make use of inactive time: You don't always have to do all your cleaning/prepping first. For example, get something sautéing while you chop stuff for the next step.

• Group together similar tasks, like vegetable prep, brining proteins, or making sauces and vinaigrettes.

• Think about how long each task takes—long cooking steps should start first while quick sautés should be last. And make dessert and breads in advance whenever possible.

3. Don't ever get too set into a game plan. Mistakes happen, steps get overlooked, so always be flexible enough to adapt as you cook.

Things to Have

These are the essentials that I think every home cook should own—*eventually.* If you're starting from scratch, buying all these items will be a significant investment, so don't feel like you must get everything right away, or at all. Most of the recipes in this book don't need any special equipment. However, if you take the time to build out your kitchen with these items, you'll be set up to cook almost anything. I've purchased most of my kitchen equipment at restaurant supply stores, auctions, and thrift stores. The great thing about high-quality kitchen equipment is that it lasts forever. You can scrub and reseason a rusty Lodge cast-iron skillet, sand down the nicks on a Boos cutting board, or polish up an old All-Clad saucepan. So with the exception of easily damaged items, like scales and thermometers, buying secondhand is often my first choice.

Core Tools

Oven Thermometer

If you buy one thing, it should be an oven thermometer. I don't care how fancy or new your oven is, I bet you anything it isn't the temperature it claims to be. I always keep a cheap analog oven thermometer hanging off the back of the center rack and check it after my oven has heated. My oven is always off by at least 10°F, not enough to affect a slow-braised short rib, but total disaster for a layer cake.

Kitchen Scale

When I was a kid, my dream was to own a pocket-sized television. All I wished for was to watch *The Fresh Prince of Bel-Air* alone in a corner when my parents dragged me to weekly dinner parties. Now, we live in a world where somehow my wildest childhood fantasy has come true, but people are still baking without a scale. The technology is readily available. You can order a backlit digital scale accurate to the gram right now and it will be on your doorstep in two days. By the time this book is published, it will probably be delivered by drone. And yet, many American cooks still fumble around with cups and spoons while asking Alexa how many tablespoons are in a pound.

I was once like you. When I first started cooking, something about using a scale made baking and pastry seem scarier. I always knew that baking wasn't something I could just wing, but having a tool with buttons and an LCD display in the kitchen really hammered it home. But once you get the hang of using a scale, I promise it's faster, easier, and (obviously) more accurate. For a hardy affordable scale, I recommend the Escali Primo scale, but if you want to level it up, reach for the Oxo Good Grips scale.

Fine-Mesh Sieves

These are a pastry must for sifting and dusting, but also to take your savory soups and sauces to the next level by ensuring they are lump-free and silky smooth. I like to have an assortment of sizes for anything from tiny tasks like dusting cookies with powdered sugar to hefty ones for straining out chicken wings after simmering for bone broth. If you have it in your budget to buy just one, choose a large and sturdy sieve that can tackle any task. Look for a sieve that's one solid metal piece rather than having a separately attached handle, which can break off after prolonged use.

Mixing Bowls
I think you know why you need these. Get as many as you can store and be sure to have at least one really big bowl. I always stick with stainless steel bowls because glass in a kitchen is risky (why do you think all chefs drink out of plastic deli containers?).

Salad Spinner
I lived a long time without a salad spinner. I'd just shove my washed greens into a clean pillowcase and take them for a whirl over my head. But let me tell you, owning one is awesome. No more wet ceilings or splatters across the TV mean I spin-dry more often, everything from button mushrooms to veggies with nooks and crannies, like broccoli or cauliflower. Without all that excess water slowing them down, they sear and sauté faster.

Sheet Pans & Racks
You can never have too many sheet pans. Not only are they a must-have for baking cookies and sheet cakes, but they're also perfect for roasting vegetables and meats—I don't even own a roasting pan. Sheet pans keep me organized while I prep, giving me a place to stage all my mise en place. And the combo of sheet pan and wire rack is absolutely necessary when dry-brining meat, resting a steak, or draining fried items. Unlike cookie sheets and the like, sheet pans come in standard sizes, allowing them to stack easily and fit wire racks seamlessly. Half-sheet pans (the ones that are 18 × 13 inches) are the ones that fit in a standard home oven, but I love having stacks on stacks of quarter- and eighth-sheet pans for tasks like toasting nuts, baking one cookie on-demand, and organizing my tools (and office supplies, and makeup, and dog medication . . .). Look for ones made of heavy-gauge aluminum with rolled edges, which are less likely to warp over time.

Stiff Silicone Spatula

Not a flimsy silicone spatula. A rigid, heatproof silicone spatula from a restaurant supply store won't come in cute colors or have any style, but it'll stand by you for years. The solid design can handle tough tasks, like scraping up every speck of the browned bits that develop during searing, and offers enough give to curve into the arc of a bowl.

Angle-Tipped Tiny Spatula

These have become my go-to for almost every task, even ones that they aren't well designed for, like stirring a full Dutch oven's worth of thick stew. What they are made for is getting you into tough spots—scrape that last bit of peanut butter out of a jar or scooch under the blade of a blender so nothing's left behind. I use one anytime I need to stir with precision, like when I'm swirling the eggs in a classic French omelet (page 91).

Mini Offset Spatula

It flips! It spreads! It smooshes! The thin, sturdy blade on this mighty 4½-inch spreader can frost a cake, butter toast, and flip small items, like planks of seared tofu or mini pancakes.

Fish Spatula

Conventional rectangular metal spatulas have short heads and squat bodies, giving you less area for flipping and making it hard to get into tight spots. That type of spatula isn't designed for a pan. Instead, it belongs on a flattop griddle, slinging around large volumes of food like hash browns and carne asada—and for the home cook, it's truly only useful for pressing ground beef flat into smash burgers. If you want to cook something other than a burger, stick to the more agile fish spatula instead. Fish spatulas have flexible, long slotted heads designed to slide under delicate fillets of fish. Their blade-like angled edge can maneuver in crowded skillets, easily flipping a dozen sunny-side eggs over easy.

Big Spoons (Holey and Not-Holey)

The fastest way to feel like a five-star chef is by butter-basting something with a big spoon. Kunz spoons are the industry standard. Their large heads and short handles give you the control to precisely plate sauces and purees, while slotted versions are great for poaching, frying, testing pasta, or scooping a boiled egg out of water.

Whisk

Whisks come in all shapes and sizes and each has its own special power. Sturdy, coiled Danish whisks are masters at mixing bread dough, while the rounded tines of a ball whisk get into the tight corners of a pot or splay open across a skillet while scrambling eggs. Narrow French whisks were born to mix smooth béchamels and whip up fluffy meringues. Depending on what you cook most in your kitchen, it might be useful to own a range of whisks for various tasks, but if you want one whisk to rule them all, a balloon whisk is the way to go. While not the best for getting into corners or mixing especially thick doughs, it's a solid choice for just about everything else.

Tweezer Tongs

There are a lot of tools from my fancy restaurant days that I can't imagine using now. Dressing a salad with single-use pipettes? Who was I kidding! But one thing I'll never let go of is my tweezer tongs. They grip, grab, flip, and turn like the snappiest, clackiest tongs, but with the precision and delicate touch of—you guessed it—tweezers.

Cake Tester

Don't let the name fool you, what cake testers excel at is helping you judge the doneness of meat, fish, and vegetables. The slick metal probe doesn't allow cake crumbs to adhere to it, so you're better off sticking to toothpicks and your fingers for your cake-testing needs.

Kitchen Towels

I like a novelty alligator pot holder as much as the next person, but nothing brings a smile to my face more than

**Core Tools
(cont'd.)**

a towering stack of blue-striped cotton kitchen towels. These are the ones restaurant pros use for nearly everything, from moving hot sheet pans out of the oven to wiping down the entire kitchen at the end of every night. They are delicate enough to polish glassware but sturdy enough to survive countless wash cycles. Oh, and super cheap, so get plenty.

Plastic Bowl Scraper

Whether I'm cooking or baking, I always keep a bowl scraper by my side. It can do everything a metal bench scraper can do, the wide blade can scoop chopped onions from cutting board to skillet, but because it's flexible, you can also use it to fold and scrape doughs.

Spider

Nothing is better at scooping pasta and eggs out of boiling water, and it's a must-have every time you fry, safely and quickly lifting French fries and frito misto out of bubbling hot oil.

Deli Containers

Deli containers come in 1-cup, 1-pint, and 1-quart sizes. I have a full shelf dedicated to them and can't live without them. They are the ultimate kitchen workhorse. Yes, obviously, you can store stuff in them, but for a long time deli containers also stepped in as my glassware, plateware, and serviceware. I've moved up in the world and now own plates, but nothing beats them for portioning, prepping, and storage. Oh, and did I mention they stack, have universal lids, and are endlessly reuseable! In the Make-Ahead Steamed Egg Sandwiches (page 84), they're ideal for steaming the egg cakes into the perfect size and shape for sandwich stacking. You can buy them online, in restaurant supply stores, or save them from your takeout.

Wooden Cutting Boards

Cutting boards come in a wide range of materials from marble to glass to stoneware, but I recommend you stick to plastic or wood. The fastest way to dull your knife is to rock it against a hard surface, like marble or glass. Not to mention, your knife is more likely to slip and slide, adding unnecessary risk to mealtime.

Plastic and wooden boards are durable while offering a little give beneath the blade, keeping your knives sharper longer. Between plastic or wood, I'm wood all the way. They may not be dishwasher safe, but if you take care of a good wooden board it will last forever and be a beautiful addition to your kitchen. Any deep scratches that develop over time can always be sanded away, while a plastic board will need to be replaced after suffering too many lacerations. But if you like the convenience of a lightweight dishwasher-safe board, then plastic might be for you.

I have three wooden cutting boards, a papa bear, a mama bear, and a baby bear. The big papa (24 × 36 inches) is my go-to board for almost everything, almost all of the time. It allows me to sprawl out my prep, slicing and piling onions in one corner while grating cheese on the opposite. I can set up all my mise en place for an average meal on it, so cleanup is just a quick rinse or thorough wipe down. Because this board sees a lot of action, I prefer one that's at least 1½ inches thick (but thicker is better), which is less likely to warp and offers plenty of girth to sand down over time as needed.

The medium board (13 × 18 inches) is reserved for breaking down raw meat and fish—the smaller size makes it easier to scrub down in a sink. Contrary to popular belief, research has shown that plastic cutting boards are not safer for butchering raw proteins. Wood has natural antibacterial properties making it difficult for bacteria to live on its surface. Because the surface is porous, through capillary action, bacteria is pulled into the board where it starves and dies. However, a plastic cutting board with lots of deep cuts and slashes (which can easily develop over time) gives bacteria places to lurk and thrive. The best way to prevent contamination is to always use a separate board for raw meat and sanitize it and the surrounding surfaces before continuing with any other prep.

My little baby board (6 ×10 inches) is great for a last-minute lemon wedge or to slice up an apple snack. It's my in-between-meals board when I don't want to get the big one messy. It also steps in for the dirty tasks, like mincing fresh turmeric or chopping beets, to keep the main board stain-free.

Cutting Board Maintenance

Moisturize!
Once a month I spend some quality time, just me and my cutting board family. Wood is porous and kind of alive—it expands and contracts, absorbs moisture and dries out. Without any TLC even the best wooden cutting board can crack, warp, or even rot from the inside. Luckily, all you need to prevent all of that is monthly moisturization.

1. Start with a clean and dry board: Using a soft dish sponge, scrub clean with dish soap. Remove any tough stains with a mixture of baking soda and water. Never use any harsh abrasives like bleach or steel wool. Rinse and then dry the board with a towel and leave it standing on its edge to fully dry. (If you can, it's best to store your board standing on its edge when not in use so moisture doesn't fester underneath.) When washing your board, be sure to wet both sides. This ensures that both sides are equally moist and dry at the same rate to prevent warping.

2. Apply a generous layer of food-grade mineral oil: Lay the board flat so excess oil doesn't run off, and use your hands to spread a thick layer of mineral oil all over one side, rubbing into the edges and any grooves. Why mineral oil? Unlike most other oils, such as canola, olive, or coconut, mineral oil is totally flavorless and won't grow rancid over time.

3. Give it time to soak in: Let it sit for a few hours and preferably overnight to drink in as much oil as possible.

4. Buff and repeat: Use a towel to rub away any excess oil the board didn't soak up. Next, buff the board, rubbing in any last remnants of oil. It should not feel slick or greasy when you're done. Flip and repeat on the other side.

• Level up: To give your board an almost velvety feel, after oiling both sides, rub them down with board cream. Board cream is a mixture of food-grade mineral oil and beeswax that you can purchase or make yourself. Using a towel, rub a thin, even layer all over the board. No need to wipe it off after.

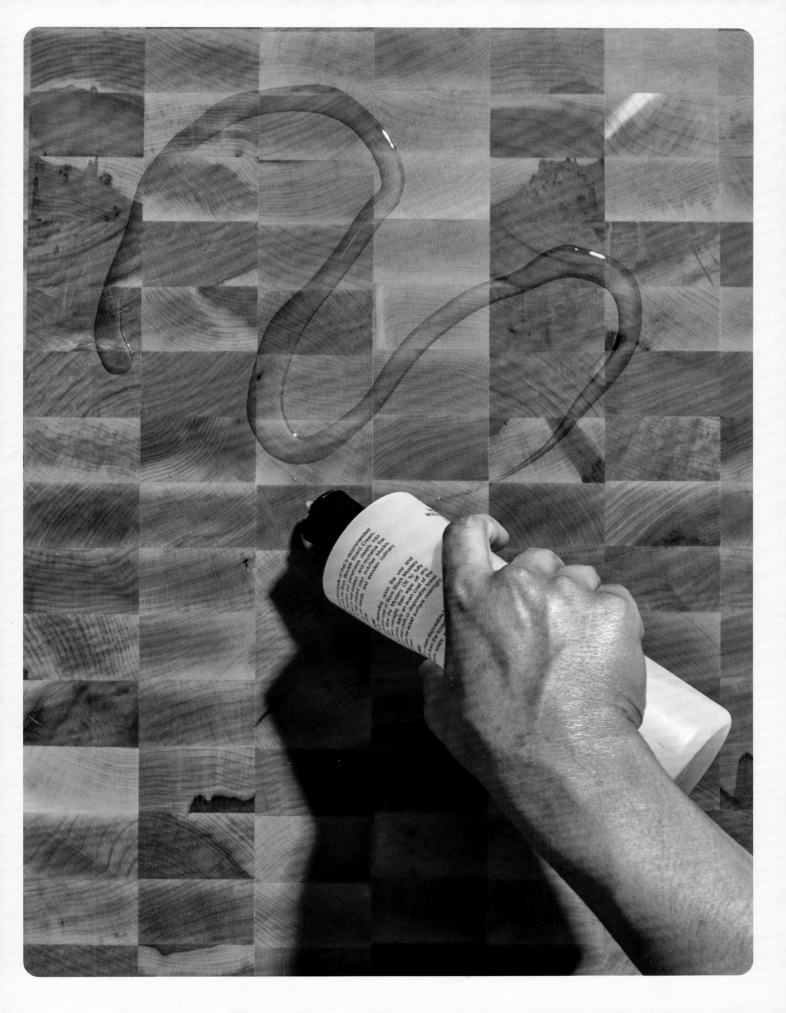

Cookware

6- to 8-Quart Enameled Cast-Iron Dutch Oven

These thick-walled pots are excellent at retaining heat, just what you need for deep brown sears and keeping fryer oil at the right temperature. The heavy, snug-fitting lid minimizes evaporation, making the Dutch oven any moist cooking method's best friend. Simmering beans, braises, and stews are all easier because you won't need to top them off with water as much (or at all) compared with braising in a pot with a lightweight stainless steel lid. Dutch ovens can range wildly in price, but you're really just paying for looks, so pick the one that fits your style and budget. If you're not picky about color, you can often find last season's colors available for sale online and at thrift stores.

10-Inch Stainless Steel Skillet

Most of my sautéing and searing happens in a cast-iron skillet, but I keep a stainless steel skillet around for when I'm cooking something that needs a lot of tossing, like a stir-fry or sautéed mushrooms. The sloped sides allow food to flip in the pan while the light weight keeps it easy on the forearms.

3-Quart Stainless Steel Saucier

This rounded-bottom saucepot allows whisks and spatulas to get flush into corners, making it the perfect pan for soft scrambled eggs, custards, and béchamel. Many home cooks haven't gotten to know this pan, but it's up there for me, right next to my cast-iron skillet. Look for one with a heavy bottom and sturdy construction, like the ones made by All-Clad, Misen, or Made In, so it can handle all that metal on metal whisking action without a single scratch.

8-Inch Nonstick Skillet

No matter how well-seasoned I keep my cast-iron skillets, they can't do what a nonstick skillet can. High-quality, heavy, nonstick pans don't scratch or flake easily, so they can handle sitting in a stack among other pans and even delicate use with metal tools. I like the small size because it's perfect for a classic 3-egg French omelet and for cooking 2 eggs any way you like.

Cookware (cont'd.)

Bamboo Steamer

When I'm in a hurry, I reach for my tiered bamboo steamer. There's no faster way to get creamy winter squash, fluffy sweet potatoes, and crisp-tender greens. Sure, the veggies aren't all that exciting straight out of the steamer, but all it takes is a quick dressing or flavorful oil to spice things up. If you are microwave-less like me, you can even use it to reheat food.

10-Inch Cast-Iron Skillet

My desert island cooking vessel, the only pan I have eyes for, is a 10-inch Lodge cast-iron skillet. This affordable workhorse can do it all: skillet-fry the craggiest chicken, sear broccoli spears until charred and blackened, bake up fluffy biscuits, braise tender turkey meatballs, and even fry an egg. I started with one pan but eventually got hooked and snagged the 6-inch skillet, 12-inch skillet, 10-inch griddle pan, pie plate, pizza stone, and Dutch oven. I'm clearly a hardcore cast-iron believer. They may not be trendy or come in cool colors, but they are cheap, can do it all, and will literally last forever.

How to Season Cast-Iron Pans

• **Forget Everything You've Heard!**
I avoided cast-iron pans for a while. They've got a reputation for being moody, "Don't wash me! No acidic foods! I'm so hard to season!" I believed all the lies. I kept those babies dry, scrubbing the pans with salt after every use to clean them. I filled the skillets to the brim with oil to season them. I hardly ever used them. Thankfully, none of those rumors ended up being true. You *can* wash cast iron! They *are* easy to maintain and season! A well-seasoned cast-iron pan can handle anything from metal tools rubbing on its surface, to deglazing with red wine, to simmering a tomato sauce—no metallic aftertaste, I promise. But the key is to keep them seasoned, and it's easier than you think (well, definitely easier than *I* thought).

• **What is seasoning?** This is one of the questions I'm more frequently asked, especially when I've baked something sweet, like cinnamon buns, in cast iron. Seasoning doesn't mean you're adding flavor to the pan. If you fry chicken in your skillet, it won't make your next batch of corn bread taste like chicken (although, that doesn't sound half bad). Seasoning is achieved by heating a cast-iron pan with several thin layers of oil. The heating transforms the fat in a process called polymerization, which makes it bond to the iron and create a protective layer, making it nonstick-ish, resistant to rust, and less reactive to acid.

• **Fresh out of the box**: Even if you've purchased a preseasoned skillet, it's always good to season it before you use it. Place your cast-iron pan in the oven and heat to 450°F (230°C). Once hot, remove it and use a towel to rub a thin layer of neutral oil all over both sides and the handle. Return to the oven, flipped over so excess oil can't pool anywhere, and heat until the pan stops smoking, about 45 minutes. Repeat with as many thin layers of oil as needed until it's matte black and slick. Don't try to rush the process with thick layers of oil, which leave the pan with sticky spots.

• **After every use:** I wash my cast iron immediately after use with just a soft dish sponge, soap, and warm water. Harsh abrasives like Bar Keepers Friend or steel wool can scrape off the seasoning. Next, towel-dry the pan and heat it on the stove or oven until no moisture remains. Finally, buff a small amount of oil into the hot pan and you're all set.

• **When disaster strikes:** You can lose the seasoning of your cast-iron pan if it's scrubbed too hard or if it gets white-hot. The pans can also become rusty if left wet or unused for a long time. In that case, you will need to scrub off the rust with steel wool and rebuild the seasoning.

Just for Baking

Stand Mixer

Sorry, but you and a wooden spoon (or even a hand mixer) are no match for the creaming, whipping, and kneading capabilities of a stand mixer. Many of the textures we know and love in modern pastries are only made possible thanks to mechanical horsepower. Butter and sugar simply can't get to the level of fluffy required for a fine-textured yellow cake. Dense maple syrup meringues can't whip into ethereal clouds. Hand mixers are only slightly better than mixing by hand, designed for light work such as whipping cream or beating eggs. Most of the recipes in this book don't need a stand mixer. But for the ones that do, know that there is no substitute for it. If you don't have a stand mixer, don't attempt the recipes that require it. Luckily, if you don't care about the color of your stand mixer, it's easy to find one on sale. Keep your eyes peeled after the holidays when seasonal colors are often available at half the price.

Cake & Pie Pans

Always opt for metal over glass, as they conduct heat faster, preventing soggy bottoms and gummy crumbs. I like all my cake pans to be 3 inches in depth. These deeper cake pans lead to taller cakes that brown less on top because the high sides of the pan act like a heat shield. The sizes I like to have in my kit are an 8-inch round, an 8-inch square, a 9 × 5-inch loaf, a 9-inch pie pan, and a 9 × 13-inch rectangle. If you don't have a cake pan, you can bake cakes and pies in a skillet or Dutch oven. Keep in mind, they'll bake at a different rate, so keep an eye on sensory rather than time cues.

Rolling Pin

The naturally coarse surface of wooden rolling pins minimizes sticking. Wash them by hand and never in the dishwasher, where the harsh detergents can cause them to splinter. Just like with a wooden cutting board, be sure to dry your rolling pin right away and rub it with mineral oil every few months to prevent cracking and mold. In general, bigger pins are better for rolling bigger things. I have two straight, handle-less rolling pins: a larger one for cookies and pie doughs, and a smaller one for roti, paratha, and dumpling wrappers. But if you don't want to get specialized, one large rolling pin can do it all.

Metal Ruler

Accurate sizes are important to how a pastry bakes up. If you roll pie crust too thick, it'll be tough or chewy, even if made properly. Pita that's too thin won't develop a pocket when baked. Sugar cookies rolled out too thick will take too long to bake and end up soft instead of crisp. Using a ruler is vital to being as precise as possible. I always use a metal one so I can easily wash it with soap and water.

Pastry Brush

Essential for dusting away flour and painting on egg wash. Wash them like a paintbrush, by massaging in a bit of soap and rinsing until clean (as it happens, mine actually is a 2-inch natural bristle paintbrush from Lowe's). Lay flat to dry, especially if the brush has a wooden handle, which can allow moisture to seep in, causing the wood to expand, resulting in the bristles falling out. I don't recommend silicone-bristled brushes. They might be easy to clean, but they don't work well at brushing things, so what's the point?

Knives & Sharp Objects

Mandoline
Regardless of how killer your knife skills may be, there are occasions when you've just got to give it up to the mandoline. Crispy fried shallots and garlic chips are prime examples. The smallest inconsistencies mean the difference between a pile of evenly golden brown and crisp glory or burnt, soggy, oily results. The simple, single-blade Japanese mandoline is the one that's earned its keep in my kitchen. It's easy to adjust thickness and disassemble for sharpening, so I reach for it as often as any other knife.

Box Grater
I admit it—sometimes I buy preshredded cheese. No, it does not melt as well or taste as good as the shreds you grate yourself, but it's perfect for that late-night quesadilla. For every other shredded cheese occasion, I grate my own. Besides my cheese needs, a box grater can quickly break down tomatoes and onions for sofrito or mirepoix without the need to pull out an appliance.

Fine Grater
In many, many recipes I will ask you to finely grate garlic, ginger, lemon zest, and more. When I say fine I mean Microplane fine. Microplane is the original manufacturer of these handheld, fine graters. They easily transform dense parmesan into a flurry of cheese and stringy ginger to a pulp. Unfortunately, they cannot be sharpened, so be sure to replace them as they grow dull. I use mine every day and replace them once a year.

Kitchen Shears
Kitchen shears make quick (and safe) work of tough jobs, like snipping the fins off fish or the wing tips off chicken. And they do all the things scissors can do, from cutting parchment paper to line a pan, to snipping chives and chilies into perfect little rings. Joyce Chen's kitchen shears are my favorite. They are sturdy enough to spatchcock a chicken while their thin blades can slip beneath a shrimp shell without damaging the flesh.

Knives & Sharp Objects (cont'd.)

Serrated Bread Knife

Obviously great for slicing bread and cake, but also tomatoes and tender fruit, like a ripe peach, which can easily squish under a blunt blade. Some people insist that a serrated knife can be sharpened, but I disagree. Instead, I stick with the affordable Tojiro serrated bread knife and replace it as needed.

Tourné & Petty Knife

I avoid paring knives and instead opt for the combo of a tourné and petty knife. A tourné knife has a short, curved blade, used in fine-dining kitchens to carve potatoes into football shapes, an utterly useless skill. A better use of its curved blade is for peeling garlic cloves, onions, and shallots. A petty knife has a thin blade that's about 6 inches in length. I use it for anywhere I might traditionally have used a paring knife, boning knife, or filleting knife, so anything from mincing a shallot, to breaking down a chicken, or even filleting mackerel.

Chef's Knife

Traditionally, a chef's knife was defined as having an 8- to 9-inch heavy curved blade, and was usually from a German manufacturer. But that was because the term "chef" meant European guys wearing tall white paper hats. As the idea of who a chef is has expanded, so has the definition of a chef's knife. These days, a chef's knife is whatever you feel comfortable using for the majority of your slicing, dicing, chopping, and mincing needs. Working in professional kitchens, I saw people use all kinds of knives as their "chef's knife," from a thin and long 11-inch Japanese slicer (sujihiki) to a broad and wide Chinese cleaver (caidao). For a long time, my chef's knife was a 7-inch Misono UX10 santoku (the blade design combines both Eastern and Western knife styles), but lately I've really been digging my 6½-inch Togiharu nakiri (the square blade makes vegetable prep extra efficient).

The knife you pick to be your "chef's" knife should be what feels comfortable in your hands and suits your cutting style. If you like to rock the blade from tip to heel while you chop, look for something with a curved blade. If you chop with more of an up and down motion, look for a square-edged knife. And if you go both ways, then a Western-style Japanese knife with its slightly curved edge might be right for you. Find a store that will let you hold knives in your hand to see if the handle fits your palm and the weight is right for your build. Picking a chef's knife is a very personal thing, so go with your gut and don't just buy a knife because someone told you to. Most important, pick a knife you can sharpen. A dull knife will always be useless. (See page lix for sharpening directions.)

Pantry Essentials

If you stock up on these ingredients, you can make almost everything in this book.

Salty & Savory
Kosher salt, MSG, soy sauce, miso paste, anchovies, fish sauce, flaky salt, chicken bouillon powder, powdered nori, capers, olives, nutritional yeast

Sweet
Honey, white sugar, brown sugar, maple syrup, molasses, dates

Hot
Black pepper, hot chili flakes, mild chili flakes (like gochugaru or Aleppo), chipotle peppers in adobo sauce, Kashmiri chili powder, cayenne pepper, fresh ginger, Thai green chilies

Tart
Apple cider vinegar, red and white wine vinegars, rice vinegar, lemons, limes, tomato paste

Fats
Neutral oil (safflower or grapeseed), fancy extra-virgin olive oil for finishing, everyday extra-virgin olive oil for cooking, butter, tahini, nuts and seeds

Spices & Herbs
Saffron; cumin, coriander, and mustard seeds; turmeric; cardamom; cinnamon; bay leaves; dried oregano; fresh thyme, parsley, dill, cilantro

Baking
All-purpose flour, bread flour, baking powder, baking soda, cream of tartar, instant yeast, milk chocolate, dark chocolate, freeze-dried fruit, cocoa powder, powdered gelatin, cornstarch, corn syrup, powdered sugar, turbinado sugar

Things to Know

How to Measure for Savory Cooking

You do not need to be precise. In fact, you can't be. Even if you weigh every ingredient to the gram—the oil, the garlic, the onion, the protein, the herbs—a recipe can lead to perfection only if you use your intuition and pay attention to sensory clues. Every onion has a unique water content. Depending on when your garlic was harvested it could be sweeter or hotter. Proteins have varying levels of collagen, fat, and amino acids based on feed and farming methods.

For savory cooking, recipes are meant to help you hone your intuition and offer techniques to guide you. That's why I'm not giving you weights for most of the ingredients in the savory recipes. So what does a medium onion look like? Take a look at the onions at the grocery store. A medium anything means it's about average size, and that goes for all produce.

How to Measure for Baking & Pastry
This is a whole other game. Not packing your brown sugar will lead to a dry cookie. Twenty extra grams of water will leave you with a sticky, unmanageable roti dough. A heaped rather than level teaspoon of baking powder will totally F up a cake. And worst of all, with baking and pastry you can rarely go back and fix your mistakes. Yes, every brand of butter, flour, and sugar is slightly different, but if you don't start by measuring as accurately as possible you don't stand a chance.

If you don't have a scale, here are some tips for measuring with cups and spoons:

- **For flours:** Fluff up the flour with a whisk, then spoon into a cup until heaped, and use the flat edge of a small offset spatula or butter knife to level it off.

- **For granulated sugar, baking powder, baking soda, cream of tartar, kosher salt:** Scoop up the ingredient, then level it off.

- **For easily packed ingredients (like powdered sugar, cocoa powder, and cornstarch):** Sift the ingredient into a bowl, then spoon into a cup until heaped and level it off.

- **For brown sugar and nut butters:** Tightly pack into a cup.

But you really should get a scale, and here's why:
The US government states that 1 cup of water weighs 237 grams. Some popular recipe sites say 1 cup of water weighs 235 grams, others round up to 240 grams. In this book, I say that 1 cup of water weighs 225 grams because that's what I consistently landed on throughout my testing. And every recipe developer, media outlet, magazine, newspaper, and YouTuber has their own volume to gram conversions for every single ingredient. Beyond that, every measuring cup out there is a little bit different, varying as much as 20 grams in either direction depending on the cup, with novelty heart or Mickey Mouse–shaped ones being the absolute worst. Trust me, I once had a really boring job helping test measuring

Egg Sizes

Eggs come in the following sizes: Jumbo, Extra-Large, Large, Medium, Small, and Peewee. All the recipes in this book were developed using large eggs. A whole large egg, out of the shell, weighs roughly 55 grams. The white weighs about 35 grams and the yolk weighs about 20 grams. If you're using farmers' market eggs, they likely don't follow any size standards, so I've provided egg weights for all the baking recipes (but not for the savory egg recipes, because that much precision isn't necessary).

cups. It was miserable, but from all that agony, I learned that you can't trust anyone.

What I'm trying to say is, even if you do everything right, carefully fluffing, spooning, and leveling off flour and evenly packing brown sugar, you might still be off because when you measure by volume all the odds are against you. Precision doesn't matter that much with savory cooking. You can be a splash off when measuring water for rice and still be okay. Your medium onion might be bigger or smaller than mine, and you will still have tasty food. If you want consistently delicious pastries, please get a scale. I have given you volume measurements for most of the pastry recipes because, well, I really don't want to get called an elitist prick, but measure at your own risk.

Keeping Your Knives Sharp

The best knife is a sharp one. Wondering why you can't get a super-fine chop on your garlic, make perfect little potato squares, or cleanly cut a fish fillet? The problem is most likely a dull knife. A sharp knife is vital to creating crisp cuts and working efficiently in the kitchen. Sharp knives are also much safer. You're less likely to slip and they require significantly less pressure to make a cut. If you're hands are calloused after a day of cooking, your knife is dull and putting too much pressure on your palms. When I worked in a professional kitchen, I had to sharpen my knives every morning. As a recipe developer, I sharpen my knives once a week. For a home cook, you'll be in good shape if you take the time to sharpen once a month. But keep in mind, certain tasks can make your knife dull faster, like cutting on a glass or marble board, breaking down tough winter squash and root vegetables, and going through the bones and skin on protein. In those instances, you may need to sharpen more frequently.

Note that honing steels do not sharpen a knife. They just realign the edge, which can fall to one side through use. A few strokes can get that point to straighten out, but it won't grow any sharper than it already is. A honing steel is useful to keep your blade aligned in between sharpening sessions.

Manual & Electric Knife Sharpeners

These are easy to use and require no maintenance or skill. However, they only work for knives that have symmetrical edges, meaning their sharp edge comes to a V-shaped point. That's because these sharpeners remove an equal amount of material from both sides of the blade. They will not work for most Japanese knives, which have an asymmetrical edge. (That unique shape is part of the reason Eastern-style knives are sharper and stay sharp for longer.) But the main downside to these sharpeners is that they take a lot of the blade off with every use. You'll visibly see your blade grow thinner and thinner every time you sharpen it. I do not recommend these sharpeners if you've invested in expensive high-quality knives that you want to last.

To use a manual or electric sharpener, move your blade through the sharpener at a steady speed with even pressure all the way from the heel to the tip. Wash with soap and a soft dish sponge, then dry with a towel to remove any shards of metal, and finish with a few strokes on a honing steel.

Whetstones

Whetstones are more difficult to use and they require skill and practice to master. However, when used correctly, a whetstone can get your knife significantly sharper than a manual or electric sharpener and you lose very little of the blade, so your knives can last a lifetime. Most important, they allow you to have full control of the angle of your edge, vital when sharpening single-beveled knives, like many Japanese knives. When I first learned how to sharpen with a whetstone, I started out with inexpensive stones and knives (because in the beginning, you will mess them up). As I grew more skilled, I upgraded to more premium stones and knives. They can range widely in price, and you get what you pay for.

To start, you'll need:

• **Two stones:** One with a coarser grit (no more than 800 grit) and one with a finer grit (between 4000 to 6000 grit)

• **Stone corrector:** This is used to sand down and level off your stones, so they are perfectly flat. As you use your stones, they can wear down unevenly or accidentally get nicked, which will prevent you from evenly sharpening the edge of your knife.

• **Extra but not essential:** A stone holder will prevent you and your stone from slipping, but you can also use a wet towel.

lx

Get Sharpening

1. Start with the coarse-grit stone. First soak it in cool tap water for 30 minutes. (The finer grit stone should just be splashed with water as you sharpen.)

2. Secure the coarse-grit stone either with a wet towel or a stone holder, with the short side closest to you. Have some more water handy to wet the stone as you go.

3. Get your blade grip down: Use the thumb and forefinger of your dominant hand to hold the handle and spine of the knife. Use the fingertips of your nondominant hand to hold the edge of the blade against the stone.

4. Figure out the angle of your blade by pressing the edge against the stone with your fingertips. Tilt the blade gently until you feel the edge lay flat against the stone. It takes practice to figure out exactly how it should feel.

5. Starting at the farthest side of the stone, press the heel of the knife against the stone, and in one even stroke, maintaining consistent pressure and an even angle, pull the blade down across the entire stone until you reach the tip of the knife.

6. Repeat. You will develop muddy silt along the blade of your knife. The silt is what's doing the sharpening. Add water a splash at a time if it feels dry.

7. Continue until you feel a slight burr on the edge of your knife. Then flip and sharpen the opposite side.

8. Continue sharpening both sides of the knife, using fewer and fewer strokes on each side until the desired sharpness is achieved.

9. Repeat on the finer-grit stone.

10. Wash with soap and a soft dish sponge, then dry with a towel to remove any shards of metal, and finish with a few strokes on a honing steel (or leather strop).

How to Hold a Knife

For the most control, use your thumb and forefinger to firmly grip the base of the blade, while your remaining fingers lightly hold onto the handle. When supporting ingredients with your free hand, always form a claw. This tucks your fingertips away and protects them from the blade.

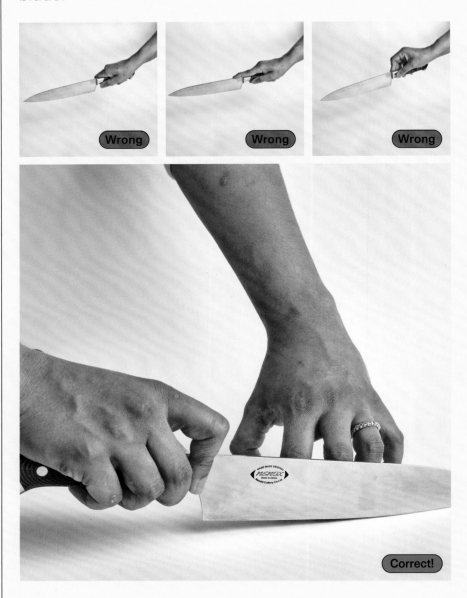

How to Use a Microplane Grater

Always use the entire length of the grater. For citrus, apply light pressure and roll the fruit while you move it along the grater. This way you get all the colorful zest (where the oils and flavor reside) while avoiding the stringy and bitter white pith. For ginger, garlic, and other ingredients where you're grating the entire item, apply firm pressure. Tap the grater to dislodge everything stuck on the underside.

Cutting Garlic

The flavor you get from garlic is heavily dependent on how you cut it. When more of the cell walls are ruptured, the flavor becomes more intense, spicy, and pungent. These cuts are in order of most pungent to least.

- **Finely Grated:** All the cell walls are ruptured, releasing the spiciest garlicky flavor. Garlic broken down this way is too moist to evenly caramelize, but easily melts into a dish.

- **The Smash-Chop:** This produces roughly chopped garlic used for sweating, sauces, stews, and when precise browning doesn't matter. Depending on how fine you want the garlic, you run your knife through it repeatedly, breaking down more cell walls, and resulting in more pungent flavor.

- **The Perfect Fine Chop:** This is to make teeny squares of finely chopped garlic when you're after even coloration and distribution throughout a dish. You don't run your knife through the garlic after the initial cuts, so it stays relatively mellow even though it's finely cut.

- **Thinly Sliced:** This cut produces garlic that evenly browns but stays distinct yet mellow in a dish.

- **Peeled and Whole:** This is where that tourné knife comes in handy. To peel off the garlic's paper husk without breaking it, trim off a sliver of the dry root end, then use the tip of the knife to slip between the paper husk and the flesh and pry off the husk. Great when you want mild garlic flavor without the burn.

Peeled and Whole

Thinly Sliced

The Perfect Fine Chop

Finely Grated

Introduction

Cutting Ginger

Unlike garlic, whose flavor profile changes depending on how the cell walls are broken down, with ginger the flavor stays the same. Instead, the way you cut ginger affects texture and how much flavor is extracted. Ginger has tough fibers running lengthwise throughout it, which do not break down with cooking. For tender bites of ginger, it's important to cut it across the grain.

• **Finely Grated:** This gives you a smooth, wet pulp, leaving the tough fibers behind. Good for when you want the ginger thoroughly incorporated in a dish and aren't looking for browning.

• **Sliced Crosswise:** Adds lots of ginger flavor, can easily be sautéed because it isn't wet, but the pieces are large and stringy. This cut is best when you don't plan to eat the ginger and are using it just for flavor.

• **Matchsticks:** Infuses a dish with spicy ginger flavor, while having distinct pieces throughout the dish that are tender and pleasant to eat.

• **Chopped:** Thoroughly incorporates ginger throughout a dish while still being able to sauté and brown.

• **Split and Smashed:** Good for moist cooking methods, like stews, braises, or a pot of beans when you want ginger flavor without any texture.

Peeled

Sliced Crosswise

Matchsticks

Split and Smashed

Cutting
Onions

Because onions have layers, the best way to get even cuts is to work with the onion's natural shape.

• **Sliced:** Peel and cut the onion in half through blossom to root end. Trim off the blossom end. To remove all of the root end (so your slices separate) make a V-shaped cut. Make lengthwise slices, moving your knife along the radius of the onion.

• **Chopped:** Peel and cut the onion in half through blossom to root end. Trim off the blossom and root ends, while keeping the root mostly intact so the onion doesn't fall apart. Make lengthwise cuts, moving your knife along the radius of the onion, without going through the root. Cut crosswise to yield little square pieces.

Trimming the Root

Peeling

Sliced

Chopped

Cutting
Herbs

Soft Herbs, like Parsley, Cilantro & Dill
All of a soft herb is edible! In fact, the stem (and root, if you find them attached) tends to have the most flavor. The stems can be slightly tough when raw, so use them in cooked applications, or finely chop or blend them to break them down. If the ends of the stems seem dry and especially tough, trim and discard only the part that's looking rough.

- **Leaves and Tender Stems:** These are just the tippy tops of the herbs. They are the softest and mildest part, best for salads and garnishes.

- **Roughly Chopped:** Gather everything into a tight ball and run your knife through it all once or twice.

- **Finely Chopped:** Just keep chopping, repeatedly running your knife through the herbs until super fine.

Tough Herbs, like Thyme or Rosemary
The stems of these herbs are too tough to eat, even if you blend or chop them. You can add the whole sprigs to dishes to infuse them with flavor, then pluck them out after cooking. Or strip the leaves off the stems and finely chop.

lxx

Separating

Leaves and Tender Stems

Roughly Chopped

Finely Chopped

How to Make Bone Broth

Being stocked up on bone broth means you're always just a few steps away from a flavorful and nutritious meal. I use it for simmering grains and beans, steaming vegetables, making sauces, and as a base for soup. And since reliable brands like Brodo and Bonafide Provisions have made bone broths accessible (always shop for your bone broth in the freezer aisle), I rarely make bone broth at home. But I always store spare chicken backs and clipped wing tips in the freezer and end up making a batch whenever I have enough.

The process for making bone broth is simple; the main ingredient is time:

1. Use bones with a lot of meat/cartilage attached, like wings, backs, knuckles, and feet.

2. Cover the bones with 1 to 2 inches of cold filtered water.

3. Add ½ tablespoon vinegar per 1 pound of bones. (Recipes I've seen claim this maximizes collagen extraction. I don't know if it actually does anything, but it doesn't hurt!)

4. Bring to a gentle simmer and cook, skimming any froth/scum/fat regularly and topping off with water as needed, until the bones start to fall apart (12 hours for chicken, up to 18 hours for beef, pork, and lamb).

5. If you want to use aromatics (like carrot, celery, onion, and herbs), add them an hour before the cooking time is over.

6. After simmering, strain through a fine-mesh sieve and taste. If looking for a more concentrated flavor, return the bone broth to the pot and continue to simmer until reduced to your liking.

Simmering vs. Boiling Water

Simmering water is gentle, with just a few small bubbles breaking the surface. Boiling is very active, with big bubbles rapidly breaking to the surface of the water.

How to Line a Cake Pan

For round pans, use the bottom of the pan as a guide to cut parchment paper to fit inside the bottom. For rectangular, square, and loaf pans, cut parchment into one long sheet that can line the bottom and two long sides of the pan. Lightly grease the pan with softened butter or cooking spray. This helps the parchment paper stick to the pan. Place the parchment into the greased pan and use your hands to adhere it to the pan. Crease the edges into the corners and make sure the paper is flush with the pan. If the paper isn't well adhered, thin batters can flow underneath the paper, making your cake stick to the pan and bake up with parchment inside it.

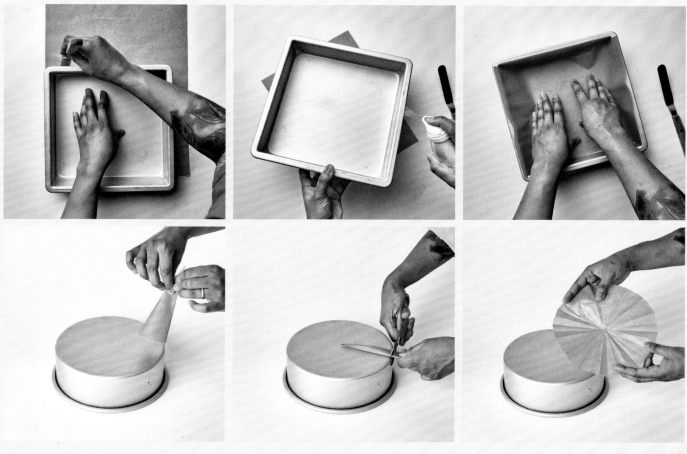

Culinary
Lessons

Taste

How else are you gonna know if your food's any good?

Taste

The first step in learning how to cook is learning how to taste. Seriously! Tasting is a skill you have to intentionally develop. I don't mean taking a bite of something and deciding if you like it or not. I mean being able to decipher *why* you're not into it so you can make it better. I first learned how to taste by spending time in the kitchen with my amu. From one bite, she could tell you not only everything that's in a dish but exactly what it needs to be better. I'd taste along with her and listen as she'd analyze her own cooking. I would try my hardest to understand what she was talking about, but for a very long time I was totally clueless. This needs more lime juice? Sure, if you say so.

In most professional kitchens, new cooks start out making cold stuff, like salads and vinaigrettes. In fancy restaurants they call this station garde manger (anywhere else you're just making salad). My amu was not a professional chef, but she ran her kitchen like one. She wrote prep lists, game plans, and kept me working garde manger for most of my life. Cooks don't start here because it's easy. Seasoning a vinaigrette—learning how to taste through all that sharp acid and slick fat—is one of the toughest tasks. They start here because mistakes are cheap and often fixable. Working on the hot line cooking meat isn't actually very difficult. I know there are big flames that make you feel so cool, but all you really do is shower stuff with salt, throw it on the grill (or skillet or plancha), and cook until it's done. But messing up a steak means you're throwing out money and making a table wait for their food. Many of the dishes on garde manger can be made in advance, before the pressure of service, so a novice cook can take their time with tasting. It's the same when you're cooking at home (but maybe without the

6

angry Yelp reviews). Starting your culinary journey with salads and dressings allows you to focus on the most important and difficult part of cooking: seasoning. Developing your palate is tough, so why add the pressure that cooking with heat can bring? Keep it chill and start by focusing on flavors first.

I started training my tastebuds by making raithas and cucumber salads in my amu's kitchen and whisking together dressings and mayonnaise alongside Chef Erin at the Apple Pie Bakery Café, where I worked during culinary school. It was the same drill with both of my first teachers: I'd stir or toss something together, march over with a spoonful, and wait for a response—more salt, more sugar, or more acid. I would taste, tweak, and triumphantly return with another spoonful only to get more feedback. This back-and-forth would continue five, ten, even a dozen times until the seasoning was just right. It probably took forever because as a new cook, the amount of salt, sugar, and acid required to properly season food can appear excessive. My nervous fingers would add only a pinch at a time. I (then) would have driven me (now) crazy! Somehow, neither teacher ever lost patience with me. They simply kept nudging me in the right direction until I finally met them at tasty town. Adding a little, bit by bit, and tasting with every addition had its advantages. At first I didn't understand their feedback, but by following their commands, I got to study how flavors transform. With master tasters by my side guiding me to my flavorful destination, I became the best damn salad girl. Now when I cook with amu, she asks *me* what I think something needs. I can't think of a better compliment.

How to Season

Even though I can't be there to usher you through your seasoning odyssey, here are some of the lessons they taught me, so you can use them in your kitchen, too. Remember, the most important thing is patience. I know tasting spoonfuls of gloppy mayonnaise is gross. You're gonna wanna settle for whatever tastes good enough. Don't. Cold food gives you time, so use that to taste, tweak, and keep pushing.

- **Make it rain:** Whether you pinch salt, sugar, and other seasonings between your fingers or scoop it up by the spoonful, evenly shower it from on high. This makes it easier to distribute onto whatever you're seasoning.

- **Take your time:** Seasonings need a moment to dissolve and become one with the food. Before you get in there and start making judgments, toss, whisk, and stir things up so you can get a true idea of how something is seasoned.

- **Season in stages:** Add seasonings a pinch at a time and have a moment of silence. Focus on what you're tasting and think about what's missing. Not sure? Portion a small bowlful and play around without the risk of spoiling the full batch.

- **Taste! Taste! Taste!:** Taste before you add salt, taste after you add salt, taste all the times in between. Especially when you're first honing your palate, you can never taste too much. Sometimes your tastebuds burn out from trying the same thing over and over again. Have a bland cracker and a sip of seltzer to reset, then dive back in. Before you know it, you won't just recognize if something needs salt or sugar, but also understand complex flavors, like if you're missing smoky cumin or the funk of fish sauce. Tasting throughout the cooking process gives you insight into how flavors develop and transform through heat, time, and layering. Bitter spices, harsh onion, and fiery chili magically meld and mellow as they cook out and are balanced with proper seasoning. You'll better understand how that magic works if you keep tasting.

- **Salt isn't always the answer:** Often when a dish falls flat, it's not salt you're missing. Don't forget about the power of sugar, acid, and spice. Acid can temper heat, perk up a dish, or freshen flavors. Sugar can mellow out the sharpness from acid, spice, and salt. Spice livens things up while adding complexity. Salt takes the edge off bitterness. Seasoning is about more than making something salty—it's about balancing all these flavors for maximum deliciousness. It can seem complicated at first, but just keep tasting, and soon it will become instinct.

Extra Credit!

Eat other people's food as much as possible. Eat at that aunt's who might ask too many personal questions at dinner but makes the best roast lamb in the family. Eat at that co-worker's who won't stop talking about their trip to Italy but came back obsessed with making fresh pasta at home. Eat at the diner across the street that's open 24 hours, that gas station that also sells carne asada burritos, and save up for that place that costs way too much for tiny portions on giant plates. I know this is a book about cooking, but you can't make your food good until you know what good food is, and you won't know until you eat a lot of it. It's easy to end up in a food bubble, just eating your own cooking and going to a few favorite spots, but your palate can grow only so much in isolation.

If you don't have the resources to frequently eat out, try to cook recipes from various sources. Different websites, cookbooks, and recipe developers each have their own style—get to know them. And actually follow the recipe. Based on the reviews of my own recipes, it's obvious some people glance at a recipe, then go off and do their own thing. ("I swapped the chicken for carrots, omitted the rice, baked on a sheet pan instead of cooking in a skillet, and didn't use any salt. This recipe sucks. Zero stars.") Look, that's fine if you're looking for weeknight meal inspiration, but if you want to get better, sometimes you gotta let someone else take the wheel, while you sit back and taste. It doesn't matter how long I've been cooking or how much I think I know—I still cook other people's recipes and I learn something new every time.

Let me introduce you to my core seasoning team: Flavor Makers Assemble!

Diamond Crystal Kosher Salt

This is the best salt in the game and the one most used in professional kitchens and by recipe developers alike. Why is it the gold standard? The big fluffy flakes are easy to pinch and evenly shower over whatever you're seasoning, allowing you to clearly see how much you're using. Diamond Crystal is less dense than other kosher salts, dissolving quickly into liquids and readily dispersing into sautés. It's also completely free of additives (which are not always required to be listed on the packaging!), like the anticaking agents found in many popular brands. These additives can cause crystallization in caramels and discolor proteins that are brined for an extended period. I can't buy Diamond Crystal kosher salt where I live, so I order it in bulk online. Luckily the packaging is so darn cute, I consider the row of boxes part of our home decor.

All the recipes in this book have been developed with Diamond Crystal kosher salt. If you are using Morton kosher salt, reduce the quantities to just over half. One cup of Diamond Crystal kosher salt is equal to ½ cup plus 2 tablespoons of Morton kosher salt. That's because the individual crystals in Morton kosher salt are dense squares, rather than light flakes. This makes it saltier by volume and it takes longer to dissolve into food. For table and fine sea salt, reduce the quantities by 75 percent—or better yet, consider switching to a coarser salt. Even if I can't get you into that DC life, maybe I can convince you to join the kosher salt club. Fine salt sticks to your fingers, clumps, and makes it way too easy to oversalt.

I don't offer weights for ingredients used in smaller quantities, such as baking soda, baking powder, MSG, and, often, salt. That's because I don't recommend using a scale for ingredients that weigh less than 15 grams. For most common ingredients this is less than 2 tablespoons. If you're not using a micro scale that's designed to be accurate to the tenth or hundredth of a gram, volume is a far more accurate method of measurement. (Read more about measurements on pages lv–lvii.)

Flaky Salt

Most salt tastes the same, regardless of color or shape. What flaky salt brings is a pop of crunch and salinity to dishes that need it, like sliced steak, ripe avocado, or silky custard. Flaky salt tends to be pricier than kosher salt because harvesting is a delicate process that's often done by hand. Use it for finishing dishes where you can highlight the salt's texture rather than for general seasoning. My favorites are Maldon Sea Salt Crystals from England, Salina Crystal Salt from New York, and Jacobsen Co. Pure Flake Sea Salt from Oregon.

MSG

In the beginning, there were four: Salty, Sour, Sweet, and Bitter. Then one evening, as biochemist Kikunae Ikeda sipped on a bowl of dashi, he thought, "What's making this taste so good?" You know the flavor—mouthwatering, meaty, savory, and addictive. That's when he found the fifth . . . Umami! Monosodium glutamate was discovered in kelp and eventually synthesized from it in 1907. Other naturally occurring sources of MSG include tomatoes, parmesan cheese, anchovies, asparagus, and much more. MSG became a staple in Asian cuisine, bringing instant umami to whatever it touched, and by the 1950s it was in most packaged food throughout the world.

But it wasn't happily ever after. In 1968, Dr. Robert Ho Man Kwok wrote a letter to the *New England Journal of Medicine* noting symptoms he felt after eating at Chinese restaurants, which included numbness and heart palpations. (Later on, conflicting evidence arose questioning whether Dr. Robert was even a real person.) That one letter turned the tide against MSG and the term "Chinese Restaurant Syndrome" took off. MSG was blamed for everything, from making you crazy to giving you cancer. Although multiple double-blind studies have not shown there to be any negative side effects from consuming standard quantities of MSG (if you have ½ cup of it on an empty stomach without food, you might feel ill, as you would from eating ½ cup of salt), the seasoning never fully got its groove back.

For me, MSG has become as important to cooking as salt and sugar. It allows me to season in stereo, adjusting the level of savoriness in dishes, along with salty, sour, bitter, spicy, and sweet. I most often use it alongside other already savory ingredients, to heighten their natural flavor, such as in dry brines for meats, in tomato sauces and salads, and in anything with cheese. The key is to have a light touch—too much MSG makes things taste funny—so sprinkle it on sparsely, a pinch at a time.

Sugar & Other Sweeteners

I think it's easy to forget about sugar in savory cooking, but a touch of sweetness can help balance a dish the same way a pinch of salt goes a long way in dessert. Sweetness acts like a base note, rounding out all the other flavors at play, adding depth to salty, bitter, spicy, and tart. Why do you think so many recipes start with cooked down onions, garlic, or carrots? Their natural sugars help all the other savory flavors pop. For dry brines or subtle dishes, where the floral flavor of honey might get in the way, I stick to plain granulated sugar. Otherwise, mild honey, like clover or orange blossom, is my first choice. It adds body and richness, along with sweetness, to vinaigrettes, sauces, stews, and crackly glazes. When I want the flavor of a sweetener in the forefront, I'll reach for a smoky dark maple syrup or blackstrap molasses. Many traditional savory dishes from South America, South Asia, and Southeast Asia rely on unrefined sugars to balance spice and acid, like panela in Mexico or palm sugar in Thailand. Since they keep for a long time in the fridge, I like to stock up on various raw sugars for regional cooking. (Read more about sugars in What Is Sugar?, page 438.)

Freshly Ground Black Pepper

Are you still using the preground stuff out of a can? It's okay, I did, too. A pepper mill was too expensive for me for a long time. I didn't understand the glory of freshly ground black pepper until I splurged on the Unicorn Magnum Pepper Mill. It was worth every penny and has lasted through the years. The pepper just flies out and it's easy to adjust from coarse to fine grind—oh, size does matter. Finely ground pepper offers delicate flavor and disappears into food, ideal for finishing scrambled eggs or a smooth gravy, while barely cracked pepper adds texture and heat, standing up to a meaty steak or adding pop to long-braised greens. Freshly ground pepper packs a punch. It's floral, spicy, and pungent, but only right after grinding. The flavor quickly dissipates, so get a pepper mill today.

Citrus & Vinegar

If something is tasting dull or flat, don't only reach for salt. Acids are the cheerleaders in your pantry, always bringing the pep. Lemon juice and apple cider vinegar play well with flavors from most parts of the globe and are my go-to pucker-uppers. Other acids, like lime juice, unseasoned rice vinegar, or balsamic vinegar are more cuisine specific, which can be exactly what you want when deployed appropriately. Always stick to fresh citrus juice, which gets nasty fast if you squeeze in advance. Wanna be a real pro? Expand your horizons into the fancy vinegar world, like white balsamic, artisanal apple vinegar, ramp vinegar, and so much more. I always keep my pantry stocked with a few seasonal vinegars from Lindera Farms.

Spices & Dried Herbs

I always try to buy high-quality spices, store them properly, and deploy them with care. The main spices and dried herbs I reach for daily are ground turmeric, bay leaves, cumin seeds, coriander seeds, cinnamon (both ground and in stick form), cardamom pods, onion powder, garlic powder, saffron, dried oregano, and an assortment of chili powders. At minimum, you should have one hot and one mild chili powder/flake. On the spicy side I like cayenne pepper and the classic chili flakes you shake on pizza. I can get out of hand with milder chilies, stocking up on gochugaru, Kashmiri red chili powder, many varieties of paprika, Aleppo pepper, silk chili, and cobanero chili flakes, to name a few. And I can't live without za'atar, the earthy spice blend that is all you need to turn yogurt and pita into a satisfying meal.

Technically, ground spices should be used within three months, while whole spices can last a year. But honestly, I almost never throw out spices. As they get old, they lose subtle aromatics and become less flavorful, so you might need more than a recipe suggests. Spices never literally "go bad" but rather go bland, so just use your best judgment. However, even if you do everything right (buy in small quantities, store them properly, use them up quickly), you might be set up to fail from the moment you pick up a jar. Did you know that sometimes, depending on the distributor, it could be years after harvest before a spice ends up on a grocery store shelf? That's why I always buy online from reputable distributors who are transparent about their sourcing. For saffron I turn to Regalis Foods and for everything else I rely on Burlap & Barrel. Keep spices in a cool and dark place, not in a cabinet directly next to the stove even though it seems oh so convenient.

How to Use Spices

Dried herbs, chili powders, and chili flakes are usually fine added directly to dishes, saffron needs special attention (see What Is Saffron?, page 26), while most spices need direct contact with heat to bloom. Here are a few ways to get the best flavor out of your spices:

• **For adding to batters, doughs, sauces, or dressings:** Dry-toast whole spices in a skillet over medium-high heat until they are aromatic and slightly darkened. Some seeds, like mustard, will pop to let you know they've reached their full potential. Once cool, blitz in a spice grinder or with a mortar and pestle and add to dishes.

• **For finishing dishes:** Sizzle whole or ground spices in oil in a process often found in South Asia called vaghar, tadka, or chhonk (depending on the region). This will bring out all the oil-soluble flavors and make the spices crunchy, adding texture to dishes like dal or soup. Be sure to use oil, ghee, or clarified butter—whole butter will burn at the high temperatures needed to fully bloom the spices. Add the spices to the fat and cook over medium-high heat, stirring the entire time, until they are aromatic and slightly darkened. Then scrape the flavorful fat and all the spices into your dish.

• **If the recipe starts with you cooking spices in fat:** When a recipe calls for this as a first step (for example, as in Coconut Cauliflower Korma, page 182, or the Chickpea & Swiss Chard Stew, page 166), feel free to forge ahead with raw spices. They will bloom as they cook. Toasting the spices before these steps would be overkill, causing you to lose some delicate aromas. Many traditional spice-heavy dishes, like curry goat from the Caribbean and countless stews in South Asia, start with a step called bhuna. Here, raw spices are mixed with the aromatics and/or meat and cooked down, repeatedly being caramelized in fat then deglazed with water. This process brings out all the flavor of the spice. These dishes are often finished with more spices sizzled in fat to layer flavors.

Seasoning Lessons

Learning how to make cucumber salad and raitha (and make them your own) is the perfect lesson in seasoning. Individually, cucumbers and yogurt are blank canvases ready to transform with a few sprinkles of this and dashes of that. Best of all, it's easy to recover if anything tastes unbalanced—just add more yogurt or cucumbers! Once you become a raitha and cuke expert, you'll be armed with the skills to easily round out any meal with these two versatile sides.

CHOOSE ONE

Raitha
Start with a cool and creamy base of fermented dairy (or faux dairy)—anything from yogurt, labne, buttermilk, sour cream, or even a combo.

Cucumber Salad
Slice, dice, or chunk your cucumbers. (Small Persian/mini cucumbers are my favorite.) For an extra-saucy salad, gently smash whole cucumbers with a rolling pin, then cut into coins.

SEASON IT TO TASTE WITH:

1. enough salt to make it savory
2. and a pinch of MSG to make you say "mmmmm"
3. and fresh citrus or vinegar to liven it up
4. and just enough sweetness to balance everything

Taste! Add more of any of the above, then repeat, until it tastes just right.

ADD OPTIONAL SPICES + MIX-INS

Spices (toast or sizzle in fat if needed): cumin, paprika, black pepper, chipotle, dried oregano, mild chili flakes

Mix-ins: fresh herbs, diced fruit, chili crisp, onion, garlic, cooked or raw vegetables like potatoes or peppers

OR TRY THESE COMBOS

Onion Raitha Dip
1. Mix strained yogurt with kosher salt, sugar, MSG, and lemon juice.
2. Add onion powder, garlic powder, thinly sliced scallions, and caramelized onions.
3. Top with sliced chives.

Hot & Tingly Smashed Cucumber Salad
1. Gently smash whole cucumbers and slice into ½-inch-thick coins.
2. Season with kosher salt, sugar, MSG, and rice vinegar.
3. Toss with chili crisp and top with Crispy Shallots (page 83).

Dill Pickle Cucumber Salad
1. Halve cucumbers lengthwise and slice into ¼-inch-thick half-moons.
2. Season with kosher salt, sugar, MSG, and dill pickle brine.
3. Add sliced dill pickles, torn dill, chopped white onion, toasted and coarsely crushed coriander seeds, and good extra-virgin olive oil.

Citrus Raitha
1. Mix labne with kosher salt, honey, MSG, orange juice, and lemon juice (freshly squeezed, please!).
2. Add lemon zest, orange zest, and mild chili flakes, like Aleppo pepper or gochugaru.
3. Top with pomegranate seeds.

Sweet, Smoky & Hot Raitha
1. Mix sour cream and buttermilk with kosher salt, sugar, MSG, and freshly squeezed lime juice.
2. Add chopped chipotle peppers in adobo, diced fresh pineapple, and chopped cilantro.

Greek-ish Cucumber Salad
1. Peel and cut cucumbers into ½-inch cubes.
2. Season with kosher salt, sugar, MSG, and red wine vinegar.
3. Add chopped red onion, chopped parsley, halved cherry tomatoes, pitted black olives, dried oregano, and good extra-virgin olive oil.
4. Top with crumbled feta.

Clockwise from top:
Onion Raitha Dip; Hot & Tingly Smashed Cucumber Salad; Citrus Raitha; Dill Pickle Cucumber Salad; Sweet, Smoky & Hot Raitha; Greek-ish Cucumber Salad

House Salad

(Makes as much as you want)

(Active: 20 mins. | Total: 20 mins.)

(Easy) (Vegan) (Gluten-free)

Ingredients:

assorted torn, tender greens: such as red or green leaf lettuce, butter lettuce, lollo rossa, Little Gem

assorted soft herbs with tender stems: such as parsley, dill, cilantro, chervil, tarragon

kosher salt

pick one: ground sumac, toasted and cracked black peppercorns, toasted and cracked coriander, or dried oregano

freshly squeezed lemon juice

extra-virgin olive oil (now's the time to break out the good stuff)

flaky salt

→ This is the salad we eat when we're not eating cucumber salad (or sometimes even when we are). Serve with practically anything. The real secret to salad perfection is to wash and dry lettuce from heads, rather than using prewashed, bagged greens. I promise it's well worth the effort—that bagged stuff is never as crisp or flavorful.

It's so simple, I can't dare give you an exact recipe, so use it as an opportunity to calibrate your palate, really focusing on what tastes right. Just toss and taste, taste, taste. Add enough salt to turn up all the flavors: bitter and vegetal, bright and citrusy, all mellowed out with a touch of extra-virgin olive oil.

---

1. Fill a large bowl or clean sink with cold water and ice cubes (the ice makes the greens extra crisp). Add the greens and herbs and gently swish with your hands to rinse.

2. Lift the greens and herbs out of the water with your hands and transfer to a salad spinner to spin dry. (Alternatively, place the greens in a clean kitchen towel or pillowcase and spin over your head outside.)

3. Wrap in a kitchen towel and refrigerate until ready to serve. (Storing lettuces wrapped in a towel helps them last longer by wicking away excess moisture while also preventing them from drying out.)

4. When ready to eat, place the washed and dried lettuces and herbs into a large bowl and season with salt and sumac (or pepper or coriander or oregano). Toss and taste: The flavor of the lettuce and herbs should be heightened and savory from the salt. The spice should add a pop of background flavor without overpowering the greens. If you're unsure, add more salt and spice just to one leaf. Taste and evaluate before adding more salt and/or spices to the entire bowl.

5. Squeeze over the lemon juice and drizzle with olive oil. Toss and taste: The lemon should brighten the flavors while the oil should round everything out. If you're unsure, add more juice and oil just to one leaf. Taste and evaluate before adding more to the entire bowl. You may want to go back and add more salt and/or spice.

6. Divide among plates, sprinkle lightly with flaky salt (for crunch), and serve right away.

How to Wash Greens

Super-Savory Tomato Salad

with nori & sesame

(Serves 2 to 4)
(Active: 5 mins. | Total: 15 mins.)
(Easy) (Vegan) (Gluten-free)

Ingredients:

2 large heirloom tomatoes (about 1 pound/450 grams), cut into rough chunks, or an equal weight of halved cherry tomatoes

¾ teaspoon Diamond Crystal kosher salt, plus more to taste

¼ teaspoon sugar, plus more to taste

¼ teaspoon MSG (optional)

1 tablespoon unseasoned rice vinegar, plus more to taste

1 tablespoon tamari or soy sauce

extra-virgin olive oil

1 tablespoon toasted sesame seeds

1 tablespoon finely ground nori (see What Is Nori Powder?, below)

→ Tomatoes naturally contain a lot of MSG. That's why they pair so well with other savory ingredients, like the salty parmesan cheese you shower on a NY pizza slice. This salad is all about upping the umami by dressing the tomatoes in other hidden sources of MSG (tamari and ground nori), and of course, some actual MSG. Every tomato is different, so use these measurements as a starting place. Taste as you go, adding more sugar, salt, and vinegar as suits you and your tomatoes.

1. In a large bowl, toss the tomatoes with the salt, sugar, and MSG (if using) and marinate for at least 10 minutes and up to 3 hours. (This gets the tomatoes extra juicy and gives the seasoning time to dissolve.)

2. Before serving, add the rice vinegar and tamari and toss to dress the tomatoes. Taste and add more salt, sugar, or vinegar if needed.

3. Transfer to a large dish or divide among shallow bowls, pouring over any liquid left in the bowl. Drizzle with olive oil and sprinkle over the sesame seeds and nori. Serve right away.

What Is Nori Powder?

Nori is made from shredded red algae that's pressed and dried in sheets in a process similar to papermaking. It's used in Japanese cuisine to wrap sushi, garnish soups, and flavor snacks. I like to lightly toast the sheets over a gas burner (or under a broiler) before tearing them into small pieces and blitzing them up in a spice grinder or high-powered blender to make nori powder. Ground nori adds an ocean-y brine to everything you put it in. It's delicious stirred into rice, tossed into noodles, topping roasted veggies, and of course, sprinkled on popcorn. Store the nori powder in an airtight container with the desiccant from the nori package thrown right in. It will stay clump-free and ready for you to stir into anything that needs a savory hit.

Waldorf Salad

with buttermilk honey-mustard dressing

(Serves 1 to 4)

(Active: 15 mins. | Total: 15 mins.)

(Easy) (Vegetarian) (Gluten-free)

For the dressing:

⅓ cup buttermilk or kefir

2 tablespoons Dijon mustard

1 tablespoon mild honey, such as clover or wildflower

2 teaspoons extra-virgin olive oil

freshly squeezed lemon juice

kosher salt and coarsely ground black pepper

For the salad:

8 medium celery stalks, leaves plucked and reserved

1 small sweet and crisp apple, such as Fuji, Gala, or Honeycrisp

1 cup seedless grapes

¼ cup walnuts, toasted

¼ cup coarsely crumbled blue cheese

→ This is my take on the Waldorf salad, which is said to have been invented at the Waldorf-Astoria Hotel in New York City. The classic version combines apples and celery in mayonnaise. Here I've lightened it up with a buttermilk honey-mustard dressing in place of the traditional mayo and kept the modern additions of walnuts, grapes, and blue cheese. Sometimes I'll top it off with leftover rotisserie chicken, a hard-boiled egg, or even roasted cubes of tofu. But most often I eat it just as it is, straight out of the mixing bowl, usually without pants on. This is my favorite salad. Even though it's not flashy or cool, it's crisp, crunchy, sweet, salty, and everything I want most of the time. Season it aggressively with spicy bites of coarse black pepper and lots of lemon juice to balance the sweet grapes and punch up all that grassy celery.

1. Make the dressing: In a large bowl, whisk together the buttermilk, mustard, honey, and oil. Add lemon juice, salt, and pepper to taste. It should be on the perky side with a peppery bite to balance the sweetness of the fruit.

2. Make the salad: Thinly slice the celery on a diagonal. Slice the apples into thin wedges. Cut the grapes in half. Break the walnuts into coarse pieces with your fingers.

3. Add the celery, apple, and grapes to the bowl of dressing and toss to combine. Taste and add more lemon juice, salt, and pepper as needed.

4. Divide among serving plates and pour over any dressing remaining in the bowl. Top with the blue cheese, walnuts, and celery leaves and serve right away. Store leftovers in the fridge for 1 day.

What Is Kefir?

Originally from Eastern Europe, kefir is a fermented dairy product that can be made with cow, sheep, or goat milk. Unlike yogurt or buttermilk, which are soured with bacteria alone, kefir is inoculated with kefir grains, which ferment the dairy with a combo of both bacteria and yeast. That's why it's not only sour, but also slightly alcoholic and a touch fizzy—like beer! Kefir can be used anywhere you use buttermilk and is also great on its own for all your sipping and smoothie needs.

Citrus & Saffron with Bitter Lettuces

Serves 2 to 4

Active: 30 mins. | Total: 30 mins.

Easy | Gluten-free

Vegetarian (can be made vegan)

Ingredients:

1 small head radicchio, leaves separated and torn into large pieces

1 medium head Belgian endive, leaves separated and torn into large pieces

2 medium Cara Cara oranges

1 medium lemon

Pinch of saffron

½ teaspoon Diamond Crystal kosher salt, plus more to taste

1 tablespoon mild honey, such as clover or wildflower, plus more to taste (see Note)

2 tablespoons extra-virgin olive oil

¼ cup pistachios or another nut/seed, toasted and roughly chopped (or coarsely ground with a mortar and pestle)

Special Equipment:

salad spinner (optional)

Microplane grater

mortar and pestle (or spice grinder)

→ I used to save my saffron for special occasions, keeping the crimson threads tucked away for most of the year, and only busting them out for holidays. But saffron goes bad, and before I realized it, *my precious* grew oxidized, dry, and dusty. Now, after I buy a tin for a festive tahdig or panna cotta, I used it freely in my day-to-day cooking. I figure, that hefty price tag was for that special meal, and whatever's left is fair game for any weeknight risotto, pudding, or even salad. Saffron's musky aroma transforms an ordinary mix of lettuce and citrus, turning any night into something special.

Radicchio and Belgian endive have a hearty crunch I can't get enough of, but they are both quite bitter. That's why you often see the two paired with citrus. The acidity and fresh sweetness of citrus, combined with salt and fat, will mellow it out. However, bitter flavors aren't for everyone, so feel free to swap in mild and crisp Little Gem lettuce leaves or torn romaine instead.

1. Rinse the salad greens in plenty of cold water and spin in a salad spinner until dry (or lay out on kitchen towels, pat dry, and once dry, stack the leaves in a pile and gently roll in a kitchen towel). Store in the fridge until ready to use.

2. Using a Microplane grater, finely grate the zest of half of one orange and half the lemon (about 1 teaspoon of each) into a large bowl. Squeeze the lemon, measure out 2 tablespoons of juice, and add to the bowl.

3. With a small mortar and pestle (or in a spice grinder), grind the saffron and salt into a fine powder. Transfer to the bowl.

4. Add the honey and whisk to combine. Set the bowl on a wet towel coiled into a nest to secure it (see page 45 for photos of this technique). While whisking constantly, stream in the olive oil.

5. Suprême the oranges: Using a sharp knife, trim off the top and bottom of the oranges. Stand the oranges upright on your cutting board and slice off the peel, moving the blade along the curve of the oranges, taking care to remove all of the outer membrane and spongy white pith. Working over the bowl with the dressing, slide the knife in between the membranes to remove each segment, dropping in the segments as you cut and collecting any juices that drip out. Squeeze the remaining orange skeleton to add every last bit of juice to the bowl.

6. Use your hands to toss to combine (so the segments stay intact). Add the salad greens and toss to combine. Taste a leaf with an orange suprême and add more salt, honey, or lemon if needed.

7. To serve, transfer to a platter or divide among plates. Pour over any dressing left in the bowl and garnish with the pistachios. Serve right away.

Note: Make it vegan by swapping the honey for orange marmalade.

What Is Saffron?

Saffron threads are the stigmas plucked from the centers of the saffron crocus, a vibrant purple flower that originated in either Greece or Iran. The flowers bloom one week out of the year and each produces just three stigmas. There is no automation in the process of collecting saffron. The flowers and stigmas are still harvested by hand, hence the steep price even the smallest container can command.

Luckily, if you get the good stuff, a pinch is all you need to add its musky aroma and golden hue to a dish. Avoid powdered saffron or anything that seems cheap; it's likely cut with dye, safflower stigmas, or tree bark. High-quality saffron threads will be uniform in size, a deep, saturated red, incredibly aromatic, and expensive. Here's how to use saffron:

- For maximum color and flavor, grind it into a powder with sugar or salt, then dissolve in hot water. You'll find this technique used in Iranian and Middle Eastern dishes, like tahdig and khoresh-e morgh.

- Make a tea by steeping the stigmas in hot water or milk, as seen in South Asian dishes like biryani and korma.

- Crumble it with your fingers and add it directly to dishes with a lot of liquid. This method releases the least aroma and color and is used in Spanish and European dishes, like paella and risotto.

How to
Suprême Citrus

Taste

Cannellini Beany Melt

(Makes 1 quart bean mixture)

(Enough for 8 toasts)

(Active: 20 mins. | Total: 20 mins.)

(Easy) (Vegetarian) (Gluten-free)

Ingredients:

3 cups cooked cannellini beans, home-cooked or two 15.5-ounce cans

3 scallions, thinly sliced

2 medium celery stalks, finely chopped

⅓ cup celery leaves (if available), roughly chopped

1 large dill pickle, finely chopped

2 tablespoons Dijon mustard

1 tablespoon pickle juice, plus more to taste

1 tablespoon extra-virgin olive oil

8 to 10 dashes Tabasco sauce

kosher salt and freshly ground black pepper

sliced bread (any kind will work, even gluten-free)

American or Muenster cheese slices

→ It's just like the tuna melt you know and love, but made with beans instead of tuna. I always have canned beans in the pantry, so this recipe combines them with a few other staples for a creamier and vegetarian take on the classic. You can store the bean mixture in the fridge for up to 3 days and make your toasts as you need them. As the mixture sits, the beans soak up the seasoning, so be sure to taste it before making each toast. Add more mustard, pickle juice, and salt as needed. Out of toast? Try the beans piled onto a double-toasted Eggo waffle. It's a sweet and salty delight. Trust me.

1. Position an oven rack just below the broiler element and set the broiler to high.

2. In a medium bowl with a fork or potato masher, mash 1 cup of the beans until it becomes a paste. Stir in the scallions, celery, celery leaves (if using), pickle, mustard, pickle juice, oil, and Tabasco and mix until well combined.

3. Taste the mixture and season with salt and pepper to taste, adding more pickle juice if it needs more acidity. Fold in the rest of the beans and gently toss to combine. Taste again for seasoning and adjust as needed.

4. Toast bread slice(s) under the broiler to your desired level of crunch (both sides if you like a lot of crunch).

5. Place the toast on a sheet pan and heap on the bean mixture, making sure you cover the toast from edge to edge. Top with a slice of cheese and place under the broiler until the cheese has fully melted, about 1 minute. Serve the open-faced sandos immediately.

Save Your Pickle Brine!

Already packed with salt, sugar, acid, and seasonings, pickle brine makes an excellent base for a dressing or a bright finish to a soup or sauce. It's also a ready-made brine for fish: Submerge any fish steak or fillet, such as cod or salmon, in pickle brine for 15 minutes prior to cooking. Then drain, pat dry, season, and cook as usual. The brine makes cooking fish more forgiving, preventing overcooking while also keeping the flesh firm and evenly seasoned. That's because the salt and acid in the brine denature some of the proteins in the fish, transforming them into a moisture-retaining net and kicking off the cooking process. But don't leave the fish in there for too long or it will pickle!

Ranch Dressing (aka The Only Dressing That Matters)

Makes ¾ cup

Active: 10 mins. | Total: 10 mins.

Easy | Vegetarian | Gluten-free

Ingredients:

¼ cup mayonnaise

¼ cup sour cream

¼ cup buttermilk or kefir

¼ cup finely chopped fresh dill

¼ cup thinly sliced fresh chives

1 garlic clove, finely grated

¾ teaspoon garlic powder

¾ teaspoon onion powder

½ teaspoon Diamond Crystal kosher salt, plus more to taste

½ teaspoon freshly ground black pepper

pinch of MSG (optional)

→ Before I moved to New York, I thought everyone dipped their pizza, burgers, and samosas into ranch, but I guess it's an LA thing? I don't care that I'm an official East Villager now, I'll never stop. Homemade ranch is absolutely next level, and luckily stupid-easy to make. You start with something creamy—I found that a mix of equal parts mayo, sour cream, and buttermilk gives me exactly the balance of richness and tang I crave. Then stir in chopped dill and add an onion/garlic situation. In the spring we make ranch with ramps, garlic scapes, and every young allium we can find. Play around with the ratios to make it your own and soon you'll be dunking eggrolls in here like a true SoCal-er!

In a medium bowl, whisk together the mayonnaise, sour cream, buttermilk, dill, chives, garlic, garlic powder, onion powder, salt, pepper, and MSG (if using). Taste and add more salt as needed. (Ranch keeps in the fridge for up to 3 days—or 1 week if you omit the fresh garlic.)

Collards & Corn with Ranch Dressing

(Serves 4)

(Active: 20 mins.) | (Total: 20 mins.)

(Easy) (Vegetarian) (Gluten-free)

Ingredients:

1 cup corn nuts

1 large bunch collard greens (about 12 ounces/350 grams)

½ teaspoon Diamond Crystal kosher salt, plus more to taste

1 tablespoon freshly squeezed lemon juice, plus more to taste

3 ears fresh corn, shucked

¼ cup Ranch Dressing (page 30), plus more to taste

½ cup lightly packed fresh dill, leaves and tender stems, plus more for garnish

½ cup sliced chives, plus more for garnish

Special Equipment:

mortar and pestle (or a bowl and heavy rolling pin)

→ I know raw collards don't get the same love as kale, but once the hearty leaves are cut into strips, they transform into silky strands ready to soak up sauce just like slippery noodles. To convince you to give collard salad a chance, here I've paired them with the best dressing and snack food there is, ranch and corn nuts.

1. With a mortar and pestle (or in a bowl with the end of a rolling pin), coarsely crush the corn nuts.

2. Working with one collard leaf at a time, hold the stem firmly in one hand, and strip the leaf off the stem and midrib with your other hand. Discard the stem pieces; wash and dry the leaves. Stack the collard leaves, roll into a fat cigar, and slice crosswise into thin strips. Transfer to a large bowl. (You will have about 8 lightly packed cups.)

3. Add the salt and lemon juice and use your hands to gently massage the collards until silky, darkened, and wilted, about 2 minutes. (The salt, acid, and massaging action break down the cellulose in the leaves, making them tender without cooking.)

4. Working with one ear at a time, stand the corn up in the bowl of collards and use a sharp knife to cut the kernels off the cob, letting them fall into the bowl. Use the back of the knife to scrape any corn milk from the cob.

5. Add the dressing to taste and toss with your hands to combine. Add the dill and chives and toss to combine. Taste and add more salt, lemon juice, and dressing as needed.

6. Transfer to a platter or divide among plates. Top with more dill and chives to garnish and sprinkle with the corn nuts. Serve right away. (Without the corn nuts, the collard salad will keep refrigerated for up to 3 days.)

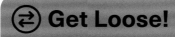 **Get Loose!**

- Try this salad with any tough green, like kale, cabbage, or escarole. The massaging action breaks them down, making them great to eat raw.

- If you don't have corn nuts, swap them out for any other crunchy snack, such as crushed Fritos, kettle chips, or pretzel sticks.

**Collards & Corn
with Ranch Dressing**

**Nutty & Salty
Gunpowder Spice**

Nutty & Salty Gunpowder Spice

for dunking, sprinkling & fun-dipping

(Makes about 1 cup)

(Active: 20 mins. | Total: 30 mins.)

(Easy) (Vegan) (Gluten-free)

Ingredients:

¼ cup chana dal (hulled and split chickpeas)

¼ cup urad dal (hulled and split black gram)

¼ cup white sesame seeds

¼ cup unsweetened coconut flakes

1 tablespoon cumin seeds

1 tablespoon flaxseeds

20 curry leaves

coconut sugar or brown sugar

kosher salt

Kashmiri red chili powder or cayenne pepper

pinch of MSG (optional)

Special Equipment:

spice grinder (or blender or mortar and pestle)

→ Gunpowder spice, also known as idli podi or milagai podi, is not a spice blend but instead a dry chutney found in South India. It's most often eaten with dosa or steamed rice cakes called idli. Around our house we just call it "fun dip." I reach for this stuff daily to dunk apple wedges, spicy radishes, and crunchy cucumbers in, or to sprinkle over hard-boiled eggs and roasted potatoes. The toasted lentils and seeds give the gunpowder a nutty and savory flavor, while there's just enough salt, sugar, and chili to keep you coming back for more. This recipe uses a mix of chana dal and urad dal, which are both hulled and split lentils. Since they are already processed, they readily toast and blitz into a powder. This won't work with a whole lentil. (Read more about dal and lentils on page 108.)

There are no measurements for the final seasoning, because how salty, sweet, and spicy you want this gunpowder spice is a personal decision and you need to go on this journey alone. Take your time: Add the salt, sugar, and chili a fat pinch at a time and taste after every addition. You want the chili heat to hit you first, with the sugar rounding out that fire, and enough salt to make everything pop. Serve with raw or cooked vegetables, with fruit, over eggs, on a savory yogurt bowl, in a dosa, or sprinkled on buttered roti (page 488).

1. In a small skillet, toast the chana dal over medium heat, stirring constantly, until it's golden brown and smells toasty. Transfer to a plate to cool. Toasting each ingredient separately, repeat with the urad dal, sesame seeds, coconut flakes, cumin, flaxseeds, and curry leaves until golden, aromatic, and crisp. Transfer them to the same plate as you go. (Each ingredient will take a different amount of time to toast, so let sight and smell be your guide.)

2. Once cool, in a spice grinder, blend all the toasted ingredients in batches until they form a coarse powder, similar in size to bread crumbs or coarse cornmeal. Transfer to a medium bowl.

3. Season with sugar, salt, chili powder, and MSG (if using) to taste. It should taste savory, spicy, and slightly sweet. Store gunpowder spice at room temperature for up to 6 weeks.

What Are Curry Leaves?

Curry leaves are an herb and are not at all related to curry powder. They are, however, related to citrus and have an incomparable musky and pungent aroma. They are often crisped in oil or toasted before adding to a dish. You can find fresh curry leaves in Indian or specialty grocery stores and keep them in the freezer until you need them.

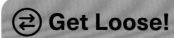 Get Loose!

You might not find all the ingredients needed for this at your average grocery store, so use this recipe as an inspiration to make your own fun dip instead. Try blending together various toasted seeds, nuts, seasonings, and spices (really, anything dry) and then season it in stages with salt, sugar, and (optional) MSG. Think of it like a dry dip you can keep at room temperature, ideal for lunchboxes and road trips. These are a few of my favorites.

Sweet Peanut & Cinnamon Fun Dip

Great for dunking anything you'd eat with peanut butter: apple wedges, celery sticks, dates, grapes . . .

½ cup peanuts

2 sheets graham crackers, broken into small pieces

1 tablespoon ground cinnamon

dark brown sugar

kosher salt

Toast the peanuts and grind with the crackers. Toss with the cinnamon, then season to taste with brown sugar and salt.

Funky Cashew & Shrimp Fun Dip

This tastes like satay sauce, which is traditionally made with peanut butter, fish sauce, chili, coconut milk, and lime. Here, dried shrimp brings that fish sauce funk to ground cashews and coconut. It's perfect for dipping cucumber spears spritzed with lime, chilled poached shrimp, and crisp sweet peppers.

½ cup cashews

¼ cup unsweetened coconut flakes

2 tablespoons dried shrimp, soaked in cool water, drained

¾ teaspoon garlic powder

pinch of MSG

coconut sugar

chili flakes

kosher salt

Toast the cashews, coconut, and shrimp separately, then grind. Add the garlic powder and MSG and season to taste with coconut sugar, chili, and salt.

Cool Pistachio Ranch Fun Dip

Because I love ranch.

½ cup pistachios

¼ cup nutritional yeast

4 teaspoons dried dill

1 tablespoon granulated onion

2 teaspoons granulated garlic

pinch of MSG

kosher salt

sugar

Toast the pistachios, then grind with the nutritional yeast and dill. Toss with the granulated onion, granulated garlic, and MSG, then season to taste with salt and sugar.

Watermelon Chaat

with lime, ginger & cashew clumps

Serves 4

Active: 30 mins. | Total: 30 mins.

Easy Vegetarian Gluten-free

Ingredients:

¾ cup cashews or any nut/seed, toasted and finely chopped

1½ teaspoons Diamond Crystal kosher salt

1 teaspoon cumin seeds, toasted and ground

1 teaspoon freshly ground black pepper

pinch of MSG (optional)

¼ cup mild honey, such as clover or wildflower

1 mini seedless watermelon (about 3½ pounds/1.5 kg)

sugar (optional)

⅓ cup freshly squeezed lime juice (from about 3 limes)

2-inch piece fresh ginger, peeled and cut into matchsticks

2 to 4 Thai green chilies or serrano chilies, very thinly sliced (or snipped with scissors)

1 cup lightly packed fresh cilantro leaves and tender stems, coarsely chopped, plus sprigs for garnish

→ Chaat is the name for a variety of snacks found throughout South Asia. They come in many forms from bhel puri, which is a mix of puffed rice, peanuts, and green chili, to the nacho-like papdi chaat, streaked with sweet and hot chutneys. Chaat masala is the one thing they all have in common—a seasoning blend made with funky black salt, tart green mango powder, cumin, and other spices. The key to chaat is chaatpati flavor, which is so tart and hot it'll make your tongue curl and your mouth pucker, with just enough sugar and salt to keep those punchy vibes in check.

My abu loves chaat and makes one for himself every day after work with whatever's around. He'll toss together pretzel sticks, cereal, crushed crackers, and fruit with chilies, lime, and ginger. As long as you've got those sour, sweet, hot, and salty flavors, you've got chaat. I want you to have chaat in your life even if you don't have chaat masala, so this bright and fresh watermelon version uses ingredients you can find in any grocery store. Shake things up by swapping in different in-season fruit in place of the watermelon, from peaches to pineapple, cantaloupe or honeydew, or even a mix. Be sure to get aggressive with your seasoning here for the ideal chaatpati flavor.

---

1. In a small bowl, stir together the cashews, salt, cumin, black pepper, and MSG (if using). Add the honey and mix until the nuts clump together.

2. Trim off the blossom and stem ends of the watermelon rind and stand the watermelon upright. Holding your knife at an angle, trim off the rind and white flesh, moving the knife along the curve of the melon. Continue until you've cut off all the rind.

3. Cut the melon in half and place it on the cutting board cut-side down. Slice into ½-inch-thick planks. Stack the planks and slice crosswise into ½-inch-wide sticks. Transfer to a large bowl along with any juices that have collected on the board.

4. Taste the watermelon. If it's not ripe and sweet, add sugar to taste. The watermelon needs to be sweet in order to balance the other aggressive flavors.

5. Using your hands, gently toss the watermelon with the lime juice, ginger, chilies, and chopped cilantro. (Some watermelon pieces will break, that's okay.)

6. Just before serving, add the nut/honey mixture and gently toss, breaking up the clumps into pea-sized pieces as you go.

7. Transfer to shallow bowls, pouring over the juices left in the bowl. Garnish with cilantro sprigs and serve right away.

Grated Beet & Crispy Chickpeas

with lemon, oregano & feta

(Serves 2 as a main or 4 as a side)

(Active: 40 mins. | Total: 40 mins.)

(Easy) (Vegetarian) (Gluten-free)

Ingredients:

1 medium lemon

1 tablespoon coriander seeds

2 large beets (about 1 pound/
450 grams)

¼ cup extra-virgin olive oil, plus more
for drizzling

1½ cups cooked chickpeas, home-
cooked or one 15.5-ounce can,
patted dry

1 teaspoon Diamond Crystal kosher
salt, plus more to taste

6 garlic cloves, finely chopped

4 scallions, thinly sliced on the
diagonal, light and dark-green
parts kept separate

2 teaspoons dried oregano, plus more
for garnish

1 tablespoon red wine vinegar, plus
more to taste

1 big hunk of feta cheese (about
6 ounces/170 grams)

Special Equipment:

mortar and pestle (or small bowl and
heavy rolling pin)

box grater

→ This salad leans into the savory side of beets with an abundance of garlic and pungent oregano. The warm olive oil and wilted scallions bring enough heat to temper the beets' raw starchiness while keeping the shreds crisp and fresh. If you don't have feta, plate the salad over a generous swipe of salted strained yogurt for a similarly creamy tang. Beets can easily taste excessively earthy and sweet, so be sure to balance this salad with plenty of vinegar and salt after everything has been combined. While you're seasoning the salad, don't forget about the salty and acidic feta that'll be joining the party later. Try this salad with any bean, like kidney, cannellini, or lima. You can even swap out the beets for an equal weight of any hardy vegetable, like carrots, parsnips, kohlrabi, or rutabaga.

1. Using a vegetable peeler, remove the zest from the lemon in long strips. Cut the lemon in half and squeeze the juice into a small bowl. With a mortar and pestle (or in a small bowl with the end of a rolling pin), crack the coriander seeds.

2. Using the same peeler, peel the beets. Using a box grater, coarsely grate the beets into a large bowl.

3. In a medium skillet, heat the oil over medium heat until shimmering. Add the chickpeas and lemon zest, tossing occasionally, until lightly browned, crackly, and crisp, 5 to 7 minutes. Remove from the heat. Using a slotted spoon, transfer the chickpeas to a plate and season with the salt. Reserve the oil in the skillet (discard the lemon zest).

4. Add the garlic to the skillet with the reserved oil and return to medium-low heat. Cook, stirring constantly, until barely golden, 4 to 5 minutes. Add the scallion whites and coriander. Increase the heat to medium-high and cook, stirring frequently, until the scallions wilt and the coriander seeds pop and become aromatic, about 1 minute. Remove from the heat and add the oregano and vinegar. Use the vinegar to scrape up anything sticking to the skillet and scrape everything over the grated beets.

5. Add the garlic/scallion mixture, the lemon juice, salt, and half the scallion greens to the beets and toss everything together. Taste and add more salt and vinegar as needed. (You can store the salad at this point in the fridge, with the chickpeas and feta stored separately, for up to 3 days.)

6. Divide the beet salad among plates, top with the chickpeas, and break over pieces of feta. Garnish with the remaining scallion greens, drizzle with olive oil, and sprinkle with oregano.

Bravas Potato Salad

Makes 1½ quarts

Active: 20 mins. | Total: 40 mins.

Easy | Vegetarian | Gluten-free

Ingredients:

35 small potatoes, like baby Yukon Golds, fingerlings, or creamers (about 2 pounds/900 grams)

½ cup Diamond Crystal kosher salt, plus more to taste

1½ tablespoons smoked paprika, plus more for dusting

1 teaspoon freshly ground black pepper

¾ teaspoon cayenne pepper

⅓ cup extra-virgin olive oil

4 garlic cloves, peeled

3 tablespoons sherry vinegar or red wine vinegar

3 tablespoons spicy or Dijon mustard

3 tablespoons mild honey, such as clover or wildflower

½ cup fresh parsley leaves and tender stems, plus sprigs for garnish

1 medium bag (about 9 ounces/ 250 grams) kettle-style potato chips

Special Equipment:

Microplane grater

→ I know this is gonna sound so cliché, but I backpacked through Europe, and yes, it changed my life. This was a time before Airbnb, when I had to go to an internet café to log on and I carried an international phone card to call home. I took a one-way flight, bounced around with no itinerary, and had my *Eat, Pray, Love* moments. I ate papas bravas daily, the iconic tapa that you'll find at every bar and restaurant. They are crispy fried potatoes covered in a spicy sauce that is either mayonnaise- or tomato-based, or even a combination of both. It gets a subtle warmth from pimentón picante, Spanish hot paprika, and an intense smolder from Pimentón de la Vera (PDO), a smoked variety from the Extremadura/La Vera region of Spain. Paprika is essential to Spanish cuisine, used in chorizo, paella, and stews, and as a dusting for nearly every tapa.

This potato salad is inspired by the flavors of all those papas bravas, even providing a fried crunch from crushed potato chips. If you can find real-deal Spanish pimentón, do go for it, but to keep things accessible, I opted for a combo of smoked paprika and cayenne pepper instead. The dressing will taste aggressively acidic at first, but add a pinch of salt at a time, toss, and taste. The salt will temper and balance the vinegar's perky punch, while the potatoes gently break down into a creamy sauce.

---

1. Wash the potatoes and place them in a medium or large pot. Add enough cool tap water to cover, add the salt, cover, and bring to a simmer over high heat. (Don't be scared by all the salt, most of it will go down the drain, see How to Salt Cooking Water, page 43.) Reduce the heat to maintain a gentle simmer and cook until easily pierced by a fork or cake tester, 17 to 20 minutes.

2. Meanwhile, have a large heatproof bowl nearby. Measure the paprika, black pepper, and cayenne into a small bowl so you can easily dump them all into the oil once hot.

3. In a small skillet, heat the olive oil over medium heat. Using a Microplane grater, grate the garlic into the oil and cook, stirring constantly, until the garlic begins to sizzle, about 1 minute. Add the spices and cook, stirring constantly, until aromatic, about 30 seconds. Scrape the content of the skillet into the heatproof bowl.

4. Whisk the vinegar, mustard, and honey into the spiced oil and set aside.

5. Once the potatoes are tender, drain them in a colander. While still warm, use a fork and your hands to roughly break each potato in half and add to the bowl with the dressing.

6. Toss well to evenly coat in the dressing and taste. Add salt a big pinch at a time, toss, taste, and add more. Continue seasoning, tossing, and tasting until all the flavors are balanced and the potatoes are evenly coated in a creamy sauce. (If it tastes too acidic or spicy, you probably need more salt.)

7. Serve warm or refrigerate for up to 3 days and serve chilled.

8. Just before serving, roughly chop the parsley and stir in. Transfer to a shallow bowl and top with a couple big handfuls of crushed potato chips, dust with smoked paprika, and top with sprigs of parsley. Serve with extra chips on the side for guests to add more if needed.

So Much Paprika

There are two other types of paprika used in Spanish cooking: Pimentón dulce (sweet paprika) and Pimentón agridulce (bittersweet). Pretty wild when you realize peppers are native to America and didn't make their way to Spain until that whole 1492 thing, but, oh boy, did they make an impression.

How to Salt Cooking Water

When you're simmering, boiling, or poaching anything in a seasoned liquid, most of that salt ends up straight down the drain. That's why you need to use a lot to get enough into whatever you're cooking. How much salt depends on several factors:

› How absorbent or porous is the ingredient? How much surface area is exposed to the salt water?
  • Whole unpeeled potatoes need more salt than peeled and diced potatoes.
  • Whole Brussels sprouts need more salt than cabbage leaves.

› How long will it simmer? A shorter cook time often requires more salt.
  • Quick-cooking green beans need more salt than poached artichokes.
  • Parboiled basmati rice needs more salt than long-simmered beans.
  • Quick-poached shrimp need more salt than long-braised octopus.

› The ratio of water to stuff you're cooking. Less water means you need less salt because more of that salt will get absorbed into the food.
  • If you boil 1 pound of pasta in a huge stockpot of water, the water will need to be more heavily seasoned than if you boil 1 pound of pasta in just enough water to cover.

For recipes that require heavily seasoned liquid, I give you measurements for the salt. Have a sip of the salted liquid before anything gets cooking, so you can learn what seasoned water should taste like. With enough practice and gulps of unpleasantly salty water, you'll be tossing fistfuls in like the best of 'em. (Remember, I use Diamond Crystal kosher salt, so make the necessary conversions if you use a different salt; see page 10.)

Homemade Mayonnaise (Is Worth It)

(Makes 1 cup)

(Active: 10 mins. | Total: 10 mins.)

(Intermediate) (Vegetarian)

(Gluten-free)

Ingredients:

1 large egg yolk

1 teaspoon Dijon mustard

1 tablespoon freshly squeezed lemon juice, plus more to taste

1 tablespoon cold water

1 teaspoon Diamond Crystal kosher salt, plus more to taste

¾ cup neutral oil, such as safflower or grapeseed

→ There are certain dishes that demand store-bought mayo, like grilled cheese, BLTs, or burgers. But when I'm treating mayonnaise as more of a sauce rather than a condiment, nothing tops the richness and depth of homemade. It's perfect for dunking vegetables, mixing with capers and cornichons for tartar sauce, or dolloping onto rice (like the Spanish do with paella). Seasoning mayonnaise can be challenging. It's tough tasting through all that fat, but take your time and add salt a pinch at a time, tasting every step of the way. Once you master how to taste and season mayo, everything else is a cinch.

1. Coil a wet kitchen towel into a nest and rest a medium bowl on it. In the stabilized bowl, whisk together the egg yolk, mustard, lemon juice, water, and salt until well combined.

2. Slowly stream in the oil, whisking constantly. Start by dripping in droplets, making sure each drop is well incorporated before adding the next. Once half of the oil has been incorporated, you can pour in the rest in a thin stream, still whisking the entire time.

3. Once all the oil has been incorporated, the mayonnaise should be thickened and spreadable. Taste for seasoning and adjust with salt and lemon juice as needed. Not sure if it's seasoned? Play around with a big spoonful, adding little pinches of salt, before proceeding with the whole batch. Store mayonnaise in the fridge for up to 1 month.

What the Hell Happened?

Did your mayo break? Is it greasy and liquidy instead of creamy and spreadable? You probably overwhelmed the emulsion by adding the oil too fast or whisking too slowly. Don't worry, here's an easy fix:

1. In a new bowl, whisk together 1 tablespoon water with 1 tablespoon of the broken mayo.

2. While whisking constantly, slowly add the broken mayo to the water mixture 1 teaspoon at a time.

3. Once all the broken mayo has been incorporated, it should be thick and spreadable.

Still Broken?
Start again with a new yolk, slowly whisking the broken mayo into the yolk until thick and spreadable.

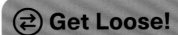 Get Loose!

You can use this base mayo to make all kinds of different sauces and condiments. In a medium bowl, combine the mayonnaise with mix-ins listed below and whisk to combine. Let the flavored mayonnaise sit in the fridge for at least 6 hours before using to allow the flavors to meld. (It's also totally cool to make these variations with 1 cup of store-bought mayonnaise instead.)

Dijonnaise
Great on sandwiches, with grilled meats, and (of course) chicken fingers.

1 cup Homemade Mayonnaise (page 44), or store-bought

¼ cup Dijon mustard

2 tablespoons mild honey, such as clover or wildflower

½ teaspoon smoked paprika

Saffron Mayonnaise
Dollop it on eggs, rice, pasta, and shellfish.

1 cup Homemade Mayonnaise (page 44), or store-bought

¼ teaspoon saffron threads, crushed between your fingers

2 garlic cloves, finely grated

freshly squeezed lemon juice and grated zest, to taste

Tartar Sauce
For all your fried fish needs!

1 cup Homemade Mayonnaise (page 44), or store-bought

¾ cup lightly packed fresh parsley leaves and tender stems, finely chopped

⅓ cup cornichons, finely chopped

¼ cup drained capers, finely chopped

3 tablespoons extra-virgin olive oil

1 tablespoon Dijon mustard

freshly squeezed lemon juice and grated zest, to taste

Mayo & Sardines on Toast

(Makes 6 toasts)

(Active: 10 mins. | Total: 10 mins.)

(Intermediate)

Ingredients:

6 pieces thick-cut country or
    sourdough bread

1 batch Homemade Mayonnaise
    (page 44)

2 tins oil-packed sardines

1 small red onion, sliced

parsley sprigs

→ For this simple sardine toast, the homemade mayonnaise is what takes things to the next level.

Char the bread under the broiler or directly over a gas flame until crusty and blackened in places. Thickly spread on the mayo. Divide the sardines and onion between the toasts and top with parsley. Serve right away.

How to Make a Velvety Vegetable Soup out of Anything

Up until now, this chapter has been about cold food, so why soup? Because soup is a great place to learn about seasoning since it's mostly water. Water that we make flavorful with vegetables, aromatics, and, most important, salt. I think great soup is the most impressive thing you can make and luckily, with some patience, it's something anyone can do with whatever they've got on hand. Pour yourself a bowl and take your time tasting as you add pinches of salt and MSG, splashes of vinegar or lemon, and just a touch of sweetener. Keep in mind that the seasoning in soup builds as you eat it, so you can tell if it's spot-on only after tasting a bowlful.

Here's my guide to making a creamy and flavorful pureed soup:

Step 1: Sweat
Not you, your vegetables! Sure, you could just boil a bunch of stuff and blend it, but many flavorful compounds are only accessed when direct contact with fat happens.

Roughly chop whatever vegetables and aromatics you're feeling (carrots, squash, onion, cauliflower) and toss them all into a pot with just enough fat to lightly coat everything (olive oil, butter, ghee, coconut oil) and a big pinch of salt. Cook, stirring often, until everybody weeps and wilts. You don't need browning here, so go ahead and crowd the pan. Sweating is a vital step for developing flavor not only in soups, but also in sauces, braises, and stews.

Add spices now! They need direct contact with fat to bloom.

Step 2: Simmer
Cover everything with water, broth, or stock and simmer until completely tender.

Step 3: Blend
If you want to cut to the chase, blend everything until smooth with a handheld immersion blender right in the pot. For silky perfection, blend the soup in batches in a stand blender. Take care to fill the blender jar only halfway for each batch and start on the lowest speed to prevent soup explosions.

Some souper inspiration:

Honeynut & Miso Soup

Step 1: Sweat—chopped, peeled Honeynut squash, onion, ginger, Fresno chili, and apple

Step 2: Simmer—with water

Step 3: Blend

Step 4: Adjust & Season— adjust thickness. Season with salt, miso paste, and maple syrup.

Step 5: Garnish—with strained yogurt and pecans toasted in oil and seasoned with chili flakes and salt.

Step 4: Adjust & Season & TASTE!

Return the soup to the pot. (Pass it through a fine-mesh sieve if you want it restaurant-level smooth.)

Add water if the soup it too thick or simmer it down over medium-high heat if it's too thin. Add a touch of cream or coconut milk if you want more body.

Season with salt (see Note). Taste and add more salt. Repeat. Pretend you're carrying a spoonful of soup to an angry chef to taste and imagine what they'd grunt at you. When you feel like you're close, take it to the next level: Pour yourself a bowlful and play around with additional MSG, acid, and sugar. Now maybe add more salt. If the angry chef in your mind is pleased, go for it and finish seasoning the whole pot just like your experimental portion.

Note: Salt doesn't have to mean "salt." Try seasoning your soup with miso paste, instant dashi powder, soy sauce, or powdered bouillon.

Step 5: Garnish (If You're Feeling Extra)

Pour the soup into bowls and top with:

• a dollop of something creamy, like yogurt, crème fraîche, or sour cream

• bring on the crunch with crushed Fritos, toasted nuts or seeds, crumbled crackers, or croutons

• freshen things up with diced raw onion, chopped fresh herbs, or sliced chilies

• go wild with mini grilled cheese, a spoonful of chili crisp, slices of Poached Chicken Breast (page 210), or fried oysters

Step 6: Store

Store ungarnished soup in the refrigerator for up to 5 days or freeze for up to 3 months. For easy thawing, I freeze my soup preportioned into 1- or 2-cup containers. After reheating the soup, taste and adjust the seasoning.

Temperature Management 101

Master heat by cooking eggs all the ways

Temperature Management 101

I didn't cook much meat or fish until I was an adult with my own kitchen and credit card (what parent's gonna bankroll a twelve-year-old's request for whole turbot?), but I don't think I missed a thing. Instead, I made eggs—lots of them. I made scrambled eggs with American cheese from my first culinary guide, *Better Homes & Gardens New Junior Cookbook*. I went through countless cartons trying to perfect the classic French omelet. Nailing one with no color, creamy curds, and a thin skin kept me busy all through middle school. And I ate so many weird, messed-up eggs trying to get down that poached egg Martha Stewart made look so easy. But all those eggs taught me everything I needed to know about how to manage heat and time, skills vital to cooking pretty much anything. By the time I got my first job working the egg station at a pub, I was so ready for those full English breakfasts, getting bangers, rashers, stewed mushrooms, grilled tomatoes, and, of course, eggs all the ways on a plate at once. (Okay, after my first service I went home and cried, but I got there eventually.)

Eggs cook quickly and can attain a wide variety of textures and consistencies. Crack an egg into a skillet of hot shimmering oil, and watch it instantly frizzle and brown, while plopping one into barely quivering water will yield a delicate white with a molten yolk core. Stir beaten eggs leisurely over moderate heat for a fluffy diner-style scramble, or briskly whisk them while cooking low and slow for the creamiest curds. You can whip egg whites into a light foam that bakes up crisp, chewy, soft, or all of the above, and use the egg yolks to enrich a custard or curd (but that's for another chapter).

Eggs allow you to explore many techniques without dedicating much time or money, which is especially important when you're starting out. Use them to learn what a gentle simmer or shimmering hot oil should look like, before you start poaching halibut or searing scallops. Practice timing and planning with eggs, working toward getting a collection of hot dishes on the table all at once, before you attack a high-stakes holiday meal. Every egg is an opportunity to get to know your burner and pan better, so you can develop a deep understanding of the subtle differences between low heat and medium-low heat or cooking in a cast-iron skillet verses a stainless steel one. Here's the hard-boiled truth, no matter how detailed a recipe is, in the beginning, you will mess up. It takes time and practice to get to know your tools, kitchen, and ingredients. Be prepared to make sloppy, un-Instagrammable dishes. But in the end, you will have breakfast (or lunch, or dinner) on the table and you will be a better cook tomorrow. Even if it means breaking a few eggs.

The Anatomy of an Egg

Shell

Eggshells are made of calcium carbonate secreted by the hen's uterine lining—wow, chickens really are incredible! The color of an eggshell is no indication of the egg's flavor or nutritiousness and is determined, instead, by the hen's breed. If I happen to have eggshells lying around, I add them to my bone broth (see How to Make Bone Broth, page lxxii) in the last 30 minutes of simmering. The residual egg white protein on the shell will bind to any foam or impurities, resulting in a clearer broth. As a bonus, the broth gets a calcium boost from the minerals leeched from the shells.

Membrane

Between the eggshell and the egg white is a thin but tough membrane that acts as a barrier against bacteria and contamination. It's made from keratin, the same stuff as human hair.

Air Gap

This little pocket exists to give a baby chick its first gulp of air. As an egg ages, it will lose moisture through the shell's many microscopic perforations, resulting in the membrane pulling away from the shell, and creating an even larger air gap. You know an egg is old if its blunt end floats when you submerge it in water, which happens because the air gap has grown. This is likely why older eggs seem easier to peel (but even a fresh egg is easier to peel if you start at the blunt end).

Cuticle

Freshly laid eggs have a thin cuticle covering, preventing bacteria from entering through their porous shells. If this cuticle is left intact, you can safely store eggs at room temperature. In the US, eggs are washed and sanitized before selling. This strips off the cuticle, so the egg needs to be stored refrigerated. On the plus side, refrigerated eggs deteriorate more slowly and last longer. So even if you buy eggs with the cuticle intact, it might be a good idea to store them refrigerated.

ANATOMY OF AN EGG

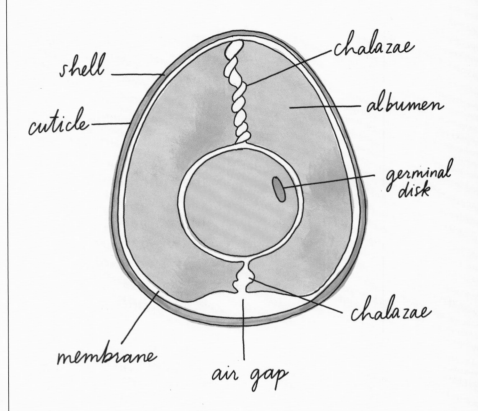

Egg White/Albumen

Egg whites are mostly water with a small percentage of protein and sparse quantities of vitamins, minerals, fatty acids, glucose, and enzymes. The egg white not only provides food and water for the growing baby chick, but also protects it physically and chemically. It might look like one uniform mass, but an egg white is actually made up of alternating layers of thin and thick white, that cushion the egg yolk. For cooking, that thick and thin egg white is why it takes a moment to thoroughly whisk an egg. Fresher eggs have a higher ratio of thick to thin white, giving you a plump poached egg or a sunny-side with a yolk that rides high.

Chalazae

This is that thick, white knot you might find clinging to an egg yolk. It's a cord made up of two entwined protein strands that keep the egg yolk centered in the egg white by tethering it to the shell. Although flavorless, its tough texture won't break down with any amount of blending or cooking. It's not noticeable in an omelet or scramble, but is an unpleasant surprise in a silky smooth pudding. Get that chalazae out of there by pouring egg-thickened sauces and custards through a fine-mesh sieve after cooking.

Egg Yolk

The yolk's purpose is to feed the baby chick, so this is where most of the egg's calories, vitamins, minerals, and fats live. Yolks give sauces and puddings richness, make cakes and cookies tender or chewy, create creamy scrambles and omelets, and, I think, are just the best damn part. They also contain incredible emulsifiers that can hook up fat and water to make thick and stable mixtures—like mayonnaise, hollandaise, and cake batter—possible. One thing to watch out for: Egg yolks contain a starch-digesting enzyme called amylase that can make pudding or pastry creams become watery if not heated sufficiently.

Germinal Disk

Ever notice a small dark spot on your egg yolk? This is the germinal disk that if fertilized, will develop into a baby chick. It doesn't affect the flavor or texture of an egg and has no culinary purpose.

Egg Meets Heat

A cracked egg is mainly little bundles of coiled-up protein floating in water. Like, a lot of water. Water molecules outnumber the proteins by 1,000 to 1. Though there are other free-flowing sources of protein, like milk and bone broth, aside from throwing a chicken breast into a blender, there isn't another fluid form of protein that transforms as dramatically and diversely. With the addition of heat, eggs can set up jammy, tender, or tough. Whisk the whites alone and they'll stiffen up. Dilute eggs into milk or cream and they add body and structure. Let's take a closer look at what's going on when an egg meets heat:

Raw Egg

Protein molecules are made up of long strands of amino acids, the building blocks of all proteins. In a raw egg, each one is tightly coiled, knotted, and tangled together like a bundle of Christmas lights. Most of the proteins carry a negative electric charge and repel each other, so they freely float throughout the water molecules far from one another.

Add Some Heat

Heat is like the DJ at a dance party, getting molecules moving and grooving. This causes the protein bundles to bounce into one another.

Add the Right Amount of Heat

After enough heat and bumper-car action, the coils begin to unravel. This unraveling is coupled with protein strands linking together, forming a loose, three-dimensional network with the water molecules trapped within. This is when the egg goes from looking translucent to opaque and is called protein coagulation. With the water snugly trapped within the protein network, you end up with tender and moist scrambled eggs, omelets, and sunny-sides. It's all about applying the right amount of heat.

But Add Too Much Heat . . .

If you continue to heat up the egg, the proteins link up tighter and closer together, eventually squeezing out all the water. This is how you end up with dry and watery eggs.

1. RAW EGG

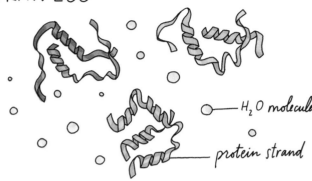

— H_2O molecule

— protein strand

2. ADD SOME HEAT

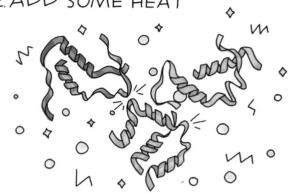

3. ADDING THE RIGHT AMOUNT OF HEAT

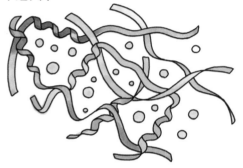

4. TOO MUCH HEAT

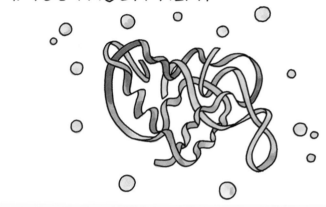

Salt & Acid on Eggs

There is myth that salting your eggs will make them tough, while in fact, the complete opposite is true. Whisking salt or acid into eggs up to 15 minutes in advance of cooking will yield a moister and more tender scramble or omelet by neutralizing the negative charge between the egg proteins. This does two things: First, it makes the proteins uncoil and more readily hook up, setting at a lower temperature. Second, it prevents them from overcoagulating, or forming a network that's so tight that the water is squeezed out. This fact is also why cream of tartar (an acid) is added to egg whites to prevent overwhipping (more on whipping later). The myth likely persists because the addition of salt or acid makes beaten eggs *appear* watery, but what's really happening is the salt breaks up the thick and thin whites, causing them to look less cloudy. Don't believe me? Try out a side-by-side test of scrambled eggs. Salt one 15 minutes before cooking and salt the other after cooking. The results are pretty hard to deny.

How to Boil Eggs for Easy Peeling & Perfect Doneness *Every Time!*

Nope, you don't need old eggs or magic to cook your eggs just right and make them easy to peel. Instead, this method uses the anatomy of the egg to your advantage. Remember that thin membrane between the eggshell and egg white? By starting with eggs straight from the fridge, dropping them into water at a rolling boil, then shocking them in ice water, that membrane relaxes and contracts, pulling away from the shell. Once in ice water, gently crack the eggs all over with the back of a spoon, which drives water between the membrane and the egg white. *Boom,* easy shell removal without any divots or dimples. The key is those dramatic changes in temperature. Make sure you have enough boiling water, so the temperature doesn't drop after adding the eggs, and use plenty of ice in a big enough ice bath.

1. Bring a pot of water to a rolling boil: Saucepan size matters—for 1 to 2 eggs, I use a small 1-quart saucepan. For a dozen eggs, I use a 6-quart saucepan. Any more than 12 eggs, and I bust out the stockpot. If you don't have enough water, the eggs won't cook evenly and the water temperature will drop drastically, throwing off cook times. You've also gotta make sure the eggs have room to groove, or they'll smack against the pot and crack prematurely.

2. Prepare an ice bath: Fill a big bowl with tons of ice and just enough water to cover.

3. Drop in the eggs and set a timer: Use a slotted spoon, or if you're cooking a lot of eggs, a spider, to gently lower all the eggs into the boiling water at once. Immediately set a timer for the desired doneness (see opposite).

4. Temperature management: You want to keep the water at a gentle boil throughout the cooking. Covering the pot helps the water come back to a boil faster, but you may need to reduce the heat, so the eggs aren't knocking into one another.

5. Remove and shock: Once the timer is up, remove all the eggs at once. Immediately, gently crack each egg all over with the back of a spoon and dunk in the ice bath. Chill the eggs in the bath for at least 1 minute and up to 2 hours.

6. Peel and reheat (if necessary): Peel off the eggshell, starting with the blunt end. If you need your eggs warm, give them a quick dunk in hot water to reheat.

The following times are for large eggs:

3 to 5 minutes
Soft and runny—for eating out of the shell and dunking toast soldiers

6 minutes
Set white with a runny yolk—ideal for dishes requiring continued cooking, such as Scotch eggs, egg korma, and doro wat

7 minutes
Set white with a jammy yolk—good on salads, tacos, eating cut in half

9 minutes
Set white and yolk, with a fudgy core—perfect for deviled eggs, egg salad, slices for sandwiches

11 minutes
Fully set white and yolk—optimal for grating into sauces

Three Ways to Scramble Eggs

Teeny creamy curds

You can make these scrambles with as many eggs as you need. I typically aim for 2 eggs per person. I use a scant teaspoon of butter and a big pinch of salt per egg. (Except for the dreamy teeny creamy curds, which get an extra hit of fat at the end.)

These are super-luxe, restaurant-style eggs. They are cooked similarly to a custard, with a whisk and preferably in a saucier (a saucepan with sloped sides). Since this type of pot has no corners, it's easy to keep everything moving and evenly cooking. You can make it in a straight-sided pot if that's all you've got, just be sure to work the whisk into the corners. Low heat and constant whisking result in a super-creamy, spoonable scramble. Adding cold butter, crème fraîche, sour cream, or labne at the end cools the scramble so it doesn't overcook.

1. Beat the eggs: Whisk the eggs with salt until totally homogeneous and no streaks of white remain. Set aside for at least 2 minutes and up to 15 minutes.

2. Temperature management: In a medium saucier or pot, melt butter over medium-high heat until foamy. Add the eggs and reduce the heat to medium-low.

3. Whisk constantly: Cook, whisking constantly until the eggs begin to look thickened with lots of small curds running throughout, 3 to 5 minutes.

4. Keep it creamy: Remove from the heat and whisk in cold butter and/or a dollop of something creamy, like crème fraîche or sour cream (about ½ teaspoon per egg).

Big fluffy egg clouds

Moderate heat with minimal folding and scraping will give you big fluffy curds, the kind you can pick up with a fork. If you want to make them extra fluffy, whisk in a splash of milk or half-and-half (about 1 teaspoon per egg). You will need a nonstick or very well-seasoned cast-iron/carbon steel skillet, along with a stiff silicone spatula.

---

1. Beat the eggs: Whisk the eggs with salt until totally homogeneous and no streaks of white remain. Add a splash of milk or half-and-half to make them extra fluffy. Set aside for at least 2 minutes and up to 15 minutes.

2. Temperature management: In a small or medium nonstick or well-seasoned cast-iron/carbon steel skillet, melt butter over medium-high heat until foamy. Add the eggs and reduce the heat to medium.

3. Fold gently: Use a stiff silicone spatula to scrape the outer edges of the egg into the center in a sweeping motion. You are bringing the cooked egg toward the center and replacing it with the raw egg from the center. Keep doing this until you have large fluffy curds.

Silky marbled ribbons

Here whole eggs are cracked directly into and scrambled in the pan. If your pan starts out too hot, the egg whites will quickly dry out. Get the heat just right and the egg white sets into tender ribbons, all coated in glossy egg yolk. You will need a nonstick or very well-seasoned cast-iron/carbon steel skillet, along with a stiff silicone spatula.

---

1. Temperature management: In a small or medium nonstick or well-seasoned cast-iron/carbon steel skillet, melt butter over medium heat until foamy. Crack the eggs into the skillet and reduce the heat to medium-low. Lightly sprinkle the eggs with salt.

2. Barely set the whites: Cook the eggs, undisturbed, until the whites are partially set on the bottom, with some runny white on top, and totally raw yolks.

3. Temperature management: Reduce the heat to low.

4. Scramble: Use a stiff silicone spatula to gently break up the eggs, coating the whites with the yolks and warming the yolks through. They should look marbled and glossy.

Crispy-Edged, Oil-Basted, Blistered Eggs

I think this is the best way to cook an egg, displaying a wide range of textures all at once. The edges become lacy, crisp, and brown, while the yolk stays warm and runny. If I don't know what to eat, I crispy-fry an egg and put it on anything. For best results, use a well-seasoned cast-iron/carbon steel skillet. A nonstick skillet will never get hot enough, while stainless steel is likely to stick. Use a big metal spoon to baste the top with the hot fat, so it cooks before the bottom overcooks from the intense heat. The thin blade of a slotted fish spatula makes it easy to cleanly lift the egg out of the pan without cracking the yolk.

1. **Temperature management:** In a medium or small cast-iron/carbon steel skillet, heat enough oil to generously coat the pan over medium-high heat until shimmering and almost smoking. Carefully crack the eggs into the skillet and lightly season with salt.

2. **Baste:** Tilt the skillet toward you so the oil pools and, using a big spoon, baste the eggs with the hot oil until the white is set and the egg browns, frizzles, and puffs.

3. **Plate:** Carefully slide a fish spatula under the egg and tilt to drain away the excess oil, then transfer to a plate.

Sunny-Side Up, Over-Easy, Over-Medium & Over-Hard

These eggs are all cooked in essentially the same way, with the same pan temperature and tools. The only difference is time. For a sunny-side up egg, you want totally set, tender egg whites with a warm and runny yolk. Over-easy, over-medium, and over-hard require you to cook them slightly longer for yolks that are more cooked and covered in fully set egg white. Traditionally, all these eggs (other than sunny-side up) are flipped to quickly give the yolk more heat. Flipping eggs without breaking the yolks is pretty tricky, especially if you're cooking more than two eggs at once. That's why, except for an over-hard egg, I don't bother with flipping my eggs, and cover the skillet with a lid instead. This method makes the cook times significantly longer, but you're at home and not working a busy egg station at a restaurant, so a few extra minutes won't kill you. (Unless you *are* working the egg station at a restaurant. In which case, you better get that flip down or you will not last a day.) You'll need a nonstick or very well-seasoned cast-iron/carbon steel skillet, a lid (or sheet pan that's big enough to cover the skillet), and a slotted fish spatula.

1. Temperature management: In a small or medium nonstick or well-seasoned cast-iron/carbon steel skillet, melt butter (about 1 teaspoon per egg) over low heat until foamy. Crack the eggs into the skillet, lightly sprinkle the eggs with salt, and cover the skillet.

2. Cook: Check for doneness every 30 seconds.

> **Sunny-side up:** about 2 minutes (totally set white, bright yellow and runny yolk)
>
> **Over-easy:** 3 to 5 minutes (thin layer of set white covering totally runny yolk)
>
> **Over-medium:** about 6 minutes (thin layer of white covering jammy yolk)
>
> **Over-hard:** after 5 minutes, flip the egg over and cook for another minute (fully set white and yolk)

Sunny-side up

Over-easy

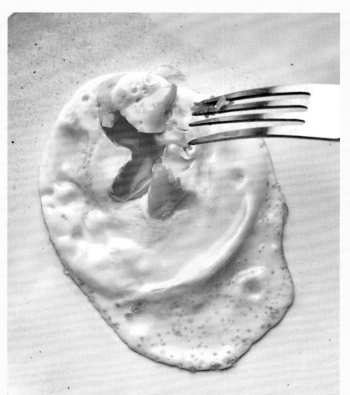

Over-medium

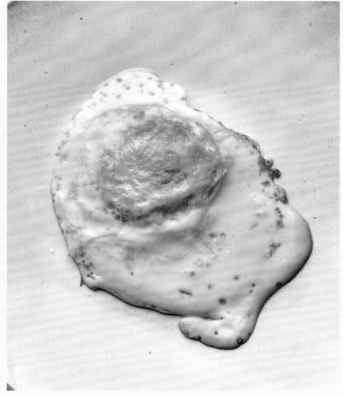

Over-hard

Temperature Management 101

Tender Poached Eggs with Runny Yolks

You don't need vinegar or salt or anything but water bubbling just right to poach an egg. Poached eggs require water at a bare simmer—no wild bubbles, but more than a still and steamy bath. For that ideal, compact shape, it's key to use a fine-mesh sieve to drain away the thin, runny white. That's the stuff that makes your poaching water cloudy and streaked, and can even cause a pocket of water in your final poached egg. Fresh eggs are vital for a picture-perfect plump poach because they have a higher ratio of thick to thin white. (See photos of this technique on page 89.)

1. Bring a pot of water to a bare simmer: You'll need at least 4 inches of water. Bring it to a boil over high heat, then adjust the dial to get the water to stay steamy with a few gentle bubbles, but not an active boil.

2. Set up: While the water is heating up, crack each egg into a small bowl or deli container. Set a small or medium fine-mesh sieve over a bowl. Have a slotted spoon and clean kitchen towel handy for egg evacuation and landing.

3. Strain: Working with one egg at a time, place the cracked egg into the sieve to drain away the thin white.

4. Poach: Swirl a spoon in the water to create a slow vortex. Roll the egg out of the sieve into the center of the vortex. Once in the water, use the spoon to give the egg a few gentle spins to center the yolk. Repeat with more eggs. Unless you're an experienced poacher, I don't recommend dropping more than 4 eggs at a time.

5. Temperature management: Adjust the heat as needed to maintain a gentle simmer; the more eggs you add, the higher you'll need to crank the heat. As the eggs get closer to doneness, you'll have to turn down the heat. Keep those gentle bubbles going throughout the cooking.

6. Test for doneness: After 3 minutes, use a slotted spoon to lift one egg out at a time. Press the egg gently with your finger. The outer edges should feel set, and the center will feel like it's filled with pudding. If the middle feels very liquidy, the egg white is undercooked, so keep poaching.

7. Remove and reheat (if necessary): Use the slotted spoon to transfer the eggs to the kitchen towel as they are done. If you're making a lot of poached eggs, you may need to cook them in batches. Eggs can be poached in advance and held at room temperature for 2 hours or overnight in the fridge. Reheat in gently simmering water.

Frizzled Desi Omelet with Onion & Chilies

(Makes one 3-egg omelet)

(Active: 15 mins. | Total: 15 mins.)

(Easy) (Vegetarian)

(Gluten-free)

Ingredients:

3 large eggs

tiny pinch of MSG (optional)

kosher salt

¼ cup lightly packed roughly chopped
cilantro

¼ cup sliced red onion (about
¼ small onion)

1 medium Thai green chili, very thinly
sliced (or snipped with scissors)

1 tablespoon ghee, clarified butter,
or neutral oil, such as safflower or
grapeseed

Special Equipment:

fish spatula

What Are Thai Green Chilies?

→ This is the omelet I grew up with. When I was a kid, I'd use a fork to painstakingly pluck out every single speck of chili and onion. Now as an adult, they are my favorite bites. This omelet cooks real quick, barely warming the onion through without losing its peppery bite. Be sure to preheat your skillet and fat, so once the eggs hit the pan they quickly grow browned and crisp without drying out. And because this is a high-heat cooking method, do not use butter, which will burn before it becomes hot enough to brown the eggs.

1. Crack the eggs into a medium bowl and season with the MSG (if using) and kosher salt (I like to go for a light sprinkling evenly across all 3 eggs). With a whisk, beat until well combined and no streaks of egg white remain. Add the cilantro, onion, and chili and whisk to combine.

2. In a medium cast-iron or nonstick skillet, heat the fat over medium-high heat until shimmering. (Add a drop of the egg mixture to the skillet to check the pan's temperature. It should sizzle immediately.)

3. Once hot, pour the egg mixture in all at once, tilt the pan to evenly distribute the mixture, then do not disturb until the bottom is lightly golden brown and set enough so that you can slide the omelet in the pan easily, 30 seconds to 1 minute. Using a fish spatula, flip the omelet over and cook until set, about 30 seconds. Transfer to a plate and serve right away.

Also known as bird's eye chilies, these peppers are small but mighty, packing a lot of prickly heat in a small package. They are vital to South and Southeast Asian cuisines, but like all peppers, originated in the Americas. The green chilies are unripe and taste grassier than when allowed to grow red and ripe, but they are both very spicy. You can find them in most Asian grocery stores. I like to buy them in bulk and store in the freezer so I'm always stocked. Use kitchen shears to snip them when frozen directly into soups, sautés, and desi omelets.

70

Four Fat Jammy Egg Tacos

(Makes 8 tacos)

(Active: 30 mins. | Total: 30 mins.)

(Easy) (Vegetarian)

(Gluten-free)

Ingredients:

4 large eggs

3 tablespoons unsalted butter

½ cup roughly chopped nuts, such as almonds, cashews, and/or hazelnuts

1 teaspoon chili flakes, plus more to taste

2 tablespoons freshly squeezed lemon juice, plus more to taste

1 teaspoon grated lemon zest

2 tablespoons finely chopped fresh parsley

kosher salt

8 corn tortillas

1 medium avocado, sliced

flaky salt

Special Equipment:

spider (or slotted spoon)

→ Fat enhances and prolongs other flavors, making everything you add it to a better version of itself. One fat is good, but multiple fats are better. When you layer various fats—olive oil, butter, chicken fat, egg yolks—in the same dish, they end up building on one another for exponential flavor potential. This taco brings together four fats: brown butter, nuts, avocado, and egg yolk. Be sure to season the brown butter sauce aggressively with chili, lemon, and salt to balance all the fat. For perfect jammy eggs every time, start with cold eggs, plunge them straight into boiling water, and set a timer. Adjust the heat to maintain an active simmer throughout the cook, then shock the eggs in a big bowl of ice water to instantly stop the cooking and make them easy to peel.

1. **Cook the eggs:** Bring a medium saucepan of water to a boil and fill a medium bowl with cool water and ice. Using a spider (or slotted spoon), lower the eggs into the boiling water, cover, and set a timer for 7 minutes. (If the boiling becomes too vigorous, turn down the heat. You want gentle bubbles or else the eggs will knock into one another and crack.)

2. When the timer is up, use the spider (or slotted spoon) to lift out the eggs. Lightly crack each egg with the back of a spoon and transfer to the ice bath. Let cool slightly in the ice water, about 1 minute. Starting at the blunt end, peel each egg and gently pat dry with a clean kitchen towel.

3. **While the eggs cook:** Place a small cast-iron or stainless steel skillet over medium heat. Add the butter and nuts and cook, stirring occasionally, until the nuts and butter become deeply browned, 4 to 5 minutes. Remove from the heat, add the chili flakes, lemon juice, lemon zest, and parsley and season generously with kosher salt. Taste and add more chili, lemon, and salt as needed—it should be aggressively spicy, tart, and salty to cut through the fat.

4. **Once the eggs are cooked and peeled:** Warm the tortillas over a burner, in a hot dry pan, or wrapped in a damp towel in a microwave for 15 seconds.

5. Divide the sliced avocado among the tortillas. Cut the eggs into quarters and place 2 quarters on each tortilla. Spoon the nuts and brown butter sauce over the eggs, season with flaky salt, and serve right away.

Deviled Egg Dip

(Serves 6 to 8)

(Active: 30 mins.) | (Total: 1½ hrs.)

(Easy) (Vegetarian)

(Gluten-free)

Ingredients:

12 large eggs

4 tablespoons full-fat cream cheese, preferably Philadelphia brand, at room temperature

2 tablespoons unsalted butter, melted

½ small white onion, finely chopped (about ¼ cup)

kosher salt and freshly ground black pepper

6 tablespoons mayonnaise, store-bought or homemade (page 44)

1 tablespoon Dijon mustard

10 dashes of Tabasco sauce, plus more to taste

smoked paprika

butter crackers for serving

Special Equipment:

spider (or slotted spoon)

fine-mesh sieve

After many years of hosting, I've learned that people get most excited over the classics: a cheese platter, shrimp cocktail, and deviled eggs. I like to make this crowd-pleaser even easier by turning it into a dip. Feel free to double or triple the quantities if you have big egg heads coming to dinner and portion the dip in multiple bowls to refresh the table throughout the night. When it's a party for people I really like, I'll skip the paprika and top the dip with big dollops of trout roe instead.

---

1. **Cook the eggs:** Bring a large saucepan of water to a boil and fill a large bowl with cool water and ice. Using a spider (or slotted spoon), lower the eggs into the boiling water, cover, and set a timer for 9 minutes. (If the boiling becomes too vigorous, turn down the heat. You want gentle bubbles or else the eggs will knock into one another and crack.)

2. When the timer is up, use the spider (or slotted spoon) to lift out the eggs. Lightly crack each with the back of a spoon, transfer to the bowl of ice water, and let fully cool, about 5 minutes. Starting at the blunt end, peel each egg and gently pat dry with a clean kitchen towel.

3. **While the eggs cook:** In a medium bowl, stir together the cream cheese and melted butter until smooth. Fold in the onion. (This will be mixed with the egg whites.)

4. Using a sharp knife, cut the eggs in half lengthwise. Using a spoon, scoop out the yolks and place in a fine-mesh sieve; set aside.

5. Roughly chop half of the egg whites (12 halves or 6 whole eggs' worth) into ¼-inch chunks and combine with the cream cheese mixture. (Reserve the extra egg white halves for another use or feed them to your dog.)

6. Taste the cream cheese mixture and season with salt and pepper as needed. Scrape into a shallow serving bowl and evenly spread into one layer. Place in the fridge to chill while you mix the egg yolk topping.

7. Place the sieve of yolks over the bowl you just used to mix the egg white base (no need to clean it out) and use a rubber spatula to press the yolks through the sieve. Add the mayonnaise, mustard, and Tabasco and mix until smooth. Taste and add salt to taste and more Tabasco as needed.

8. Scrape the yolk mixture over the white and use the back of a spoon to make swoops and swirls like you're frosting the top of a cake. Cover and refrigerate for at least 1 hour and up to overnight to chill before serving. Sprinkle with smoked paprika and serve with butter crackers.

Stracciatella alla Romana
(Italian Egg Drop Soup)

(Serves 2 to 4)

(Active: 10 mins. | Total: 15 mins.)

(Easy) (Gluten-free)

Ingredients:

2 large eggs

1 tablespoon extra-virgin olive oil

¼ cup finely grated parmesan cheese
   (use the small holes of a box
   grater)

1 quart high-quality chicken bone
   broth, store-bought or homemade
   (see page lxxii)

3 tablespoons freshly squeezed
   lemon juice (from about 1 lemon)

¼ cup fresh parsley leaves and stems,
   finely chopped

kosher salt and freshly ground
   black pepper

Special Equipment:

container with a spout

box grater

→ In Italy, a lot of things are called stracciatella—bulging balloons of mozzarella filled with shreds of curd and cream, smooth gelato streaked with snappy threads of chocolate, and this comforting chicken soup with fluffy clouds of egg and cheese. *Stracci* means "rags" in Italian and is the term used to describe all these striated dishes. There are many different styles of egg drop soup, but this Roman one is my favorite, salty from grated parmesan with fresh lemon and parsley to balance the richness of the broth. Because there are so few ingredients, it's all about quality. Use the best bone broth, eggs, and cheese you can find. For the best texture, grate the parmesan on the fine side of a box grater (cheese shredded on a Microplane will be too fine, causing the fat to break out of it in the hot broth). Be sure to bring the broth to a rapid boil, so the eggs instantly cook and break into strands the moment they are whisked into the hot broth.

1. In a medium bowl, whisk together the eggs, olive oil, and parmesan until evenly combined. Scrape the egg mixture into a container with a spout and set aside.

2. In a medium pot, bring the bone broth to a rapid boil over medium-high heat. While constantly whisking, slowly stream in the egg mixture. When all the egg is in the pot, keep whisking until the soup comes back up to a simmer, then remove from the heat.

3. Add the lemon juice and parsley. Taste the soup and season with salt and black pepper as needed. Serve immediately.

Spicy Tomato Sauce
Poached Eggs
with Beans, Greens
& Tortillas

Spicy Tomato Sauce Poached Eggs

with Beans, Greens & Tortillas

(Serves 3 to 4)

(Active: 30 mins. | Total: 40 mins.)

(Easy) (Vegetarian)

(Gluten-free)

Ingredients:

8 corn tortillas

4 tablespoons neutral oil, such as safflower or grapeseed

kosher salt

1 large bunch mustard greens (about 12 ounces/350 grams)

1 medium yellow onion, chopped

3 garlic cloves, chopped

1 teaspoon ground cumin

½ to 1 teaspoon chili flakes or cayenne pepper, plus more to taste

1 pint cherry tomatoes (about 10 ounces/280 grams)

1 cup tomato passata or puree

¾ cup water

1½ cups cooked pinto beans, home-cooked or one 15.5-ounce can

3 to 6 large eggs

½ cup coarsely grated sharp cheddar cheese

To Serve:

diced avocado

strained yogurt or sour cream

fresh cilantro leaves and tender stems

→ Chilaquiles are a traditional Mexican dish in which leftover corn tortillas are fried before tossing in salsa. For something to be chilaquiles, that's truly all you need, but many people gussy it up with cheese, eggs, or sliced onion. Shakshuka is a dish originating in North Africa where eggs are poached in a spicy tomato sauce. I guess because the words shakshuka and chilaquiles just roll off the tongue, recipe developers have begun calling anything with poached eggs shakshuka and anything with tortillas chilaquiles. I love both those dishes, because they're freaking delicious, and although this dish is inspired by both, it's neither of those things. That's just what happens with food as cuisines, cultures, and people interact and move across the globe.

Some chilaquiles recipes use store-bought tortilla chips instead of frying them fresh, but depending on the brand, those can get soggy fast. So I toast fresh tortillas in the oven until crisp (even I won't deep-fry in the morning). They bake up sturdy with a hearty crunch that can stand up to soaking in the sauce. The time it takes for the eggs to cook in the oven can vary depending on how many you add and how neatly you're able to nestle them into the sauce. Check them frequently to prevent overcooking. Let your fingers be your guide—the whites should feel firm and set while the yolks stay wiggly and molten underneath.

1. Position a rack in the center of the oven and heat to 350°F (177°C).

2. Toast the tortillas: Lay the tortillas on a sheet pan (it's okay if they overlap slightly), drizzle with 2 tablespoons of the oil, and use your hands to evenly coat the tortillas with the oil on both sides. Sprinkle lightly with kosher salt. Invert a wire rack upside down on top of the tortillas (this keeps them flat while they toast). Place in the oven and cook until golden brown and dried, flipping once during baking, 11 to 14 minutes.

3. Meanwhile, strip the mustard leaves from the stems and midribs. Roughly chop the leaves and discard the stems.

4. Make the spicy tomato sauce: In a large ovenproof skillet, heat the remaining 2 tablespoons oil over medium-high heat. Add the onion and a big pinch of salt and cook, stirring frequently, until softened and lightly browned at the edges, 3 to 4 minutes.

5. Reduce the heat to medium, add the garlic, cumin, and chili flakes and cook, stirring constantly, until fragrant, about 1 minute. Add the cherry tomatoes, tomato passata, and water. Simmer, stirring occasionally, until the cherry tomatoes are tender, 2 to 4 minutes. Use the spatula to lightly crack each tomato so it spills its juices into the sauce.

6. Add the chopped greens and cooked beans to the sauce and stir to combine. Cook, stirring occasionally, until the greens have wilted, 3 to 5 minutes.

80

7. Taste and add salt and more chili flakes if needed. Add more water if the sauce is too thick—it should flow freely, like a marinara sauce.

8. Once the tortillas have toasted, remove them from the oven but leave the oven on (and reserve the sheet pan, no need to wash). Break the tortillas into rough 1-inch pieces. Reserving one big handful of the crispy tortillas for garnish, add the rest to the sauce and stir to evenly combine.

9. Cook the eggs: Reduce the heat under the sauce to medium-low. Use the spatula to make slight divots in the sauce. Crack 3 to 6 eggs into the divots (depending on how many eggs each guest wants). Sprinkle each egg lightly with kosher salt. Evenly sprinkle everything with the grated cheddar.

10. Cover the skillet with the sheet pan and transfer to the oven. Bake until the whites are set but the yolks feel runny when you gently press them, 5 to 8 minutes.

11. Garnish with the reserved crispy tortilla pieces, avocado, yogurt, and cilantro. Serve right away straight out of the skillet.

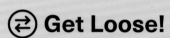 **Get Loose!**

• Swap out the mustard greens for any other tender, quick-cooking green. Try Swiss chard, arugula, watercress, or baby kale.

• Swap out the pinto beans for any bean.

• Don't eat eggs? (Sorry about this chapter.) The greens, tortillas, and beans make this a hearty meal even without 'em. Just pop the skillet under the broiler to melt the cheese.

Chili-Blistered Egg over Brothy Beans

with Fish Sauce & Lime

Serves 2

Active: 15 mins. | Total: 15 mins.

Easy · Gluten-free

Ingredients:

1½ cups beans with their cooking liquid, any kind, home-cooked or from one 15.5-ounce can

kosher salt

2 large eggs

3 tablespoons neutral oil

1 Thai green chili, very thinly sliced (or snipped with scissors)

½-inch piece fresh ginger, peeled and cut into thin matchsticks

⅓ cup lightly packed fresh cilantro leaves and tender stems

⅓ cup lightly packed dill sprigs and tender stems

freshly squeezed lime juice

fish sauce

Crispy Shallots (page 83; optional)

Special Equipment:

fish spatula

→ I worked at a Northern Thai restaurant in Brooklyn that let us order off the menu for family meal. This is totally unheard of. Family meal is typically whatever the cooks have time to make in between everything else they have to do. It can be good, it can be bad, but it's always a comfort to know that you've got one meal covered. I made a round through the menu trying everything once, but after that, I knew what I wanted. Yam khai dao, a salad of crunchy veggies and a lacy-edged deep-fried egg tossed in nuoc cham—a punchy dressing of fish sauce, chili, and lime (see page 245 for a nuoc cham recipe). Now when I see a crispy fried egg, it doesn't feel right without a kick from Thai green chili and ginger. This dish brings all those bright flavors together in a new way, so I can keep eating yam khai dao even when I'm not. A very hot pan and oil is key to getting those crackly edges. Lower the eggs from close to the skillet, so the hot oil doesn't splatter onto your hand. Have everything prepped before you start cooking because the eggs cook real fast.

---

1. In a small saucepan, warm the beans and their broth over medium heat. Season with salt to taste (if needed) and divide between two serving bowls.

2. Crack each egg into its own small bowl and lightly season with kosher salt.

3. In a medium cast-iron or carbon steel skillet, heat the oil over medium-high heat until shimmering and almost smoking. Carefully lower the eggs into the skillet, sprinkle with the sliced chili and ginger matchsticks, and cook undisturbed until the edges grow crisp and browned, about 30 seconds.

4. Tilt the skillet toward you so the oil pools and, using a big spoon, baste the eggs with the hot oil until the white is set and the egg browns, frizzles, and puffs, 1 to 1½ minutes. Using a fish spatula, transfer the eggs to the bowls of beans.

5. Divide the herbs over the eggs and season with lime juice and fish sauce to taste. Garnish with crispy shallots (if using). Serve right away.

Crispy Shallots

→ Crunchy, light, sweet, and savory, crispy shallots might be the best topping for just about anything. As a kid, my amu had to store the container out of my reach or I'd shovel them into my face by the fistful. They are used throughout the world, from Thailand and Vietnam, throughout South Asia, and into the Levant. You can buy them or make them yourself:

1. Peel and thinly slice shallots. Uniform thickness is key to getting even color. I recommend using a mandoline and aiming for ⅛-inch thickness.

2. Set a fine-mesh sieve over a heatproof bowl and have a sheet pan lined with paper towels handy.

3. Place the shallots in a small or medium pot (depending on how much you've sliced) and pour on enough neutral oil to almost cover. (As the shallots cook down, they will become fully submerged in oil.)

4. Cook over medium-high heat while constantly stirring. They'll initially foam and bubble, then quiet down as the moisture has cooked out.

5. Once the bubbling has subsided, the oil has quieted down, and the shallots are evenly light golden brown, pour into the sieve. Lift the sieve to allow the excess oil to drain and immediately spread the shallots out onto the towel-lined sheet pan. (They will continue to brown and crisp as they cool.)

6. Sprinkle with kosher salt. Once cool, transfer to an airtight container (with a desiccant if you have one). They will keep for 1 month. Use the shallot-flavored oil for sautéing and roasting vegetables.

Make-Ahead Steamed Egg Sandwiches with Tartar Sauce

(Makes 4 sandwiches)

(Active: 15 mins. | Total: 15 mins.)

(Intermediate) (Vegetarian)

For the steamed eggs:

8 large eggs

½ teaspoon kosher salt

¼ cup heavy cream or half-and-half

extra-virgin olive oil or cooking spray

For assembly:

4 soft rolls, preferably milk bread

½ recipe Tartar Sauce (page 46)

Special Equipment:

four 1-cup plastic deli containers

bamboo steamer

→ I'm not a tea or coffee person, but I must eat within five minutes of waking up or I become a monster. That's barely enough time to make toast, but if I've planned ahead, these egg sandwiches can save my morning. Mix the sauce and steam the eggs in advance. The tartar sauce can be made with mayonnaise from scratch or with 1 cup of store-bought mayonnaise. I store the cooked eggs in the deli containers they're steamed in. Come morning, I can slap together a breakfast sandwich before my inner Dr. Jekyll goes all Mr. Hyde. These steamed egg cakes are also a game changer if I have a busy week ahead. I can quickly pop one out (no need to reheat) to slice and top a salad, cube and mix into hot rice with a shake of furikake, or cut into strips and slip into a bowl of instant ramen. If you've got a lot of mouths to feed, double or triple the quantity, steaming the eggs in batches. The time the eggs take to steam can vary greatly depending on your steamer and the container you steam the eggs in. Start checking the eggs after 3 minutes; they should feel firm when you gently press the center.

1. **Steam the eggs:** Fill a medium saucepot with 1 inch of water and bring to a simmer over medium-high heat. While the water is heating up, whisk the eggs and salt in a medium bowl until no streaks of white remain. Add the cream and whisk until combined.

2. Grease the insides of four 1-cup deli containers with the oil or cooking spray and divide the egg mixture among them (about ½ cup per container).

3. Arrange the deli cups inside the baskets of a tiered bamboo steamer and place over the simmering water. Cover and cook until the eggs puff and set, switching the basket positions halfway through, 4 to 10 minutes. (Timing varies greatly depending on your steamer, so start checking early and often.) Eat hot or cover and store (in the deli cups) in the refrigerator for up to 3 days.

4. **Assemble the sandwiches:** Split the buns in half (toast if you want) and liberally spread the tartar sauce on each side. Flip the steamed egg cake (hot or cold) out onto the bottom buns, top, and eat.

Çılbır (Poached Eggs over Labne with Chili Oil)

(Serves 2)

(Active: 25 mins. | Total: 25 mins.)

(Intermediate) (Vegetarian)

For the chili oil:

1 teaspoon coriander seeds

½ to 1 teaspoon chili flakes

1 teaspoon hot smoked paprika

½ teaspoon ground cumin

big pinch of kosher salt

⅓ cup extra-virgin olive oil

2 garlic cloves, thinly sliced

For the eggs:

4 large eggs

⅔ cup labne or whole-milk Greek yogurt

flaky salt

roughly torn fresh mint leaves

roughly torn fresh parsley leaves and tender stems

1 lemon

warm pita for serving (page 502)

Special Equipment:

mortar and pestle (or a heavy knife)

small or medium fine-mesh sieve

Microplane grater

→ Çılbır is a Turkish dish that my husband, Ham, grew up eating. It's composed of poached eggs served on a bed of yogurt, sometimes topped with melted butter or olive oil, often steeped with some kind of dried chili. The different layers of richness from the chili oil, runny yolk, and creamy labne are offset with the subtle burn from the chilies, tang from the labne, and the freshness of the herbs. It is an almost paradoxical way to start your day in that it is simultaneously rich, but light enough that you are not weighed down.

Poaching eggs isn't hard; it's all about managing the temperature of the water. You want the water at a bare simmer, with gentle bubbles that quickly set the exterior of the egg without being so aggressive that the egg tears apart. Adjust the temperature throughout the cook, so you keep those little bubbles going even after dropping in the cold eggs. This recipe makes more chili oil than you need, but if you make any less it's difficult to evenly brown the garlic. Don't fret, extra chili oil is great tossed with noodles, rice, vegetables, and over eggs cooked any way. If you want to make this dish for a crowd, cook the eggs in batches and hold them at room temperature for up to 2 hours or overnight in the fridge. Reheat them with a quick dunk in simmering water just before serving.

1. **Set up for egg poaching:** Fill a medium saucepan with water and bring to a simmer over high heat. Reduce the heat to maintain a gentle simmer.

2. **Meanwhile, make the chili oil:** With a mortar and pestle (or with the side of a wide knife), coarsely crack the coriander seeds. Transfer to a small heatproof bowl along with the chili flakes, smoked paprika, cumin, and salt.

3. In a small pot or skillet, heat the oil and garlic over medium heat. Cook, swirling the pan so the garlic cooks evenly, until fragrant and lightly brown around the edges, 2 to 3 minutes. Immediately pour over the spices and stir to combine.

4. **Poach the eggs:** Adjust the heat so the water is at a bare simmer. It shouldn't be totally still or actively bubbling. You want to see sparse, gentle bubbles.

5. Crack each egg into its own small bowl (I use 1-cup deli containers). Set a small or medium fine-mesh sieve over a bowl. Drop one egg into the sieve to drain away the thin white. Swirl the simmering water with a spoon, then gently drop the drained egg into the center of the vortex. Quickly repeat with the remaining eggs, draining each and dropping it into the water and adjusting the heat as needed to maintain a bare simmer.

6. Have a clean kitchen towel beside you. Check the eggs by lifting them out of the water with a slotted spoon and pressing them gently with your finger. The whites should feel set, while the yolk inside feels molten and runny, 3 to 5 minutes. As each egg is done, transfer to the towel to drain. →

Çılbır (Poached Eggs over Labne with Chili Oil) (cont'd.)

What Is Labne?

7. **Plate the dish:** Divide the labne between two shallow bowls. Use the back of a spoon to create a nest in the labne. Place 2 poached eggs in the center of each nest, season lightly with flaky salt, and drizzle with as much chili oil as you want. Shower with the torn herbs and use a Microplane to zest the lemon over everything. Serve immediately with warm pita.

Yogurt is milk that has thickened thanks to lactic acid bacteria jumping in the pool, chomping down on milk sugar (lactose), and causing the milk to become soured. The acidic environment created by lactic acid bacteria makes the proteins in milk denature and coagulate, transforming pourable milk into something thick and spoonable. If you "strain" yogurt, some of the water in it is drained off resulting in thick Greek-style yogurt. (Although in the US it's marketed as "Greek" yogurt, this kind of drained and thickened yogurt is found all over the world.) Now, let that drain again and you've got labne! Labne can be rich and creamy like sour cream or as stiff as cheese. Variations of this type of super-strained yogurt are made throughout the globe with different names.

How to Poach
an Egg

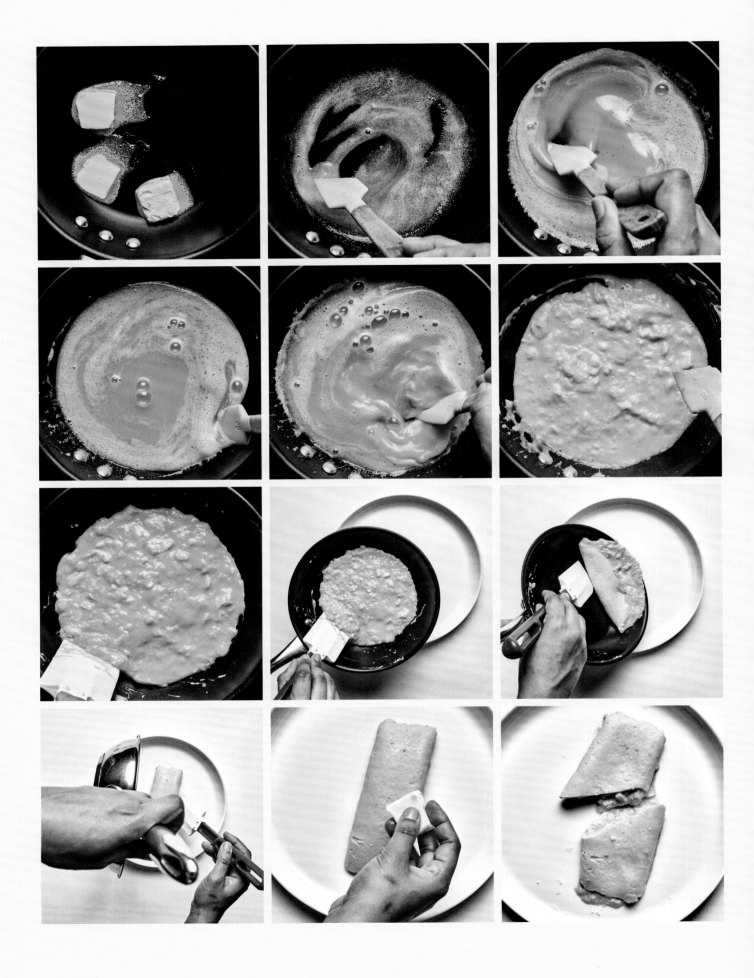

Classic French Omelet

Makes one 3-egg omelet

Active: 10 mins. | Total: 10 mins.

Advanced Vegetarian

Gluten-free

Ingredients:

3 large eggs

kosher salt

1 tablespoon unsalted butter, plus
more to finish

optional garnishes: shredded or
crumbled melty cheese (like
cheddar, Gruyère, or Boursin),
sliced chives, chopped parsley,
freshly ground black pepper,
flaky salt

House Salad (page 18) and/or crusty
bread for serving

Special Equipment:

8-inch nonstick skillet

tiny silicone spatula

What the Hell Happened?

Is your omelet brown, raw in
the middle, broken, or all of
the above? Try it again! This
recipe is all about practice,
and along the way you'll learn
about your burner, your skillet,
and everything about eggs.
If you experienced excessive
stickage, you might need a new
nonstick skillet.

→ The classic French omelet is one of the best ways to learn about temperature. Yup, this recipe is going to take a few tries, but even if you don't nail it the first time, at least all your attempts will be delicious. Perfection means a thin and tender outer skin that's about to burst with creamy curds, delicately seasoned with butter and salt. Getting it right is all about controlling your heat and knowing what you're looking for. The eggs go from runny and undercooked to dry and brown in the blink of an eye. Proper equipment is also vital. You will need a high-quality small nonstick skillet. Any scrapes or scratches in your pan will result in sticking eggs. I like to use a tiny silicone spatula for stirring the eggs into perfect little curds, then switch to a larger one to fold the omelet. If you don't have a tiny spatula, you can make it work with the one you've got (it just requires more attentiveness). Luckily, breakfast comes around every morning, so you'll have plenty of opportunities to practice, practice, practice!

1. This omelet waits for no one. Have your plate, garnishes, and accompaniments ready to go before you start cooking.

2. Crack the eggs into a medium bowl and season with kosher salt (I like to go for a light sprinkling evenly across all 3 eggs). Beat the eggs and salt with a whisk until no white streaks remain.

3. Place an 8-inch nonstick skillet over medium-high heat and melt the butter until foamy.

4. Scrape the beaten eggs into the skillet with a large spatula and reduce the heat to medium-low. Switch to a tiny spatula and stir the eggs constantly, making small, swift circles, frequently scraping the sides into the middle and shaking the pan, until the eggs begin to look thickened with lots of small curds running throughout, 1 to 2 minutes.

5. Spread the egg evenly across the skillet and let cook undisturbed until the edges look just set but the top is still creamy, 30 seconds to 1 minute. (If using cheese, add it in a layer down the center of the omelet at this point.)

6. **Now it's time to roll:** Switch to a big spatula. Run the spatula under the rim of the omelet and give the pan a few taps against the stovetop to ensure that the omelet has loosened from the bottom of the pan. With your other hand, hold the handle of the skillet with your palm facing up. Use the spatula to fold the part of the omelet closest to the handle over the center of the omelet. Tip the skillet so the unrolled edge of the omelet slides out onto the plate and tilt the skillet over to fold the omelet closed.

7. **Optional finishes:** Use a clean kitchen towel to form the omelet into a torpedo shape. (This is a totally optional, yet traditional, step I usually skip because I don't want to dirty a towel.) Rub with butter and add some sprinkles—flaky salt, freshly ground black pepper, fresh herbs—and serve right away with a house salad and/or crusty bread.

**Fancy Weekend
Scramble
with Pepper Bacon &
One Big Pancake**

Fancy Weekend Scramble

with Pepper Bacon &
One Big Pancake

(Serves 4)

(Active: 30 mins. | Total: 30 mins.)

(Advanced)

For the pancake batter:

160 grams (1⅓ cups) all-purpose flour

3 tablespoons sugar

1 teaspoon baking powder

1 teaspoon baking soda

1 teaspoon kosher salt

2 large eggs (about 110 grams)

295 grams (1⅓ cups) buttermilk

56 grams (4 tablespoons) unsalted
    butter

For the bacon:

8 slices thick-cut bacon (about
    1 pound/450 grams)

2 tablespoons maple syrup, plus more
    for serving

2 teaspoons coarsely ground black
    pepper

For the eggs:

8 large eggs

½ teaspoon kosher salt

2 tablespoons unsalted butter

3 tablespoons sour cream, crème
    fraîche, or labne

Special Equipment:

large ovenproof nonstick pan or *very*
    well-seasoned cast-iron skillet

→ Individually, all these things are easy—scramble eggs, roast bacon, make one giant pancake. The challenge is getting everything to the table at the same time for maximum enjoyment. Cold scrambled eggs are sadness, and eating a pancake held warm in the oven is never as joyful as digging in hot off the skillet. But in that moment when crispy glazed bacon, crackly caramelized pancake, and custardy eggs land on a plate in a synchronized dance, I feel like I'm skipping through a field of wildflowers with Dua Lipa singing from the clouds.

You don't need years of experience to get your timing right, you just need a game plan. I make a game plan every time I cook, whether it's salad and pasta for a weeknight meal or a holiday spread for the in-laws. I'll take an overhead view of all the steps in all the dishes I'm cooking, allowing me to weave and layer them together. Taking the time to think through my moves in the kitchen not only lets me move faster and multitask, but also get hot food on the table all at once. Also, by not having to worry about what you've got to do next, you can focus on what you're doing in the moment, which is especially important with all the temperature management going on in this recipe. Keep an eye on the bacon to figure out when to start your pancake. Adjust the heat of the pancake, using your nose and eyes to guide you, so it begins to set without burning underneath. And be extra careful with the eggs, which can go from perfectly creamy and tender to dry and curdled from excess heat.

If you haven't done much multitasking in the kitchen, breakfast is a great place to learn. The stakes are low, so you can focus on timing and execution. However, if you don't feel like starting your chill Sunday with a mini Iron Chef challenge, then make only one item from this spread. When I need cheering up, I make the pancake for dinner and drown it and myself in warm maple syrup.

Keep in mind that every package of bacon, whether thick or thin, cured or uncured, tofu or turkey, will take a different amount of time to roast, so keep a vigilant eye on it as it cooks. Because the pancake recipe is a baked good, where precise measurements are important, I've listed the gram measurements first as my not-so-subtle way of asking you to use a scale.

---

1. **Prep the oven:** Position oven racks in the upper and lower thirds of the oven and heat to 375°F (190°C).

2. **Make the pancake batter:** In a medium bowl, whisk together the flour, 2 tablespoons of the sugar, the baking powder, baking soda, and salt. In another medium bowl, whisk the eggs until no streaks of white remain, then whisk in the buttermilk. Set aside.

3. **Cook the bacon:** Line a sheet pan with foil, set a wire rack in it, and arrange the bacon on top. Set on the lower rack in the oven and cook until the fat is beginning to render, the edges are starting to curl and barely brown, but the bacon isn't fully cooked yet. This will vary greatly depending on the specific brand of bacon you're using, anywhere from 10 to 30 minutes (check the suggested cook time on the package as a guide).

Here's the game plan:

• First, prepare the wet and dry teams for your pancake batter and set aside.

• Get the bacon in the oven.

• When the bacon is nearly done, stir together the pancake batter and start cooking it in the skillet.

• Meanwhile, take the bacon out to glaze and pepper.

• Return the bacon to the oven along with the pancake to both finish cooking. (Ideally, the pancake is ready at the same time as the bacon. If the bacon is cooked before the pancake, take it out and pop it back in the oven right when you start scrambling the eggs.)

• Whisk your eggs with salt right after putting the pancake in the oven, so it can sit for a few minutes to tenderize.

• Start cooking your eggs when the pancake has 5 minutes of baking time left.

• If all goes well, the bacon, pancake, and eggs will be hot and ready all at the same time. Do you feel the warm glow of a thousand suns beaming on your chest? Because you're a breakfast hero!

4. **Cook the pancake:** When the bacon is nearly done, in a large ovenproof nonstick pan (or *very* well-seasoned cast-iron skillet) over medium heat, melt the 56 grams (4 tablespoons) butter until foamy. Remove from the heat and whisk 2 tablespoons of the melted butter into the buttermilk mixture.

5. Add the buttermilk mixture to the flour mixture and mix with a stiff spatula until just combined (some lumps are okay).

6. Return the skillet with the remaining melted butter to medium heat. Evenly sprinkle in the remaining 1 tablespoon sugar and pour the pancake batter on top. Cook the pancake, without stirring, over medium heat, until the edges begin to look set and bubbles appear across the whole surface, 3 to 5 minutes. (The pancake will still look very runny.)

7. **Glaze the bacon:** Meanwhile, take the bacon out of the oven, drizzle with the 2 tablespoons maple syrup, and sprinkle with the pepper. Return to the lower rack in the oven.

8. **Finish the pancake:** Transfer the pancake to the upper rack in the oven to bake until set, about 10 minutes.

9. **Start the eggs:** In a medium bowl, whisk the eggs and salt until no streaks of white remain. Set aside until the pancake is 5 minutes away from being done. (Presalting eggs for up to 15 minutes before scrambling makes them more tender and delicate.)

10. **Cook the eggs once the pancake has 5 minutes to go:** In a medium saucier or pot over medium-high heat, melt the butter until foamy. Add the eggs, reduce the heat to medium-low, and cook, whisking constantly, until the eggs begin to look thickened with lots of small curds running throughout, 3 to 5 minutes. Remove from the heat and whisk in the sour cream.

11. You did it! Flip the pancake onto a plate and cut into wedges. Serve alongside the bacon and eggs with maple syrup.

03

Just Add Water

(Or any liquid) to cook grains, beans & pasta

Just Add Water

Seeds are everywhere. All the grains and legumes, such as rice, corn, lentils, chickpeas, and numerous other foods at the core of our diet are seeds—tiny packets of potential, carrying everything necessary to create life. Nuts are the seeds of a tree, beans and lentils are the seeds of a legume, and grains are the seeds of a grass. (Could eggs be kind of a seed, a chicken seed? Or is everything just an egg?) And we just eat those future plant babies by the spoonful without a second thought. That's why grains and legumes are so nutritious; inside every single seed are the carbohydrates, protein, fat, vitamins, and minerals required to nourish a sprout.

Dal bhat, the combo of steamed white rice and stewed lentils, is at the heart of every Bangladeshi meal. One of my first kitchen lessons was on how to rinse rice, swishing the grains with water in the thin aluminum rice cooker insert, draining away the starchy liquid, and repeating until the water ran nearly clear. It's the same lesson many of us have had because rice is the staple food for more than half the world's population. If you're not from a rice culture, then some other seed is likely at the center of the plate, whether it's wheat berries ground into flour and formed into pasta, or corn that is nixtamalized, crushed into masa, and pressed into tortillas.

These days we're experiencing a seed revolution as an increasing number of people are trying to consume more whole grains, beans, and lentils in an effort to eat less meat. It's become easier to find sorghum, fonio, freekeh, and heirloom beans of every color. But it can also get a little confusing. What's the difference between dal and lentils? Or pearled and semi-pearled barley? And wait, buckwheat *isn't* wheat?!

Luckily, to cook any grain or legume (and any noodle made from those grains or legumes), you simply need to do one thing: hydrate! Tooth-cracking when dried, grains, legumes, and the noodles made from them plump and swell when hydrated in a liquid. They go from tough to tender, dense to chewy, and brittle to creamy. All you really need is water, but any water-like liquid will do, like unctuous bone broth or savory dashi. Yes, it is as simple as simmering, but this chapter covers a few methods that transform dried grains, pseudo-grains, legumes, and pasta into tasty morsels: the Absorption Method (page 105), the Porridge Method (page 106), Legume Lovin': Low & Slow (page 108), the Pilaf Method (page 111), and the Rapid-Boil Method (page 114). This way you'll be armed with countless ways to make meals from cheap and nutritious seeds that keep for (almost) ever in your pantry.

Grains (rice, corn, sorghum, millet, wheat, rye, barley, oats)

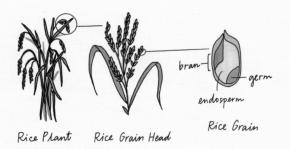

Rice Plant   Rice Grain Head   Rice Grain

Grains are the seeds of grasses. They have a fibrous outer bran, nutrient-rich germ, and starchy endosperm. I find it helpful to relate grains to eggs: Think of the bran as the protective shell, the germ is like the rich yolk, and the endosperm is like the egg white that will become food for the growing plant. The presence of the bran can make grains cook more slowly, while the fatty germ quickly oxidizes, so both are often removed to speed up cook time and increase shelf life. With the germ and bran intact, whole grains are best stored in the fridge or freezer.

Here's a Handy-Dandy Seed Guide

Grains are sold in various forms:

Whole
Brown rice, wheat berries, oat groats: The bran and germ are intact, making the cook time long.

Cracked
Steel-cut oats, cracked wheat: The grain has been broken into pieces, speeding up the cook time. The bran and germ may still be intact or may have been removed.

Polished, pearled, or semi-pearled
White rice, pearled barley: Some or all of the bran and germ have been removed, significantly decreasing cook time and increasing shelf life.

Parboiled or steamed
Bulgur, converted rice, rolled oats: The grains have been soaked, steamed, and dried, significantly decreasing cook time and, in some instances, also boosting the nutrients.

Ground
Cornmeal, semolina: The bran and germ can be intact or removed before grinding into a coarse, medium, or fine flour, ready for bread or quick porridges.

Pseudograins (quinoa, amaranth, buckwheat)

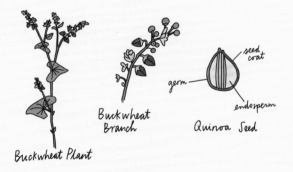

Pseudograins are the seeds of broadleaf plants. They are used just like grains in the kitchen, but their anatomy is often closer to that of a nut or legume.

Beans and Lentils (kidney beans, fava beans, chickpeas, dal, and more!)

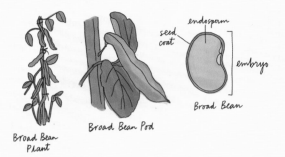

These are the seeds of legumes. Unlike grains (where the germ is the plant embryo and fed by the starchy endosperm), a legume is an embryo packed with all the nutrients needed for growth and wrapped in a protective seed coat. They are higher in protein than grains, thanks to a symbiotic relationship with bacteria in the soil.

Rice, Rice, Baby!

Rice is special to me and to many cultures throughout the world, so I'm giving it extra attention here. Most of the rice we consume today is related to *Oryza sativa*, which was first domesticated in China at least eight thousand years ago, before conquering the rice game across the globe. There are two main subspecies of *Oryza sativa*. The first are the short and chubby grains of *japonica*, which are major players for sushi and risotto, and the second are the medium and long grains of the *indica* variety, best for dishes like pilaf, jambalaya, and paella.

Two distinct molecules make up the starch granules in all grains and legumes but are especially notable in rice: amylose and amylopectin. Amylose are long, straight chains of carbohydrates that are relatively small and easily arrange themselves into stiff and orderly structures. Amylopectin are big, bushy molecules with branches of carbohydrates that do not want to line up in neat clusters. It's the ratio of amylose and amylopectin within each variety of rice—and not the length of the grain—that dictates whether the rice will cook up fluffy and hold its shape (like basmati, bomba, or Carolina Gold) or become sticky and creamy (like sushi, Carnaroli, or glutinous rice). Rice with a higher ratio of highly organized amylose will also require more water to tenderize those sturdy starch frameworks.

Rice is most often found in two forms: brown (with the bran and germ intact) and white (grains of pure starchy endosperm, with the bran and germ removed before polishing). You can also find rice with just the bran removed and the germ still intact or ground into a coarse or fine flour. But most of the time when we're talking about rice, we mean those pearly white grains that cook up quickly and last a long time in the pantry. White rice can also be converted, which means that it has been parboiled and dried. This process boosts nutrition, increases shelf life, and changes the texture through a process called retrogradation, where the carbohydrate molecules realign themselves to become stronger than before. Converted rice cooks up fluffier with fewer broken grains, ideal for the twice-cooked process of tahdig (page 150) or for pilafs (page 138) that incorporate meat or dense vegetables and therefore require extended cooking.

The Absorption Method

With this method, we cook grains, legumes, and small pasta with a measured amount of liquid, covered and without stirring, until they absorb all that liquid and become tender. Since the cooking liquid is fully absorbed, this is a great place to bump up nutrition and flavor by using bone broth (page lxxii) or vegetable stock as the cooking liquid. Unlike the Rapid-Boil Method (page 114), you'll have to look up the ideal ratio of liquid and cook time. It can vary widely, from 1:1 and 15 minutes for short-grain white rice, to 3:1 and 45 minutes for wheat berries. Nope, I'm not gonna give you a chart with all the ratios. There are so many different grains and pseudograins, not to mention all the various forms that they come in, so it's best to look it up on the back of the package.

Step 1: Rinse & Soak (If You've Got Time)

To ensure fluffy and distinct grains, place them in a large bowl and **rinse with cool water.** Take your time to agitate the grains with your hands, washing off any loose starch. As the grains get jostled around during production and transport, they rub up against one another and end up coated in a fine dust of starch. If this starch isn't rinsed off, the grains will clump up after cooking. Repeatedly rinse and drain until the water runs clear enough to see your hand through it.

Next, cover the grains in cool water and **soak** (15 minutes for cracked, polished, semi-pearled, pearled, parboiled large grains, and dal, and up to overnight for whole grains, pseudograins, and lentils) before cooking. This is an optional step that helps rice and lentils cook more evenly and can speed up the cook time for other grains; you can skip it if you're tight on time. Soaking makes an especially big difference when cooking extra-long-grain basmati rice, which will expand more and is less likely to break than when cooked without a soak. No need to rinse or soak pasta. Drain and transfer to a pot that has a tight-fitting lid.

Step 2: Steam & Fluff

Add the required amount of water or bone broth and season with salt if desired. Cover the pot with the lid. Bring the liquid to a boil over high heat. Once you hear the liquid gurgling and wisps of steam escape from under the lid, reduce the heat to the lowest setting, then **simmer covered.** The time varies with each grain; check the package for specific times. No peeking! If you lift the lid, you'll release the steam and prevent the grains from cooking fully. After the initial cook time, remove from the heat and get in there with a fork and **fluff up the grains** to prevent them from clumping together. Cover again and allow them to **rest for 10 minutes.** While resting, the grains will absorb any remaining moisture and firm up, so they stay distinct. If the grains are not tender after absorbing all the liquid, add a splash of hot water and continue cooking.

Best for:

- pretty much everything but pasta, but most often associated with rice, oats, or ground grains, like semolina and cornmeal

Water ratios: Use a liquid ratio just as a starting point.

The Porridge Method

Similar to the Absorption Method, all the liquid used when making a porridge stays in the final dish, with nothing drained off. What's different here is we're aiming for tender grains in a thick sauce made up of their own sloughed-off starches. Porridge is one of the most forgiving things you can possibly cook. It's helpful to start with a rough liquid to grain ratio, but you honestly don't need to measure. Add the liquid in stages, adding more until everything is tender and the porridge is the consistency you want. This is another place where bone broth (page lxxii), vegetable stock, or dashi can be used as the primary cooking liquid. Make things extra creamy with milk and butter.

Step 1: Toast & Soak (If You Want, but You Totally Don't Have to)

Toasting grains in a dry skillet or in fat helps enhance their nutty flavors, or you can skip it for a mild-flavored porridge. Many traditional rice porridges, like congee and juk, are intentionally bland to help soothe your stomach when you're sick (or even just sad). Soaking whole, cracked, and pearled grains and legumes helps shorten cooking time, but is an optional step. Soaking ground grains, like cornmeal or semolina, shortens cook time, makes the porridge creamier, and prevents lumps, but is, once again, an optional step.

Step 2: Add Aromatics (If You Want, but You Totally Don't Have To)

Create a base of flavor by sweating down aromatics, like onion, garlic, and ginger. Keep everything cut small. You don't want a big wedge of onion floating in a pot of porridge. This is spoon food, so everything you put in the pot should be spoonable. Or don't add any aromatics at all if you want a mellow-flavored porridge.

Step 3: Simmer, Season & Stir

If ground grains aren't soaked, you need to take extra precaution against lumps. Add your cooking liquid to the aromatics (if using) and bring to a rapid boil, then shower in the ground grains while whisking constantly. If you've soaked the ground grains, they have had time to slowly hydrate with cool water, and there's no risk of clumping, so you can add them (and the liquid they've soaked in) straight to the pot and bring up to a simmer. Whole grains can also be added directly to the liquid or given a chance to toast in fat before adding the liquid in stages. Be sure to season early and aggressively. Porridges are mostly water and need a lot of help in the seasoning department. Stir frequently to prevent the bottom from scorching and promote even cooking.

Step 4: Finish with Fat (or Don't!)

Enrich your porridge with a pat of butter, spices sizzled in ghee, grated cheese, or a dollop of sour cream. Or don't! Porridge can be rich and creamy or mild and delicate. It's totally up to you.

Confusing Legume Terms Defined

- *Legume:* the name for the plant and the seed. All beans and lentils are legumes.

- *Pulse:* a "government" word for any legume harvested only for selling in dried form. Therefore, the term *pulse* does not include peas or green beans, which are frequently eaten fresh, or soybeans and peanuts, which are often pressed to extract their oils.

- *Lentil:* any lens-shaped legume. In the past, they were categorized as beans.

- *Dal:* any legume that is split, so it can be a bean or a lentil. The seed coat can be removed or left on. This is a common form of legume in South Asia, prized for quick cooking.

Legume Lovin': Low & Slow (& Preferably with a Salt Water Soak)

Lentils are small, enabling you to cook them using the Absorption Method (page 105) or Pilaf Method (page 111), but beans need special attention. Sure, you can boil them, you can pressure cook them, but if you want perfectly intact beans and lentils so silken on the inside they pop like caviar, you gotta go low and slow. Simmer legumes too vigorously, and their stiff seed coats can't keep up with the swelling interior starches and burst, spilling all their precious creamy, beany guts into the cooking liquid. Sometimes you want this for a silky soup or dal, and if that's the case, feel free to crank up that heat or use a pressure cooker.

To soak or not to soak? Legumes take so long to cook because water can penetrate only via a tiny hole in their seed coat, unlike whole grains, where seepage happens across the entire husk. Soaking them speeds up the cook time by giving the water a head start. (Dal don't need a soak because they're split, exposing their endosperms.) If beautiful unburst beans are what you're after, soak them in salted water. Nope, salt will not make beans take longer to cook! I'm sure you've heard this myth and it couldn't be further from the truth. Salt helps tenderize legumes by breaking down the pectin that gives them their structure. Starting with a soak in salt water makes the seed coat more flexible, like your bean is switching from those stiff leather pants you haven't worn since college into stretchy leggings. When they are hit with heat, the hydrated starches gelatinize and expand, and the seed coat is primed to accommodate the plumping, keeping cooked legumes intact. But if you don't have time to soak, it's totally okay! They will simply take longer to get tender, and you might find a broken bean here or there.

Acid is another ingredient that gets demonized around legumes, but not all acid affects them the same way. Citric acid, which is found in tomatoes and lemon juice, will make legumes more tender, while the acetic acid found in vinegar will toughen them. Always add vinegar at the end with your final seasonings, but feel free to run wild with the tomato puree. If you're struggling with getting a pot of legumes tender, they're most likely old. Technically, beans and lentils never go bad, but the older the legume, the longer it will take to soften, and it's not just because they're drying out. Over time, the starches in legumes stored at room temperature will transform into lignin—the same stuff that gives wood it's stiff structure. Legumes over one year old will take significantly longer to cook, while very old beans and lentils may never get there.

If your plan is to blitz your legumes into a velvety oblivion for hummus or masoor dal, then baking soda is your best bet. A teeny bit of baking soda added to the cooking liquid makes beans and legumes more smooshable. I don't recommend this addition if you want your legumes to remain intact, and be cautious not to add too much, which will make them taste soapy and bitter. I never add more than **½ teaspoon baking soda per 1 pound legumes.**

Step 1: Rinse (Always) & Soak (If You've Got Time)
Rinse the legumes in cool water and soak if you have time. (No soak needed for dal!) When soaking, cover the legumes with several inches of cool water (or bone broth if you plan to use the cooking liquid), giving them plenty to drink up. (Chickpeas are especially thirsty.) I add roughly **1 tablespoon kosher salt per 1 quart water** and swish to dissolve. Store them in the refrigerator overnight; beans can quickly ferment at warm room temperature.

Step 2: Simmer (with Aromatics If You Want)
Add the legumes and all the soaking liquid to a pot, bring to a boil, and reduce the heat to **gently simmer.** During the first minutes of simmering, depending on the legume, the cooking liquid may get foamy and require some skimming. Use a large spoon or ladle to scoop off any accumulating foam. Stir occasionally and simmer until tender, adding more water to the pot if the liquid level gets too low. Be sure to **taste and add salt**

throughout the cook so the legumes are seasoned to the core, instead of just swimming in a salty broth.

For a pot of legumes I plan to eat all week, I keep it simple: bay leaves, crushed garlic cloves, a halved onion, and black pepper. But you can get creative by adding dried chilies, herbs, and aromatic vegetables or simmering in dashi, bone broth, or vegetable stock. I prefer my beans and lentils to cook up flavorful but without a specific identity, allowing them to fit into any dish. Although it doesn't take much to fully transform them: Finish a pot of beans with lemon zest, extra-virgin olive oil, and parsley for a Mediterranean feel. Add red wine vinegar and cumin to make punchy Taco Party Black Beans (page 133) for serving alongside stewed and grilled meats. Drizzle ghee sizzled with spices and curry leaves into masoor dal for serving over rice.

Save Your Bean Broth!
If you're keeping it meat-free, in many instances bean broth makes a better alternative for bone broth than vegetable stock. Bean broth is loaded with starch, which can help emulsify pan sauces and provide a rich base for stews and braises, much like the gelatin and collagen in a high-quality bone broth. I don't recommend using it for cooking rice pilaf, risotto, and other grains, where things can get too starchy and scorch. If you're not a vegetarian, bean broth is just delicious. I love a bowl of it seasoned with lots of black pepper and topped with a poached egg for a comfy winter breakfast. Just be warned, the stuff in beans that makes you gassy is especially concentrated in the cooking liquid. Pass on the bean broth if you're worried about excess flatulence, but as the owner of a bulldog I'm not afraid of some farts.

110

The Pilaf Method

Whatever you want to call it, pilaf/pulao/poloa/plov/polow is a dish and a method typically used for cooking rice that works well with other grains, too. In France it's called pilaf and is often scented with thyme and bay leaves and finished with snipped chives. Then there's the palaw in Afghanistan, fully loaded with mutton or beef, raisins, carrots, and nuts. In the Caribbean, pelau is studded with pigeon peas, corn, carrots, and sometimes simmered with coconut milk. And I would never forget "the San Francisco treat," Rice-A-Roni, with flavors like jalapeño cheddar and simply, beef. Pilaf can be as straightforward as toasting grains in butter before adding water, or a meal in itself with vegetables, meat, spices, and nuts. Most recipes follow the same template; once you learn one you can cook them all.

Step 1: Rinse (Always) & Soak (If You've Got Time)
Pilaf starts the same as the Absorption Method: To ensure fluffy and distinct grains, place them in a large bowl and **rinse with cool water.** Take your time to agitate the grains with your hands, washing off any loose starch. As the grains get jostled around during production and transport, they rub up against one another and end up coated in a fine dust of starch. If this starch isn't rinsed off, the grains will clump up after cooking. Repeatedly rinse and drain until the water runs clear enough to see your hand through it.

   Next, cover the grains in cool water and **soak** (15 minutes for cracked, polished, semi-pearled, pearled, parboiled large grains, and dal, and up to overnight for whole grains, pseudograins, and lentils) before cooking. This is an optional step that helps rice and lentils cook more evenly and can speed up the cook time for other grains; you can skip it if you're tight on time. Soaking makes an especially big difference when cooking extra-long-grain basmati rice, which will expand more and is less likely to break than when cooked without a soak. No need to rinse or soak pasta.

Step 2: Build a Flavor Base (Optional)

You will be toasting the grains in fat, so now is the time to make that fat extra flavorful through the addition of aromatic vegetables, spices, and woody herbs. It's a totally optional place to bump up the flavor, but I think it's worth it. I recommend keeping additions minimal at this stage, opting for those that highlight the grain and don't overpower it: chopped onion or fennel; finely grated ginger or garlic; thyme, bay leaf, or rosemary; and spices like turmeric, cumin, fennel, and black pepper. When you're chopping up the vegetables, try to keep everything small so it easily distributes throughout the pilaf, while keeping sprigs and leaves whole so you can pluck them out after cooking. Sweat any vegetables first until tender and translucent (or dark brown and jammy if that's your thing), then add whole or ground spices or woody herbs to quickly bloom in the fat.

Step 3: Toast

This step is what separates pilaf from any old pot of steamed rice. After the grain is drained, add it to the pot with the fat (and aromatics and spices if you choose) and **toast the grains,** tossing and stirring constantly, until it smells toasty, looks dry, and just begins to grow translucent around the edges. This step is called *parching* and it achieves two things: It develops aromatic flavors, similar to when you toast spices or nuts, while also deactivating the surface starches to further prevent clumping. This happens because with direct heat, starches rapidly break down and lose their thickening power; exactly what you need to get to fluff city.

Step 4: Steam & Fluff

You can simmer the pilaf with water or opt for a more flavorful choice, like bone broth (page lxxii), dashi, or even brewed tea. For liquids with more body, like tomato puree and coconut milk, it's best to combine them with water to prevent scorching. Once you've added the cooking liquid of your choice, add salt and bring the mixture to a rapid boil. Then reduce the heat to the lowest setting, **cover, and simmer.** The cooking time varies with each grain, but white rice typically cooks in

15 minutes. Check the package for specific timings. No peeking! If you lift the lid you'll release the steam and prevent the grains from cooking fully. After the initial cook time, get in there with a fork and **fluff up the grains** to prevent them from clumping together, before covering again and allowing them to **rest for 10 minutes.** While resting, the grains will absorb any remaining moisture and firm up, so they stay distinct. If the grains are not tender after absorbing all the liquid, add a splash of hot water and continue cooking. Just before serving, pull out any inedibles, like thyme sprigs, bay leaves, and cinnamon sticks.

Get Extra: When to Add Mix-Ins
Mix-ins that are fully cooked or good to go with just a hit of that residual heat—like toasted nuts and seeds, frozen peas or corn, and tender herbs—can be tossed in when you fluff, to steam as the pilaf rests. Additions that need time to cook—like vegetables, fish, and meat—should be added at the same time as the liquid so they can simmer together with the seeds or pasta. If you're adding a mix-in that needs more time to cook than the seeds or pasta, like chicken thighs or potatoes, you can increase the total cook time but you may also need to add more liquid. The toasting step gives you a buffer, allowing the grains to cook longer without becoming mushy. You'll have to play around with ratios and cook times here, but after a couple of tries you'll be inventing your own pilafs like a pro.

The Rapid-Boil Method

If you've made pasta before, even a box of Kraft mac and cheese, you already have the skills needed to cook any grain—boil it! Some folks even refer to this as the pasta method. This is the best place to start when you want to get to know a grain or pseudograin you're cooking for the first time. No need to look up ratios or cook times.

Step 1: Boil & Season Water

Bring a pot of water to a rolling boil and add salt. How much salt? Definitely not as salty as the sea, but be much more aggressive than if you were making a tasty soup. I've found **¼ cup kosher salt for every 1 quart water** to be a good midpoint. It can seem like a lot, but remember, most of it will be poured down the drain. **Taste the water** every time so you can learn your own preferences and eventually season the water without measuring.

Step 2: Cook Your Grain/Pseudograin/Pasta

Add the grain or pasta to the boiling water and **cook until tender.** Since the cooking liquid will be drained away along with any excess starch that sloughed off during cooking, there's no need to prerinse most grains. The one exception is quinoa, which contains a high quantity of a bitter, soapy substance called saponin. Saponins protect plants from fungus and insects (and taste freaking terrible). Check your package of quinoa. Some brands are sold prerinsed, which are good to go, otherwise a rinse is all that's needed to remove it.

Step 3: Drain & Dress (or Crisp!)

That's it! **Drain your grain** and it's ready to eat. Toss it in a dressing or sauce while warm so it'll soak all that flavor up. You can also chill cooked grains, then toss with oil to crisp in a nonstick skillet or the oven. Crisped grains offer fun pops of texture to salads, soups, porridge, and roasted veggies. Cooked grains will keep refrigerated for 5 days, making them an awesome meal prep move.

How to Sauce Pasta & Grains

Sauce up rapidly boiled grains or pasta following these steps:

1. Cook pasta and polished, pearled, or parboiled grains until al dente (or slightly underdone). They will finish cooking in the sauce and soak up all that flavor. Whole grains hold on to their chew, so it's best to fully cook them before draining.

2. Save some starchy cooking liquid to help emulsify the sauce.

3. Add the drained pasta/grain to a sauce or aromatic base along with some of the reserved starchy water. (You can even finish it in the starchy water alone.) Simmer, stirring and tossing frequently, until the liquid has thickened, and the pasta/grains are cooked to your desired final doneness.

4. Remove from the heat and finish with butter, olive oil, and/or cheese, tossing until creamy and emulsified.

Note: To prevent cheese from breaking in your sauce, do not grate it on a Microplane. Microplane graters yield a fine flurry of cheese that melts too fast and clumps, rather than gently emulsifying into a creamy sauce. Stick with coarse cheese crumbs or shreds processed with a box grater, blender, or food processor instead.

Perfect Pot of Steamed Rice

Serves 4

Active: 10 mins. | Total: about 1 hr.

Easy | Vegan | Gluten-free

Ingredients:

2 cups rice

water (see package directions for amount)

¼ teaspoon Diamond Crystal kosher salt (optional)

Special Equipment:

pot with tight-fitting lid

→ A simple pot of steamed rice rounds out any meal, whether a pot of lentils, Seared & Braised Chicken Thighs (page 174), or just a boiled egg (page 60). If you can cook rice, you'll always have something to eat. When it comes to steaming rice, many people use the knuckle method to determine how much water to add. This means you place the rice in a pot, put your finger on top of the rice, and add enough water to reach your first knuckle. This method only works consistently with *japonica* varieties in quantities greater than 2 cups. I know this is controversial in the Asian community, but I'm going to ask you to measure your rice and water—and take notes. Why? Because there's a big, wide world of rice out there! I encourage you to go out and explore more than what your momma made and figure out precisely how you like it cooked.

Every single brand and variety of rice has a unique texture, aroma, hue, and flavor, and requires a different level of hydration. I've read articles that claim that any rice can be cooked with the simple ratio of 1 part water to 1 part rice. Sure, this will result in rice that's cooked through and edible, but I want my rice to be more than just edible. I want it to be tender, chewy, and fluffy. I love the bite of Tsuyahime rice, but I've found it needs 1 more tablespoon of water than the package suggests to become utterly impeccable. No other rice has grains that cook up as distinct as Daawat rice, but it needs a whopping 2 parts water to 1 part rice. I believe the best way to cook rice is to start with the package's suggested water ratio and cook time, then make adjustments for future batches based on the results. The amount of water and time needed to cook any variety of rice will vary based on your pot, stovetop, and personal preferences. Once I know how I want a particular brand of rice cooked, I like to keep notes written on the container it's stored in.

---

1. Rinse and soak the rice: Place the rice in a medium bowl. Cover with cool tap water, use your hand to gently agitate the grains, and drain. Repeat at least two more times until the water runs clear enough to see your hand through it. Cover with cool tap water and soak for at least 15 minutes and up to 2 hours. (Brown rice can be soaked up to overnight in the fridge.)

2. Cook: Thoroughly drain the rice (I recommend using a fine-mesh sieve) and add to a medium pot with a tight-fitting lid. Add water (see package directions) and salt (if using), cover, and bring to a boil over high heat. Once you can hear the water gurgling and see wisps of steam escaping from under the lid, reduce the heat to the lowest setting and cook, without peeking, for the time indicated on the package (white rice usually takes about 15 minutes).

3. Once the time is up, uncover and check the rice: The water should be fully absorbed and the grains should be tender. Depending on the variety, the rice may look slightly wet and mushy at this point—don't worry. As long as the grains are tender and there isn't excessive water left, you are good to move to the next step. If not, follow the steps on page 119 to troubleshoot: →

Perfect Pot of Steamed Rice (cont'd.)

Troubleshooting:

• If there's excessive water left (as in, things are looking soupy), uncover the pot and continue cooking to drive off excess moisture.

• If all the liquid has absorbed but the grains are still tough, create a hole in the rice by driving the end of a wooden spoon through it to the bottom of the pot. Pour an additional 1 to 4 tablespoons hot water into the hole (depending on how raw the rice seems). Cover and continue cooking until tender.

4. **Fluff and rest:** Remove from the heat and use a fork to fluff the rice, being sure to reach all the way to the bottom of the pot. Cover and rest for at least 10 minutes before serving. As the grains cool slightly, they'll firm up, absorb the last remnants of moisture, and grow distinct and fluffy. (That's because of starch retrogradation.)

Quinoa Crunch Salad

(Serves 4)

(Active: 30 mins. | Total: 30 mins.)

(Easy) (Gluten-free)

(Vegetarian (can be made vegan))

For the quinoa:

2 cups white quinoa

3¾ cups water

1 teaspoon Diamond Crystal kosher salt

3 tablespoons neutral oil

For the salad:

4 small Persian (mini) cucumbers, cut into a fine dice

3 scallions, thinly sliced

2 small heads Little Gem lettuce, torn into bite-sized pieces

½ medium avocado, cut into a fine dice

cilantro leaves and tender stems, roughly torn

dill leaves and tender stems, roughly torn

Green Goddess Dressing (page 122)

→ This salad is everything I want to eat all the time. Oven-toasting quinoa gives it a super-satisfying snack-food crunch, while the punchy dressing is fatty, fresh, and savory thanks to lots of lemon juice, tamari, and MSG. It's practically a Dorito in salad form. Okay, not really, but it's got the same I-can't-stop-eating-this vibe.

I prefer to cook the quinoa using the Absorption Method (page 105). Since all the water is absorbed, none of the nutrients end up down the drain. If you want to make things extra savory, swap the salt in the quinoa for instant dashi powder instead. This recipe takes a little time up front, but is perfect for meal prepping: The cooked quinoa, toasted quinoa, and dressing all keep for 5 days. Then just before serving, toss everything together with freshly cut veggies. Feel free to multiply the batch as needed.

---

1. **Cook the quinoa:** Place the quinoa in a medium bowl. Cover with cool tap water, use your hand to gently agitate the grains, and drain. Repeat two more times. (Quinoa is covered in a bitter and soapy substance called saponin. It should be rinsed off before cooking—unless you've purchased a prerinsed quinoa.) Drain. Transfer to a medium pot with a tight-fitting lid. Add the water and salt, cover, and bring to a boil over high heat. Once you hear the water gurgling and see wisps of steam escaping, reduce the heat to the lowest setting and cook, without peeking, for 15 minutes. Uncover, fluff, and rest for at least 10 minutes. (Store in the fridge for up to 5 days.)

2. **Crisp the quinoa:** Heat the oven to 350°F (177°C). In a medium bowl, toss half the cooked quinoa with the oil, breaking up any clumps. Spread out in one even layer on a sheet pan and bake, tossing every 10 minutes, until golden brown and crisp, about 30 minutes. Remove from the oven and let cool completely before using. (Store the toasted quinoa in an airtight container at room temperature for up to 5 days.)

3. **Assemble the salad:** In a large bowl, toss the remaining cooked quinoa, the crunchy quinoa, the cucumbers, scallions, lettuce, avocado, cilantro, and dill until evenly dispersed. Add the dressing a spoonful at a time to avoid overdressing until evenly coated. Serve with more dressing on the side. (Or toss together individual servings as needed.)

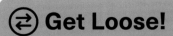 **Get Loose!**

- Try this out with any grain or pseudograin, like farro, buckwheat, or amaranth (water ratio and cook time will vary, check the package).

- Toss the grains and dressing with any combo of crunchy vegetables, like sliced radishes, torn watercress or iceberg, jicama or carrot matchsticks, or thinly sliced celery.

Green Goddess Dressing

(Makes 2 cups)

(Active: 15 mins.) (Total: 15 mins.)

(Easy) (Gluten-free)

(Vegetarian (can be made vegan))

Ingredients:

1 cup buttermilk or kefir

½ medium avocado

1 cup lightly packed fresh cilantro leaves and tender stems

1 cup lightly packed fresh dill leaves and tender stems

3 scallions, roughly chopped

1 jalapeño, roughly chopped

1 garlic clove, smashed and peeled

⅓ cup freshly squeezed lemon juice (about 2 lemons), plus more to taste

2 tablespoons extra-virgin olive oil

2 tablespoons soy sauce or tamari

1½ teaspoons Diamond Crystal kosher salt, plus more to taste

1 teaspoon sugar, plus more to taste

½ teaspoon MSG (optional)

→ Once you round up the ingredients, this creamy and fresh dressing whizzes up in a snap. To keep it vegan, swap the buttermilk with ¾ cup plant-based yogurt and ¼ cup water. Use it to dress a salad, as a dip for veggies, or tossed into cooked grains. It'll keep in the fridge for up to 5 days.

Place all the ingredients in a blender and blend on high speed until smooth. (Take care not to blend the dressing for so long that it gets warm, which will cause the herbs to grow muddy and brown.) Taste and add more salt, sugar, or lemon juice if needed. It should be tart, savory, and salty, with just enough sugar to mellow things out. Store the dressing in the refrigerator for up to 5 days.

Basic Pot of Creamy Legumes

(Serves 6 to 8)

(Active: 15 mins.)(Total: varies)

(Easy)(Gluten-free)

(Vegetarian (can be made vegan))

Ingredients:

1 pound (450 grams) any type dried
    beans or whole lentils

2 quarts water, plus more as needed

2 tablespoons Diamond Crystal
    kosher salt, plus more to taste

¼ cup olive oil

aromatics, such as quartered onions
    or shallots, peeled garlic, fresh
    ginger split lengthwise and
    crushed

herbs, such as bay leaves and sprigs
    of thyme, rosemary, parsley

if you're feeling extra: chunk of
    parmesan rind or bacon, ham
    hock, dried chilies (like guajillo or
    pasilla), lemon zest, anchovies

freshly ground black pepper

→ If you don't know what to cook, the best thing you can do for yourself is make a pot of beans. We try a different legume every week—snappy-skinned Ayocote Morados, teeny black-eyed peas, gargantuan Royal Coronas, mossy green Puy lentils, inky black beluga lentils—we never get bored. The first day I eat them straight out of the pot with a dollop of yogurt. I'll drain and add them to salads, sautés, and soups. I'll crisp them in oil or mash them with butter like potatoes. I'll wilt greens in the bean broth for a quick stew. Add as many or as few aromatics, herbs, and additions as you want. I usually keep things relatively neutral, with bay leaves, onion, and garlic. This gives me a blank canvas to work with all week long. If you have time, soaking the legumes in advance in salted water ensures that they stay intact while growing tender. The cook time and amount of water required greatly varies with each legume, so keep an eye on the pot, adding more water anytime the level looks low. Don't be tempted to crank up the heat; keeping the water at a gentle simmer allows the beans to evenly hydrate without bursting.

---

1. Rinse and soak: Rinse the beans or lentils in cool water. If you have time, transfer to a large container, add the water and salt, and stir to dissolve the salt. Soak overnight in the fridge (or however long you have time for).

2. Add the aromatics: Transfer the legumes and all the soaking liquid to a large or medium pot. (If you didn't have time to soak, start here, combining the water, legumes, and salt in the pot.) Add the oil and whatever aromatics, herbs, and extras you're feeling.

3. Simmer: Bring to a simmer over medium-high heat, then reduce the heat to maintain gentle bubbling. Use a ladle or spoon to scoop off any foam that accumulates on the surface, then partially cover with a lid.

4. Checking the legumes periodically, and adding water if the level gets too low, cook until totally tender. The cook time varies with type and age of legume and soak time. Once tender, taste and season with pepper and more salt as needed.

Note: If you plan to eat the legumes within 3 days, you can cool them at room temperature and then store in the fridge. If you want the legumes to last all week, cool leftovers rapidly by transferring to a large metal bowl set over an ice bath. Legumes go bad quickly if not cooled and stored properly.

The Creamiest Polenta

(Makes 4 cups)

(Active: 1 hr. | Total: 7 to 25 hrs.)

(Easy) (Gluten-free)

(Vegetarian (can be made vegan))

Ingredients:

1 cup coarse or medium grind
   cornmeal

2 cups cold water or bone broth
   (page lxxii), plus more as needed

kosher salt

2 cups milk, any percentage (or
   any heat-stable plant milk, see
   page 403)

freshly ground black pepper

4 tablespoons unsalted butter (or
   extra-virgin olive oil, coconut oil,
   or vegan butter)

No Time to Soak?

How to Make It Cheesy

Need More or Less?

→ Polenta is one of my favorite sides because it's good with nearly anything. Top a bowl of creamy polenta with Steamed & Sizzled Greens (page 197) and a Crispy-Edged Egg (page 65) for a fast, cheap, and satisfying dinner. Nothing is better at sopping up the briny sauce from my Broiler Turkey Meatballs in Perky Puttanesca Sauce (page 261). I even dig a big bowl all on its own for those nights when I just want some comforting mush.

Toasting the cornmeal enhances its sweet and nutty flavor, while a soak in cool water allows the grains to hydrate evenly, preventing lumps and maximizing creaminess. Try this method with any coarse or medium ground grain like semolina, grits, or masa harina; or any small grain like millet or teff; or any cracked grain, like steel-cut oats or cracked wheat. Depending on the grain, grind size, and how thick you want the final dish, you may need to add more water or increase the cook time. Use this recipe as a starting point. Be sure to add salt in stages during the cook, for even seasoning throughout. Polenta and porridges of all kinds need lots of salt to taste good, so don't be shy.

1. Toast and soak the cornmeal: In a medium skillet, toast the cornmeal over medium heat, stirring frequently with a spatula, until hot and nutty-smelling, about 5 minutes.

2. Place the toasted cornmeal in a container, add the cold water and a generous pinch of kosher salt and stir well. Cover and refrigerate for at least 6 hours and up to 24.

3. Simmer: In a medium saucepan, bring the milk and a big pinch of salt to a simmer over medium-high heat. Add the cornmeal and all the soaking liquid, whisking constantly until the mixture returns to a simmer.

4. Switch to a spatula and reduce the heat to medium-low. Taste and add salt as needed. Cook, stirring and scraping occasionally, until the polenta is fully cooked, creamy, and no grittiness remains, 45 minutes to 1 hour. Add water if the mixture seems too thick. Taste and season with pepper and more salt as needed. Remove from the heat and stir in the butter.

No problem! Bring the water (or bone broth), milk, and salt to a vigorous boil and rain in the toasted cornmeal while stirring vigorously. Season and cook, stirring frequently, until tender.

Add 1 to 2 cups (4 to 8 ounces/112 to 224 grams) shredded melty or hard grating cheese, such as cheddar or parmesan, off the heat once the polenta is totally tender. Do not use cheese grated on a Microplane, which is too fine and will clump rather than become creamy.

Feel free to scale this recipe up or down as needed. Just remember the basic ratio of 1 part cornmeal to 4 parts liquid. The procedure and cook time will remain the same.

124

How to Make Polenta

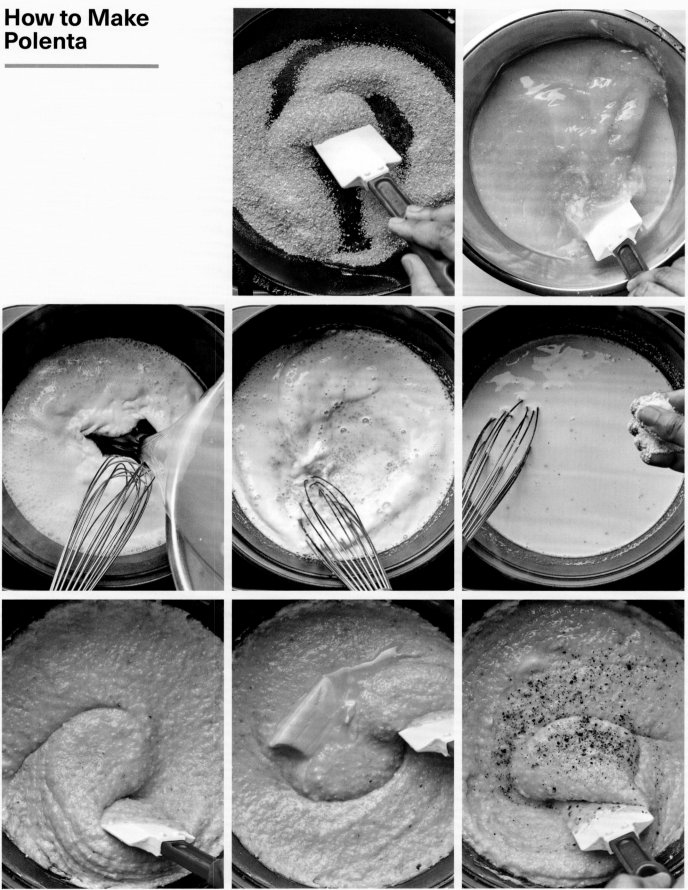

Ginger & Turmeric Rice Porridge

with Cilantro Chutney

(Serves 4)

(Active: 30 mins. | Total: at least 1½ hrs.)

(Easy) (Gluten-free)

(Vegetarian (can be made vegan))

For the porridge:

¾ cup medium-grain white rice, such as jasmine or Carolina Gold

2 tablespoons ghee, butter, or vegan butter

2-inch piece fresh ginger, peeled and cut into matchsticks

1 teaspoon ground turmeric

¼ to ¾ teaspoon chili powder or flakes

¼ cup hulled and split lentils, such as masoor, toor, or chana dal

8 cups water or bone broth (page lxxii), or a combination, plus more as needed

kosher salt and freshly ground black pepper

1 medium russet potato (about 10 ounces/280 grams), peeled and cut into ½-inch pieces

For the cilantro chutney:

1½ cups lightly packed fresh cilantro leaves and tender stems, very finely chopped

1 to 2 green chilies, such as Thai or serrano, very finely chopped

¼ cup freshly squeezed lime juice (about 2 limes)

¼ cup extra-virgin olive oil

kosher salt

→ My amu would make me a rice porridge just like this one anytime I was sick. Where I'm from it's called gulothi, but every rice-eating region has their own take, from mild okayu to vibrant khichdi. The small quantity of rice and lentils almost fully breaks down, thickening the water or broth into a velvety bowl of comfort. I prefer it with jasmine rice and masoor dal (hulled and split red lentils) because that's what amu made, but you can use any combination of polished, pearled grain, or cracked grain and split lentil. Try it with pearled barley and split peas or bulgur and chana dal. The amount of liquid and time to cook it may change, but regardless of the grain, the goal is the same: You want to simmer the grain and legume until they swell and rupture, spilling their starches into the liquid, making it silky and thick.

1. **Wash and soak the rice:** Place the rice in a medium bowl. Cover with cool tap water, use your hand to gently agitate the grains, and drain. Repeat at least two more times until the water runs clear enough to see your hand through it. Cover the rice with fresh, cold water and set aside to soak for at least 15 minutes and up to 24 hours.

2. Drain the rice, then roughly crush it with a pestle or the end of a rolling pin, breaking the grains into uneven pieces ranging from cornmeal-sized bits to larger pieces that are cracked in half.

3. **Cook the aromatics:** In a medium pot, melt the ghee over medium heat until foamy. Add the ginger, turmeric, and chili and cook until fragrant, about 1 minute.

4. **Simmer the porridge:** Add the rice, lentils, and water to the pot. Season with salt and black pepper to taste. Bring to a boil, then reduce to a simmer and cook, uncovered, until the rice and lentils are tender, about 30 minutes.

5. Add the potato and gently simmer, stirring occasionally, until the potato is totally tender and the porridge has thickened, about 20 minutes. If the porridge has thickened too much, add water to thin. If it's too thin, continue simmering until it reduces to your desired consistency.

6. **While the porridge simmers, prepare the cilantro chutney:** In a small bowl, mix the cilantro, green chilies, lime juice, and olive oil. Stir to combine, taste, and adjust seasoning with salt.

7. Taste the porridge and adjust seasoning with salt and black pepper. Divide into bowls, garnish with the cilantro chutney, and serve immediately.

Charred Lemon Risotto

(Makes 8 cups)

(Active: 45 mins. | Total: 45 mins.)

(Easy) (Vegetarian) (Gluten-free)

Ingredients:

2 cups short-grain rice, such as
    Arborio, Carnaroli, or sushi rice

6 cups water, plus more as needed

2 teaspoons Diamond Crystal kosher
    salt, plus more to taste

¼ cup olive oil

2 medium lemons

2 teaspoons coarsely ground black
    pepper

1 cup coarsely grated
    parmesan cheese (about
    4 ounces/112 grams)

4 tablespoons cold unsalted butter,
    cut into ½-inch cubes

Special Equipment:

fine-mesh sieve

→ I was always taught that good risotto starts with high-quality bone broth, but what if I don't want to spend twenty bucks on dinner? Here I skip the broth and instead deeply char cut lemons in olive oil until the fat is speckled with bits of burnt flesh. Don't be alarmed, the bitterness from the blackening, once combined with salty parmesan and butter, adds unbelievable depth and richness. The charred lemon juice also slaps you with its brightness, so even with all that creaminess, your palate is never weighed down. This recipe makes a generous quantity, so feel free to cut the recipe in half if you're only serving 2 or 3; the timing of the steps will remain the same.

Risotto should have the al dente bite of properly cooked pasta with the saucy body of comforting rice porridge. This creamy texture is built by the starches hanging on to the outside of each grain of rice. As you stir and cook the rice, that starch is sloughed into the broth, making it thick and lush. However, before adding the broth, the rice is toasted in fat to turn up its nutty aroma. This direct heat deactivates some of those exterior starches, leaving the risotto less creamy than it could be. In order to take advantage of every speck of sauce-forging starch, I've adopted J. Kenji López-Alt's technique of rinsing the rice in the risotto cooking liquid. Just a quick swish makes the risotto that much creamier.

---

1. Rinse the rice: Put the rice in a fine-mesh sieve and set it over a medium saucepan. Slowly pour the water over the rice, gently swishing with a spatula, and collecting the starchy liquid in the saucepan below. Once drained, lift off the sieve and set aside. Season the starchy liquid with 2 teaspoons kosher salt and bring to a simmer over high heat. Cover and reduce the heat to low to keep warm.

2. Char the lemons: In a medium Dutch oven, heat the oil over medium heat until shimmering. Cut the lemons in half and place them cut-side down in the oil. Cook, undisturbed, until deeply charred (blackened bits will speckle the oil, that's just what you want), 6 to 8 minutes. Flip and lightly sear the lemon rinds to flavor the oil, about 1 minute. Transfer the lemons to a cutting board to cool.

3. Toast the rice: Add the drained rice and pepper to the Dutch oven and stir to coat with the oil. Cook, stirring constantly, until the rice looks dry, smells toasty, and sizzles and pops, 3 to 5 minutes.

4. Simmer: Reduce the heat to medium-low and add enough of the warm starchy water to barely cover the rice. Cook, stirring frequently, until most of the liquid has been absorbed. Add the rest of the water in stages, each time adding enough to barely cover and stirring until absorbed before adding more.

5. Cook, stirring frequently, until the rice is almost tender but with a raw bite left at the core, and the water is thickened into a starchy sauce that generously immerses the rice. (If you've used up all the water before the rice is cooked, or need more starchy sauce, add hot tap water as needed. Err on the side of too loose, as the risotto will thicken as it cools.) Depending on the type of rice, this will take between 14 and 19 minutes. →

How to Make
Charred Lemon
Risotto

130

Charred Lemon Risotto (cont'd.)

6. **Enrich the risotto:** Add the parmesan and stir vigorously until mostly melted. Add the butter and continue stirring until creamy and emulsified. Remove from the heat. Squeeze the charred lemons into the risotto through a fine-mesh sieve, pressing to push through any tender pulp; discard the rinds. Taste and add salt if needed. Serve right away.

Taco Party Black Beans

Makes about 4 cups

Active: 20 mins. | Total: 20 mins.

Easy | Vegan | Gluten-free

Ingredients:

¼ cup neutral oil

1 medium yellow or white onion, finely chopped

kosher salt, plus more to taste

3 tablespoons tomato paste

4 garlic cloves, finely chopped

1 to 2 canned chipotle peppers in adobo sauce, finely chopped, plus adobo sauce to taste

2 teaspoons ground cumin

2 teaspoons dried oregano

½ teaspoon freshly ground black pepper

3 cups cooked black beans, home-cooked or two 15.5-ounce cans, drained but unrinsed and bean broth reserved

freshly squeezed lime juice

Special Equipment:

potato masher (or sturdy whisk)

→ . . . cause they make anything you put them on a party! These black beans are sautéed in seasoned fat before lightly smashing, much like Mexican refried beans, which are traditionally cooked in lard. You can make this with any bean or lentil you've simmered from scratch, but it's also a great way to quickly jazz up any canned bean. I'm amping up the flavor with the same seasoning I'd typically add to beef when I'm going for a Taco Bell–style taco. Try them smooshed on a tostada, topped with a crispy fried egg, or in a warm tortilla with cheese. But my favorite way to enjoy these beans is in a taco salad. I'll smear the bottom of a bowl with a big spoonful of beans, top with shredded cheddar cheese, sliced radishes, chopped lettuce and tomato, sliced avocado, hot sauce, lime, sour cream, and a crowning glory of crushed Fritos.

---

1. **Cook the aromatics:** In a medium Dutch oven or saucepot, heat the oil over medium-high heat until shimmering. Add the onions, season lightly with kosher salt, and cook, stirring often with a wooden spoon, until frizzled and charred in spots, 9 to 11 minutes.

2. Add the tomato paste, garlic, chipotle, cumin, oregano, and black pepper. Stir well and cook until fragrant and the paste begins to stick to the bottom of the pot, about 1 minute.

3. **Simmer with the beans:** Add the black beans and use the wooden spoon to scrape up the spice mixture from the bottom of the pot and evenly coat the beans. Add enough reserved bean broth to make the mixture as saucy as you'd like and bring to a simmer, about 1 minute. (I usually start with ½ cup, then add more as needed.)

4. Use a potato masher (or whisk) to roughly smash some of the beans. Season with salt, add more bean broth and adobo sauce to taste.

5. Remove from the heat and add lime juice to taste. Serve right away or store in the fridge for up to 3 days.

Brothy Black Lentils

with Dandelion Greens & Tons of Toasted Garlic

(Serves 4)

(Active: 30 mins. | Total: 1 hr.)

(Easy) (Vegetarian)

Ingredients:

⅓ cup olive oil

30 garlic cloves, peeled (from about 3 heads)

2 bunches dandelion greens (12 ounces/336 grams), ends trimmed and cut into bite-sized pieces

1 cup black lentils

4-inch piece parmesan or pecorino rind

1 teaspoon Diamond Crystal kosher salt, plus more to taste

6 cups water, plus more as needed

4 thick-cut pieces crusty bread, deeply toasted

grated parmesan or pecorino cheese for serving

→ I know, 30 cloves is a lot of garlic, but by deeply caramelizing it in a generous amount of olive oil you can develop an intensely savory broth without much else. This trick works with any allium (all those aromatic wonders in the onion family, including shallots, scallions, leeks, and onions) and has become my go-to move when the fridge is looking bare. Take care to keep the cloves whole instead of going for a smash-peel situation, which activates the compounds in garlic that make it hot and harsh. (See page lxv for pictures of how to peel garlic.) Black lentils keep their shape even when tender for pops of texture among the silky greens and inky broth, but you can give this recipe a whirl with any bean or whole lentil you've got. You just might need to add more water and increase the cook time for some legumes.

---

1. Caramelize the garlic: Heat a medium Dutch oven or pot over medium-high heat. Add the olive oil and garlic cloves and cook, stirring constantly, until the garlic cloves are deeply browned all over and lightly charred in spots, 4 to 7 minutes. (Getting deep color on the garlic is key to this dish's flavor. Not brown enough and the broth will taste unpleasantly bitter.)

2. Wilt the greens: Add the dandelion greens and toss until wilted, about 1 minute.

3. Simmer: Add the lentils, cheese rind, salt, and water. Bring to a boil, then reduce to a bare simmer and cover. Use a ladle or large spoon to scoop off any foam that accumulates on the surface of the pot. Cook until the lentils are totally tender, 30 to 40 minutes. Taste and add salt if needed. (If the broth tastes too bitter, you probably need more salt.)

4. Divide the bread among four shallow bowls, ladle the lentils over, and top with grated cheese. Serve right away.

134

Baked White Beans with Dates

(Serves 6 to 8)

(Active: 20 mins. | Total: 4½ hrs.)

(Easy)

(Vegetarian (can be made vegan))

Ingredients:

1 pound (450 grams) dried small white beans (like navy or Great Northern)

2 quarts water, plus more as needed

1 tablespoon Diamond Crystal kosher salt, plus more to taste

2 tablespoons neutral oil

1 medium yellow onion, chopped

5 garlic cloves, chopped

2¾ cups tomato passata or puree (24.5 ounces/670 grams)

8 medium Medjool dates, pitted and roughly chopped

1 tablespoon freshly ground black pepper

2 tablespoons classic or vegan Worcestershire sauce, plus more to taste

2 tablespoons apple cider vinegar, plus more to taste

brown sugar (optional)

→ Heinz beans, the kind you get piled on toast at a sticky pub that's always got footy playing on the tube, is my favorite way to bean. I know we've got our own baked beans here in the States, but the sweet tomato vibes from across the pond have always been my favorite. This is my version of those, syrupy with melted Medjool dates and smoky with plenty of unpronounceable Worcestershire sauce (if you want to keep this vegan, use soy sauce, tamari, or better yet, vegan Worcestershire sauce instead).

Because we want intact and creamy beans, the hydration is gonna happen nice and slow, first through an overnight soak in salted water, then in the gentle heat of the oven. Baking beans does take a long time, but if cooked on the stovetop the thick tomato sauce would scorch without frequent stirring. In the oven, the beans don't need any babysitting. Depending on how fresh your beans are, they may take more or less time and liquid to hydrate. Follow the notes on how to adjust the sauciness of your baked beans after the initial 2-hour bake time. Serve on toast, in a baked potato, or alongside hot dogs, BBQ, or grilled meat.

---

1. **Rinse and soak:** Rinse the beans in cool water. Transfer to a large container, add the water and salt, and stir to dissolve the salt. Soak overnight in the fridge for at least 6 and up to 12 hours.

2. Position a rack in the lower third of the oven and heat to 325°F (163°C).

3. **Cook the aromatics:** In a large Dutch oven, heat the oil over medium-high heat until it shimmers. Add the onion and a big pinch of salt and cook, stirring frequently, until wilted and barely golden, about 3 minutes. Add the garlic and cook, stirring frequently, until the garlic wilts and the onions brown, about 2 minutes.

4. **Simmer and bake:** Add the tomato passata, dates, black pepper, and the beans with all their soaking liquid. Bring to a boil, cover, transfer to the oven, and bake until totally tender, about 2 hours.

5. Remove from the oven and check the beans' doneness:
- If they are tender but too saucy, simmer on the stovetop until thickened.
- If they are tender and too thick, add water to adjust.
- If they are underdone and dry, add more water, bring to a boil, then return to the oven.
- If they are tender and glazed in a thick sauce, proceed with final seasoning.

6. **Season the beans:** Stir in the Worcestershire and vinegar, then taste, adding some brown sugar if using or more salt, Worcestershire, or vinegar if needed.

Black Sesame & Nori Rice Pilaf

(Serves 4 to 6)

(Active: 20 mins.) (Total: 1 hr.)

(Easy) (Gluten-free)

Ingredients:

2 cups jasmine rice

3 tablespoons unsalted butter

3 cups dashi or high-quality bone broth (page lxxii)

1 teaspoon Diamond Crystal kosher salt

2 sheets nori

1 tablespoon toasted black sesame seeds

→ This is hands down my favorite pilaf. It's super savory and briny, with rice that's simmered in dashi before fluffing with ground, toasted nori. You can make your own dashi, use instant dashi powder, or stick with bone broth. All I need to make this the most satisfying dinner is a pile of steamed greens, but the rice is laid-back enough to play background to broiled fish, steamed clams, or even a whole roasted chicken. Take your time toasting the grains in butter—this is the essential step to a pilaf. The grains will develop a nuttier flavor, be less prone to sticking, and become less likely to overcook and break. Once you get in the pilaf groove, try out the variations that follow or make up your own. Any rice, pseudograin, or pearled or polished grain can pilaf! Liquid ratios and cook times will vary, but it's always the same as if you're just going for a simple steam. Use the ratios on the package to guide you.

1. **Rinse and soak the rice:** Place the rice in a medium bowl. Cover with cool tap water, use your hand to gently agitate the grains, and drain. Repeat at least two more times or until the water runs clear enough to see your hand through it. Cover the rice with water and let soak for at least 15 minutes and up to 2 hours.

2. Drain the rice in a fine-mesh sieve.

3. **Toast the rice:** In a medium Dutch oven or saucepot, heat the butter over medium-high heat until shimmering. Add the drained rice and cook, stirring constantly, until the rice is coated in the butter, starting to look translucent and smell toasty, and you can hear it sizzle and pop, 2 to 3 minutes.

4. **Simmer:** Add the dashi and salt, increase the heat to high, and bring to a rapid boil. Cover, reduce the heat to the lowest setting, and simmer for 15 minutes. (No peeking! Lifting the lid will release steam and throw off the hydration.)

5. Meanwhile, lightly toast the nori sheets over a gas burner or under a broiler until they look slightly darkened and smell aromatic, about 30 seconds. Tear into small pieces and blitz in a spice grinder until fine.

6. **Fluff and rest:** Remove the lid of the pot, add the sesame seeds and ground nori, fluff the rice with a fork, put the lid back on, and rest for 10 minutes. Serve while hot. Sauté leftovers in oil for fried or crispy rice.

Tomato & Turmeric Rice Pilaf

Vegan Gluten-free

Ingredients:

2 cups jasmine rice

3 tablespoons olive oil

1 small yellow onion, finely chopped

2 garlic cloves, finely chopped

½ teaspoon ground turmeric

½ teaspoon smoked paprika

1½ cups tomato puree or passata

1½ cups water

1 teaspoon Diamond Crystal kosher salt

Coconut & Pea Rice Pilaf

Vegan Gluten-free

Ingredients:

2 cups jasmine rice

2 tablespoons virgin coconut oil or neutral oil

3 scallions, thinly sliced

1-inch piece fresh ginger, peeled and finely grated

one 13.5-ounce (400 mL) can full-fat coconut milk

1½ cups water

1 teaspoon Diamond Crystal kosher salt

¾ cup cooked pigeon peas

More Easy Pilafs!

Try these variations following the directions in the previous recipe as a guide.

1. Rinse and soak the rice.

2. In the Dutch oven, heat the oil and cook the onion and garlic until tender. Add the spices and cook until aromatic.

3. Add the drained rice and toast.

4. Add the tomato puree, water, and salt and simmer as directed on page 138.

5. Fluff and rest.

1. Rinse and soak the rice.

2. In the Dutch oven, heat the oil and cook the scallions and ginger until tender.

3. Add the drained rice and toast.

4. Add the coconut milk, water, and salt and simmer as directed on page 138.

5. Fluff the rice, folding in the peas at the same time. Cover and rest.

Chicken-y Chive Rice Pilaf

(Gluten-free)

Ingredients:

2 cups jasmine rice

3 tablespoons rendered chicken fat or unsalted butter

1 small yellow onion, finely chopped

3 sprigs fresh thyme

1 bay leaf

½ teaspoon freshly ground black pepper

3 cups high-quality bone broth (page lxxii)

1 teaspoon Diamond Crystal kosher salt

¼ cup thinly sliced chives

1. Rinse and soak the rice.

2. In the Dutch oven, heat the chicken fat and cook the onion until tender. Add herbs and pepper and cook until aromatic.

3. Add the drained rice and toast.

4. Add the broth and salt and simmer as directed on page 138.

5. Fluff the rice, folding in the chives at the same time. Cover and rest. Remove the thyme sprigs and bay leaf before serving.

Korma-ish Rice Pilaf

(Vegetarian) (Gluten-free)

Ingredients:

2 cups jasmine rice

3 tablespoons ghee or unsalted butter

1 small yellow onion, finely chopped

2 teaspoons garam masala

one 13.5-ounce (400 mL) can full-fat coconut milk

1½ cups water

1 teaspoon Diamond Crystal kosher salt

½ cup Crispy Shallots (page 83)

½ cup golden raisins

1. Rinse and soak the rice.

2. In the Dutch oven, heat the butter and cook the onion until tender.

3. Add the garam masala and drained rice and toast.

4. Add the coconut milk, water, and salt and simmer as directed on page 138.

5. Fluff the rice, folding in the shallots and raisins at the same time. Cover and rest.

Cheesy Macaroni Pomodoro

(Serves 1 or 2)

(Active: 15 mins.) | (Total: 15 mins.)

(Easy) (Vegetarian)

Ingredients:

kosher salt

1 cup any short dried pasta, such as elbow or cavatappi

2 tablespoons extra-virgin olive oil

2 garlic cloves, thinly sliced

1 cup tomato passata or puree

¾ cup coarsely grated parmesan cheese (about 3 ounces/85 grams)

2 tablespoons cold unsalted butter, cut into ½-inch cubes

roughly torn fresh basil

→ This extra saucy cross between mac and cheese and pasta pomodoro and tomato soup is probably an abomination, but it's my go-to bowl of comfort on those days when I want to feel like a kid again. Nope, there aren't even chili flakes, because sometimes I can't handle even the slightest prickle. This recipe serves two (or one on a really bad day), but you can scale it up endlessly. Just make the sauce in a Dutch oven rather than a skillet so you've got plenty of room to groove when it comes time to toss and sauce. Oh, and for maximum nostalgia, eat with a spoon. I'm using the rapid-boil method here to cook the pasta, but you can make this with any whole, polished, semi-pearled, pearled, or parboiled grains, or pseudograins. Remember, the cook times for grains can greatly vary, so follow visual rather than time cues when swapping in other grains.

1. **Cook the pasta:** Bring a medium saucepan of water to a boil and season aggressively with salt. Add the pasta and cook, stirring occasionally, until somewhat tender but with a distinct bite still left at the core. (The pasta will finish cooking in the sauce, so drain it when it seems a few minutes away from al dente. At this point, it's better to undercook rather than overcook the pasta.) The timing will vary with each pasta brand; begin tasting for doneness a few minutes before the package says it will be cooked. Reserve 1 cup of the starchy cooking water and drain the pasta.

2. **Make the sauce:** Meanwhile, in a medium skillet, combine the oil and garlic and cook over medium heat, stirring frequently, until barely golden, about 2 minutes. Add the tomato passata and increase the heat to medium-high. (If your pasta isn't ready yet, cover the skillet and remove from the heat.)

3. **Bring it together:** Bring the sauce to a boil, add the drained pasta and ½ cup pasta cooking water, and cook, stirring frequently, until the pasta is al dente (mostly tender with a slight bite at the core) and the sauce is slightly thickened, adding more pasta water if needed.

4. Reduce the heat to low and add the parmesan, stirring frequently until melted. Remove from the heat and add the butter and basil, stirring until combined. Taste and add salt if needed. Divide between bowls, top with more torn basil, and serve immediately.

Grating Cheese for Melting

I love my Microplane rasp grater for many things: instant garlic or ginger paste, a flurry of lemon zest, or freshly grated nutmeg. But one thing it's not great at is grating cheese. A Microplane rasp grater will grate cheese so extremely fine that it melts too fast, clumps, and ultimately leads to a broken rather than an emulsified sauce. For pasta, risotto, or any dish where your goal is creamy, cheesy glory, stick with the small holes on a box grater (or even blitz in a food processor or blender) instead.

How to Make Cheesy Macaroni Pomodoro

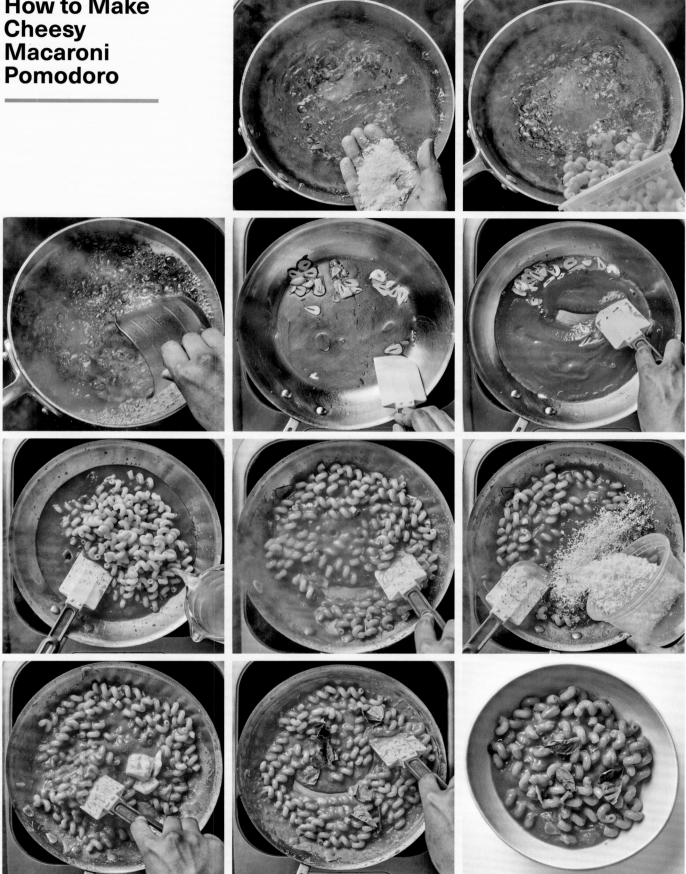

Chilled Green Tahini Soba

(Serves 2 or 3)

(Active: 30 mins.) | (Total: 30 mins.)

(Intermediate) (Vegan)

For the red onion slaw:

1 small red onion, thinly sliced

½ cup lightly packed fresh parsley leaves and tender stems

3 tablespoons freshly squeezed lemon juice (about 1 lemon)

1 tablespoon sumac

½ teaspoon Diamond Crystal kosher salt, plus more to taste

For the green tahini dressing:

½ cup well-stirred tahini

8 scallions, cut into rough 1-inch pieces

¾ cup lightly packed fresh parsley leaves and tender stems

¾ cup lightly packed fresh cilantro leaves and tender stems

1 garlic clove, smashed and peeled

1 Thai bird's eye chili, stemmed

6 tablespoons freshly squeezed lemon juice (about 2 lemons)

1 teaspoon ground coriander

½ teaspoon ground cumin

1 teaspoon Diamond Crystal kosher salt, plus more to taste

1 teaspoon sugar

¼ teaspoon MSG (optional)

For the soba and assembly:

10 ounces (280 grams) dried soba noodles

1 cup cashews, toasted and roughly chopped

→ Soba noodles are made with buckwheat, often in combination with wheat flour, and have a rich and earthy flavor. Unlike Italian pasta, which is made from 100 percent wheat flour, you want to cook soba in lots of unsalted boiling water until tender, then immediately rinse under cold water to halt the cooking. If you skip this step, the soba doesn't just become mushy, it fully disintegrates in front of your eyes. This dish is a great make-ahead meal: Prep the dressing, cook the soba, and mix the red onion slaw today to easily eat well for days. The dressing is heavy on lemon juice to brighten up the soba and rich tahini, so be sure to balance all that acid. If the dressing tastes too sharp, it probably just needs a fat pinch of kosher salt.

---

1. **Make the red onion slaw:** In a medium bowl, combine the red onion, parsley, lemon juice, sumac, and salt. Toss together, taste, and add more salt if needed.

2. **Make the green tahini dressing:** In a blender, combine all the ingredients and blend until smooth. (Take care not to blend the dressing for so long that it gets warm, which will cause the herbs to grow muddy and brown.) Taste and add more salt if needed.

3. **Cook the soba:** Fill a large pot with water and bring to a boil. Add the soba and cook according to the package directions. Drain in a fine-mesh sieve and thoroughly rinse under cold water, gently tossing the noodles with your hands. Place the sieve on top of the pot to drain the remaining water.

4. **Assemble the dish:** In a large bowl, toss the soba noodles with the dressing, adding a splash of water at a time if the dressing is looking too thick. Divide into serving bowls, top with the red onion slaw, sprinkle with the cashews, and serve. Alternatively, dress as much soba as you like and reserve the cooked soba, dressing, and red onion slaw in separate containers in the fridge for up to 5 days. Dress and top each portion of soba as needed.

Spaghetti with Zucchini, Pecorino & Mint

(Serves 6 to 8)

(Active: 30 mins.) (Total: 1 hr.)

(Intermediate) (Vegetarian)

Ingredients:

½ cup extra-virgin olive oil

10 garlic cloves, thinly sliced

8 medium zucchini (about 3 pounds/
   1.3 kilograms), halved lengthwise
   and thinly sliced crosswise

kosher salt

1 cup water

2 teaspoons chili flakes

1 pound (450 grams) spaghetti

½ cup lightly packed fresh mint
   leaves, plus more for garnish

1½ cups coarsely grated Pecorino
   Romano cheese (about 6 ounces/
   170 grams), plus more for garnish

→ Don't be alarmed by how much zucchini is in this recipe. Once it cooks down, the squash collapses into a silky sauce for pasta, leaning more into luxe Alfredo ambiance than a delicate primavera. This transformation from watery and bland to rich and nuanced is possible for practically any vegetable. Cook down cabbage, cauliflower, peppers, or eggplant until they collapse and caramelize, then add pasta, water, cheese, and boom—it's freaking delicious. It does take some time to fully cook down the zucchini, but you can prep that part in a big batch and store in your fridge or freezer until you're ready to pasta. Just as with the Cheesy Macaroni Pomodoro (page 142), here we boil the pasta in salted water until it's barely tender, with plenty of bite left at the core. This allows the pasta to finish swelling and tenderizing in the sauce, soaking up flavor and getting the sauce glossy and emulsified with help from the starches in the pasta.

1. **Cook the zucchini:** In a medium Dutch oven, warm the olive oil over medium-high heat until fragrant and shimmery. Add the garlic and cook, stirring frequently, until the garlic is fragrant and browned along the edges, 2 to 4 minutes.

2. Add the zucchini, a large pinch of salt, and the water. Cover and cook, stirring occasionally until the zucchini collapses and grows wilted and soft, about 8 minutes. Uncover and cook until the water has evaporated and the zucchini has cooked down to a thick paste and has started to brown, 25 to 30 minutes. (If the zucchini is sticking to the pot, add a splash of water and use a wooden spoon to scrape it up.) Add the chili flakes and stir well to incorporate. Remove from the heat and cover. (Or store in the refrigerator for 1 week or in the freezer for 3 months. Reheat before adding the pasta.)

3. **Cook the pasta:** Bring a medium pot of water to a boil and season it aggressively with salt. Add the pasta and cook, stirring occasionally, until somewhat tender but with a distinct bite still left at the core. (The spaghetti will finish cooking in the sauce, so drain it when it seems a few minutes away from al dente. At this point, it's better to undercook rather than overcook the pasta.) The timing will vary with each pasta brand; begin tasting for doneness a few minutes before the package says it will be cooked. Reserve 2 cups starchy cooking water and drain the spaghetti.

4. **Bring it together:** Add the spaghetti and 1½ cups cooking water to the zucchini and cook, stirring frequently, until the pasta is al dente (mostly tender with a slight bite at the core) and the sauce is slightly thickened, adding more pasta water if needed. Remove from the heat, add the mint leaves and Pecorino, and stir again until the cheese is melted and the spaghetti is well coated in the sauce.

5. Divide among plates, garnish with more Pecorino and mint, and serve immediately.

Chicken Soup with Masa Dumplings

(Serves 4)

(Active: 25 mins.) (Total: 1 hr.)

(Intermediate) (Gluten-free)

For the chicken:

2 boneless, skinless chicken breasts (about 12 ounces/350 grams total), cut into bite-sized pieces

2 teaspoons Diamond Crystal kosher salt

1 teaspoon sugar

For the soup:

2 tablespoons unsalted butter

1 medium jalapeño, finely chopped (seeds removed if you want)

1 medium yellow or white onion, finely chopped, plus more for serving

6 garlic cloves, finely chopped

kosher salt

1 medium bunch kale, stemmed and roughly chopped

2 quarts high-quality chicken bone broth, store-bought or homemade (page lxxii)

1½ cups cooked black beans, home-cooked or from one 15.5-ounce can

2 bay leaves

½ teaspoon dried oregano

For the dumplings:

1½ cups (180 grams) masa harina

1¼ cups boiling water

3 tablespoons unsalted butter, melted

1 tablespoon Diamond Crystal kosher salt

→ This recipe is based on a classic Mexican dumpling called chochoyotes, where the masa harina is mixed with water and fat before simmering in broth. The dumplings thicken the soup as they cook up tender and flavorful. You can also simmer them in water and sauté them just like gnocchi. Once you've got your hands on masa harina, try swapping it in for half the wheat flour in baked goods for a boost of corny flavor. If you want to level this soup up, treat it like a taco and top each bowl with sour cream, avocado, cilantro, and a squeeze of fresh lime.

1. Season the chicken: In a medium bowl, toss the chicken breasts with the salt and sugar and let sit in the fridge.

2. Make the soup: Heat a large Dutch oven or large pot over medium heat. Add the butter, jalapeño, onion, garlic, and a big pinch of salt and cook, stirring occasionally, until the vegetables are tender and translucent, 3 to 5 minutes.

3. Add the kale and cook, stirring occasionally, until wilted and darkened, 2 to 3 minutes.

4. Add the bone broth, beans, bay leaves, oregano, and 1 teaspoon Diamond Crystal kosher salt and bring to a simmer over high heat. Cover, reduce the heat to medium-low, and cook until the kale is silky and tender, about 30 minutes.

5. Meanwhile, make the masa dumplings: In a medium bowl, combine the masa harina, boiling water, melted butter, and salt and mix well with a rubber spatula. Once everything is evenly combined, knead with your hands until the mixture comes together into a smooth ball.

6. With a #60 scoop (or two spoons), scoop the dumpling dough into generous 1-tablespoon portions onto a sheet pan or large plate. With wet hands, roll each dumpling into a smooth ball. Use a chopstick to press a divot into each dumpling (this helps them cook evenly).

7. Taste the soup and add more salt if needed. Gently add all the dumplings to the simmering soup. Cover, adjust the heat to maintain a gentle simmer, and cook for 10 minutes.

8. Add the chicken and simmer, stirring gently to distribute the heat, until cooked through, 6 to 9 minutes.

9. Ladle the soup into bowls and top with chopped onion.

Zhaleh's Classic Saffron-Stained Tahdig

Serves 4 to 6

Active: 30 mins. | Total: 1½ hrs.

Advanced | Gluten-free

Vegetarian

Ingredients:

2½ cups aged extra-long basmati rice, preferably sella rice

¾ cup plus ½ teaspoon Diamond Crystal kosher salt

A big pinch of saffron threads

1 teaspoon sugar

1 large egg yolk

2 tablespoons whole-milk Greek yogurt

6 tablespoons melted ghee, clarified butter, or neutral oil

⅓ cup dried barberries, currants, or cranberries

Special Equipment:

large, lightweight nonstick pot with lid

mortar and pestle

→ Tahdig is the crunchy layer you end up with at the bottom of the pot when steaming basmati rice. Sometimes the pot is lined with potatoes or bread, but this is my favorite version, where the rice itself turns into a caramelized and crackly cake. The rice goes through two cooking steps here: First we boil it in lots of salted water until it's al dente—mostly tender with a bite left at the core. Next, some of the rice is mixed with yogurt, egg, and fat and spread onto the bottom of the pot. The remaining rice is piled on top, and the pot is placed onto super-low heat, crisping the bottom while steaming the rice on top. This is how you get the fluffiest, longest grains of basmati rice with a crunchy tahdig underneath.

I struggled with this dish for years until Ham's stepmother, Zhaleh, taught me her secrets. She's an incredible cook, an expert in all the Persian classics, and makes the best tahdig I've ever had. The secret: a lightweight, nonstick pot with a tight-fitting lid. Nothing expensive or fancy. You know I love Dutch ovens, but this dish was born in thin aluminum Persian pots. A heavyweight enameled or stainless steel pot is less responsive to changes in heat, making it hard to control the browning of the rice. I almost didn't put this recipe in the book because you need a special pot, but I think it's so worth it. Once you master this technique, the riffs are endless and I guarantee you'll be making tahdig on repeat. This is a recipe that takes several tries to get right. The cook times vary greatly depending on your pan and cooktop, and you can't peek, so you've got to rely on sound and smell to guide you.

Key things to keep in mind:

- When you cook the rice, wrap the lid with a clean kitchen towel to collect the steam and prevent it from condensing and rolling down the sides of the pan.

- Seek out high-quality aged basmati rice, preferably parboiled or sella, which is steamed and dried. Sella rice cooks up fluffier and is more forgiving, but regardless of the type of basmati you get, the cooking method remains the same.

- Whole butter won't work here; the milk solids will burn. Be sure to use ghee, clarified butter, or a neutral oil, like safflower or grapeseed.

1. Rinse and soak the rice: Place the rice in a medium bowl. Cover with cool tap water, use your hand to gently agitate the grains, and drain. Repeat at least two more times until the water runs clear enough to see your hand through it. Cover with cool tap water and soak for at least 15 minutes and up to 2 hours.

2. Parboil the rice: In a large nonstick pot, bring 3 quarts water and ¾ cup of the salt to a rapid boil over high heat. Add the drained rice all at once to the boiling salted water. Initially the water will stop boiling and the rice will sink to the bottom. Stir a few times with a wooden spoon to prevent sticking, then stop stirring. After a couple of minutes, the water will return to a simmer and a few grains will begin appearing near the surface. The rice is ready to drain when the grains have nearly doubled in size, the water returns to a boil, and most of the rice rapidly bubbles to the surface. When you bite into a grain, you want to see a small white core; just like pasta cooked al dente, the grains should remain firm. Depending on the quality of your rice, this →

Zhaleh's Classic Saffron-Stained Tahdig (cont'd.)

can take anywhere from 3 to 7 minutes, so begin tasting the grains early and often. Drain the rice and rinse under cool running water to stop the cooking. Wash and dry the pot. Set aside.

3. The rice can be parboiled in advance and stored in the refrigerator for up to 2 days; just be sure to take the chill off by either letting it sit at room temperature or running it under warm tap water in a colander before proceeding.

4. Mix the tahdig layer: With a small mortar and pestle, grind the saffron threads and sugar into a fine powder. Add 2 tablespoons hot tap water and stir to dissolve to make a saffron tea.

5. In a medium bowl, stir together the egg yolk, yogurt, 1 tablespoon of the saffron tea, 3 tablespoons of the ghee, and the remaining ½ teaspoon salt. Add 1½ cups of the parboiled basmati rice and gently stir to combine. Spread the rice mixture with the back of a spoon in one even layer in the clean nonstick pot.

6. Assemble: Fold the barberries into the remaining rice. Using a large spoon, mound the remaining rice on top in a small hill, taking care that the rice does not touch the sides of the pot. Using the back of a wooden spoon or a chopstick, make a hole in the center of the mound all the way to just above the tahdig layer. (This helps the steam circulate throughout the rice.) Drizzle on 2 tablespoons hot tap water, the remaining saffron tea, and remaining 3 tablespoons ghee. Wrap the lid of the pot with a clean dish towel so the towel covers the underside of the lid (the side toward the rice), securing the ends of the towel to the lid handle with a rubber band or twine. Cover the pot with the lid.

7. Steam: Place the pot over medium-high heat. Do not open the lid at any point—you need to rely on sound, smell, and time cues from this point forward. Cook until the sides of the pot are very hot to the touch and you can hear simmering inside the pot, about 5 minutes. Reduce the heat to medium-low and cook, undisturbed, until the rice begins to smell toasty (not burnt) and the simmering sounds have subsided, 40 to 45 minutes. (If it's your first time making this, start checking for audio and olfactory cues after 25 minutes. Timing can vary greatly depending on the thickness of your pot and the strength of your burners.)

8. Now, remove the lid and check for doneness; the rice should be fully cooked and fluffy. Using an offset spatula or fork, lift up the base and take a peek to see if the crust has formed. If it has not, re-cover the pot and continue cooking for another 10 minutes. If it has, remove the pot from the heat and let it rest, covered, for 10 minutes.

9. Open the lid and scoop the rice off the tahdig layer to a serving platter. Loosen the rice crust with an offset spatula and either flip it out onto another plate or break it into large pieces in the pot and place on top of the rice. Serve hot.

Let's Break It Down

These are the main steps to master in this recipe:

1. Parboiling the rice until it is just al dente
- You know the rice is cooked just enough when it all quickly bursts to the surface of the water, the grains have nearly doubled in size, and when you bite into a grain you see a tiny white hard core remaining.

2. Mixing and spreading the tahdig layer
- If you parboiled your rice in advance, make sure it has come to room temperature before continuing.
- Combine the yogurt/egg yolk mixture before adding the rice, so you don't have to overmix once the rice joins the party.
- Gently fold the rice to prevent the grains from breaking.

3. Mounding the rice
- Avoid contact with the sides of the pot, where the rice can grow dry and hard.

4. Steaming the rice until the grains are tender and the layer on the bottom of the pot is crisp and crunchy
- This part is about getting to know your pot and burners. It will take some trial and error to determine what heat level and time will get you that crisp crust.
- Use your senses: The sides of the pot will grow hot, the rice will go from simmering to sizzling, and you'll smell the toasty tahdig forming.

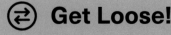 **Get Loose!**

Once you've got the steps down, add mix-ins to change up the flavors.

Double Dill Tahdig
Omit the saffron and barberries. Instead, after laying down the tahdig layer, fold ½ cup finely chopped dill and ⅓ cup chopped dill pickles into the rice. Then mound, steam, and proceed as usual. This bright and herby rice is perfect alongside grilled or broiled fish.

Summer Corn Tahdig
Omit the saffron and barberries. Shave the kernels off 3 ears of corn. Using the back of your knife, hold the cob upright and also scrape out the corn milk. Mix the corn milk into the tahdig layer. Fold the corn kernels along with 3 tablespoons chopped tarragon and freshly ground black pepper into the remaining rice. Mound and steam as directed.

04

Break It Down & Get Saucy

How to stew & braise

Break It Down & Get Saucy

The words "braise" and "stew" both have their roots in eighteenth-century French. Braise is derived from the word for lit coals (from the practice of surrounding cooking vessels with hot embers) and stew comes from the word for stove. Regardless of when or where the names originated, both techniques have long histories in every culture in every part of the world. Richly spiced curry goat from the Caribbean, smoky chicken paprikash from Hungary, savory kimchi-jjigae from Korea, floral bouillabaisse from Provence, and even meaty chili from Texas are all stews and braises. It's the most forgiving and hands-off cooking technique. While braising and stewing take time, that can be remedied by planning ahead. The flavor of braises and stews vastly improves when fully cooled in their cooking liquid and gently reheated—I rarely eat a braise on the same day I cook it. You don't need any special equipment and aren't cooking things to a specific internal temperature, so you can simmer a delicious stew over a fire pit just as easily as on the most expensive induction burner around. Cave people did it, and so can you.

Although almost anything can be braised or stewed, these methods make the most out of tough cuts of protein. The key to braising/stewing meat is knowing how to manipulate time, temperature, and moisture to break down collagen. Collagen is the stretchy connective tissue in skin and surrounding muscle fibers holding them in place. The harder a muscle works (like your hammies on leg day), the more collagen it has. That's why muscles that get a lot of action, like shanks, shoulder, and legs, are better suited to braising than less active muscles, like a tenderloin or breast, which have less connective tissue. Applying heat breaks down the collagen, and it dissolves into unctuous gelatin. Without the collagen holding them in place, the muscle fiber bundles fall apart, leading to fork-tender meat, while the gelatin melts into the sauce, giving it body and a sticky texture, and gelling once cooled.

I know braising and stewing may sound a lot like poaching, but they are entirely different cooking methods. With poaching, the liquid is primarily a vehicle for transferring heat. It is seasoned to make sure that everything tastes good but isn't often eaten, while with a stew or braise, the sauce is the real star. Foods that are better off poached are usually leaner and low in collagen because they don't release much precious gelatin into the liquid. For example, chicken breasts and lean halibut fillets are better poached, while chicken thighs and catfish steaks (from the more active, collagen-heavy part of the animal) are better stewed or braised.

You are not limited to only braising/stewing meat or fish. A well-seared and slow-braised dense vegetable can pack as much flavor as its meaty counterparts. While they don't have collagen, hard root vegetables and hardy greens benefit from having their tough fibers broken through braising or stewing. Winter squash and rutabaga absorb the flavors of the cooking liquid and go from being crisp to creamy. Collards and kale melt into silky strands. Cruciferous vegetables, like cauliflower, cabbage, and Brussels sprouts lose their grassy bite, becoming savory and rich instead. Spicy radishes lose their spicy, watery crunch, turning mellow and sweet.

What's the difference between a braise and a stew?

It's all about the size of the main ingredient you are cooking and how much liquid it's submerged in. That's it. Braises involve larger pieces of meat or whole vegetables gently cooked in enough liquid to cover them half to three-quarters of the way up. (Think lamb shoulder, pork butt, or a full head of cabbage.) Because the ingredients aren't entirely submerged, long-cooked items can develop deep browning even in a steamy situation. Stews have smaller, bite-sized, or even spoonable pieces of meat or vegetables totally immersed in liquid, like the cubes of chuck in a classic beef stew, the pork shoulder in a spicy vindaloo, or the clams and shrimp in cioppino. Both braising and stewing are low and slow methods that rely on gentle, moist heat to break down protein and vegetables.

Given their similarities, how do you know when to stew or braise?

It comes down to three main factors:
1. How much time you have
2. How saucy you want things
3. How fancy you're feeling

Stews cook faster because they use ingredients cut into small pieces. They also have a higher liquid ratio, giving you more sauce and stretching an ingredient to feed a crowd. They are a great everyday option, especially when you have a fridge full of things you don't know what to do with and need to throw together a meal. Braises use either whole ingredients or keep them cut into larger pieces, bringing the drama to the dinner table. Who doesn't love showboating a large chunk of jiggling short rib on the bone? Not to mention the added pleasure you get from cutting into a honkin' hunk o' something. Cooking tough cuts of meat in larger chunks makes them less likely to overcook as they heat up more slowly. But braising a big cut takes significantly longer than stewing the same item cut smaller. Braising also results in less sauce, although it will be more concentrated and flavorful. I'll pull out a braise on the weekend when I'm cooking to impress.

How to Braise Big Hunks & Stew Little Dudes

Both braises and stews follow the same steps. The variations in ingredient size and the ratio of liquid will get you one or the other.

1. Choose Your Braise/Stew Players

Meats: Opt for collagen-rich active muscles and other tough stuff, like beef, lamb, and pork shanks, shoulder, leg, belly, ribs, tails, and cheeks. Chicken thighs and wings, fish heads and skin-on fish steaks, octopus, and squid. Steer clear of lean cuts, which will quickly overcook and become tough, like beef, lamb, or pork loin, chicken breast, shrimp, and scallops.

If you've got time, dry-brine larger cuts of meat before braising (this is not needed for the smaller cuts used in stews). To dry-brine: Evenly season the meat with salt, then rest in the fridge on a wire rack set into a sheet pan for at least 6 hours and up to 2 days (depending on how sizable a hunk you're dealing with). The salt draws moisture out of the protein, dissolving into a concentrated liquid brine on the surface of the meat. Over time, this brine is drawn back into the food, seasoning it while denaturing protein fibers. This helps render fat and break down collagen, and creates a moisture-trapping net, guaranteeing a juicy and tender braise.

Non-meats: Anything goes! Tender veggies like lettuce and cucumber will cook very quickly, while dense and hardier vegetables, like winter squash, beets, and collards, take longer to break down.

2. Pick Your Braise/Stew Pot

You can make any pot/high-sided skillet/roasting pan/casserole dish work, but I love my Dutch oven. No matter what you choose, make sure it has:

- A heavy bottom for even searing (unless you're searing in the oven)

- A tight-fitting lid to keep all that steam sealed in (or crimp on some foil)

- For a braise, make sure everything can fit in one layer (this is less important with a stew because there is enough liquid to evenly heat everything)

160

3. To Sear (or Not to Sear)

Cooking food with direct heat until it develops a dark brown crust is called searing. Searing results in a more intense braise or stew thanks to the Maillard reaction, a process in which sugars and proteins break down from heat and get busy making loads of new savory flavor babies. (Read more about browning in the Go to Brown Town chapter, page 225.) In French cooking, nearly every braise/stew starts with a sear, but many braises/stews in parts of the world that rely on spices or chili puree skip the searing step, which can get in the way of those other already complex flavors. Think critically before deciding to sear the ingredients for your stew/braise: What else is in the braise/stew, what are the flavors you want to highlight, and how will searing add or detract from the dish?

My method for searing changes based on what I'm cooking. Does it have an uneven shape, like an unwieldy lamb leg or an entire knobby head of cauliflower? For those, the oven offers an easy way to get golden all around. There's no worry about flipping something around in hot fat, potentially cannonballing scalding oil all over the place. When searing in the oven, rub the food with a thin layer of neutral oil to help conduct heat and give you even coloration. For the smaller, even-sized pieces usually found in stews, I sear in the same pot that I am going to simmer in. Be sure to work in batches; maintaining the heat of your pan is crucial for a good sear. Overcrowding leads to drops in temperature, leaving you with steamed meat and veggies. Steaming can be delicious, but not when you're looking for golden brown and crusty.

4. Add Aromatics & Cooking Liquid

Aromatics refer to the large group of ingredients that add flavor and aroma when heated (get it? aroma-tics), contributing complex layers to your braise or stew. Many regional cuisines have a base set of aromatics that you can be inspired by: In Western Europe, you'll find varying ratios of carrots, celery, and onion; in Southeast Asia, dishes often start with a flavorful base of shallots, garlic, chilies, and lemongrass; and in South Asia, braises and stews begin with a paste of ginger, garlic, and onion. If

Why I Hate Pressure Cookers

Yeah, you save some time, but at what cost! Cooking in a pressure cooker is the opposite of low and slow, rocking meat with so much heat that it wrings every bit of moisture and flavor out of it. You inevitably end up with very flavorful liquid with tender (maybe too tender?), bland chunks swimming around in it. If your plan is to fully break down something, like with chili, dal, or haleem, then totally go live that #pressurecookerlyfe. But if you're after the best of braise, nothing beats going low and slow. (Yes, this goes for Instant Pots, too!)

How to Braise
Big Hunks & Stew
Little Dudes
(cont'd.)

there's a part of the world you want your cooking to take you just figure out the aromatics that'll get you there. But don't feel limited to those combos, either. Make your own aromatic mixture, or just focus on one or two flavors. Anything braised in a lot of garlic is always a good move.

Aromatics can be browned (or not) for added flavor. Deeply coloring them in this step does the same as searing, intensifying savory notes via the Maillard reaction. Sweating (cooking aromatics over medium to low heat until they soften without developing color) gently coaxes out the flavors of the aromatics for more subtle undertones. And aromatics aren't just limited to vegetables; I like to harness the umami-laden powers of anchovies or kombu in many of my braises and stews.

The cooking liquid in a braise/stew serves as a conduit for heat and is yet another opportunity to add flavor. Wine, beer, and liquor unlock alcohol-soluble flavors; tomatoes bring acidity and umami; a gelatinous bone broth adds body and richness and can reinforce the flavor of the meat being cooked. Water is the best option when you want to keep things light or if there are lots of spices in play. You can braise/stew with pretty much any liquid, but seasoning is key regardless of whether you are using a combo of wine and stock, a hoppy IPA, or just plain water. I'm talking about salt. Adding salt early ensures that your ingredients themselves are seasoned to the core and not just floating around in a seasoned sauce. However, braising and stewing involve a lot of liquid reduction, which intensifies the flavors and concentrates salt. When you are starting out and learning how to adjust salt, season on the lighter side and always taste and adjust right before serving.

As mentioned above, the amount of liquid and the size of the ingredients are the main factors behind the differences between a braise and a stew. When adding the cooking liquid to a braise, make sure the largest pieces are in one even layer, then add enough liquid to come one-half to three-quarters of the way up the depth of the ingredients. When adding the liquid to a stew, add enough to fully cover all your ingredients.

5. Simmer (Very Gently) on the Stove (or in the Oven)

Now that all your ingredients are in the pot, it's time to slow-cook your way to the finish line. Bring the liquid to a boil, then reduce the heat to maintain a bare simmer and put on a tight-fitting lid. If you don't have a lid, tightly crimp on a layer of foil to keep the steam in the pot.

You can take the braise/stew all the way to tender and saucy glory right on your stovetop or transfer the pot to a 250° to 325°F (120° to 163°C) oven (where it will be less likely to scorch). Choose a higher temperature for stews and quicker cooking items, like chicken or vegetables, and aim for lower temperatures for braises and larger cuts, like a short rib plate or lamb shoulder. The lower temperatures ensure even heating all the way through. Keep an eye on the liquid level periodically to make sure it hasn't reduced too much and isn't bubbling aggressively. If things are looking dry, just add water. If the simmering gets rowdy, turn the heat down.

Keep that mellow bubbling going until meats are falling apart and wiggly and hardy vegetables are floppy and easily forked. For vegetable and seafood braises/stews, you can dig in now, but with more meaty ones, like beef, chicken, lamb, or pork, it's best if you take a few extra steps (or not, it's up to you!).

Get Extra: Chill, Skim & Reduce

For beef, lamb, chicken, and pork braises/stews, take things to the next level and let them fully cool before reheating and serving. This does two things: First, as the muscle fibers cool, they will loosen and relax, absorbing the tasty sauce around them like a sponge, resulting in meat that's exceptionally juicy and flavorful. Also, this gives the fat in the sauce time to rise to the top and solidify, so you can easily scoop it right off. Removing the fat lightens the braise/stew, allowing its more subtle flavors to shine. (Keep that fat in the fridge for up to 1 month or in the freezer for 3 months. Use it for roasting vegetables!)

Reheat gently over low heat on the stovetop or in a 325°F (163°C) oven. If your sauce isn't as concentrated and sticky as you want, use a slotted spoon to scoop out the ingredients (so they don't overcook), then reduce the sauce before returning the party to the pot.

Cooking with Booze

Flavors are finicky. Some are soluble in water, others in fat, and there's an entire set of tiplers that needs booze to come out and play. Cooking with wine, beer, and liquor is key to unlocking the alcohol-soluble flavors within a dish. In addition, they add their own character as well. Deeply tannic red wine adds richness and sweetness, crisp dry white wine adds acidity and brightness, fortified wines like sherry bring subtle notes of raisins and dried fruit, and a hoppy beer adds malty depth. The main rule is to never use something that you wouldn't enjoy drinking, as anything you add will play a role in the final flavor. When cooking with booze, you've got the option to cook out the alcohol or keep it in. Simmering alcohol down until syrupy enhances its sweetness and negates that harsh alcohol burn. But if using an exceptional wine or cooking very fatty meat, there can be instances where you want to keep some of that liquor taste.

Time to Eat! Add crisp, fresh, and acidic garnishes

Braises/stews tend to be rich, heavy, and tender, so eating them can get boring. Keep things interesting by adding final bright and crunchy pops for contrast. Try torn fresh herbs, like parsley, mint, and dill. Add a zing of acid with citrus zest, capers, or pickles. Crackly fried shallots on an allium-heavy braise can add another layer of oniony goodness and a good dose of crunch. Olive oil–fried bread crumbs, toasted and chopped nuts, or a simple celery salad all add a lively final flourish.

Supporting cast

Traditionally, braises and stews are served with carb-y sides like mashed potatoes, polenta, or rice because they are great for sopping up all that sauce. I also like lighter options that can take advantage of the intense flavors at play, like crisp-tender steamed broccoli (the fluffy florets act as sauce sponges), quick-sautéed spinach or pea leaves, or raw, crunchy radishes and cucumbers for palate-cleansing bites in between hearty spoonfuls of stew.

HOW TO BRAISE and STEW

1. CHOOSE YOUR BRAISE & STEW PLAYERS

Meat: collagen-rich active muscles and other TOUGH stuff

Veggies:

} These tender veg. cook very quickly

} Dense & heartier veg. take longer to cook

2. TO SEAR or NOT TO SEAR?

ask: "Are there other flavors I'd like to highlight?" —OR— "Am I after that savory Maillard Reaction?"

↓ DON'T SEAR   ↓ SEAR

3. ADD AROMATICS & COOKING LIQUID

Aromatics

Western Europe
- carrots
- celery
- onions

Southeast Asia
- shallots
- chilies
- garlic
- lemongrass

Get Crazy
- fennel · turmeric
- parsnip · leeks

South Asia
- Paste of ginger, garlic & onion

Liquids
- wine, beer & liquor → alcohol-soluble flavor
- tomatoes → umami & acidity
- bone broth → body & richness
- water → reinforces meat flavor

4. SIMMER ON THE STOVE (or in the oven)

(very gently)

250°-325°F

550 500 450 400 350 300 250

→ lower temps. for braises & longer cuts
→ higher temps. for quick-cooking items like chicken or veggies

4B. Extra: chill, skim, and reduce

5. GARNISH & SERVE!

freshly torn herbs

drizzle of olive oil

bread crumbs

fried shallots

toasted nuts

citrus zest

capers

pickles

celery salad

Chickpea & Swiss Chard Stew

(Serves 4)

(Active: 30 mins. | Total: 40 mins.)

(Easy) (Gluten-free)

(Vegetarian (can be made vegan))

Ingredients:

1 large bunch Swiss chard

2 teaspoons coriander seeds, ground

2 teaspoons ground turmeric

2 teaspoons Kashmiri red chili powder or ¾ teaspoon cayenne pepper

1 teaspoon cumin seeds, ground

1 teaspoon freshly ground black pepper

3 tablespoons ghee or neutral oil

1 medium yellow, white, or red onion, thinly sliced

2 garlic cloves, finely chopped

2-inch piece fresh ginger, peeled and finely chopped

3 cups drained chickpeas, home-cooked or two 15.5-ounce cans

kosher salt

4 cups water

½ cup lightly packed fresh cilantro leaves and tender stems, roughly chopped

2 tablespoons freshly squeezed lemon juice (about 1 lemon)

2 tablespoons unsalted butter or vegan butter

To Serve:

Steamed Rice (page 116)

plain yogurt or raitha (page 17)

→ Chana masala goes by several names with countless variations: channay, chole masala, chhole masala, chole, chholay, and nowadays, chickpea curry. It originates from South Asia, a diverse region where many languages are spoken, so one dish can have many names or conversely, one name can belong to many dishes. No matter what it's called, chana masala is made up of spiced and stewed chickpeas that can be brothy enough to spoon over rice or dry and thick enough for scooping up with roti. My simple version gently simmers everything together with just water. This allows the flavors to meld, while the greens wilt down, and the liquid grows thick and creamy from the starch of the chickpeas. Traditionally, stews rich with spices don't need much browning, which can muddle their intense flavor.

1. Strip the leaves off the stems of the Swiss chard. Trim off the dry ends of the stems and cut the stems into bite-sized pieces. Roughly chop the leaves. In a small bowl, combine the coriander, turmeric, chili, cumin, and black pepper.

2. In a large Dutch oven or heavy pot, combine the ghee, onion, garlic, ginger, and Swiss chard stems. Cook over medium-high heat, stirring frequently, until fragrant and the onions start to frizzle and become golden brown along the edges, 8 to 10 minutes.

3. Add the spice mixture and cook, stirring constantly, until fragrant, about 1 minute.

4. Add the chickpeas, a large pinch of salt, and the water. Bring to a simmer and add the Swiss chard leaves. Cook, stirring occasionally, until the leaves are tender and the gravy has reduced and thickened, about 10 minutes.

5. Remove from the heat, add the cilantro, lemon juice, and butter. Taste and adjust with more salt or lemon juice if needed. Serve over rice with a large dollop of yogurt.

⇄ Get Loose!

- Swap the Swiss chard for another quick-cooking green, like arugula, mustard greens, dandelions, beet or turnip tops, spinach, or a combination of whatever is wilting in your fridge.

- Instead of water, simmer the stew in tomato puree, bone broth, or a mixture of equal parts water and coconut milk.

- Swap the chickpeas for an equal amount of any other cooked bean, like cannellini, kidney, or black beans.

166

Brothy Same-Day Slow-Roast Whole Chicken

(Serves 4)

(Active: 30 mins. | Total: 1½ hrs.)

(Easy) (Gluten-free)

Ingredients:

3 tablespoons unsalted butter

2 large yellow onions (about 1½ pounds/680 grams), thinly sliced

8 garlic cloves, thinly sliced

kosher salt

4 bay leaves

One whole chicken (3½ to 4 pounds/ 1.5 to 1.8 kilograms)

1 tablespoon olive oil

1½ cups dry white wine, sake, or vermouth

To Serve:

flaky salt

softened butter

baguette

House Salad (page 18)

Special Equipment:

instant-read thermometer (optional)

→ I almost always want you to dry-brine every protein before cooking. It seasons the meat to the core, helps retain moisture during cooking, prevents overcooking, helps render fat, and promotes browning. But I get that it's not always possible to plan ahead, so here's a same-day roast chicken that's still moist and flavorful. I braise a whole chicken, covered, in a Dutch oven with white wine, onions, and butter. The moist environment helps the chicken cook evenly and stay juicy, while the acidity from the wine keeps the meat tender, even if you overcook it a touch. In fact, I want you to take it a little further than normal to at least 170°F (77°C). This helps the connective tissue break down and the meat fall right off the bone. This isn't a browned and crispy chicken, but a jammy and brothy one, perfect with a crusty baguette on a cold day. And if you've got time, go ahead and dry-brine, it will make this chicken even better; just season with salt and refrigerate for 12 to 36 hours! (Read more about dry-brining on page 258.)

1. Position a rack in the lower third of the oven and heat to 325°F (163°C).

2. In a large Dutch oven, melt the butter over medium heat until foamy. Add the onions, garlic, and a large pinch of salt. Cook, stirring frequently, until the onions are wilted and translucent, about 10 minutes. Add the bay leaves.

3. **While the onions cook:** On a cutting board, pat the chicken dry, inside and out, with paper towels. Rub with the oil and season liberally with salt all over, making sure to season the inside cavity as well. (If you have time, you can place the seasoned chicken on a sheet pan fitted with a wire rack and dry-brine in the fridge, uncovered, for 12 to 36 hours.)

4. Add the wine to the onions, bring to a simmer, and place the chicken in the Dutch oven, breast-side up. Cover and transfer to the oven to cook until the thickest part of the chicken breast and the joint between the drumstick and the thigh register at least 170°F (77°C) on an instant-read thermometer (or when you wiggle a leg it feels like it wants to pull right off), 40 to 45 minutes.

5. Remove from the oven and set the broiler to high. Return the pot to the oven, uncovered, and continue cooking until the skin is dry and golden brown in some spots, about 10 minutes.

6. Remove from the oven and let the chicken rest, uncovered, for 10 minutes.

7. Transfer the chicken to a cutting board, cut it into pieces, and transfer to a serving platter. Pour the onion broth over the chicken. Serve with flaky salt, butter, baguette, and house salad alongside.

Braised Eggplant with Parm Vibes

(Serves 4)

(Active: 30 mins.) | (Total: 30 mins.)

(Easy) (Vegetarian) (Gluten-free)

Ingredients:

3 medium Japanese eggplants (about 1¼ pounds/560 grams total), tops trimmed and halved lengthwise

kosher salt

5 tablespoons extra-virgin olive oil

4 garlic cloves, thinly sliced

1 teaspoon chili flakes

1 pint cherry tomatoes (12 ounces/340 grams)

¾ cup water

4 ounces (112 grams) part-skim mozzarella cheese, torn into ½-inch chunks

⅓ cup coarsely grated parmesan cheese

⅓ cup lightly packed fresh basil leaves

To Serve:

crusty bread, buttered pasta, or The Creamiest Polenta (page 124)

→ Who doesn't love eggplant parm? But all that breading, frying, and layering can be a lot. This braised eggplant has all those savory parm-y flavors, but in an easy any-night form. Dense and meaty Japanese eggplant gets seared until lightly charred before simmering until tender in a quick burst-cherry tomato sauce. The eggplant becomes silky and lush before a final trip under the broiler melts and blisters the cheese. Eggplant is a sponge that wants to sop up all the oil you add, so be sure to preheat the skillet until ripping hot, which will prevent sticking and minimize all that oil-sucking. Have creamy polenta (page 124), buttered pasta, or crusty bread alongside.

1. Position a rack in the center of the oven and set the broiler to high. Heat a large cast-iron or broilerproof stainless steel skillet over medium-high heat until barely smoking. While the skillet heats, season the cut sides of the eggplant with salt.

2. Add 3 tablespoons of the olive oil to the pan and swirl to coat the pan. Quickly arrange the eggplant in the pan cut-side down. Use a fish spatula to firmly press the eggplant pieces down. Cook until lightly charred and starting to soften, about 5 minutes.

3. Remove the skillet from the heat and transfer the eggplant to a plate. Add the remaining 2 tablespoons olive oil, the garlic, and chili flakes to the skillet. Cook over medium heat, stirring constantly, until fragrant, about 1 minute.

4. Add the cherry tomatoes and water and cook until the tomatoes are softened, pressing them with the back of the spatula to burst them all, 4 to 6 minutes. Season with salt.

5. Return the eggplant to the skillet and cook until tender and the sauce has reduced and thickened slightly, about 5 minutes. (Add more water if the pan goes dry before the eggplant are tender.) Taste the sauce and add salt if needed. Remove from the heat.

6. Dot the pan with the torn mozzarella and sprinkle with the parmesan. Transfer to the oven and broil until the cheese melts and browns, about 1 minute.

7. Tear the basil leaves and scatter on top. Serve immediately with crusty bread, buttered pasta, or polenta.

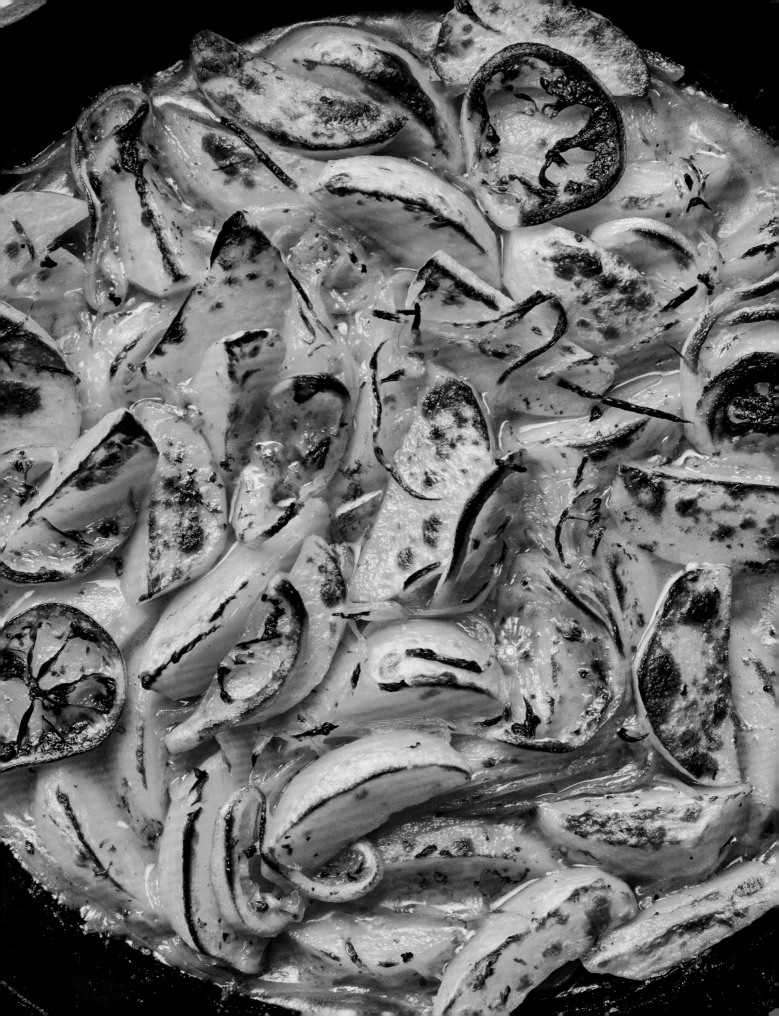

Turmeric Potatoes with a Whole Lotta Lemon

(Serves 4 to 6)

(Active: 25 mins. | Total: 1½ hrs.)

(Easy) (Vegetarian) (Gluten-free)

Ingredients:

4 lemons

8 tablespoons unsalted butter

1 teaspoon ground turmeric

2¼ pounds (1 kilogram) Yukon Gold potatoes (about 8 medium), peeled and cut into 1-inch wedges

1 medium yellow onion, very thinly sliced

2 teaspoons Diamond Crystal kosher salt, plus more to taste

1 teaspoon freshly ground black pepper, plus more to taste

1 cup water

Special Equipment:

large cast-iron or broilerproof stainless steel skillet with lid (or use foil)

→ Crispy potatoes get all the attention, but I think these tart, rich, and creamy braised Yukon Golds are the best spud in town. By braising them in a moist and comfy skillet, the onions grow jammy and sweet, the water reduces into a thick and starchy glaze, and the potato wedges become creamy and fluffy, speckled with bits of golden brown. Don't be tempted to cut back on the butter. It's key to balancing all that tart lemon juice, helps the potatoes to cook evenly, and creates a creamy sauce.

When prepping the ingredients, get everything ready before you peel and cut the potatoes, so you get them cooking right away without worrying about discoloration. Depending on the size and material of your skillet (stainless verses cast-iron), the potatoes can take a wide range of time to cook through. Start checking them for doneness after 30 minutes. You should be able to easily pierce them with a cake tester or fork. And yes, you can cook with acid in a cast-iron skillet! If your pan is seasoned, there's nothing to worry about (read about it in How to Season Cast-Iron Pans, page xlv).

1. Position a rack in the center of the oven and heat to 375°F (190°C).

2. Scrub and thinly slice 1 lemon and remove any seeds. Halve and squeeze the remaining lemons until you have 6 tablespoons of juice (you may not need all the lemons).

3. In a large broilerproof skillet, melt the butter over medium heat until foamy, about 2 minutes. Add the turmeric and cook until aromatic, stirring constantly, about 30 seconds. Add the potatoes, onion, salt, and pepper and toss to combine.

4. Add the water and bring to a simmer. Remove from the heat, top with the lemon slices, and drizzle with 3 tablespoons of the lemon juice. (If you don't have a big enough skillet to hold all the potatoes, toss everything together in a large broilerproof baking dish.)

5. Cover the skillet with a lid, transfer to the oven, and cook until the potatoes are tender enough to easily pierce with a cake tester or fork and the liquid has slightly reduced, 35 to 55 minutes. (The cook time greatly varies depending on the size and material of the skillet, so focus more on visual cues than time.)

6. Remove the skillet from the oven and set the broiler to high. Uncover the skillet, toss the potatoes with a spatula or wooden spoon (some might break and that's okay), and broil until lightly charred in spots, 8 to 10 minutes.

7. Remove from the oven and drizzle with the remaining 3 tablespoons lemon juice. Taste and add salt and pepper if needed. Serve immediately.

Seared
& Braised
Chicken
Thighs

with Zucchini & Salsa Verde

(Serves 4)

(Active: 30 mins. | Total: 1 hr.)

(Easy) (Gluten-free)

Ingredients:

1 pound (454 grams) tomatillos (about 8 medium), husked and roughly chopped

2 garlic cloves, smashed and peeled

1 medium jalapeño, roughly chopped (seeds removed if you like)

2 medium zucchini

2 tablespoons neutral oil

4 bone-in, skin-on chicken thighs (about 30 ounces/800 grams total)

kosher salt

1 medium yellow onion, thinly sliced

3 medium poblano peppers, seeded and cut lengthwise into slices

To Serve:

cilantro

sour cream

warm tortillas (page 491)

lime wedges

Special Equipment:

stand blender

→ Seared and braised is the best way to chicken thigh. The initial direct heat from the sear develops browning and renders the fat from the skin, so there's no flabby chicken here. Then the thighs are gently braised in a bright tomatillo salsa while floating on a zucchini raft, so all that connective tissue can break down for tender and juicy meat. As always, if you've got the time, season the chicken with salt in advance and let it dry-brine, uncovered, in the fridge, resting on a wire rack for at least 12 and up to 24 hours for even better rendering, browning, and breaking down of those connective tissues. (Read more about dry-brining on page 258.)

1. In a blender, combine the tomatillos, garlic, and jalapeño and blitz into a smooth puree. (You should not need to add water, the tomatillos have plenty of moisture. Just keep blending and it will get there.)

2. Cut the zucchini crosswise into 2-inch sections. Cut each section lengthwise into ½-inch-thick planks. Stack the planks and cut lengthwise into ½-inch-thick sticks (you want them to look like zucchini fries).

3. Position a rack in the lower third of the oven and heat to 325°F (163°C).

4. In a large Dutch oven (or heavy-bottomed ovenproof pot), heat the oil over medium heat until it shimmers, about 2 minutes. Season the chicken thighs with salt and sear, skin-side down, until golden brown, 8 to 10 minutes. Flip the chicken and sear on the other side until browned, 5 to 7 minutes longer. Transfer the chicken to a plate and set aside. (If there's excess fat in the pot, scoop out and discard all but about 2 tablespoons.)

5. Add the sliced onion and poblanos to the pot and cook, scraping up any browned bits from the chicken, until translucent and tender, about 10 minutes.

6. Increase the heat to high, add the tomatillo puree and zucchini, and bring to a simmer. Taste and season with salt. Return the chicken to the pot along with any accumulated juices, resting it skin-side up on top of the zucchini so that the skin remains above the surface of the liquid.

7. Transfer the pot to the oven and bake, uncovered, until the chicken is cooked through and the zucchini is tender, 30 to 35 minutes.

8. Serve right away with cilantro, sour cream, warm tortillas, and lime wedges. →

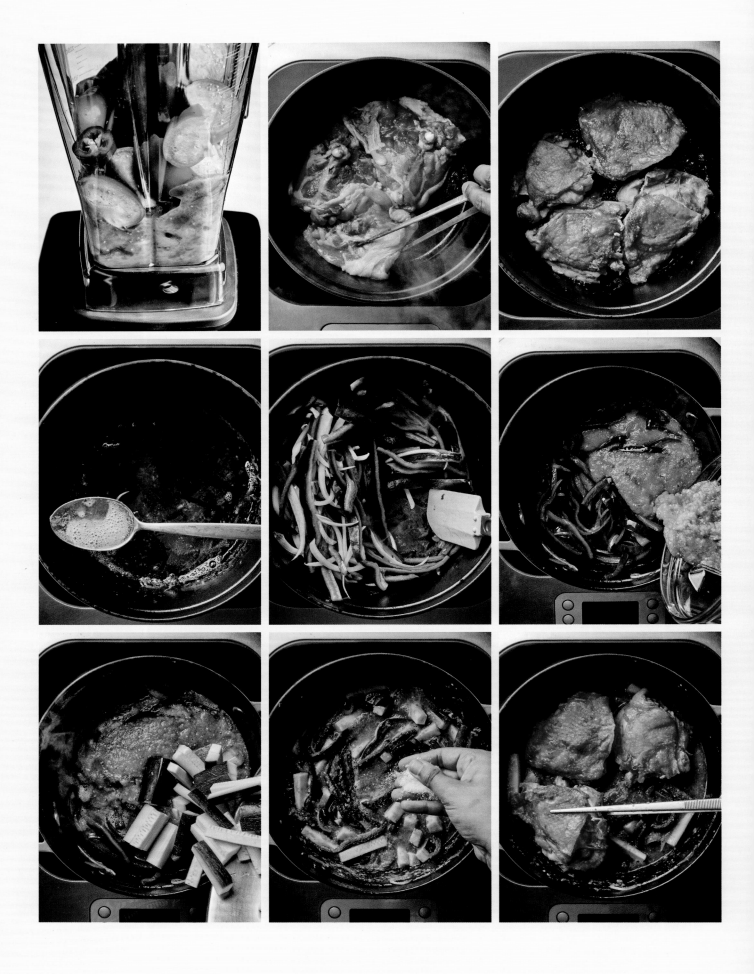

Seared & Braised Chicken Thighs (cont'd.)

 Get Loose!

Use this recipe as a template to cook chicken thighs with whatever you've got. Just follow these key steps:

1. Season (or dry-brine) the chicken, then sear to brown the skin and render the fat. Remove from the pan.

2. Cook a base of aromatics in the same pan, adding spices if you like, while scraping up any browned bits.

3. Add a cooking liquid, like a quick salsa, coconut milk, marinara sauce, or bone broth.

4. Add hearty vegetables for the chicken to rest on: Try cabbage wedges, cauliflower, sweet potato, squash, or beets.

5. Taste and season well with kosher salt, then rest the chicken on top, and place in the oven to braise until the chicken is cooked through and the veggies are tender.

• Try it with Jammy Carrots
After browning the chicken, in the same pan, cook chopped garlic, onion, and celery until browned. Add tomato paste and cook until caramelized. Add 2 cups of bone broth and scrape up any browned bits. Add 1 bunch of peeled and halved carrots along with 1 packed cup chopped carrot tops and top with the chicken thighs. Braise everything together in the oven.

• Try it with Cabbage Curry
After browning the chicken, in the same pan, cook chopped scallions, ginger, and garlic until wilted. Add 2 to 3 tablespoons green curry paste and cook until caramelized. Add 1 can of coconut milk, 1 can of water, and 1 small cabbage cut into wedges. Season with salt. Rest the chicken on top. Braise everything together in the oven.

Braised Short Ribs

with Anchovy & So Much Garlic

(Serves 6 to 8)

(Active: 1 hr. | Total: at least 20 hrs.)

(Intermediate) (Gluten-free)

Ingredients:

2 tablespoons plus 1 teaspoon Diamond Crystal kosher salt, plus more to taste

1 tablespoon freshly ground black pepper

6 pounds (2.72 kilograms) bone-in short ribs, at least 1½ inches thick

6 tablespoons extra-virgin olive oil

40 garlic cloves, very smashed and peeled

12 anchovy fillets

one 750 ml bottle dry white wine

6 cups high-quality chicken or beef bone broth

torn fresh parsley

finely grated lemon zest

To Serve:

steamed vegetables

Special Equipment:

sheet pan fitted with a wire rack

→ Short ribs are one of the best cuts of beef because they are packed with flavorful connective tissue while being meaty and substantial. You're not picking through bone and tendon, like with oxtail or neck, but you still get all that sticky and rich flavor. They are a pricey cut, so this is more of a special-occasion dish reserved for good friends and holidays. Since it is so special, take the time to dry-brine the beef, salting it and letting it rest for at least 12 and preferably a full *48* hours. It will be so worth it! This will give the salt time to dissolve and be drawn into the meat, seasoning it, tenderizing it, and drying out the surface for better browning and rendering.

Instead of searing the short rib in a skillet, we'll be searing the pieces in a hot oven, getting even color all around without any splatter or mess. The longer you dry-brine the meat, the faster it will get to tender and wiggly glory because the salt has already done much of the work for you. You know it's done when you can easily pierce the meat with a cake tester and it's falling off the bone. Don't let all the garlic and anchovies frighten you off. The long cook time mellows everyone out, so the result is sweet, savory, and salty. Serve this alongside simple steamed or boiled vegetables and a crisp leafy salad.

1. In a small bowl, stir together the salt and pepper. Line a sheet pan with foil and place a wire rack on top. Season the short ribs on all sides with the salt/pepper mixture, arrange on the rack, and refrigerate, uncovered, for at least 12 and up to 48 hours.

2. Position a rack in the center of the oven and heat to 450°F (230°C). Evenly coat the short ribs with 3 tablespoons of the olive oil. Place the rack with the short ribs in the oven and roast until deeply golden brown all around, about 50 minutes, flipping over the ribs halfway through. Remove from the oven and reduce the oven temperature to 325°F (163°C).

3. In a large Dutch oven, heat the remaining 3 tablespoons olive oil over medium-high heat until shimmering, about 1 minute. Add the garlic and anchovies and cook, stirring and smashing with a stiff silicone spatula, until the anchovies are broken down and the garlic is starting to brown, 2 to 3 minutes. Add the white wine and boil until it fully reduces, glazes the garlic, and the mixture switches from simmering to sizzling, 15 to 20 minutes.

4. Add the broth and bring to a simmer. Add the roasted short ribs and any rendered fat and juices from the sheet pan, making sure the liquid comes halfway up the sides of the ribs. (If it doesn't, add enough water until it does.)

5. Return to a simmer, taste, and add salt if needed. (You want the liquid lightly seasoned at this point. It will reduce and the flavors will concentrate during cooking.) Cover, transfer to the oven, and braise until the short ribs are wiggly and tender and easily pierced with a fork, 2 to 3 hours (this varies greatly with how big the short ribs are cut and how long they have been dry-brined). →

Braised Short Ribs (cont'd.)

6. Let the short ribs cool fully in the liquid, at least 4 hours and ideally overnight in the fridge, then scrape off the fat on top. For leaner grass-fed beef, I prefer to keep some of the fat in the braise. (Reserve the fat in the fridge for up to 1 month or in the freezer for 3 months. Use it for roasting vegetables, potatoes, or making pilaf.)

7. Reheat the short ribs, covered, over medium heat or in a 350°F (177°C) oven until warmed through, about 30 minutes. Taste and add salt if needed. Top with the torn parsley and lemon zest before serving alongside steamed vegetables.

Note: Make sure you have a pot big enough to fit the short ribs in one layer. If you don't have one, braise the short ribs in a roasting pan tightly covered with foil.

Coconut Cauliflower Korma

(Serves 4)

(Active: 1 hr.) (Total: 1½ hrs.)

(Intermediate) (Vegan)

(Gluten-free)

Ingredients:

1 large yellow onion, peeled

2-inch piece fresh ginger, peeled and thinly sliced

4 garlic cloves, smashed and peeled

¼ cup neutral oil, plus more as needed

¼ cup pistachios or slivered almonds

1 medium head cauliflower (about 2 pounds/900 grams), leaves removed, cut into quarters through the stem

kosher salt

1 tablespoon ground coriander

1 bay leaf

one 3-inch cinnamon stick, snapped in half lengthwise

3 green cardamom pods, cracked

one 13.5-ounce can full-fat coconut milk, shaken

3 Thai green or serrano chilies

8 pitted prunes

To Serve:

Steamed Rice (page 116), Flaky Brown Butter Lachha Paratha (page 507), or Thin & Chewy Roti (page 488)

cucumber salad (see page 17)

→ Korma is a type of braise/stew found throughout South Asia. Some versions are made with yogurt for a light and delicate sauce, while a wedding korma is rich with cream, nuts, and saffron. The main thing tying all korma together is an aromatic base of onion, garlic, and ginger with warm spices such as cardamom and cinnamon. This korma is influenced by the one my mom made almost once a week when I was growing up, with chicken, shrimp, or hard-boiled eggs. Hers was made with yogurt, but I wanted to give some heft to the cauliflower, so I'm simmering it here in coconut milk instead. The key to properly developing the flavors is time. Take your time frizzling the onions, browning the cauliflower, cooking down the onion puree, and simmering everything together, otherwise the aromatics will taste harsh and acrid.

---

1. Cut the onion in half lengthwise, trim off the root, and thinly slice one half lengthwise from root to stem. Set aside.

2. Roughly chop the remaining onion half and puree it in a blender along with the ginger and garlic, adding as little water as is needed to blend until smooth. Set aside.

3. Make the frizzled onions: In a medium Dutch oven or heavy pot, combine the oil and reserved sliced onions and cook over medium-high heat, stirring often, until crisp and deeply browned, 10 to 12 minutes. (The onions will continue to brown after removing them from the heat, so scoop them out of the pot when they are a shade lighter than the desired final color.) Remove the pot from the heat and use a slotted spoon to transfer the onions to a plate, leaving behind the fat in the pot. Spread them out so they cool down quickly and don't clump together.

4. Return the pot to medium heat and add the nuts. Cook, stirring frequently, until lightly browned, 3 to 5 minutes. Remove from the heat and use a slotted spoon to transfer them to a plate, leaving the fat behind.

5. Sear the cauliflower: Return the pot to medium heat and arrange the cauliflower wedges in one even layer, working in batches if necessary. Sprinkle generously with salt. Cook until very deeply browned on the cut sides, 5 to 7 minutes per side. (If the pot looks too dry at any point, add more oil.) Transfer to a plate.

6. Caramelize the base: Add more oil if the pot looks dry. Add the pureed onion, coriander, bay leaf, cinnamon stick, cardamom pods, and a big pinch of salt and cook over medium-high heat, stirring frequently, until deeply browned, most of the moisture has cooked out, and the paste begins sticking to the pot, 5 to 8 minutes. →

Coconut Cauliflower Korma (cont'd.)

7. Braise: Add the coconut milk, ½ can water, green chilies, and prunes and bring to a simmer, scraping up any browned bits. Taste and add salt if needed. Return the cauliflower wedges to the pot, reduce the heat to maintain a bare simmer, and partially cover. Cook until the cauliflower is totally tender and the sauce is thick and the flavors have melded together, 20 to 30 minutes, flipping the cauliflower once during cooking. (Some of the cauliflower might fall apart, that's okay. If the liquid has reduced too much before the cauliflower is tender, add more water.)

8. Top with the frizzled onions and nuts. Serve with steamed rice, paratha, or roti and cucumber salad.

Stuffed Squid with Sofrito & Saffron

(Serves 4)

(Active: 1 hr.) | (Total: 1½ hrs.)

(Advanced) (Gluten-free)

Ingredients:

1 cup short-grain rice, such as Calasparra, bomba, Arborio, or sushi rice

1½ pounds (680 grams) squid tubes and tentacles (ideally 8 to 12 tubes)

5 tablespoons extra-virgin olive oil

6 garlic cloves, very finely chopped

2 medium yellow onions, very finely chopped

2 medium red bell peppers, very finely chopped

3 teaspoons smoked paprika

large pinch of saffron

2 teaspoons Diamond Crystal kosher salt, plus more to taste

one 28-ounce (794 grams) can crushed or pureed tomatoes

1 cup clam juice

2 cups water

1 cup frozen peas (no need to thaw)

1 cup lightly packed fresh parsley leaves and tender stems, roughly chopped

To Serve:

crusty bread

House Salad (page 18)

Special Equipment:

pastry bag (or small spoon)

→ Sofrito is a base of aromatic vegetables that are cooked down until wilted, caramelized, and deepened in flavors. It's the starting point for countless stews, braises, and rice dishes in Europe and Latin America. The mix of vegetables can vary depending on what country you're in, often containing onion, garlic, peppers, and tomato. What they all have in common is that the veggies are cut very small, sometimes even pureed before cooking, then stirred and scraped until they become one. This recipe uses a Spanish-style sofrito that's finely chopped by hand, which keeps the mix from getting too wet and allows for better browning. If you're not up for all that chopping, feel free to pulse the ingredients in a food processor; just keep in mind that the sofrito will take longer to cook down and won't caramelize as deeply. Squid are unique in that you need to either cook them hot and fast (like with fried calamari) or low and slow to be tender. Here we're simmering them gently, which makes the bodies tender while the rice plumps. The toughest part is filling the tubes, so take your time and don't overfill them.

1. **Rinse and soak the rice:** Add the rice to a medium bowl and cover with cool water. Gently swish with your hands to rinse. Drain and repeat until the water mostly runs clear. Cover with cool water and set aside to soak for at least 20 minutes and up to 2 hours. Drain.

2. **While the rice soaks, prep the squid:** Rinse the squid under cold running water until you don't feel grit on them. Pat the tubes and tentacles dry with paper towels. Pull off any wings that may still be on the tubes and discard. Rip off the super-long tentacles near the mouth (there are usually two and they remain tough, even after braising) and discard. Roughly chop the tentacles. Keep chilled while you make the sofrito.

3. **Make the sofrito:** In a medium Dutch oven (or heavy pot), heat 3 tablespoons of the olive oil over medium heat until it shimmers. Add the garlic, onions, and bell peppers and cook, frequently stirring, until softened, beginning to brown, and sticking slightly to the bottom of the pot, about 20 minutes. This is the sofrito. Remove from the heat. Scoop out half the sofrito and set aside. (Half will be for the filling, while the other half is for the braising liquid.)

4. **Make the filling:** Return the pot to medium heat. Add the chopped tentacles, drained rice (reserve the bowl), 2 teaspoons of the smoked paprika, the saffron, and salt and cook, stirring frequently, until the rice smells fragrant and toasty, about 5 minutes. Scrape into the bowl. Return the reserved sofrito to the now-empty pot and set aside while you stuff the squid. →

Stuffed Squid with Sofrito & Saffron (cont'd.)

5. **Stuff the squid:** Using a small spoon or piping bag, stuff each squid tube three-quarters of the way with the rice mixture, gently compacting the rice with your fingers. Using a toothpick, thread the top of the squid closed. Repeat until all the squid is stuffed. (If there are any ripped squid that can't be stuffed, don't worry about them. Slice them into rings and toss into the pot with the reserved sofrito.)

6. **Braise the squid:** Place the pot with the reserved sofrito over medium-high heat. Add the remaining 2 tablespoons olive oil and 1 teaspoon smoked paprika and cook until aromatic, about 1 minute. Add the crushed tomatoes, clam juice, and water and bring to a simmer. Taste and season with salt as needed. Add the stuffed squid tubes. Cover, adjust the heat to maintain a gentle simmer, and cook for 20 minutes. (The squid will plump and the rice will become tender.) Uncover and increase the heat to medium. Simmer until the sauce has slightly thickened, about 5 minutes.

7. **Finish:** Add the peas and parsley and cook until the peas are warmed through, about 5 minutes. Serve immediately with crusty bread and salad.

Steam & Poach

Quick cooking & clean flavors

Steam & Poach

Steaming and poaching are both moist cooking methods. Steaming transfers heat to food through, you guessed it, steam, while poaching submerges food entirely in a liquid and cooks it gently, well below the boiling point. I'll admit it, I wasn't a poaching and steaming believer until six months into the pandemic. I'll accept my public shaming with grace. It never seemed to me like a punchy or flavorful method of cooking, but what's actually holding these remarkably versatile techniques back is bad branding. Steaming and poaching immediately make me think of all the fat-free diets of the '90s, obsessed with steaming broccoli and poaching chicken. Now, I *am* about to give you some recipes for steaming broccoli and poaching chicken, but I promise you they are killer. There's nothing wrong with the techniques; it's how you use them.

As it turns out, steaming and poaching are almost unrivaled at capturing the truest essence of a food. Now whenever I come across a new vegetable at the farmers' market, my first step is to try it steamed and seasoned with salt, so I can taste its flavor in its purest form. Steaming and poaching are fast, require minimal cleanup, and don't need you to turn on an oven. When sheltering in place and forced to cook every meal every day, steaming and poaching came to the rescue.

Since both steaming and poaching cook stuff by transferring heat through a liquid, we're limited in how much heat we can transfer to our food by the temperature of the liquid. Boiling water can't exceed 212°F (100°C). Depending on how saturated it is, steam can get significantly hotter than boiling water, but at normal pressure it's still less than the rip-roaring intensity of dry-heat methods like broiling or roasting. Browning reactions don't begin until at least 250°F (121°C) and don't get serious until 300°F (149°C)—unless we're talking about very prolonged cooking times or highly alkaline environments. Because of this, steamed and poached foods tend to be mild and delicate. This is what I want when I'm working with high-quality ingredients and I want to taste them without anything in the way, like seasonal market produce. It's also great when I want a lighter dish to go alongside something rich or intensely flavored, like Braised Short Ribs (page 178) or Coconut Cauliflower Korma (page 182).

Get Steamy: Hot & Fast Moist Heat

Often lumped together because they're both moist-heat methods, steaming and poaching are actually pretty different, like sisters from the same mister. Because steam gets hotter than water, steaming is a faster, more aggressive cooking method than poaching, best for foods that benefit from that kind of intensity, such as:

• Vegetables you want to remain crisp-tender: broccoli, asparagus, cabbage wedges, green beans, carrots, bok choy

• Tender greens you'd like to quickly wilt without becoming watery: spinach, pea shoots, arugula, or watercress

• Bivalves that require high heat to pop open: mussels, clams, and cockles

• Dense vegetables that take a long time to cook and can become waterlogged if boiled: winter squash, sweet potatoes, and potatoes

Steaming over Water

The primary way to steam is by suspending food above actively simmering water. There are pots that come with perforated inserts or, as every mom had in the '80s, a collapsible metal contraption with feet to hold your food in a basket above the water. My preferred way to steam is in an inexpensive, and easy-to-find, Chinese bamboo steamer. You've probably seen these used to steam dumplings and bao buns, but you can use them for practically anything—tamales, baby potatoes, and even for reheating leftovers. Because bamboo is a poor conductor of heat, the food is heated by the steam alone, allowing it to cook evenly. With a flat base, these steamers are easy to line with parchment for anything that might want to stick or make the steamer funky, like fish or doughs. Best of all, these steamers are multitiered units, allowing you to cook an entire dinner with just an inch of simmering water. If you don't have any type of steamer, grab a foil pie tin and riddle it with holes. Flip it over into a large saucepan of simmering water, place your food on top, and cover. This hack only works with food heavy enough to weight the pie plate down, like sweet potatoes or squash.

If you spring for a bamboo steamer, I've found that a 12-inch one with three tiers is great for most things. I also have a small 8-inch steamer for solo or small meals. Traditionally, these steamers are set inside a wok with enough water to reach just below where the steamer rests. If you don't have a wok, you can use a saucepan with a rim that's wide enough to allow the steamer to just barely fit over it. If the pot's too small, the steam won't evenly fill the basket; if it's too big, much of the steam will escape. There must be a tight seal between the bottom of the steamer and the rim of the pot, otherwise, your food will cook unevenly and take significantly longer. If you're buying a steamer and don't have a wok, let the size of your saucepan guide what size steamer to purchase.

Steaming in Liquid

Another way to steam is by cooking *in* a small amount of liquid, rather than setting food above it. This way, the liquid ends up becoming the sauce or broth for your final dish. It's still a fast method, unlike poaching, which totally submerges an ingredient and takes things low and slow. Here, you heat a small amount of flavorful liquid, then add the ingredients and tightly cover with a lid to trap the steam. Or you seal food in a pouch with a flavorful liquid, then pop the whole thing in the oven where the food cooks from the steam trapped inside. (The French term for this is *en papillote*, which is, literally, "in paper.")

Unlike when steaming over water, you want to add flavor to this liquid base, kicking it off with sautéed aromatics and using broth, coconut milk, or wine. This is how you cook bivalves, like clams or mussels, or quick-cooking vegetables, like brothy wilted greens or peas. All you need is a pot with a tight-fitting lid.

Best Steaming Practices

- **Cranking the heat won't make it hotter:** Adjust the heat so the water is at an active simmer. Turning up the heat beyond that will simmer away the water faster without necessarily creating more steam.

- **Give the steam room to groove:** Evenly space ingredients in one layer so the steam can move around everything and cook it evenly.

- **Don't let the pan go dry:** Especially for ingredients that take longer to cook, like potatoes or pork, keep an eye on the water level, adding more hot water as needed. If the pan goes dry, it can buckle and burn.

196

Steamed & Sizzled Greens

Try steaming over water with this simple, customizable, and easy side that I make almost every day:

1. Arrange any quick-cooking green in your steamer.
2. Cook until bright green and crisp-tender. Transfer to a platter.
3. In a small skillet, heat oil, ghee, clarified butter, or lard with spices or aromatics until sizzling, then scrape the hot and flavorful fat over the greens. Season with salt or something salty, like fish sauce, tamari, or Worcestershire sauce.

Some sizzling inspiration:

Hot & Tingly Cabbage
1. Cut a head of cabbages into wedges thin enough to fit in your steamer, then tuck ginger matchsticks between the leaves. Steam until the leaves have wilted and the core is mostly tender. Transfer to a plate.
2. Heat neutral oil until shimmering, then add cumin seeds, coriander seeds, cracked Sichuan peppercorns, and chili flakes and cook until aromatic.
3. Scrape the oil and spices over the cabbage and season with salt and soy sauce or tamari. Garnish with sliced scallions.

Everything Seasoned Broccoli
1. Steam broccoli spears until crisp-tender. Transfer to a plate.
2. Heat butter until foamy, then add everything seasoning (store-bought or make your own by mixing equal parts granulated garlic, granulated onion, poppy seeds, sesame seeds, and flaky salt) and cook until aromatic and the butter begins to grow nutty and brown.
3. Scrape the butter and spices over the broccoli and serve.

Caesar-ish Little Gems
1. Cut Little Gem lettuce in half lengthwise and steam, cut-side down, until just wilted, warmed, and still crisp-tender. Transfer to a plate, cut-side up.
2. Heat olive oil, anchovies, and chopped garlic until the anchovies break down and the garlic is golden.
3. Scrape the oil and all the garlic and anchovy bits over the lettuce. Squeeze over fresh lemon juice, lightly season with salt, and top with shaved parmesan.

Brothy & Glazed Vegetables

Practice steaming in a liquid by making a quick vegetable side:

1. Prepare a flavorful liquid base, either by sautéing aromatics and spices, simmering water with aromatics, simmering down wine, or concentrating broth. For quick-cooking ingredients, you want just enough liquid to cover the bottom of the pan. For things that take longer to cook, you may need up to 1 inch of liquid, adding more if the pan goes dry.
2. Add the vegetables. Tender greens, snap peas, and green beans can remain whole. Tear or chop hardy greens, like collards or kale, and chop dense vegetables, like potatoes or winter squash.
3. Cover and cook until tender, uncovering and adding a splash of liquid if the pan sounds dry. You want to end up with only enough liquid to just coat everything.
4. Finish by adding a flavorful fat, like butter or extra-virgin olive oil, and stir or toss to emulsify. For a sticky glaze, add a sweetener, like honey or maple syrup.

Some brothy & glazed inspiration:

Brothy & Garlicky Pea Leaves
1. Combine sliced garlic, salt, a pinch of MSG, and just enough water to cover the bottom of the pot. Bring to a simmer.
2. Pile in the pea leaves. Cover and steam until wilted.
3. Uncover and finish with toasted sesame oil, stirring to emulsify.

Sticky Spicy Carrots
1. In a pan, heat olive oil and cook sliced garlic and red chili until aromatic. Add white wine and simmer until reduced by half.
2. Add salt and arrange peeled carrots (halved lengthwise if thick) in a single layer. Cover and steam until tender and most of the liquid has reduced, adding water if the pan goes dry before the carrots are tender.
3. Add butter, honey, and pepper and stir to emulsify. Garnish with chopped parsley.

Fancy Restaurant–Style Glazed Potatoes
1. Peel a russet potato, trim off the ends, and cut crosswise into 1½-inch-thick coins.
2. Heat neutral oil in a pan and lightly sear both sides of all the potato pieces until golden brown, arranging them in a single layer.
3. Add 1 inch of chicken bone broth and season generously with salt. Cover and steam until the potatoes are tender and the broth has reduced into a starchy sauce, adding more broth if the pan goes dry before the potatoes are tender.
4. Uncover and finish with butter, stirring to emulsify.

Poaching: Low, Slow & Submerged

Poaching happens low and slow, well below the boiling point of water, between 160° and 190°F (71° and 88°C). This method is best for ingredients that might easily become tough. You can poach in water, broth, and even oil. Depending on who you ask, oil poaching is sometimes called confit. Traditionally, confit was a term reserved for anything that has been brined before slowly cooking in its own fat. Nowadays, many people call anything cooked in any fat (with or without brining) confit. Although oil poaching is cool for making your own preserved tomatoes or tuna, I don't think it's a very friendly method for the home cook because it requires so much oil, which you often can't reuse.

Technically, you can poach anything, but poaching is not as versatile as steaming. I only recommend it for lean meats that can easily become tough or dry, like chicken breast, halibut, and shrimp. But it's an incredible way to cook those proteins, so I think it's worth talking about just for the juiciest chicken breast, most tender halibut, and snappiest shrimp. Most vegetables end up leaching too much of their flavor and nutrients with this cooking method. Sous vide is like poaching, in that an ingredient is submerged in a liquid and cooked low and slow. However, with sous vide the food is sealed in a bag first and held at a very consistent temperature, so flavors and nutrients also stay sealed within and the cooking is extremely precise.

Best Poaching Practices

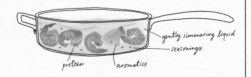

gently simmering liquid
seasonings
protein
aromatics

- **Season aggressively:** Make sure the poaching liquid is very well seasoned with salt, acid, and aromatics.

- **Dry-brine if you've got time:** Proteins cook best when dry-brined first. Even though you're not getting crispy skin or a crackly sear, a dry brine seasons proteins to the core, promotes even cooking, retains moisture, and aids in the rendering of fat. (See page 258 to read more about dry-brining.)

- **Manage the heat vigilantly:** You never want the poaching liquid to come to a simmer, which can make things tough and unevenly cooked.

- **Pick the right pot for the job:** Everything should be submerged in the poaching liquid. For something small, like one fish fillet, use a tall and narrow pot. For several chicken breasts, opt for a wide and high-sided pot.

Fluffy Kabocha

with Tahini Almond Sauce

(Serves 2 as a main or 4 as a side)

(Active: 10 mins. | Total: 40 mins.)

(Easy) (Vegan)

Ingredients:

1 small kabocha squash (about
    2 pounds/900 grams)

Tahini Almond Sauce (page 221)

cilantro sprigs for garnish

Special Equipment:

medium saucepan (or large wok)

bamboo steamer or collapsible metal
    steamer

→ Kabocha is a Japanese squash with a dark green knobby rind and rich yellow flesh that changes depending on how you cook it. In the oven it becomes caramelized and sweet, it grows silky simmered in soup, and in the steamer it gets extra starchy, like a pillowy russet potato. Steaming it is also the fastest way to cook it, so during kabocha season (late summer through early fall) I eat it this way on repeat. This hearty dish can stand alone as a meal or be served alongside a light protein, like steamed cod, poached chicken, or roasted tofu. Marconas are plump, sweet Spanish almonds often found deep-fried and salted in the cheese aisle of the grocery.

---

1. **Set up a steamer:**
- If using a medium saucepan and bamboo steamer, fill the pot halfway up with water and bring to a boil over high heat. Reduce the heat to maintain a simmer. Place the steamer on top, making sure that the bottom basket just fits over the edges of the pot. (If there's a gap, your squash will take longer to steam.)
- If using a wok and bamboo steamer, add enough water to reach 1 inch below the bottom of where the steamer will rest. Bring to a boil over high heat, reduce the heat to maintain a simmer, and place the steamer on top.
- If using a medium saucepan and collapsible metal steamer, add enough water to reach just below the steamer and place the rack on top. Cover, bring to a boil over high heat, then reduce the heat to maintain a simmer.
- Throughout the cooking, keep an eye on the water level and add more hot water as needed.

2. **While the water comes to a boil:** Using a heavy knife, trim the top and bottom from the squash. Cut the kabocha in half through the stem and spoon out the seeds and stringy bits. Cut each half into wedges that are roughly 1 inch thick.

3. Arrange the kabocha slices in the two baskets of the steamer in an even layer, with some space between them to allow steam to circulate (try not to overlap the pieces too much). Cook until completely tender and a cake tester or knife can be inserted without resistance, 20 to 30 minutes, switching the positions of the tiers halfway through.

4. Arrange the steamed kabocha on a plate, drizzle with some sauce, and garnish with cilantro sprigs. Serve right away. (Store leftover cooked squash and sauce separately in the fridge for up to 1 week.)

200

Tofu & Bok Choy

with Ginger Garlic Scallion Sauce

(Serves 4)

(Active: 10 mins. | Total: 30 mins.)

(Easy) (Vegan) (Gluten-free)

Ingredients:

two 10-ounce (280-gram) packages
firm tofu

4 baby bok choy (about 1 pound/
450 grams), halved lengthwise

Ginger Garlic Scallion Sauce
(page 222)

1 bunch scallions (6 to 8), dark green
parts, thinly sliced on a bias

Special Equipment:

medium saucepan (or wok)

bamboo steamer or collapsible metal
steamer

→ When I was a kid, I was lucky because I wasn't made fun of for having a korma sandwich for lunch. (Don't worry, I got made fun of for plenty of other things, like the mullet I accidentally had from seventh to eighth grade.) I went to a diverse school and most of my friends had cool lunches, too. We'd usually trade bites and this is where I had my first taste of kimbap, noodle kugel, spam musubi, and chocolate croissants. My favorite was tucked into my friend Celene's lunchbox: wobbly chilled tofu slices with scallions and soy. I tried to re-create it at home and never got anywhere close. It was years before I learned the secret—good tofu. Something this simple is all about ingredients, and thankfully nowadays, high-quality tofu is readily available. My favorite tofu is made by Hodo. It has a nutty and complex flavor that's sophisticated enough to stand on its own. Steaming it makes it extra silky, rich, and ready to sop up the savory ginger garlic scallion sauce. Have this hot or cold; it only gets better as it sits.

1. **Set up a steamer:**
   - If using a medium saucepan and bamboo steamer, fill the pot halfway up with water and bring to a boil over high heat. Reduce the heat to maintain a simmer. Place the steamer on top, making sure that the bottom basket just fits over the edge of the pot. (If there's a gap, your tofu and bok choy will take longer to steam.)
   - If using a wok and bamboo steamer, add enough water to reach 1 inch below the bottom of where the steamer will rest. Bring to a boil over high heat, reduce the heat to maintain a simmer, and place the steamer on top.
   - If using a medium saucepan and collapsible metal steamer, add enough water to reach just below the steamer and place the rack on top. Cover, bring to a boil over high heat, then reduce the heat to maintain a simmer.
   - Throughout the cooking, keep an eye on the water level and add more hot water as needed.

2. **Set the tofu:** Place the blocks of tofu in one basket of the steamer and cook until completely warmed through, about 20 minutes. (If using a collapsible metal steamer, you'll have to steam the tofu and bok choy separately.)

3. **When the tofu has 5 minutes left to steam:** Arrange the bok choy in another basket of the steamer, cut-side down. Cook until the leaves have wilted and the stem is crisp-tender (the tip of a paring knife should easily pierce the thickest part of the stem), about 5 minutes.

4. Transfer the tofu to a platter. Use a small offset spatula or butter knife to cut it into thick slices and fan them out. Drizzle some sauce over them and top with the scallion greens. Plate the bok choy beside it and drizzle with some sauce. Serve hot or cold with extra sauce on the side. Store for up to 3 days in a tightly sealed container in the fridge. (The tofu will absorb the sauce as it sits, so this is a great make-ahead meal.)

Loaded Sweet Potatoes

with Vegan Queso

(Serves 2)

(Active: 10 mins. | Total: 1 hr.)

(Easy) (Vegan) (Gluten-free)

Ingredients:

2 large sweet potatoes (about
    1½ pounds/680 grams total),
    scrubbed

½ medium head broccoli (about
    6 ounces/170 grams)

kosher salt

extra-virgin olive oil

Vegan Queso (page 223)

2 scallions, thinly sliced

crushed Fritos

Special Equipment:

medium saucepan (or wok)

bamboo steamer or collapsible metal
    steamer

→ Depending on the type and size of your sweet potatoes, the cook time can vary greatly, but regardless, steaming is significantly faster than roasting in the oven and doesn't leach away flavor the way boiling does. I'm not giving you an amount for the Fritos because that's personal. Maybe you want a handful or perhaps it's a whole-bag kinda night—I'm not here to judge.

---

1. **Set up a steamer:**
- If using a medium saucepan and bamboo steamer, fill the pot halfway up with water and bring to a boil over high heat. Reduce the heat to maintain a simmer. Place the steamer on top, making sure that the bottom basket just fits over the edges of the pot. (If there's a gap, your sweet potatoes and broccoli will take longer to steam.)
- If using a wok and bamboo steamer, add enough water to reach 1 inch below the bottom of where the steamer will rest. Bring to a boil over high heat, reduce the heat to maintain a simmer, and place the steamer on top.
- If using a medium saucepan and collapsible metal steamer, add enough water to reach just below the steamer and place the rack on top. Cover, bring to a boil over high heat, then reduce the heat to maintain a simmer.
- Throughout the cooking, keep an eye on the water level and add more hot water as needed.

2. **Steam the sweet potatoes:** Set the sweet potatoes in the bottom basket of the steamer. Cook until a cake tester or knife easily pierces through the thickest part. Depending on diameter and type of sweet potato, this can take anywhere from 40 to 60 minutes.

3. **Prep the broccoli:** Use a sharp knife to split the head from the stem of the broccoli. Trim the dried-out ½ inch off the bottom of the broccoli stem. Peel off the stem's tough outer skin and cut the stem into bite-sized pieces. Divide the head into bite-sized florets.

4. **Steam the broccoli:** When the sweet potatoes are fully cooked, arrange the broccoli on a second steamer basket and cook until crisp-tender and bright green, 4 to 6 minutes. (Keep the sweet potatoes in the steamer while the broccoli cooks to stay warm; they won't overcook that quickly. If using a collapsible metal steamer, you'll have to steam the broccoli and sweet potatoes separately.)

5. **Assemble:** Place the sweet potatoes on serving plates. Using a sharp knife, make a lengthwise incision halfway into each sweet potato and gently push in the sides until it splits open (like a baked potato). Season the sweet potato flesh lightly with kosher salt and drizzle with olive oil. Fill each sweet potato with the broccoli and season lightly with kosher salt. Smother with queso and garnish with scallions and Fritos.

204

Steamed Mussels with Sake & Coconut

(Serves 2 or 3)

(Active: 30 mins. | Total: 50 mins.)

(Easy) (Gluten-free)

Ingredients:

2 pounds (900 grams) mussels

1 tablespoon Diamond Crystal kosher salt

2 tablespoons neutral oil

5 garlic cloves, thinly sliced

1 small yellow or white onion, thinly sliced

2-inch piece fresh ginger, peeled and finely chopped

3 Thai bird's eye or serrano chilies, thinly sliced

½ cup dry sake or any dry white wine

one 13.5-ounce can full-fat coconut milk

2 tablespoons fish sauce, plus more to taste

3 tablespoons freshly squeezed lime juice (about 2 limes), plus more to taste

3 scallions, thinly sliced

Steamed Rice (page 116), cooked noodles, or crusty bread for serving

→ Although they can seem intimidating, mussels are one of the easiest things to cook, on top of being a cheap and sustainable source of protein. First things first, get rid of all that grit. Mussels are part of the ocean's filtration system, so they swallow a lot of sand. A quick soak in cool salt water encourages them to purge the grit, then scrub each with a clean coarse sponge, before pulling out their beards (the tough stringy bit that dangles near the hinge). Cleaning mussels weakens them, so it's best to cook them soon after. Never eat mussels that are already dead. Any open mussels should close with a sharp tap. If they don't close, they're dead and you should discard them. To cook mussels, make a flavorful base with aromatics before adding a liquid to steam them. Finally, crank up the heat, get all the liquid at a rapid boil, then cover and shake the pot to distribute that heat. Mussels need intense heat to open, but once popped, they are cooked and ready to eat.

1. Place the mussels in a large bowl and set in the kitchen sink. Rinse the mussels, then cover with cold water. Add the salt and toss with your hands to dissolve. Let sit for 10 minutes. (This gets the mussels to purge any grit lurking inside.)

2. Working with one mussel at a time, give it a scrub under cold running water with a clean scrubby and pull off any hairlike "beards" sticking out from the hinge of the shell. Once clean, transfer the mussels to a new bowl and continue until all the mussels have been cleaned. Fill up the bowl with the cleaned mussels with cold water and drain again. Cover with a damp towel and place in the fridge (for up to 12 hours) until ready to cook.

3. In a large Dutch oven, heat the oil over medium-high heat until nearly smoking, about 2 minutes. Add the garlic, onion, ginger, and chilies and cook, stirring frequently with a stiff silicone spatula, until fragrant, the garlic starts to brown, and the onions are wilted, about 2 minutes.

4. Add the cleaned mussels. Stir until the mussels are coated in the onions and everything starts to sizzle aggressively. Add the sake and coconut milk, bring to a rapid boil, and cover with a lid. Gently shake the pot occasionally until all the mussels have been opened, 3 to 5 minutes.

5. Discard any mussels that have not opened. Remove from the heat and finish with fish sauce, lime juice, and scallions. Taste the broth for seasoning and adjust with lime juice or fish sauce as needed. Immediately serve hot or remove the mussels from their shells, put the meat into the broth, and chill completely to serve as a cold soup. Serve with steamed rice, cooked noodles, or crusty bread alongside.

Saffron Cod in a Packet

Serves 1

Active: 10 mins. | Total: 40 mins.

Easy | Gluten-free

Ingredients:

tiny pinch of saffron threads

½ teaspoon Diamond Crystal kosher salt, plus more to taste

one 6-ounce (170-gram) cod fillet

1 cup cherry tomatoes, halved

1 small fennel bulb, halved, cored, and thinly sliced

½ small yellow onion, thinly sliced

1 small garlic clove, thinly sliced

1 tablespoon drained capers

5 Castelvetrano olives, crushed, torn, and pitted

2 tablespoons extra-virgin olive oil

1 tablespoon unsalted butter, cubed

¼ cup sake or dry white wine

To Serve:

torn parsley

lemon wedges

Special Equipment:

mortar and pestle

sheet pan fitted with a wire rack

parchment paper

foil

→ This packet method is called en papillote. When I became a chef, I'd put something en papillote on every menu I could. They were filled with anything from tournéed vegetables and blood sauce to pistachio cake with poached pears, each one hand-stitched closed with red and white twine, then torn open tableside. I guess somewhere along the way I lost the point; cooking in a packet should be fun and easy. Everything steams together, with all the flavors and juices locked inside. This method works with any combo of ingredients that'll cook in about the same time and doesn't need direct heat for rendering fat or browning. I like it best with lean fish and tender vegetables; avoid stuff like bacon or steak. Adding a flavorful liquid, like wine, sake, or bone broth to the packet creates the steam that cooks everything through and becomes the sauce. Because there isn't any browning, be sure to turn up the flavor with salt, fat, acid, and spices. This recipe is for one, so feel free to multiply the recipe to make a packet for every diner. (But don't make a jumbo packet, that won't cook through evenly.) Or don't follow the recipe at all and make it your own.

1. **Dry-brine the cod:** With a small mortar and pestle, grind the saffron with the kosher salt. Pat the cod fillet dry, then rub all over with the saffron salt and set on a sheet pan fitted with a rack. Let the cod sit with the seasoning in the fridge for at least 15 and up to 45 minutes. Do not rinse.

2. Heat the oven to 400°F (200°C).

3. **Meanwhile, prep the veggies:** In a medium bowl, toss together the cherry tomatoes, fennel, onion, garlic, capers, olives, and olive oil. Season with salt to taste, tossing to evenly coat.

4. **Make the papillote:** Lay one 13 × 18-inch sheet of parchment paper on top of a sheet of foil and fold the paper in half. Unfold and toward the middle, right next to the crease, place the tomato mixture. Rest the cod and cubes of butter on top.

5. Fold the parchment and foil over and crimp two sides of the packet closed. Before sealing the final side, pour in the sake. Seal the final side and make sure the edges of foil and parchment are tightly crimped shut all around. (If making ahead, you can store the prepped papillote in the fridge for up to 12 hours.)

6. **Cook the papillote:** Place on a sheet pan and bake until the fish feels tender when you pierce it through the packet with a cake tester, 18 to 22 minutes.

7. Let rest for at least 5 and up to 15 minutes, then carefully unwrap one side of the parchment pouch and slide the contents into a bowl. Garnish with parsley and lemon wedges and serve immediately.

I Promise It's Good! Poached Chicken Breast

Makes 2 chicken breasts and 3½ cups reinforced broth

Active: 45 mins. | Total: 45 mins. plus 12 hrs. brining time

Easy   Gluten-free

Ingredients:

2 bone-in, skin-on chicken breasts (about 20 ounces/560 grams total)

1 tablespoon Diamond Crystal kosher salt

4 cups high-quality chicken bone broth (page lxxii)

1 bay leaf

3 garlic cloves, smashed and peeled

1 teaspoon peppercorns

Special Equipment:

sheet pan fitted with a wire rack

→ Poached chicken gets a bad rap, but when done right, it is succulent, flavorful, tender, and anything but dry. I take every step to guard against boring chicken: Start with bone-in, skin-on breasts, dry-brine them overnight, then cook them from cold in already awesome chicken bone broth for maximum flavor. It's like a two-for-one deal: you get the best poached chicken ever and amped-up bone broth ready for soup, sauces, rice, or just sipping. If you want to cook more chicken breasts, keep in mind that you need only enough broth to cover the chicken, so you may not need to multiply the quantity of bone broth and aromatics. For large batches, be sure to cook the chicken in a large pot, stirring occasionally, and you'll be ready for Classic Curried Chicken Salad (page 213), Hainanese-Inspired Chicken Rice (page 217), Simple Chicken Noodle Soup (page 214), and anything else you can dream up.

1. Dry-brine the chicken: Place the chicken breasts on a sheet pan fitted with a wire rack and pat dry with paper towels. Evenly sprinkle with the salt, coating all sides of the chicken breasts. Place in the fridge, uncovered, to dry-brine for at least 12 and up to 36 hours. (Do not rinse.)

2. In a medium saucepan, combine the broth, bay leaf, garlic, peppercorns, and chicken breasts. (The broth should cover the chicken. If it doesn't, use a narrower pot or add water.) Gently cook over medium-low heat until the water is steamy. Reduce the temperature if needed to keep the water hot, but not bubbling (between 160° and 170°F/71° and 77°C). You may even need to turn the heat off if the liquid gets too hot. Stay vigilant! The results will be more than worth it. Poach until opaque all the way through and 160°F (71°C) in the thickest part of the breast, 25 to 40 minutes.

3. Use tongs to transfer the chicken to a plate. Strain the poaching liquid, discard the solids, and reserve the broth. (If you're not planning to eat the chicken right away, for even better results, let it fully cool in the broth.) Now you have two tender and succulent chicken breasts and about 3½ cups reinforced bone broth that you can use for anything! Fully cooled, the chicken and broth will keep in the fridge for 3 days. You can freeze the broth for up to 3 months.

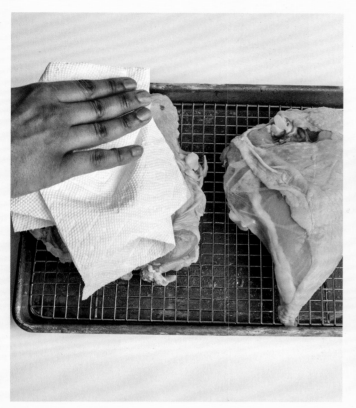

Classic Curried Chicken Salad

(Serves 2 to 4)

(Active: 20 mins. | Total: 20 mins.)

(Easy) (Gluten-free)

Ingredients:

2 tablespoons extra-virgin olive oil

¼ cup slivered almonds

¼ cup golden raisins

1 tablespoon Madras curry powder

¼ cup mayonnaise, store-bought or homemade (page 44)

¼ cup sour cream or whole-milk Greek yogurt

1 small crisp apple, such as Fuji or Honeycrisp, chopped

1 celery stalk, chopped

⅓ cup lightly packed fresh cilantro leaves and tender stems, finely chopped

2 Poached Chicken Breasts (page 210), cooled

freshly squeezed lemon juice

kosher salt and freshly ground black pepper

bread, wrap, lettuce cups, or salad, for serving

→ Nothing beats this classic combo of sweet crunchy apples, warm curry powder, and moist poached chicken. The salad only gets better as it sits, giving the chicken a chance to soak up all the flavors of the dressing, so double the batch if you like to meal prep.

1. In a small skillet, combine the oil and almonds over medium heat and cook, stirring frequently, until the almonds are toasted, 3 to 4 minutes. Remove from the heat, add the raisins and curry powder, and stir to combine. Scrape into a large bowl.

2. Add the mayo, sour cream, apple, celery, and cilantro to the bowl and stir to combine.

3. Cut the chicken breasts off the bone, remove the skin, and shred into large chunks. Add to the bowl and toss to combine. Taste and add lemon juice, salt, and pepper to taste.

4. Serve in a sandwich, wrap, in lettuce cups, or on a House Salad (page 18). Or transfer to an airtight container and store in the fridge for up to 3 days.

Simple Chicken Noodle Soup

Serves 2 to 4

Active: 20 mins. | Total: 45 mins.

Easy

Ingredients:

½ cup small pasta, such as ditalini or orzo

3½ cups reinforced broth (from Poached Chicken Breast, page 210)

2 medium carrots, peeled and cut into ½-inch pieces

2 celery stalks, cut into ½-inch pieces

kosher salt and freshly ground black pepper

1 Poached Chicken Breast (page 210)

¼ cup frozen peas

¼ cup lightly packed fresh dill leaves and tender stems, chopped

freshly squeezed lemon juice

→ When I'm sick I don't want anything complicated, and this soup hits the spot. Because the reinforced broth is extra chicken-y, so are all the veggies and pasta that get simmered in it. Here I opt for the tried-and-true combo of carrots, celery, and peas, but feel free to add whatever is in the fridge. Try adding turnips and their tops, kale and potatoes, or even mixed frozen vegetables.

1. Add the pasta to a small bowl and cover with cool water. Set aside for at least 30 minutes and up to 12 hours in the fridge, stirring occasionally. (This will allow the pasta to cook in the soup without soaking up all the broth.)

2. In a medium pot, combine the broth, carrot, and celery. Taste and add salt and pepper if needed. Bring to a simmer and cook until the carrots are almost tender, 5 to 8 minutes. Drain the pasta, add to the soup, and cook until the pasta is tender, 4 to 6 minutes.

3. Meanwhile, remove the chicken from the bone and remove the skin. Cut the meat into cubes or shred into pieces.

4. Add the chicken and peas to the soup to warm through; taste and add salt and pepper if needed. Finish with the dill and lemon juice to taste.

Hainanese-Inspired Chicken Rice

(Serves 2 to 4)

(Active: 15 mins.) | (Total: 45 mins.)

(Intermediate) (Gluten-free)

Ingredients:

2 cups jasmine rice

2 tablespoons unsalted butter

4 scallions, thinly sliced

4 garlic cloves, finely chopped

¾ teaspoon Diamond Crystal kosher salt

2½ cups reinforced broth (from Poached Chicken Breast, page 210), plus more hot broth for serving

2 Poached Chicken Breasts (page 210), cooled

Ginger Garlic Scallion Sauce (page 222)

→ This is my version of the chicken rice dishes developed by Hainanese immigrants in Singapore and Malaysia to make the most out of a chicken, with some recipes cooking the rice in rendered chicken fat so nothing goes to waste. When I want to level it up, I'll crisp the chicken skin with oil in a nonstick skillet to crumble on top of the rice. However, because dry-brining helps the skin become tender and render all its fat during poaching, it's even delicious left on the breast and eaten cold.

1. **Rinse and soak the rice:** Add the rice to a medium bowl, cover with cool water, gently swish to rinse, and drain. Repeat until the water runs mostly clear. Cover with fresh cool water and set aside for 15 minutes, then drain.

2. In a medium saucepan, melt the butter over medium heat until foamy. Add the scallions, garlic, and salt and cook, stirring frequently, until wilted, about 2 minutes. Add the rinsed and drained rice and cook, stirring frequently, until the grains are coated in fat and begin to look translucent around the edges, about 2 minutes. Add the broth, cover, and bring to a boil over high heat. Reduce the heat to low and cook, undisturbed, for 20 minutes. Remove from the heat, uncover, and fluff the rice with a fork. Cover and rest for 10 minutes.

3. **Meanwhile, prep the chicken:** Cut the breast off the bone and cut on the diagonal into thick slices with the skin on.

4. Serve the hot rice with cold poached chicken, ginger garlic scallion sauce, and extra hot broth alongside for sipping.

Snappy Shrimp

with Punch-You-in-the-Face
Cocktail Sauce

Serves 4

Active: 1 hr. | Total: 1½ hrs.

Intermediate

Ingredients:

1 pound (450 grams) U16 to U20
shell-on shrimp (see U What?,
page 220)

3 tablespoons Diamond Crystal
kosher salt

½ teaspoon baking soda

5 cups water

1 cup dry sake or any white wine

4 garlic cloves, smashed and peeled

2 celery stalks, halved

1 medium yellow or white onion,
quartered

½ bunch parsley

⅓ cup freshly squeezed lemon juice
(about 3 lemons), spent lemons
reserved

Punch-You-in-the-Face Cocktail Sauce
(page 220)

Special Equipment:

kitchen shears

sheet pan fitted with a wire rack

spider (or sieve)

→ Like pretty much all proteins, shrimp benefit from dry-brining. Rather than making them tender, tossing shrimp in a mixture of salt and baking soda keeps them snappy and offers a buffer against overcooking. All it takes is 15 minutes to vastly improve their texture. To amp up their flavor, here the shrimp are poached in a broth made from the shells simmered with aromatics and sake. If it's warm in your kitchen, keep your shrimp in a bowl set over an ice bath while you're cleaning them. Shrimp go bad super fast.

---

1. **Clean the shrimp:** Working with one shrimp at a time, use sharp kitchen shears to snip open the back. Use your hands to pull off the shell while keeping the tail attached. (Set the shells aside.) Pull out and discard the dark vein, then rinse under cold water to remove any grit.

2. **Dry-brine the shrimp:** In a medium bowl, combine the salt and baking soda. Add the cleaned shrimp and toss to evenly coat. Place a wire rack in a sheet pan and arrange the shrimp in one layer. Let the shrimp dry-brine in the fridge, uncovered, for at least 15 and up to 45 minutes. Rinse the shrimp with cold water and arrange on the rack once again. Place in the fridge until ready to cook. (If storing for more than 1 hour, tightly wrap the pan. Once wrapped, the shrimp will keep in the fridge for 24 hours.)

3. **Make the poaching liquid:** In a large pot, combine the reserved shrimp shells, water, sake, garlic, celery, onion, parsley, lemon juice, and spent lemons. Bring to a simmer over high heat, then reduce to a bare simmer. Cover and cook until flavorful, about 30 minutes. Using a spider, scoop out all the solids from the stock, pressing gently to squeeze the liquid from the shells, and discard. (Or pass through a sieve, reserving the stock and discarding the solids. Return to the large pot.)

4. **Poach the shrimp:** Fill a medium bowl with ice and add water to cover to make an ice bath. Season with a large pinch of salt.

5. Set the pot of poaching liquid over medium heat and heat until steamy but not bubbling (around 190°F/88°C). Add the shrimp all at once and stir to distribute the heat. Cook, stirring occasionally, until the shrimp are opaque and slightly curled, about 3 minutes.

6. Remove from the heat and lift the shrimp out of the liquid with a spider (or pour through a sieve) and transfer to the ice bath to halt the cooking. Once the shrimp are cooled, 5 to 8 minutes, lay them out on a sheet pan and place in the fridge to fully chill. (If storing for more than 1 hour, tightly wrap. They will keep in the fridge for 3 days.)

7. Serve chilled shrimp with cocktail sauce.

Punch-You-in-the-Face Cocktail Sauce

(Makes about 1 cup)

(Active: 15 mins. | Total: 15 mins.)

(Easy) (Gluten-free)

Ingredients:

¼ cup prepared horseradish

½ cup ketchup

1 garlic clove, finely grated

2 tablespoons freshly squeezed lemon juice (about 1 lemon), plus more to taste

2 tablespoons whiskey or brandy

2 or 3 dashes Worcestershire sauce

2 or 3 dashes Tabasco sauce

Dash of fish sauce

kosher salt

→ A splash of whiskey or brandy gives this cocktail sauce extra bite. Besides dunking your poached shrimp in here, add a dollop to chilled oysters, spread on a roast beef sandwich, or serve alongside steak.

Place the horseradish in a fine-mesh sieve and press with the back of a spoon to squeeze out any excess liquid. In a medium bowl, mix together the drained horseradish, ketchup, garlic, lemon juice, whiskey, Worcestershire sauce, Tabasco, and fish sauce. Taste the sauce and adjust with lemon and salt if needed. Store in the fridge for up to 1 week.

U What?

Shrimp are sized by how many you get in a pound. For example, U8 shrimp are big boys, with just 8 per pound, while U60 means they're teeny-weeny, with a whooping 60 per pound. For shrimp cocktail, I like U16 to U20 shrimp. At about an ounce per shrimp, they're just the right size for grabbing by the tail and dunking into sauce.

Tahini Almond Sauce

(Makes about 1 cup)

(Active: 10 mins. | Total: 10 mins.)

(Easy) (Vegan)

Ingredients:

1 tablespoon white miso paste

¼ cup well-stirred tahini

¼ cup freshly squeezed lemon juice (about 2 lemons), plus more to taste

2 tablespoons extra-virgin olive oil

1 small garlic clove, finely grated

1 to 3 tablespoons water

kosher salt

⅓ cup toasted Marcona almonds (or any other toasted nut), roughly chopped, plus more for garnish

¼ cup lightly packed fresh cilantro leaves and tender stems, finely chopped

→ This salty and tart tahini sauce, studded with buttery Marcona almonds, is great drizzled over a savory yogurt bowl, tossed with noodles, alongside grilled chicken, or thinned with water to dress a salad. Be sure to season it aggressively with salt to balance all the fat and acid from the tahini and lemon juice. If you're unsure, portion a small bowlful to play around with before seasoning the full batch.

In a medium bowl, combine the miso and tahini. Using a stiff silicone spatula, smash the miso into the tahini until smooth. Add the lemon juice, olive oil, and garlic and whisk to combine. Add 1 to 3 tablespoons water to adjust to your desired thickness. Taste and whisk in salt to taste and more lemon juice as needed. (It should taste rich and tart. If it's too acidic, bland, or garlicky, it needs more salt.) Stir in the chopped almonds and cilantro. Store the sauce in the fridge for up to 1 week.

Ginger Garlic Scallion Sauce

(Makes about 1 cup)

(Active: 15 mins. | Total: 15 mins.)

(Easy) (Vegan) (Gluten-free)

Ingredients:

2 tablespoons neutral oil

2 tablespoons toasted sesame oil

1 bunch scallions (6 to 8), white/light green parts, thinly sliced

3-inch piece fresh ginger, peeled and finely grated

4 garlic cloves, finely grated

2 tablespoons unseasoned rice vinegar, plus more to taste

2 tablespoons soy sauce or tamari, plus more to taste

pinch of MSG (optional)

1 to 3 tablespoons water

kosher salt

Special Equipment:

Microplane grater

→ This sauce gives everything a super-savory punch. Try it with dumplings, tossed into noodles, and in the Hainanese-Inspired Chicken Rice (page 217).

1. In a small saucepan, heat the neutral oil and sesame oil over medium heat until they start to shimmer and the sesame oil is fragrant, about 2 minutes. Add the scallions, ginger, and garlic. Cook, stirring and scraping frequently with a stiff silicone spatula, until fragrant and tender and the violent bubbling subsides, about 2 minutes.

2. Remove from the heat and scrape into a heatproof bowl. Add the rice vinegar, soy sauce, and MSG (if using) and stir to combine. Add 1 to 3 tablespoons water to adjust to your desired thickness. Taste and season with salt to taste and more vinegar and/or soy if needed. (The sauce will never fully emulsify; stir before serving.) Store the sauce in the fridge for up to 1 week.

Vegan Queso

(Makes about 3 cups)

(Active: 30 mins. | Total: 30 mins.)

(Easy) (Vegan) (Gluten-free)

Ingredients:

2 tablespoons extra-virgin olive oil

4 garlic cloves, chopped

1 teaspoon smoked paprika

3 cups water, plus more as needed

1 cup cashews

¼ cup nutritional yeast

1 teaspoon mustard powder

1 medium sweet potato (about
    8 ounces/224 grams), peeled and
    cut into ½-inch cubes

1 chipotle pepper in adobo sauce

1 tablespoon adobo sauce from the
    chipotle pepper can

pinch of MSG (optional)

kosher salt

Special Equipment:

blender

→ Okay, it's not really queso, but a nut puree seasoned with cheesy nutritional yeast. It needs a lot of salt to taste right, so don't be shy. If you're unsure, portion a small bowlful to play around with before seasoning the full batch. This makes more queso than you'll need for the Loaded Sweet Potatoes (page 204), but any less won't blend smoothy. Thankfully, leftover vegan queso is one of the greatest foods on earth. Have it cold as a dip for veggies, make mac and cheese, or just eat it with Fritos.

---

1. In a medium pot, combine the olive oil and garlic and cook over medium-high heat, stirring frequently, until the garlic is fragrant and light golden, about 2 minutes. Add the smoked paprika and cook until fragrant, about 30 seconds. Add the water, cashews, nutritional yeast, mustard powder, diced sweet potato, chipotle, adobo sauce, and MSG (if using) and gently simmer, stirring occasionally, until the sweet potatoes and cashews are tender, 15 to 20 minutes.

2. Carefully transfer the mixture to a blender and puree until completely smooth. Generously season with salt to taste. (It should taste cheesy, slightly spicy, and have a mellow sweetness. If it's too spicy, sharp, or bland, it needs more salt.) If the mixture is too thick, add water a tablespoon at a time. (Once cooled, the queso will keep in the fridge for 1 week.)

Go to Brown Town

Cooking with dry heat

Go to Brown Town

I had that stereotypical overprotective first-gen Asian American kid upbringing. I wasn't allowed to talk to boys who weren't my cousins, I couldn't go to dances, and I definitely didn't date living under that roof. But my parents were weirdly relaxed about other things. They were okay with me staying up all night baking cheesecakes. They let me paint not just my room, but nearly every room in the house with whatever technique I picked up that week watching home renovation shows. And neither one blinked an eye when I regularly started tiny fires in the backyard. It was my amu's fault, because she told me about how as a young girl she'd dig firepits in her yard to cook rice and lentils in makeshift walnut shell pots. So, I did, too. The rice part was tough—you can't fit much in a walnut shell—but the fire part was easy. I have no doubt these pyro playtimes were why I started cooking. I learned early on how the dry heat of flames made everything exciting. Squishy, snowy marshmallow turned into molten syrup bombs wrapped in bitter black husks and floppy Ball Park franks got plump and snappy. But you don't need to dig a fussy (and apparently illegal in Manhattan) firepit to develop dynamic flavors and textures in an ingredient; just try cooking with dry heat.

I don't want to play favorites, but only dry heat can so easily create such contrast between the interior and exterior of an ingredient, which is key to making food you want to keep eating. Unless an ingredient has bite, moist cooking methods—like steaming, poaching, braising, and stewing—can't add any crackle because everything is damp. These methods are also lower in heat because they are limited by the temperature of water and steam. Water maxes out at the boiling point, which is just 212°F (100°C), while steam can get a bit hotter (significantly so if saturated in a pressure cooker). On the other hand, low heat in a skillet is about 300°F (149°C) and if you preheat a heavyweight pan, you can easily attain surface temperatures of about 500°F (260°C). Dry heat—whether from the hot air of an oven, through intimate contact with the surface of a raging skillet, or a whip of flames jumping off a wee firepit—is just simply hotter than moist heat.

Why does that matter? High heat brings so much flavor to the party because it encourages browning through caramelization and the Maillard reaction (named after French chemist Louis Camille Maillard, who first described the process in 1912). The Maillard reaction is a complex interaction involving both carbohydrate molecules and amino acids—sugars and proteins. Not just any sugars are eager to hook up with proteins; the ones that are down to party are called *reducing sugars*. Heat breaks down their molecules and prompts numerous chemical reactions, creating that signature brown color you see on anything from a roast chicken to a beer by reconfiguring those sugars and amino acids into a series of rings that reflect light such that our eyes register it as brown. The color produced is the least exciting thing going on, though—we're here for the flavor, baby! The multitude of compounds created from this reaction account for the deep, rich, meaty, toasty, malty, and savory flavors in everything from a crusty loaf of bread to a lacy smashburger patty. The Maillard reaction really gets grooving at temperatures above 250°F (121°C), moving faster with higher heat, but it can also happen more slowly at lower temperatures, which is how a long-simmered bone broth becomes golden even without roasting the bones first. The

228

Caramelization vs. the Maillard Reaction

You may have heard the terms caramelization and Maillard reaction used interchangeably because on the surface they both look like they're doing the same thing (taking your food to brown town) and readily occur concurrently, but they are actually distinct mechanisms. They both take place when heat is applied and are both examples of nonenzymatic browning (enzymatic browning is what happens when you cut an avocado or banana and it turns black). Caramelization occurs when sugars reach temperatures of 330°F (166°C) and above, and the Maillard reaction involves both sugars and proteins. Caramelization tempers sweetness and creates countless new complex flavors—smoky, butterscotch-y, nutty, and bitter like the exterior of charred marshmallows. The number of chemical reactions that are taking place while this happens is in the hundreds, literally so many that scientists stopped trying to name them all (and we all know how much scientists love to name things). Slowly melting sugar in a pan and heating it until it starts to get golden is the clearest example of caramelization at work (to see this in action, see Golden Saffron Flan on page 467).

aromas and flavors created vary a great deal depending on the specific ratio of amino acids and reducing sugars present in the ingredient you are cooking, so the brown flavors in a roasted lamb leg taste different from those in roasted potatoes.

Besides temperature and time, alkaline ingredients encourage the Maillard reaction and promote browning. Pretzels get their signature bronze hue thanks to a quick dunk in a highly alkaline lye solution (you can fake it at home with baking soda). Some recipes use baking soda or baking powder to help speed up the browning of onions or to get a deeper color on roast chicken without cranking the heat so much it dries out.

The majority of browning happens on the surface of foods where dry heat dehydrates the outside, eliminating moisture, allowing temperatures to rise, and getting the Maillard reaction going. As long as some moisture is present on the inside, the internal temperature can't rise above 212°F (100°C), so the interior will have a totally different texture, flavor, and color than the outside. This is how you get a steak with a crusty chocolate brown sear while retaining a velvety pink middle or crisp mahogany mushrooms that are still moist and bouncy when you bite into them. Once you know how to prep food, manage your heat sources, and bring the two together, you can make the most out of any ingredient.

All this is just to say, brown food tastes good. So, how can we harness the mythical powers of the Goddess Maillard and Her Reactions? The key is figuring out how to manipulate heat to get the color and texture you want on the outside by the time the inside is just right.

Here are my golden rules to get golden

(well, brown, at least) while staying moist, juicy, tender, fluffy, soft, or crisp—you know, depending on what you want!

Rule #1: Equipment Matters

Steam is the enemy of a good sear because it drops the temperature on the surface of the ingredient, slowing or even fully blocking browning from happening. The lower sides of a skillet or sheet pan let the steam that's developed during cooking quickly escape. That doesn't mean you can't sear in a high-sided Dutch oven or roasting pan, it just might take longer. This isn't a problem for large chunks of beef short rib, which can handle a longer cook time, but it mostly certainly is a problem for Brussels sprouts, which can get mushy and sulfurous if you cook them too long.

Heavyweight stainless steel, enameled, or cast-iron cookware retain and transfer heat better than lightweight aluminum or insulating glass, keeping that Maillard reaction moving along. Cast-iron skillets heat unevenly and take longer to warm up than stainless steel, but once preheated are the best tool for searing. Since many nonstick pans have coatings that can become toxic at higher temperatures, they should be avoided for this type of cooking.

If you're roasting or searing in the oven and looking for 360 degrees of brown, a wire rack is essential. It allows hot air to circulate all around an ingredient and prevents whatever you're cooking from resting in a pool of its own juices.

Rule #2: Preheat

When food hits a hot skillet, sheet pan, or pot, the moisture on the surface of the food swiftly sizzles off, preventing sticking and getting those browning reactions going right away. Cook anything long enough and it will eventually brown, but dynamic food is all about contrast. If you want to retain moisture in the center of a salmon fillet, crisp texture at the core of a broccoli floret, or a fluffy center in a potato, while also getting crisp and browned all around, you need the food to get hot and dry quickly.

When searing or sautéing on the stovetop in a cast-iron, enameled, or stainless steel pan, let the pan heat over medium or medium-high until barely smoking before adding oil and ingredients. How long it takes to heat up depends on the pan and the burner, ranging anywhere from 3 to 8 minutes. Don't be tempted to crank the heat, which can result in uneven heating, particularly with heavy cast-iron pans. If the cast-iron gets white hot or the base of the stainless steel skillet warps, you've gone too far. Leave them to cool down before proceeding.

If searing in the oven, place your sheet pan or roasting pan in the oven to heat up while the oven comes to temperature. When roasting food on a rack, like when you're cooking larger pieces of meat such as prime rib or whole chicken, the food won't be in direct contact with the pan so there is no need to preheat it. Broiling uses such intense heat that there's no need to preheat the pan as long as you preheat the broiler.

Rule #3: Moisture Is the Enemy

Get to those high Maillard reaction–promoting temperatures fast by starting out with dry ingredients. For vegetables, beans, and tofu, this means patting them dry with clean kitchen towels before cooking. For proteins, like chicken thighs, steaks, and fish fillets, you want to pat them dry with paper towels and dry-brine them if you have time.

Dry-brining is a simple process involving seasoning the protein with kosher salt and letting it sit, uncovered, on a rack in the fridge. I generally use 1 teaspoon (3 grams) Diamond Crystal kosher salt per 1 pound and evenly sprinkle it all over the outside of the protein. The salt draws out moisture and dissolves into a concentrated brine, which gets absorbed into the protein. This process leaves the surface extra dry, which translates to brown and crispy results. (Read more in Why Dry-Brine? on page 258.)

Rule #4: Fat Is Your Friend

Fat helps browning by promoting even and efficient heat transfer. Because searing, sautéing, roasting, and broiling all involve high heat, it's best to use fats with high smoke points. Smoke point refers to what temperature you can heat up a particular fat to before it starts to break down and smoke. Lard, safflower oil, and clarified butter all have relatively high smoke points, just what you need for crispy roast potatoes, while flax oil, whole butter, or walnut oil would burn. Contrary to what you might have heard, you can use olive oil for high-heat methods, but since it is an expensive ingredient, I only use it if I'm not draining off the oil, like with a burst-cherry-tomato sauce. If a fat is particularly flavorful, like clarified butter or extra-virgin olive oil, that flavor will end up in the final dish. If that's not what you want, stick with a flavorless neutral oil, like refined peanut or grapeseed oil.

For searing and sautéing on the stovetop, it's best to add fat after heating. That's because, depending on the oil, it might smoke and begin breaking down before the pan is hot. When you add oil to the pan later, followed immediately by your ingredients, the oil is less likely to overheat. For lower-temperature cooking, like sweating onions and garlic, it's okay to add the oil right away.

When it comes to browning in the oven, I don't place the fat directly in the cooking vessel. Instead, I make sure to coat the food that I am cooking in an even layer of fat. Place it in a large bowl and drizzle on a tablespoon of fat at a time, tossing until evenly coated. This prevents too much fat from pooling on the sheet pan, which can potentially burn or even ignite when under a broiler.

Rule #5: Toss with Intent

Movement matters. Frequent tossing is good for quickly transferring heat through smaller-sized ingredients, perfect for crisp-tender sautéed green beans or roasted cauliflower. But for a dark, deep sear, like you want on a charred broccoli steak or cabbage wedge, the ingredients have got to stay put. They need consistent, direct contact with heat. Level up by using a cooking weight or heavy skillet to press food down and maximize contact. Thick proteins, like steaks and chops, need

232

Don't Waste Your Fond! (Unless You're a Monster Who Hates Flavor)

special treatment. Flip them regularly while also pressing them down, allowing them to cook evenly from both sides.

And Remember:
Throughout your roasting and sautéing adventures, you may come across a brown substance stuck to the bottom of your cooking vessel. This is known as *fond* (cue the choir of angels). It's pure bits of concentrated savory flavor. Treasure it and never let it go to waste.

You can utilize fond in a bunch of ways. The easiest is to scrape it up with a splash of liquid—hot water works, or go wild with bone broth, vinegar, or sake. Use the flat edge of a wooden spoon or stiff silicone spatula to scuff every streak free from your pan or sheet pan and dissolve it into the liquid (this step is called *deglazing*). Pour that liquid gold into whatever else you have cooking for that meal—a pot of steamed rice, simmering lentils, or a dressing or sauce. Wilt quick-cooking vegetables, like Swiss chard or bok choy, in the fond water for an easy side. Or mop it up with crusty bread. If the liquid is too watery, simmer it down in a small saucepan until it's the consistency you want.

Another option is to turn the fond into a quick pan sauce. In French culinary tradition, you deglaze the fond with wine, simmer the wine down until syrupy, then add stock and simmer it down once more until thick enough to coat the back of a spoon. Remove it from the heat and swirl in a couple of pats of butter, then finish the sauce with final seasonings like pepper, fresh herbs, or mustard. Play around with this method using any liquid to deglaze the fond, like dashi, vermouth, sake, coffee, or just plain water. Add body with butter and balance the flavors with lemon juice, herbs, fish sauce, or miso.

Whatever you do, don't waste your fond—unless it's burnt. Fond is brown, sometimes even taupe, but it's not black. Let your nose guide you. If the fond smells burned, ditch it.

Blistered Carrots

with Carrot Top Salsa Verde

(Serves 4 to 6 as a side)

(Active: 20 mins. | Total: 1 hr.)

(Easy) (Vegetarian) (Gluten-free)

Ingredients:

2 bunches medium carrots with tops
(about 2 pounds/900 grams)

6 tablespoons olive oil, plus more to
taste

kosher salt

1 garlic clove, peeled

2 lemons

freshly ground black pepper

¾ cup labne or Greek yogurt

Special Equipment:

sheet pan

Microplane grater

→ I've been rocking glasses for as long as I can remember, so my mom made me eat a lot of baby carrots. Nope, it didn't help my vision (my lenses only got thicker every year), but it did teach me to hate carrots. I was on the anti-carrot team for years, until I ate one blackened and charred. Intense, dry heat transforms their grassy and watery crunch into something meaty, sweet, and practically like fudge. Here, they're placed on a bed of cool labne and topped with bright carrot top salsa verde. Heating the sheet pan before adding the carrots prevents them from sticking and gets that browning action going right away.

1. Position a rack in the center of the oven. Place a sheet pan on the rack and heat the oven to 500°F (260°C).

2. While the oven heats, prep the carrots: Trim the tops off the carrots and reserve. Scrub the carrots, especially where the tops meet the carrot. Pat dry with a clean kitchen towel. Find the smallest carrot in the bunch, then halve or quarter the larger carrots lengthwise so they match the thickness of the smallest carrot. (If all your carrots are very thick, quarter them all. You want them no thicker than ¾ inch.)

3. Cook the carrots: Toss the carrots in a large bowl with 2 tablespoons of the oil and generously season with salt. Once the oven is hot, quickly remove the heated sheet pan and spread the carrots onto the pan (no need to be precise about evenly spacing them out, just be fast so the pan doesn't cool down). Roast until deeply browned, tossing once during cooking, until tender and the tips are charred, 30 to 40 minutes.

4. While the carrots cook, make the salsa verde: Measure ¾ cup (tightly packed) carrot tops (leaves and stems) and thoroughly wash them in a bowl of cool water until no grit remains. Drain and dry. Very finely chop the tops (be sure to repeatedly run your knife through the greens so it's almost a paste) and add them to the same bowl you used to toss the carrots—no need to wash. Use a Microplane grater to finely grate over the garlic clove and the zest of both lemons. Add the juice of 1 lemon, the remaining 4 tablespoons of oil, and generous pinches of salt and black pepper. Stir and add more lemon juice, salt, pepper, and oil to taste. It should be very lemony and assertive to balance the sweet carrots.

5. To plate: Spread the labne on a large platter. Top with the roasted carrots. Garnish with carrot top salsa verde and serve right away.

Note: Whenever you are moving something in and out of a hot oven, work as quickly as possible. Depending on the oven, the temperature can drop as much as 25°F every time you open the door.

Crisped Kale Salad

with Candied Pecans & Maple Dressing

(Serves 4 to 6)

(Active: 30 mins.) (Total: 45 mins.)

(Easy) (Gluten-free)

(Vegetarian (can be made vegan))

For the candied pecans:

1 cup pecans (whole or pieces)

¼ cup pure maple syrup

1 tablespoon unsalted butter or vegan butter, melted

½ teaspoon Diamond Crystal kosher salt

For the dressing:

2 tablespoons maple syrup

3 tablespoons freshly squeezed lemon juice (about 1 lemon)

1 tablespoon Dijon mustard

¼ to ½ teaspoon chili flakes

2 tablespoons extra-virgin olive oil

kosher salt and freshly ground black pepper

For the salad:

3 large bunches lacinato kale (about 2 pounds/900 grams)

2 tablespoons extra-virgin olive oil

kosher salt

2 medium pears, halved, cored, and sliced

freshly ground black pepper

→ Here torn leaves of kale are roasted in the oven until parts are wilted, with some leaves slightly charred, and others crisped into chips, before being tossed in a sweet and tart maple-mustard dressing. Take the time to thoroughly dry the kale and heat your sheet pan. This ensures that it won't stick, and browning can happen as soon as the kale hits the pan, giving you crisp and charred leaves, rather than chewy and steamed ones. Serve this salad alongside hearty roasted meats or stewed beans. Or make it a meal in itself by topping with leftover roast chicken or tofu.

1. **Make the candied pecans:** Heat the oven to 325°F (163°C). Line a sheet pan with parchment paper.

2. In a medium bowl, toss together the pecans, maple syrup, melted butter, and salt. Spread onto the sheet pan, pouring over all the maple syrup and butter, and bake until deeply golden brown and the syrup has reduced, 25 to 30 minutes, stirring every 5 minutes. Slide the parchment onto the counter, allow the nuts to cool completely, then roughly chop or break with your fingers. Reserve the sheet pan for cooking the kale and increase the oven temperature to 475°F (246°C).

3. **Meanwhile, make the dressing and prep the kale:** In the same bowl you tossed the pecans (no need to wash it), whisk together the maple syrup, lemon juice, mustard, and chili flakes. Drizzle in the olive oil while whisking. Season with salt and pepper to taste. It should be sweet, spicy, salty, and tart.

4. Strip the kale leaves off the stems (discard the stems). Tear the leaves into large pieces. Wash in cool water and dry in a salad spinner or pat with kitchen towels.

5. **Cook the kale:** When the nuts are out of the oven and you've increased the temperature to 475°F (246°C), slide in the reserved sheet pan (without parchment) to preheat. Meanwhile, add half the kale to a large bowl. Drizzle with 1 tablespoon of the oil, sprinkle with salt, and massage to evenly coat.

6. Working quickly, remove the hot pan from the oven, evenly spread the seasoned kale onto the pan (it's okay if the leaves overlap one another), then return it to the oven. Roast until some of the leaves have crisped, some have charred, and some have wilted, 7 to 10 minutes. Transfer the crisped kale to a large bowl (or if you don't have another bowl, stack it on the cutting board and place in the large bowl after you've seasoned the remaining kale). Repeat with the remaining kale, seasoning and crisping.

7. Reserve some pieces of crispy kale for garnish. Toss together the rest of the kale, the dressing, and the pears. Taste and season with pepper and more salt if needed. Transfer to a platter and top with the candied pecans and reserved crispy kale. Serve right away.

Cabbage & Yuba

with Spicy Peanut Dressing

(Serves 4)

(Active: 20 mins. | Total: 1 hr.)

(Easy) (Gluten-free)

(Vegetarian (can be made vegan))

For the cabbage & yuba:

1 medium head green or red cabbage (about 2 pounds/900 grams)

5 tablespoons neutral oil

kosher salt

10 ounces (280 grams) yuba

1 medium red bell pepper, sliced lengthwise into thin strips

For the dressing:

½ cup peanut butter (any kind)

¼ cup freshly squeezed lime juice (about 3 limes)

2 tablespoons fish sauce (optional)

1 tablespoon unseasoned rice vinegar, plus more to taste

1 tablespoon soy sauce or tamari

1 tablespoon mild honey or maple syrup, plus more to taste

2 garlic cloves, finely grated

1-inch piece fresh ginger, peeled and finely grated

1 to 3 Thai green or red chilies, finely chopped

kosher salt

To Garnish:

torn fresh cilantro leaves and tender stems

chopped toasted peanuts

→ You know how uncovered hot pudding can develop a skin? That's very similar to how yuba is made: It's the skin that forms when soy milk is heated. The sheets are often used in Japanese and Chinese cooking and can be thick and chewy or thin and delicate, like the strands of cheese inside burrata (my favorite brand of yuba is from Hodo foods). Yuba sheets will soak up a saucy braise, stand in for a noodle, or grow crisp and crunchy. Here are all of my favorite things, blackened cabbage wedges and blistered yuba shards teamed up with a perky peanut sauce inspired by Thai satay sauce. The dry heat transforms chewy yuba strands into shattering strands ready for dipping into the spicy sauce, perfect for those nights when I want dinner to have snacky vibes. Be sure to heat the sheet pan before adding the yuba so there's no risk of it sticking.

---

1. Position a rack in the center of the oven, place a sheet pan on the rack, and heat to 450°F (230°C).

2. Prep and cook the cabbage: Trim the root from the cabbage and remove any discolored outer leaves. Cut the cabbage into quarters through the core and place in a large bowl. Toss with 2 tablespoons of the oil, rubbing to fully coat, and season with a big pinch of salt. Carefully place the wedges on the heated sheet pan cut-side down, and roast until deeply charred, about 20 minutes. Remove the pan from the oven, flip the wedges, and roast until the other side is charred as well, 15 to 20 minutes. Divide among four plates.

3. Meanwhile, prep the yuba . . . : Separate the sheets of yuba, pat dry with a paper towel, and cut into wide strips. In the same bowl you used for the cabbage (no need to wash), combine the yuba strips, bell pepper, remaining 3 tablespoons oil, and a big pinch of salt and toss until evenly coated.

4. . . . and make the dressing: In a medium bowl, whisk together the peanut butter, lime juice, fish sauce (if using), vinegar, soy sauce, honey, garlic, ginger, and chilies. Add water a teaspoon at a time until the sauce has your desired thickness. Taste and adjust the seasoning with salt and more vinegar and honey as needed. (It should be aggressively tart and spicy, with enough salt to make the flavors pop and honey to mellow things out. If it's too spicy or tart, add more salt.)

5. Crisp the yuba: Once the cabbage is done, on the same sheet pan (no need to wash), spread out the yuba mixture and roast, tossing once during cooking, until every piece is crisp and some are browned, 20 to 25 minutes.

6. Return the crisped yuba to the large bowl (no need to wash) and toss with ¼ cup of the dressing until evenly coated. Divide the yuba onto the plates with the cabbage. Garnish with cilantro and peanuts and serve the remaining dressing alongside. Serve immediately.

Broiler-Popped Oysters with Tomato Butter

(Makes 18 oysters)

(Active: 20 mins. | Total: 25 mins.)

(Easy) (Gluten-free)

Ingredients:

18 fresh oysters in the shell

4 tablespoons unsalted butter, at room temperature

1 tablespoon tomato paste

2 garlic cloves, finely grated

1 tablespoon finely chopped fresh parsley

¼ to ½ teaspoon chili flakes

½ teaspoon dried oregano

→ When Ham and I lived in a studio apartment, my dream was to one day have a big enough place to throw an oyster party. You know, when you get a bunch of oysters and people pop 'em themselves. Well, I finally got that apartment, and threw that party, and it sucked. We invited over a group of professional chefs (who should know their way around an oyster), but maybe the party pressure got to them, because most were too shy to crack in on their own. After that, we had *broiled* oyster parties. So much easier and with no risk of accidental stabbing. Under the high heat of the broiler, oysters give up their tight grip and easily open right up. You still go through the motions of shucking, but all you need is a butter knife, so think of this like oyster shucking with training wheels on. After opening them up, if any of the oysters smell foul, are filled with grit, or have a small crab inside them, do not eat and do discard.

1. Under cold running water and with a clean scrubby, scrub the oysters of any dirt, paying extra attention to the hinge.

2. Position an oven rack 6 inches below the broiler element and set the broiler to high.

3. In a medium bowl, with a stiff silicone spatula, mix together the butter, tomato paste, garlic, parsley, chili flakes, and oregano until evenly combined.

4. Place the oysters on a sheet pan in one layer, flat-side up. (If they are wobbling a lot, place them on a bed of salt or crinkled up foil.)

5. Set under the broiler and cook until they've opened slightly, 2 to 4 minutes. Remove from the oven. Working with one oyster at a time on a cutting board, use a butter knife to slide into the hinge and turn to pop the oyster open. Wipe the blade clean, then run it along the top shell, scraping the oyster free. Scooch the butter knife under the bottom of the oyster to detach it from the shell but leave it in the shell (this makes them easier to eat).

6. Place a scant teaspoon of the butter mixture onto each oyster and return them to the sheet pan and back under the broiler. Cook until the butter is melted and the tops of the oysters are golden brown, 2 to 3 minutes.

Go to Brown Town

Broiled Whole Fish with Limey Cabbage Slaw

(Serves 2 or 3)

(Active: 20 mins.) (Total: 1 hr.)

(Easy) (Gluten-free)

For the fish:

1 whole head-on white fish (2 to 3 pounds/1 to 1.3 kilograms), such as snapper, branzino, or black bass, scaled and gutted

1 tablespoon Diamond Crystal kosher salt

2 tablespoons neutral oil

1 lime, thinly sliced

½ medium bunch cilantro leaves and stems

extra-virgin olive oil, for drizzling

For the slaw:

½ small head green cabbage (about 12 ounces/340 grams), halved, cored, and very thinly sliced

1 teaspoon Diamond Crystal kosher salt, plus more to taste

¼ cup freshly squeezed lime juice (about 3 limes), plus more to taste

1 to 2 Thai bird's eye chilies, thinly sliced or snipped with scissors

⅓ cup lightly packed fresh cilantro leaves and tender stems, roughly chopped

Special Equipment:

fish spatula

cake tester

→ If you've never cooked fish before, whole is the way to go. Unlike a delicate boneless fillet, the flesh is less likely to overcook, allowing you to pop it on a sheet pan and broil away without worry of spatter or sticking. Fresh fish will have clear eyes and smell like the ocean (you shouldn't get a whiff of fishiness). Ask your fishmonger to gut and remove the fish scales but keep the head and tail on. There's so much rich meat lurking in the cheeks and collar, while the tail transforms into a crispy chip. This method works with whole fish of any size, just be sure to follow visual rather than time cues. You know the fish is cooked through when you can easily pull off a fin and a cake tester can pierce the thickest part of the flesh without resistance.

---

1. **Dry-brine the fish:** Line a sheet pan with foil and set a wire rack on top. Pat the fish dry with paper towels and season both sides and the cavity liberally with the kosher salt. Place on the rack and dry-brine for at least 30 minutes at room temperature and up to 24 hours in the refrigerator.

2. Position a rack in the center of the oven and set the broiler to high. Rub the fish evenly with the neutral oil, including the cavity. Stuff the cavity with the lime slices and cilantro.

3. Place in the oven and broil until the edges are charred and a cake tester inserted into the thickest part of the flesh enters with no resistance, 10 to 12 minutes. Using a fish spatula, flip over and cook until the opposite side is also charred, a cake tester pierces the thickest part of the flesh with no resistance, and you can easily pull off a fin, 6 to 8 minutes.

4. **Meanwhile, make the slaw:** In a medium bowl, toss the cabbage with the salt and lime juice. Massage the cabbage until it's moist and wilted. Add the chilies and cilantro and lightly toss. Taste and adjust with more salt and lime if needed. Chill in the fridge until ready to serve.

5. Let the fish rest for at least 5 minutes before serving with the cabbage slaw on the side. Drizzle olive oil all over the fish and slaw and serve immediately.

Serving Whole Fish: For a casual weeknight dinner, I usually plop the fish on a platter in the center of the table and we go at it with chopsticks or forks. Yes, you want to eat the skin here, which will get crunchy and blistered under the broiler. If I want to fancy it up, I'll go the extra step of filleting the fish: Use two big serving spoons, one to support the fish and the other to do the filleting. Run the tip of the filleting spoon along the spine, then drive the spoon between the flesh and the bones. Then flip the fish and repeat the process on the other side, transferring the fillets with the spoons to a plate as you work. Serve alongside the slaw. Keep the head and bones in the center of the table so you can pick every bit of meat off the bones.

Crispy-Skinned Salmon

with Radishes & Nuoc Cham

Serves 4

Active: 10 mins. | Total: 40 mins.

Easy Gluten-free

For the salmon & radishes

1 large bunch radishes with tops (about 12 ounces/340 grams)

2 tablespoons neutral oil

2 teaspoons plus a large pinch of Diamond Crystal kosher salt, plus more as needed

one 24-ounce/670-gram skin-on salmon fillet

For the nuoc cham:

2 tablespoons boiling water

2 tablespoons granulated sugar, plus more to taste

2 garlic cloves, finely grated

2 Thai green or red chilies, finely chopped

3 tablespoons freshly squeezed lime juice (about 3 limes), plus more to taste

2 tablespoons fish sauce

kosher salt

To Serve:

cilantro leaves and stems, roughly chopped

Steamed Rice (page 116)

→ Salmon is remarkably rich, comfortably handling the heat of a broiler for this no mess, one bowl, one sheet pan dinner. Try to get one big fillet rather than four single-serving portions. Cooking the fish in a slab gives you more time to get the skin crispy without the flesh drying out. Don't be afraid of getting the skin charred for crackly contrast against the velvety flesh (I think the blistered skin is the best part). Nuoc cham is a sour, sweet, salty, all-purpose Vietnamese condiment that comes together quickly and packs one hell of a punch, cutting through the fatty salmon. Get to know it; you'll want it on everything.

1. Position a rack in the center of the oven and heat to 425°F (220°C). Line a sheet pan with parchment paper.

2. Separate the greens from the radishes, wash and thoroughly dry both. Cut the radishes in half and trim the greens of any dry, wilted, or yellow leaves. Place the radishes and greens in a bowl and toss with 1 tablespoon of the oil and a large pinch of salt. Spread onto one side of the prepared sheet pan. (Reserve the bowl, no need to wash.)

3. Pat the salmon dry with paper towels. Rub with the remaining 1 tablespoon oil and evenly season all sides with the 2 teaspoons kosher salt. Set the salmon on the prepared sheet pan alongside the radishes. (They cook at different rates, so the radishes will be pulled out first.)

4. Place in the oven and roast until the radish greens are wilted and charred and the radishes are tender and opaque, 12 to 15 minutes.

5. **Meanwhile, make the nuoc cham:** In the reserved bowl, combine the boiling water, sugar, garlic, and chilies and whisk until the sugar is dissolved. Add the lime juice and fish sauce. Taste and season with salt and more lime juice or sugar as needed.

6. When the radishes are done, pull out the sheet pan and transfer the radishes to a platter. Set the broiler to high. Return the salmon to the oven and broil until the skin is crisped, puffed, and charred in spots, 6 to 8 minutes. Remove from the oven and let rest for 5 minutes.

7. Serve the salmon alongside the radishes, top with cilantro, drizzle with some of the nuoc cham, and serve the rest on the side. Serve with steamed rice alongside.

Bisteeya-Inspired Phyllo Chicken Pie

(Serves 4)

(Active: 30 mins. | Total: 2 hrs.)

(Intermediate)

For the filling:

3 tablespoons neutral oil or clarified butter, plus more if needed

¼ cup slivered almonds

1 pound (450 grams) ground chicken

1 teaspoon plus a big pinch of Diamond Crystal kosher salt, plus more to taste

1 medium yellow onion, finely chopped

2 garlic cloves, finely grated

2-inch piece fresh ginger, peeled and finely grated

½ teaspoon ground turmeric

½ teaspoon ground cinnamon

½ teaspoon freshly ground black pepper, plus more to taste

¼ cup golden raisins

1 lemon

⅓ cup lightly packed fresh parsley leaves and tender stems, finely chopped

For assembly:

8 tablespoons unsalted butter, melted

eight 14 × 18-inch frozen phyllo sheets (see Note), thawed

powdered sugar

ground cinnamon

→ Bisteeya is a Moroccan pie traditionally made with braised pigeon, almonds, warm spices, herbs, and eggs. Instead of slowly braising whole cuts of poultry, here I make it with quickly seared ground chicken. By developing dark brown color on the ground chicken, I'm able to mimic the deep flavors of a long-cooked braise in a snap. For the best color, spread the ground chicken out on the skillet and walk away (well, not literally). By leaving it put, the chicken has a chance to dry out and go to brown town on one side, while the opposite side stays moist. This is how I get the best color and texture with any ground meat. If you've never used phyllo, this recipe is a good place to start. We're simply layering the phyllo and folding it over the filling. There's no complicated scrunching or rolling, and with only a few sheets, if you move quickly, there's little risk of the pastry drying out. Don't fret if any sheets tear. With all the layers, the pie can withstand a few ripped sheets.

---

1. **Make the filling:** In a medium skillet, combine the oil and almonds and cook over medium heat, stirring frequently, until the nuts are golden brown and aromatic, 2 to 4 minutes. Remove from the heat and use a slotted spoon to scoop the nuts into a large bowl, leaving the fat in the skillet.

2. Return the skillet to medium-high heat. Add the ground chicken and use a stiff silicone spatula to break it up and spread it out into one layer. Sprinkle with the 1 teaspoon kosher salt and cook undisturbed until browned on one side, about 5 minutes. Break up the chicken and cook, tossing frequently, until no pink remains, 5 to 7 minutes. Use a slotted spoon to transfer the chicken to the bowl with the nuts.

3. If the skillet looks dry, add more oil. Return to medium heat and add the onion, garlic, ginger, and a big pinch of kosher salt. Cook, stirring frequently and scraping up any browned bits that have formed on the bottom of the pan, until wilted, translucent, and browned along the edges, 3 to 5 minutes.

4. Add the turmeric, cinnamon, pepper, and raisins and cook, stirring frequently, until the spices are aromatic and the raisins plump, about 1 minute. Add 2 tablespoons water and scrape up any browned bits stuck to the bottom of the pan. Scrape the mixture into the large bowl.

5. Finely grate half the zest of the lemon into the bowl, add the parsley, and toss until everything is evenly combined. Taste and add lemon juice and more salt, pepper, and zest as needed. Set aside to cool slightly, about 30 minutes. (You can refrigerate the filling for up to 2 days.) →

Bisteeya-Inspired Phyllo Chicken Pie (cont'd.)

Special Equipment:

pastry brush

6. **Assembly:** Line a sheet pan with parchment paper. Position a rack in the lower third of the oven and heat to 350°F (177°C). Have the melted butter and pastry brush handy.

7. Stack the phyllo on a cutting board. With a sharp knife, trim and discard 4 inches of the phyllo dough, leaving you with a 14-inch square. Cover with a slightly damp towel. (Wrap up and put away any remaining phyllo immediately.)

8. Transfer one sheet of phyllo to the prepared sheet pan and evenly brush with butter. Continue layering on all the phyllo, brushing each with butter, and ending with a layer of butter.

9. Place the chicken mixture in the center of the square of stacked phyllo. Using an offset spatula, spread it into a flat, 6-inch circle. Starting with a corner, fold the edges of the phyllo up and over the filling, pleating the dough as you go. All the filling should be covered by the dough. Brush the top with the remaining butter.

10. Bake until golden brown and crisp, 45 to 50 minutes. Rest for at least 15 minutes, then serve warm or at room temperature. Dust with powdered sugar and cinnamon. To serve, use a sharp serrated knife to cut into wedges.

Note: Phyllo sheets come in various dimensions. If you can't find the size I'm using, don't fret. You ultimately want a 14-inch square of phyllo. If your sheets are larger, trim them to fit. If your sheets are smaller, use 12 sheets, staggering each as you lay them, so you end up with a wider square. The edges will be thinner than the middle, but once folded up and over the filling, you won't notice it at all.

**Broiler Lamb Kofta
with All the Fixin's**

Broiler Lamb Kofta with All the Fixin's

(Serves 4)

(Active: 1 hr.) | (Total: at least 7 hrs.)

(Intermediate) (Gluten-free)

For the lamb kofta:

1 large yellow onion, peeled

2 pounds (900 grams) ground lamb

2 teaspoons Diamond Crystal kosher salt

For the grated tomato sauce:

1 large tomato

1 garlic clove, finely grated

2 tablespoons extra-virgin olive oil

1 teaspoon sherry vinegar, plus more to taste

½ teaspoon Diamond Crystal kosher salt, plus more to taste

pinch of MSG (optional)

granulated sugar

For the onion salad:

1 medium red onion, thinly sliced

⅓ cup fresh parsley leaves and tender stems

¼ cup freshly squeezed lemon juice (about 2 lemons)

2 tablespoons sumac

½ teaspoon Diamond Crystal kosher salt

For the tahini sauce:

½ cup well-stirred tahini

¼ cup freshly squeezed lemon juice (about 2 lemons)

2 garlic cloves, finely grated

→ Koobideh is a Persian kebab made of ground meat kneaded with onion and pressed onto long, flat, sword-like skewers. It's traditionally cooked over the intense heat of very hot coals, charring the outside before the inside dries out. My husband's Iranian stepmother makes the best version I've ever tasted, and the key is high, dry heat. This broiler kofta aims to re-create those flavors and textures without a grill or special skewers. The meat mixture is like a sausage without the casing, so kneading it with salt and allowing everything to rest gives the proteins time to uncoil and reconfigure themselves for that satisfyingly springy texture. Keep the logs of lamb flat and thin, so they quickly cook through under the heat of the broiler without drying out. Just like a burger patty, the meat will plump after cooking, so press it out wider and flatter than the size you want your final kofta to be. The tahini sauce, grated tomato sauce, and sumac onion salad are the traditional sides you'll find with koobideh. If they feel like a lot of work, just make the sides you want.

---

1. **Mix the kofta:** On the large holes of a box grater, grate the onion into a medium bowl. Using your hands or a fine-mesh sieve, squeeze the pulp, wringing out as much liquid as you can, and transfer the pulp to a large bowl. Put the onion juice in an airtight container and set aside in the fridge (you will brush this on the kofta during broiling).

2. Add the ground lamb and salt to the onion pulp. Using your hands, knead the mixture, squeezing and folding it onto itself like bread dough, until homogeneous and springy, about 5 minutes. (There should be no distinguishable meat fibers left; it should be a uniform mass.) Tightly cover and rest in the fridge for at least 6 and up to 24 hours.

3. **Shortly before cooking the kofta, make the grated tomato sauce . . . :** Grate the tomato on the large holes of a box grater into a medium bowl and discard the skin. Add the garlic, oil, vinegar, salt, and MSG (if using), and whisk together. Taste and add sugar and more salt or vinegar as needed.

4. **. . . and the onion salad . . . :** In another medium bowl, toss together the red onion, parsley, lemon juice, sumac, and salt. Gently massage the mixture with your hands until the onion wilts.

5. **. . . and the tahini sauce:** In another medium bowl, whisk together the tahini, lemon juice, garlic, oil, and salt. Add water, 1 teaspoon at a time, until the consistency you desire. Taste and add salt as needed.

6. **Cook the kofta:** Position an oven rack 6 inches below the broiler element and set the broiler to high. Line a sheet pan with foil and place a wire rack on top.

252

1 tablespoon extra-virgin olive oil

½ teaspoon Diamond Crystal kosher salt, plus more to taste

To Finish:

1 tablespoon extra-virgin olive oil

flatbread, such as warm lavash or Perfectly Puffy Pitas (page 502), for serving

7. Divide the meat into 8 portions. Roll each portion into a 1-inch-thick log, then flatten it to a scant ½ inch thick and arrange on the prepared sheet pan.

8. To finish, mix the reserved onion juice with the 1 tablespoon olive oil and brush some on the top of the kofta. Place the sheet pan under the broiler and cook until crusty and deeply brown, 8 to 10 minutes. Flip, brush with more of the onion juice mixture, and cook until the other side is also crusty and browned, 6 to 8 minutes.

9. Set the kofta onto flatbread and rest for at least 5 minutes before serving alongside the tomato sauce, onion salad, and tahini sauce.

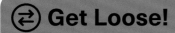 **Get Loose!**

Use the grated tomato sauce for . . .

• Pan con Tomate:
Split a baguette in half lengthwise and toast under the broiler until charred. Top with the tomato sauce, drizzle on extra-virgin olive oil, and sprinkle with flaky salt.

• Fresh Pasta Pomodoro:
Cook 8 ounces (225 grams) of pasta (any shape) in boiling salted water until mostly tender with a little bite at the core. Drain and return to the pot with the grated tomato sauce, 2 tablespoons unsalted butter, and ⅓ cup coarsely grated parmesan cheese. Stir constantly over low heat until the cheese and butter have melted. Serve right away.

Go to Brown Town

Monday Chicken Dinner for Winners

Serves 4

Active: 1 hr. | Total: 13 to 37 hrs.

Intermediate | Gluten-free

For the potatoes:

2 tablespoons Diamond Crystal
kosher salt, plus more as needed

2 pounds (about 900 grams) russet or
Yukon Gold potatoes, peeled and
cut into 2-inch chunks

For the chicken:

4 teaspoons Diamond Crystal kosher
salt

2 teaspoons powdered chicken
bouillon, like Knorr (optional)

1 teaspoon granulated sugar

One whole chicken (3½ to 4 pounds/
1.5 to 1.8 kilograms)

For roasting:

¼ cup plus 1 tablespoon olive oil

kosher salt

→ I know what you're thinking, you want me to make an ENTIRE roast chicken dinner complete with crispy potatoes and vegetables on a Monday night? Yes. It's all possible with some planning. When you've got time on Saturday or Sunday, boil your potatoes. Letting them chill in the fridge, uncovered, makes sure that they roast up extra crispy. While those potatoes are cooking, spatchcock and dry-brine your chicken. If you've never spatchcocked a chicken before, all you need are some kitchen shears to get the job done. Spatchcocked chickens are best for high-heat roasting because the legs get more direct heat and cook through before the breast dries out. Then Monday night, when you come home from work and you're miserable because its Monday, you've got a fridge full of prepped-out wonders just waiting to roast up crispy and golden for you.

I like to cook my chicken in a skillet, flipping it halfway through to make sure every bit is brown and golden. As a bonus the pan collects all the drippings and schmaltz (aka beautiful, golden chicken fat), perfect for cooking up any vegetable. Sear cut radishes in there, add grated carrots and dates, wilt down any green, and all you need to do is add a splash of water to make them their saucy, glazed, and most delicious selves.

HERE'S THE GAME PLAN:

- **1 to 2 days before (Saturday or Sunday, if you're making this for Monday)**
  - Peel, dice, and cook the potatoes.
  - Spatchcock and dry-brine the chicken.

- **1 hour before you want to eat (Monday night)**
  - Arrange the racks in the oven and heat a sheet pan on the top rack.
  - Toss the potatoes in oil and roast on the heated sheet pan.
  - Heat a skillet, add the chicken breast-side down, and roast in the oven on the bottom rack.
  - Flip the potatoes and chicken, then continue roasting.
  - Meanwhile, prep your veggies.
  - Remove the chicken and let it rest; cook your veggies in the chicken skillet.
  - Veggies and potatoes will be ready by the time the chicken has rested.

How to
Spatchcock &
Brine Chicken

How to Roast Chicken & Make Schmaltzy Veggies

For the schmaltzy vegetables:

aromatics, like chopped garlic, onion, or ginger (optional)

1 to 1½ pounds (450 to 680 grams) vegetables, halved, grated, chopped, or torn so they cook quickly (try halved Little Gem lettuce or baby bok choy; grated carrots, parsnips, or beets; halved radishes and their greens; chopped Swiss chard; broccoli florets and chopped stems; cherry tomatoes or chopped celery)

tender herbs (like dill, parsley, or cilantro), dried fruit (like torn dates or raisins), and/or freshly squeezed lemon juice (optional)

1. **Prep the potatoes:** In a medium pot, combine 2 quarts water, the salt, and potatoes and bring to a boil over medium-high heat. Reduce to a simmer and cook until the potatoes are cooked all the way through and starting to break apart on the surface, 30 to 40 minutes.

2. Drain the potatoes in a sieve and return them to the pot. Shake the pot to gently rough up their surfaces, and spread them out onto a plate or parchment-lined sheet pan. Refrigerate, uncovered, for as long as you brine the chicken.

3. **Meanwhile, prep the chicken:** In a small bowl, whisk together the salt, bouillon (if using), and sugar. Place the chicken on a cutting board, breast-side down. Using kitchen or poultry shears, cut along both sides of the backbone to remove it. Snip off the wingtips if you want. (You can save them both for stock or roast them alongside the chicken to gnaw on—the backbone is my favorite part.) Flip the bird and press firmly on the breast until it flattens and you hear the wishbone crack. Pat dry with paper towels.

4. Season the chicken with the dry brine, taking care to use all of it to evenly cover all of the chicken—in between the wings and the legs. (It may fall off, just scoop it back up and pat it on.) Transfer the chicken to a plate or (preferably) a wire rack set into a baking sheet (if you have the room) and refrigerate, uncovered, for at least 12 and up to 36 hours.

5. **When you're ready for dinner:** Position oven racks in the upper and lower thirds of the oven and heat to 450°F (230°C). Set a sheet pan into the top rack of the oven to heat.

6. **Roast the potatoes:** Transfer the potatoes to a medium bowl. Toss the potatoes with the ¼ cup oil and a big pinch of salt. Using the bowl, slide the potatoes into the hot pan that has been preheating in the oven. The potatoes should immediately sizzle. Roast until golden brown and crisp on the outside, 45 to 50 minutes, flipping the potatoes over at least once halfway through the cooking process. (Ideally, flip the potatoes over twice to make sure you get full 360-degree crunch.)

7. **Meanwhile, roast the chicken:** Heat a large cast-iron skillet over medium-high heat until slightly smoking (I've found a 3½ pound chicken fits just right in a 12-inch skillet). Add the 1 tablespoon oil and swirl to coat. Add the spatchcocked chicken, breast-side down, and press firmly to ensure maximum contact with the pan. (If you have a weight or small heavy skillet, place it on top to weight down the chicken for even better browning.) Slide the chicken and skillet into the lower rack in the oven and roast until the skin on the breast and thighs is golden brown and easily releases from the pan, about 20 minutes. →

8. Remove the skillet from the oven and carefully flip the chicken over using tongs so it is now breast-side up. Return to the oven and roast until the thickest part of the chicken breast and thigh register at least 160°F (71°C), 15 to 20 minutes. Transfer to a cutting board and rest for at least 10 minutes.

9. While the chicken rests, make the schmaltzy veggies: Heat the cast-iron skillet with the chicken drippings over medium heat. Add the aromatics (if you want) and cook, stirring frequently, until wilted, scraping up any browned bits with your spoon. Then add the veggies and cook: For halved veggies (like radishes or baby bok choy), let them cook undisturbed to develop some color. For grated, chopped, or torn veggies (like grated carrots, torn greens, or chopped broccoli), toss frequently to wilt. Add a splash of water and use a stiff spatula or wooden spoon to scrape up any browned bits and coat the vegetables. Taste and add salt if needed (the chicken fat and browned bits will be salty, so you may not need any). Level it up by finishing with torn tender herbs, dried fruit, and/or lemon juice.

10. Use a sharp knife to divide the chicken into drumsticks, thighs, breasts, and wings. Serve with the roast potatoes and veggies.

Note: Whenever you are moving something in and out of a hot oven, work as quickly as possible. Depending on the oven, the temperature can drop as much as 25°F every time you open the door.

Why Dry-Brine?

If you want a roast chicken with crisp skin *and* juicy meat, you cannot skip the dry brine. Thankfully, dry-brining is a cinch. Simply season your chicken in advance and allow it to sit, uncovered, in the refrigerator for at least 12 hours. Yes, you must plan, but you will be rewarded with the best roast chicken, and isn't that worth it? Over those 12-plus hours, the moisture from the chicken dissolves the salt, which is then absorbed by the chicken, while the cool air circulating in the fridge dries the skin for maximum browning.

The dissolved salt does a few amazing things: First off, it seasons the meat, not just on the surface, but to the bone. Second, it breaks down the fat beneath the skin, allowing it to render easily to achieve crisp and glassy skin. Finally (and most important), it tenderizes the muscle fibers, preventing them from contracting as much during cooking, and dissolves some proteins into a thick gel that retains moisture.

Chicken doesn't get to have all the fun. Dry-brining works wonders on any whole muscle protein, like duck breast, whole poultry, large roasts (pork, lamb, and beef), and even fish. Fish needs a much shorter dry-brine, between 45 minutes and 2 hours, while a big pork shoulder roast or whole turkey is best brined for 2 to 3 days. All a dry brine really needs is salt, but I love the combo of salt, sugar (to help with browning), and powdered chicken bouillon. Make a big batch of dry brine by combining (by volume): 4 parts kosher salt, 2 parts powdered chicken bouillon, and 1 part granulated sugar. You'll use it on everything, I promise!

How to
Carve Chicken

Broiler Turkey Meatballs

in Perky Puttanesca Sauce

(Serves 8)

(Active: 1 hr. | Total: at least 7 hrs.)

(Intermediate)

(Can be made gluten-free)

For the meatballs:

2 cups regular or gluten-free panko bread crumbs

1 cup heavy cream

3 tablespoons olive oil, plus more for oiling the meatballs

2 medium shallots, finely chopped

8 garlic cloves, finely chopped

5 anchovy fillets

2 pounds (900 grams) ground turkey

1 large egg

⅓ cup lightly packed fresh parsley leaves and tender stems, finely chopped

2 teaspoons chili flakes

2 teaspoons Diamond Crystal kosher salt

1 teaspoon dried oregano

For the puttanesca sauce:

¼ cup olive oil

4 pints (48 ounces/1.3 kilograms) cherry tomatoes

8 anchovy fillets

¼ cup drained capers

8 garlic cloves, thinly sliced

2 teaspoons chili flakes

2 teaspoons dried oregano

⅔ cup Castelvetrano olives, smashed, pitted, and torn

⅓ cup lightly packed fresh parsley leaves and tender stems, roughly chopped

→ Panade is a mixture of any carb-y crumbs and liquid, ranging from broken crackers and water to the panko and cream used here. It is the key to moist and tender meatballs, even if you start with lean ground meat or overcook them a touch. Take your time and thoroughly knead the meatball mixture together, which, as in the Broiler Lamb Kofta (page 252), is more like a sausage than the ground beef you gently patty together for a burger. Letting the meatball mixture rest before cooking gives the flavors time to deepen and the proteins time to uncoil and reconfigure themselves for the best flavor and texture.

1. Prep the meatballs: In a large bowl, combine the panko and cream, kneading it with your hands until the crumbs are broken down and the cream is well incorporated. Let sit for at least 5 minutes.

2. In a medium cast-iron or stainless steel skillet, heat the olive oil over medium-high heat until shimmering. Add the shallots, garlic, and anchovies and cook, stirring frequently, until the shallots are translucent and the anchovies have broken down, about 5 minutes. Scrape out of the skillet onto the panko/cream mixture and stir to combine.

3. Add the turkey, egg, parsley, chili flakes, salt, and oregano and knead together with your hands until completely homogeneous. Press plastic wrap directly onto the surface of the mixture (or transfer to an airtight container) and chill in the refrigerator for at least 6 hours and preferably 24 hours.

4. Cook the meatballs: Position an oven rack 8 to 12 inches below the broiler element and set the broiler to high.

5. Portion the meatball mixture with a #16 disher or a ¼-cup measure. Roll each one between your hands to form a smooth ball (dip your hands in cold water if the mixture sticks). Arrange on a sheet pan and rub each meatball with a thin layer of oil with your hands.

6. Place the meatballs in the oven and broil, flipping them over halfway through the cooking, until cooked through and browned, 14 to 16 minutes. (An instant-read thermometer should read at least 160°F/71°C at the center or when you cut one in half, no pink should remain.) If your broiler has hot spots, you may need to rotate the meatballs on the edges of the pan with ones in the center so they all cook evenly.

7. While the meatballs cook, prepare the puttanesca sauce: Heat a large Dutch oven or heavy pot over medium-high heat. Add the olive oil, cherry tomatoes, anchovy fillets, capers, garlic, chili flakes, and oregano. Cook, stirring constantly, until the cherry tomatoes begin to burst, 6 to 8 minutes. →

Broiler Turkey
Meatballs
(cont'd.)

To Serve:

pasta, crusty bread, or The Creamiest
   Polenta (page 124)

8. Once the tomatoes are tender, gently crush each one to release their juices. Reduce the heat to low, add the olives and parsley, partially cover, and gently simmer until the flavors meld, about 10 minutes.

9. Add the meatballs to the puttanesca sauce, stir gently to coat, and simmer, partially covered, for 5 minutes. Serve over pasta, polenta, or with crusty bread. (Store leftovers in the fridge for up to 5 days or freeze for 3 months.)

Seared Scallops with Pepperoni, Sungolds & Corn

(Serves 4)

(Active: 30 mins.)

(Total: 30 mins. to 2½ hrs.)

(Intermediate) (Gluten-free)

Ingredients:

4 ears corn, shucked

1 pound (450 grams) dry-packed U16 sea scallops

kosher salt

2 tablespoons neutral oil

2 garlic cloves, thinly sliced

2 ounces (56 grams) pepperoni, sliced into thin strips

2 cups Sungold or grape tomatoes (about 12 ounces/340 grams)

sugar (optional)

1 teaspoon dried oregano

½ to 1 teaspoon chili flakes

½ cup lightly packed fresh basil leaves, torn

finely grated parmesan cheese

extra-virgin olive oil

→ Scallops can be sold without any additives, called dry-packed, or after being treated with sodium tripolyphosphate, labeled as wet-packed. Treated scallops absorb moisture, increasing their weight and making them harder to sear. Always look for dry-packed scallops if your goal is a deep sear because as you know by now, moisture is the nemesis of golden brown color. Just like shrimp, scallops are sized according to how many make up a pound. If you're cooking scallops for the first time, look for big U16 scallops (each weigh about 1 ounce, so there are 16 per pound). Scallops are easy to overcook, so starting with bigger ones will make it easier to develop good color without drying them out.

1. Invert a small bowl into a large bowl. Working with one at a time, stand an ear of corn up on the inverted bowl. Use a sharp knife to shave the kernels off the cob. Then use the back of the knife to scrape out any corn milk from the cobs.

2. If the scallops have their abductor muscle still attached, tear off and discard. (It looks like a little flap stuck to the side of each scallop; they are often sold with this part already removed.) With a paper towel, pat the scallops dry. Lightly season both sides of the scallops with salt. Cook right away, or if you have time, set on a sheet pan fitted with a wire rack and place in the fridge for at least 45 minutes or up to 2 hours.

3. Heat a medium cast-iron skillet over medium-high heat until lightly smoking. Add the oil, swirl to coat, and place the scallops in the pan, making sure they are flat-side down. Cook, undisturbed, until one side is deeply golden brown, 1 to 2 minutes. Flip over and let the second side cook undisturbed for another minute, then remove to a plate, making sure the side with the best sear is facing up.

4. Add the garlic and pepperoni to the pan and cook, stirring frequently, until the pepperoni starts to crisp, about 2 minutes. Add the corn and corn milk and cook, stirring frequently, until the corn is plump, tender, and no longer tastes raw, about 2 minutes. Add the tomatoes and cook, stirring frequently, until slightly softened, about 3 minutes. Press the tomatoes with your spatula until they burst. Taste and season with salt (and sugar if the corn and tomatoes aren't sweet enough) as needed. Add the oregano and chili flakes. Place the corn mixture on a serving platter and top with the scallops. Garnish with torn basil, freshly grated parmesan, and olive oil. Serve immediately.

(Any) Steak & Salad Dinner

Serves 2

Active: varies | Total: varies

Intermediate | Gluten-free

For the marinated tomatoes:

2 medium heirloom or beefsteak tomatoes, cut into large chunks

3 tablespoons freshly squeezed lemon juice (about 1 lemon)

1 tablespoon sherry vinegar, plus more to taste

1 tablespoon extra-virgin olive oil

kosher salt

For the steak:

1 beef, pork, or lamb steak/chop (bone-in or boneless), at least 1 inch thick

kosher salt

neutral oil

2 to 4 tablespoons unsalted butter (use the larger amount for a bigger steak)

3 garlic cloves, smashed and peeled

3 sprigs fresh thyme

flaky salt

For the salad:

4 radishes, halved lengthwise and thinly sliced into half-moons

1 medium head romaine lettuce, torn into forkable pieces

½ cup lightly packed fresh tender herbs (such as dill, parsley, chives, basil, etc.), roughly chopped

→ When my husband, Ham, and I worked in restaurants, we didn't have much money or time to spend together, so our big splurge was a steak dinner for two. It's a fast way to feel fancy and, depending on the cut you choose, can be relatively affordable as well. (My favorite affordable steak is bavette; ask your butcher about it. It's incredibly flavorful, but lean and tough, so best cooked medium-rare to medium.) I'm keeping this recipe vague, just calling for "steak," because regardless of what meat—beef, pork, lamb, whatever—or cut you buy, they all cook the same way:

- Pat the steak (or chop) dry with paper towels to ensure a good sear.

- Season very liberally with kosher salt (use more salt than you think you'd need because it will fall off while cooking).

- Develop a brown crust in a hot cast-iron skillet with neutral oil, flipping every minute for even cooking.

- Add butter, garlic, and herbs and baste, gently riding medium heat until 5°F away from your desired internal temperature—meat continues to cook a few degrees while resting. (For steaks/chops more than 2 inches thick, finish cooking in the oven after a quick butter baste.)

- Rest for 5 to 15 minutes (depending on thickness), slice against the grain, season with flaky salt, and serve with brown butter drippings.

Just note that the thicker the steak, the more it will continue to cook after being removed from the heat and the longer time it will need to rest. Pull thick steaks off the heat when they are 10°F away from the target internal temperature and make sure they rest for at least 15 minutes before carving. While the steak rests, finish up a simple bright and crisp salad to counter all that butter-basted action. Because steak is such a special-occasion dish, an instant-read thermometer is a must. Depending on whether your steak is corn-fed, grass-fed, or grass-finished, a conventional or heritage breed, a tough or tender cut, medium-rare will feel different every time, so ditch that poke test. You have a computer in your pocket; you should have a thermometer in your kitchen drawer, too.

1. **Marinate the tomatoes:** In a large bowl, combine the tomatoes, lemon juice, vinegar, and olive oil. Use the back of a large spoon to gently crush the tomatoes so they release their juices. Toss together and season generously with kosher salt. Set aside to marinate while you cook the steak.

2. **Set up:** Heat a medium cast-iron skillet over medium-high heat. Fit a wire rack in a sheet pan and set aside. (If your steak is more than 2 inches thick, position a rack in the center of the oven and heat to 350°F/177°C.)

3. **Season:** Using paper towels, pat the meat dry. Season very liberally on all sides with kosher salt (it will look like too much salt, but don't worry—much of it falls off during searing). →

4. **Sear:** Once the pan is hot, add enough oil to liberally coat. (How do you know your pan is hot? As soon as you add the oil, it should spread across the surface and lightly smoke.) Carefully lay the steak/chop in the pan away from you and firmly press it down with a fish spatula. Flip the steak/chop every minute (literally, use a timer), pressing it down each time to ensure full contact with the pan.

5. **Temp:** Use an instant-read thermometer to check the meat's internal temperature. Once 20°F away from your target internal temperature, it's time to butter baste. (For thick cuts, you'll develop a crust before getting close to your target temperature. That's okay, it will finish in the oven. Begin basting once the crust is ready.)

6. **Baste (and roast in the oven for thick cuts):** Reduce the heat to medium and add the butter, garlic, and thyme to the side of the skillet that's farther from you. Tilt the skillet toward you and, using a large spoon, baste the steak with the butter and drippings. Flip the steak every minute and continue basting until 5°F away from your desired internal temperature. (For steaks over 2 inches thick, after basting both sides, transfer to the wire rack and finish cooking in the oven. Remove from the oven once 10°F away from your target temperature.)

7. **Rest:** Transfer the steak to the wire rack and pour the pan drippings over it. Set aside to rest for 5 to 15 minutes (depending on thickness).

8. **Finish the salad:** While the steak rests, add the radishes, romaine, and herbs to the tomatoes. Toss to combine. Taste and add salt or more vinegar if needed.

9. **Slice and serve:** Slice the rested steak against the grain and season with flaky salt. Serve alongside the salad and brown butter drippings.

Target Internal Temperatures

Rare	120°F or 49°C
Medium-Rare	130°F or 54°C
Medium	140°F or 60°C
Medium-Well	150°F or 66°C
Well	160°F or 71°C

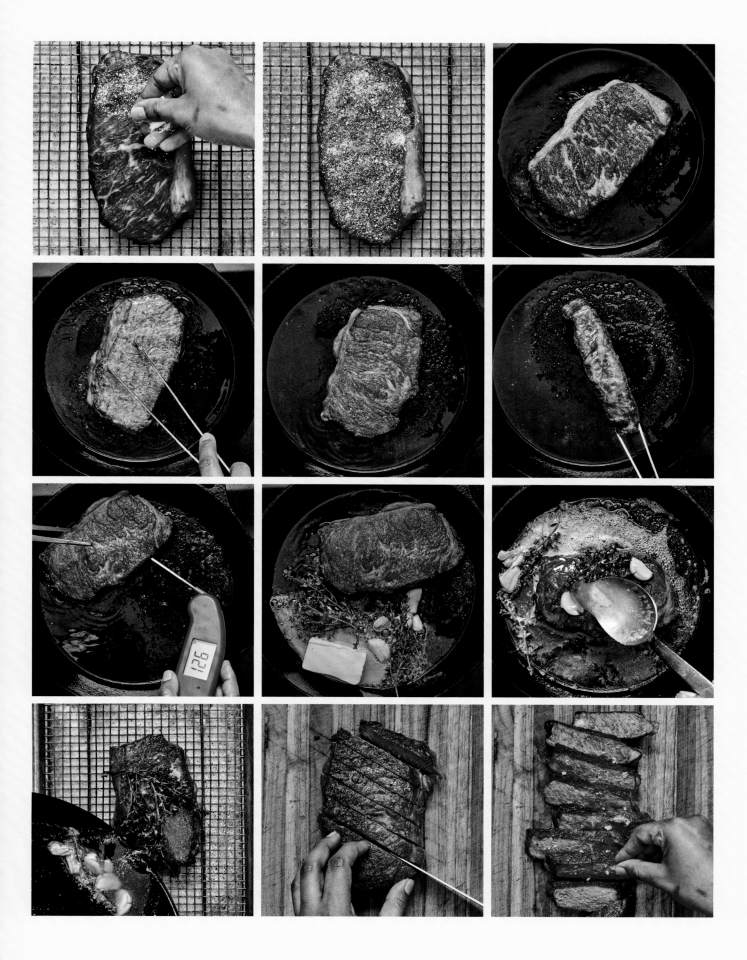

Baking
& Pastry
Lessons

All About Butter

And how to mix & cream it right

All About Butter

We have a Shiba Inu named Vito. Living with him feels less like owning a pet and more like having a fussy roommate who hates us. He's usually ignoring me from a corner of the room and gets lively only if there's butter around. No other food grabs his attention, whether we're talking about the fanciest freeze-dried, grass-fed lamb treat or a classic peanut butter KONG. But for butter, he instantly drops the I'm-too-good-to-be-your-dog act and gets up on both hind legs. I can't blame him. There's no other ingredient out there like butter. It's the only naturally occurring fat that's not a pure fat, but rather an emulsion of fat, water, and protein.

Oh, emulsions don't excite you? Well they should! Fluffy cake batters and buttercreams are only possible thanks to the magic of emulsion, keeping the water and fat hooked up and happy. Unlike liquid fats, like olive oil or peanut oil, butter is flexible and bendy. This lets you whip and cream it full of teeny air bubbles that translate to chewy, crispy, and crumbly cookies. At the right temperature, you can literally fold butter into doughs that bake up into flaky and light pastries. It's these unique qualities that make butter a foundational ingredient for many of the pastries and baked goods we know and love. Vito is right, it is something to get excited about, that's why I'm starting the sweet side of this cookbook with butter. In this chapter I'm going to give you the full lowdown on butter—what it is, why it's awesome, and what kind to buy. Then we'll get into the different mixing methods and best practices when making batters and doughs that rely heavily on butter.

But before we get baking . . .

276

What Exactly Is Butter?

Whole milk is a mixture of water, milk fat, and milk solids, which include proteins, lactose (milk sugar), and several vitamins and minerals. It's not the most stable emulsion, similar to the oil and vinegar in a simple dressing. As it sits, the fat-rich cream rises to the top. However, milk fat is unique because, unlike that oil and vinegar dressing, the fat never entirely breaks out into a straight-up oil slick. Instead, it separates into cream, which is just milk with more fat concentrated in it. That's because each milk fat globule is surrounded by phospholipids—two-sided molecules that have equal affinity for both fat and water. The phospholipids' fat-favoring side attaches to the fat globules while their water-loving side keeps the fats flowing freely in milk and cream, rather than clumping together. In order to make butter, we've got to get those phospholipids out of the way.

As cream sloshes around in a churn, some of the phospholipids protecting the fat globules are sloughed off and the milk fat begins to group together, trapping air bubbles and thickening into fluffy whipped cream. Keep churning and more phospholipids are moved out of the way so the milk fat can clump together into butter, squeezing out most of the water. The liquid that's left behind is buttermilk. After the buttermilk is drained off, the butter is kneaded in cold water to rinse off any residual buttermilk for a longer shelf life.

What we have left is still an emulsion of fat, protein, and water, but we've turned that emulsion inside out. Whole milk starts out with about 4% fat dispersed throughout what is mostly water—an oil-in-water emulsion. Heavy cream has between 35% to 40% fat, still dispersed throughout the water. But with butter, we changed the game. Clocking in at 80% to 86% fat, butter is a water-in-oil emulsion with the water dispersed throughout the fat.

Types of Butter

Salted vs. Unsalted Butter
This one's easy: One butter has salt added while the other doesn't. For all cooking and baking, I prefer to use unsalted butter, which gives me full control over seasoning. If all you have is salted butter, be sure to cut back on some of the salt in the recipe.

Sweet Cream Butter

This twentieth-century addition to the world of butter was made possible only by the advent of the centrifugal cream separator. Because cream could then be separated before the milk had time to culture, that cream could be churned into a mild, uncultured butter. Sweet cream butter is milky in flavor and ironically, since it's the butter I grew up with, tastes nostalgic for a relatively brand-new product.

Cultured Butter

In the past, cultured butter was made with cream that spontaneously fermented thanks to the countless wild bacteria present in the environment. Nowadays, culturing is a very controlled process. Specific cultures are added to the cream after skimming or to the butter after churning. Every brand has its own unique process and resulting level of tang, aroma, and funk.

Plant-Based Butter

What does butter add to your cooking and baking? Well, because it is at least 80% fat, butter does what fat does—helps keep cookies tender and cakes moist, and transfers heat, so that bread, vegetables, and proteins can evenly brown. The bit of water in butter helps aerate cookie doughs and emulsify cake batters. Many plant-based butters have gotten that emulsion of fat and water down, but what they are missing (for now) is flavor.

Like I mentioned before, it's the emulsion of fat, water, proteins, minerals, and vitamins that makes butter truly unique, and, I believe, irreplaceable. The milk solids in butter brown and toast when you bake or cook with it, adding its signature toffee depth to everything. Unique aromatic compounds from the enzymes and minerals in butter give it its milky and butterscotch-y taste. Plant-based products have come a long way in a very short time, so who knows, maybe soon there will be a brand with solids that brown and toast and whip just like the real thing. For now, feel free to swap in plant-based butter (my favorite brand is Miyoko's) in any recipe that doesn't require browned butter. Just be aware that you'll miss out on some flavor, and the texture might not be quite the same.

Temperature Matters

I understand the urge to zap a stick of butter in the microwave to quickly soften it, or even slam cold butter around in the mixer until it looks creamy. Who wouldn't want to shorten the distance between themselves and dessert? However, there is a difference between butter that has had the time to sit and evenly come to a perfectly pliable room temperature and one that's faking it. Room-temperature butter, specifically butter that is between 65° and 70°F (18° to 21°C) throughout, is soft and flexible. You can easily smush it around with a spatula, but it's not so warm that the delicate emulsion of fat, protein, and water has broken. It's the ideal texture for whipping up light and trapping tons of air bubbles. When you warm butter in the microwave, it heats unevenly, resulting in pockets of cold and melted, broken butter, with maybe some parts that are just right. This stuff will never, *ever* get as light or fluffy as the real-deal, let-it-sit-and-hang-out, room-temp butter.

Room-temperature butter is vital to any recipe that calls for mixing butter and sugar together until light and doubled in volume, a process called creaming. After a minute in a mixer, softened butter and sugar will look creamy and smooth, but don't stop here. Keep going for 4 to 6 minutes and watch it transform, becoming pale, less gritty, and almost like a glossy buttercream. Why is this fluffy-city moment so important? Creaming makes thin, crunchy cookies light and crisp rather than dense and hard, it gives soft cookies chew, and makes cakes light and tender. Not every recipe benefits from a long creaming, so take note of the time and visual cues for each individual recipe. Melted butter makes my Add-Anything Drop Cookies (page 294) dense and fudgy, while cold butter is key to flaky laminated pastries, like my Rough Puff Pastry (page 324).

To soften butter:
Cut however much you need into 1-tablespoon pieces and lay them out on a plate at cool room temperature for about 30 minutes.

Are you a planner? Leave the butter wrapped and whole out at room temperature the night before you plan to use it. When I'm baking a lot, I just have pounds of butter waiting for me on a sheet pan in a cool room for up to 48 hours.

Hello, My Name Is Sohla, and I Was a Chronic Undermixer

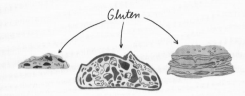

For some reason, when it comes to baking, everyone is so worried about overmixing (I certainly was). But what does that even mean? My theory? I think we all grew up making pancakes and brownies from a box that stressed the hell out of us with their directions that screamed, "Do not overmix! Lumps are okay!" Relax, brownies. What we're really worried about is gluten, the stuff that makes pizza chewy and people in LA scatter, but what is it?

There are two main proteins in wheat: glutenin and gliadin. In flour they're like dried sea monkeys, waiting for a splash of water to wake them up. Once water comes along, the glutenin and gliadin hook up to create a stretchy and elastic protein network called gluten. Agitation from mixing or kneading makes the protein network stronger, but with enough time and hydration, gluten can get busy all on its own, too. (Read more about gluten in So What the Heck Is Gluten? on page 479.) Gluten gives cookies their chew, gives bread dough the strength to capture every yeasty burp, and makes puff pastry crisp and flaky. We need it in most baking, otherwise gluten-free baking wouldn't require a mix of so many starches and gums that we have to buy a pricey blend to come close to the texture that wheat flour alone can deliver.

Okay, so there are times when overmixing is a problem, like with pancakes. But not everything is a pancake and there are many times when undermixing is exactly the move that'll lead to a dense, dry, and sad birthday cake. Depending on how butter is incorporated into a dough or batter, it can wrap itself around flour granules, slowing down gluten development and requiring extra-long mixing times. What we need is the right amount of gluten development to give our cakes the strength to rise. Instead of worrying about over- or undermixing, let's talk about the three cake-mixing methods in this chapter and how to stir each just the right amount.

The Muffin Method: minimal mixing, high risk of gluten development

In one bowl, you assemble your dry team: Traditionally this includes the flour, leavening, and salt. If there's

Hello, My Name Is Sohla, and I Was a Chronic Undermixer (cont'd.)

anything else dry, like cocoa powder or spices, it's whisked into the flour as well. In another bowl you assemble your wet team: eggs, oil, melted butter, milk, extracts, and sugar. (Yes, sugar is considered a "wet" ingredient because it moistens and hydrates baked goods.) No stable emulsion is formed between fat and water, and the flour is not protected by sugar or fat. Because of this, once the wet and dry teams join forces, they race to form gluten. Too much agitation, or simply letting the batter sit for too long before baking, will quickly form tough gluten bonds resulting in a dense, tough, and shrunken cake.

For batters mixed using this method, overmixing is a serious issue. Use a stiff spatula to fold the dry into the wet only until all of the flour is hydrated. Batters mixed with the muffin method tend to be thin and pourable, baking up with significant doming and with an open crumb. All the lift comes from chemical leavening, so you usually don't need to worry about having room-temperature butter and eggs, making it a great method if you want to make cake on the fly.

The Creaming Method: moderate mixing, moderate risk of gluten development

Here you start by mixing room-temperature butter and sugar until fluffy and light in a process called creaming—this takes longer than you think. For creamed cakes, the majority of the lift comes from the pockets of air developed during creaming. The leavening works to expand those bubbles while baking, but if you don't produce enough of them during this first step, your cake will bake up dense. For smaller batches of batter, you can beat enough air into the butter with a hand mixer, but for a larger batch, like the Base Yellow Cake (page 530), nothing but a stand mixer will get you there. Be sure to scrape your paddle and bowl so the butter and sugar are creamed evenly, otherwise dense pockets of butter can erupt out of the cake while baking.

Next, room-temperature eggs are added one at a time. If you add the eggs too quickly or use cold eggs, the mixture will not emulsify properly. Remember, butter is mostly fat, while eggs are mostly water, so they need coaxing to come together. Once the eggs are evenly

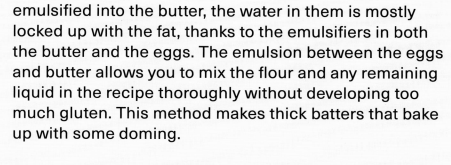

emulsified into the butter, the water in them is mostly locked up with the fat, thanks to the emulsifiers in both the butter and the eggs. The emulsion between the eggs and butter allows you to mix the flour and any remaining liquid in the recipe thoroughly without developing too much gluten. This method makes thick batters that bake up with some doming.

The Reverse-Creamed Method: extended mixing, low risk of gluten development

This is a modern method that was developed in the early twentieth century for industrial cake making, so a stand mixer is required. (Sorry, hand mixers can't handle this much action.) It works only for cakes that have a higher ratio of sugar to flour, which prevents too much gluten from developing during the long mixing times. It results in a rich cake with a tight and tender crumb, with minimal doming and a long shelf life. I grew up eating Little Debbie and Betty Crocker cakes, so this is hands down my favorite style of cake.

To start, the dry ingredients are combined with sugar and room-temperature butter until the fat completely disappears. The softened butter coats each granule of flour with fat, giving it a protective layer against the water, and distributes the sugar to prevent a strong gluten network from forming. Cold butter won't disperse evenly, while melted butter will clump, so room-temperature butter is vital. Be sure to stop and scrape the paddle and the bowl so the butter is evenly mixed, or you'll end up with tunnels and batter erupting out of the cake pan.

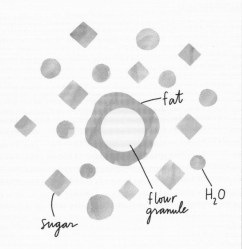

Next, the room-temperature liquids are added in phases while mixing for anywhere from 30 seconds to 3 minutes, depending on the batch size. Extended mixing emulsifies and aerates the batter. It should look mousse-y and smooth. If you don't mix the batter long enough, or if you use cold liquids, it will look broken and greasy, and bake up dense and dry. Proper mixing time and ingredient temperatures are especially important with this advanced method. But get it right and you'll have an exceptionally delicate cake that stays moist for days, perfect for baking in advance for special occasions.

Basic Shortbread
(That You Can Make Unbasic)

(Makes 16 cookies)

(Active: 20 mins. | Total: 1 hr.)

(Easy)

(Vegetarian (can be made vegan))

Ingredients:

113 grams (1 stick) unsalted butter or vegan butter, cut into cubes, at room temperature

50 grams sugar: powdered (7 tablespoons) or granulated (¼ cup)

¼ teaspoon Diamond Crystal kosher salt

120 grams (1 cup) all-purpose flour

Special Equipment:

parchment paper

stand mixer (or medium bowl and stiff silicone spatula)

offset spatula

bench scraper (or knife)

skewer (or fork)

→ I'm starting the baking and pastry section with butter, because without butter, most cookies, cakes, and pies wouldn't be possible as we know them now. And the ultimate expression of butter is shortbread. Shortbread is just a way to eat butter—held together with flour and sweetened with sugar. Best of all, once you've got a shortbread recipe you trust and love, the possibilities are endless. Shortbread can take on many forms and flavors, from the classic finger-shaped crumbly Scottish style to vanilla and citrus scented, and even loaded with chocolate chips.

The simple combo of butter, sugar, and flour can shape-shift based on minor adjustments to the ratios and on additions like eggs or starch. I'm letting you decide whether to use powdered sugar, for a more tender cookie, or granulated, for more crunch. Once you get comfortable, play around: Try swapping 1 tablespoon of flour for cornstarch or rice flour for a melt-in-your-mouth texture. Add an egg yolk for chewy cookie vibes. Don't forget to check out all the variations below so you can get inspired and develop your very own shortbread recipe.

1. **Set up:** Position a rack in the center of the oven and heat to 325°F (163°C). Line a sheet pan with parchment paper.

2. **Make the dough:** In a stand mixer fitted with the paddle (or in a medium bowl with a stiff silicone spatula), combine the butter, sugar, and salt and beat until creamy and combined, scraping down the paddle and the bowl once during mixing. (Don't overmix—we don't want to incorporate air into the cookie dough.)

3. Add the flour and mix until it comes together into a dough. (Don't worry about overmixing here; there's so much butter, the dough will not become tough.)

4. **Form the dough and score:** Gather the dough into a ball. Place on the lined sheet pan and use your hands and an offset spatula to flatten it into a round about 6 inches across and a scant ½ inch thick. Using a lightly moistened bench scraper or knife, cut the round into 16 wedges.

5. **Bake and cut:** Bake until set, dry to the touch, and lightly browned around the edges, about 25 minutes.

6. Remove from the oven and reduce the oven temperature to 300°F (150°C). Using a bench scraper or knife, cut the shortbread once again along the same lines. Use a skewer or fork to decoratively prick the top of the shortbread. Return to the oven and bake until the center is barely golden, 10 to 12 minutes. Allow the shortbread to cool completely on the sheet pan. Stored in an airtight container (with a desiccant if you have one), shortbread will keep at room temperature for 2 weeks.

Note: Shortbread, like all butter-rich cookies, are always best the day after they are baked.

Two Ways to Form Cookie Dough

What the Hell Happened?

- *Did your shortbread bake up with dimples and/or bubbles across the surface?* The butter was too cold and not properly mixed with the sugar.

- *Does your shortbread have ridges along the edges instead of baking flat?* The butter and sugar were overmixed, incorporating too much air into the cookie dough.

- *Is the shortbread chewy in the center?* It was underbaked.

- *Did the fat melt out of the cookie during baking, leaving you with a greasy and tough shortbread?* The dough was undermixed, so not all the flour was evenly combined.

⇄ Get Loose!

- Add citrus zest (lemon, lime, or grapefruit), finely minced fresh woody herbs (like rosemary, thyme, or sage), spices (cracked toasted coriander, black peppercorns, cured sumac, or fennel seeds), and extracts (vanilla or almond) while mixing the butter, sugar, and salt.

- Swap out *up to* ¼ cup of the flour for an equal *volume* of another powdery addition, like matcha, cocoa, wheat germ, rice flour, or oat flour to change up the texture and flavor.

- Swap out *up to* half the sugar for an equal *weight* of another granulated sugar, like brown sugar, grated gur or piloncillo, or date sugar. Be aware that darker sugars will cause the shortbread to brown deeply and greatly change its texture (which can be super fun).

- Add mix-ins just when the flour is nearly incorporated, like chopped chocolate, nuts, dried fruit, pretzels, or potato chips.

- Roll the dough into a log, chill until firm, then brush the exterior with beaten egg white and roll in sugar, sprinkles, seeds, or finely chopped nuts before slicing and baking.

Some shortbread inspiration:

Creamsicle Shortbread

Add the seeds scraped from ½ vanilla bean, ½ teaspoon vanilla extract, and 1 teaspoon grated orange zest while mixing the butter, sugar, and salt.

Sweet & Salty Nigella Shortbread

This is my favorite variation and a take on a classic Bangladeshi tea cookie. Increase the kosher salt to ½ teaspoon and add 1½ teaspoons nigella seeds while mixing the butter, sugar, and salt.

Chocolate Chip Shortbread

Substitute half of the sugar for dark brown sugar. Add ½ teaspoon vanilla extract while mixing the butter, sugar, and salt. Add 112 grams (¾ cup) chopped semisweet or dark chocolate after the flour is mostly incorporated.

Slice & Bake Shortbread

After mixing the cookie dough, form it into a log using parchment paper or plastic wrap. For circular cookies, chill the log as it is. For triangular or rectangular cookies, flatten the sides of the log using a bench scraper. Wrap tightly and chill in the refrigerator for up to 3 days or in the freezer for 1 month.

   When ready to bake, slice crosswise into ¼-inch-thick slabs with a sharp knife, giving the log a quarter turn after each slice to maintain the shape of the log. (If the dough cracks, let it soften slightly at room temperature, then proceed with slicing.) Arrange the cookies on a parchment-lined sheet pan spaced 1 inch apart and bake at 350°F (177°C) until set, dry, and barely golden around the edges, 12 to 15 minutes.

Basic Crumble
(That You Can Make Unbasic)

(Makes about 1½ cups)

(Active: 10 mins. | Total: 25 mins.)

(Easy)

(Vegetarian (can be made vegan))

Ingredients:

90 grams (¾ cup) all-purpose flour

55 grams (¼ cup packed) light or dark
brown sugar

35 grams (⅓ cup) old-fashioned rolled
oats

¼ teaspoon Diamond Crystal kosher
salt

¼ teaspoon baking powder

56 grams (4 tablespoons) unsalted
butter or vegan butter, melted

→ Making a crumble is so freaking easy and has saved me countless times when I needed to whip up a fast dessert. You can use it to give a pie or cake extra texture, roll cookies in, or be the star of the dessert itself. Get creative and use it to top grilled pineapple, stewed apples, ice cream, or yogurt. This ratio is just a starting point, but after you've got a few crumbles under your belt, it is one of those rare sweet treats that can easily be eyeballed. You want the mixture to be relatively dry so that it bakes up crisp and, of course, crumbly. Too much butter or sugar can get in the way of that, but don't be shy to play around, and be sure to check out the crumble riffs that follow.

---

1. In a medium bowl, use your hands to toss together the flour, brown sugar, oats, salt, and baking powder, breaking up any brown sugar clumps with your fingers. Add the melted butter and rub it into the dry mixture with your fingers until it holds together in large clumps when squeezed in your palms. (Alternatively, you can mix the crumble in a stand mixer fitted with the paddle.) The unbaked crumble will keep in the refrigerator for 5 days and frozen for 2 months.

2. Bake on top of or in another dessert or spread onto a parchment-lined sheet pan and bake at 350°F (177°C) until dry and lightly browned, tossing once during cooking, 12 to 15 minutes. Baked crumble will keep at room temperature for 1 week (with a desiccant if you have one) or frozen for 2 months.

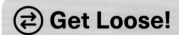 **Get Loose!**

- Swap out *up to ¼ cup* of the flour for an equal *volume* of another absorbent powdery ingredient, such as cocoa, masa harina, cornmeal, or ground crackers.

- Swap the brown sugar for an equal *weight* of any other granulated sugar, such as coconut sugar, grated piloncillo, or maple sugar.

- Swap out the rolled oats for an equal *volume* of another mix-in, such as chopped nuts or seeds, shredded coconut, crushed pretzels, potato chips, or crackers.

- Add ground spices to taste, such as cinnamon, nutmeg, cardamon, and/or star anise.

288

💡 Some crumble inspiration:

Try out these crumble variations with the Mix & Match Jammy Cookie Bars (page 290), Fruity-Doodle Cookies (page 297), or as a topping for ice cream, pie, yogurt, layering in cake, and whatever else you can dream up. For all these, use the same quantities of flour, salt, and baking powder as the basic crumble (except the corny crumble). Some quantities are measured by volume and others by weight. When making swaps in baking you need to use both because different sugars, flours, and starches have various densities.

	Swap the brown sugar for:	Swap the oats for:	Swap the fat for:	Other:
Funfetti Crumble	55 grams granulated sugar	⅓ cup rainbow sprinkles	Keep same	Add ½ teaspoon clear (imitation) vanilla
Brown Butter Cinnamon Pecan Crumble	Keep same	⅓ cup finely chopped pecans	56 grams (4 tablespoons) butter (not vegan), browned	Add 2 teaspoons water and 2 teaspoons ground cinnamon
Matcha Almond Crumble	55 grams granulated sugar	⅓ cup sliced almonds	Keep same	Add 2 teaspoons matcha
Maple Coconut Crumble	55 grams maple sugar	⅓ cup unsweetened shredded coconut	28 grams (2 tablespoons) unsalted butter and 28 grams (2 tablespoons) virgin coconut oil	—
Corny Crumble	Keep same	⅓ cup crushed Fritos	Keep same	Swap ¼ cup flour for ¼ cup masa harina

Mix & Match Jammy Cookie Bars

(Makes 16 bars)

(Active: 30 mins. | Total: 1½ hrs.)

(Easy)

(Vegetarian (can be made vegan))

Ingredients:

softened butter or cooking spray for the pan

dough from Basic Shortbread (page 284) or any of the variations (page 287), at room temperature

200 grams (⅔ cup) jam, jelly, or preserves

kosher salt

unbaked Basic Crumble (page 288) or any of the variations (page 289), at room temperature

Special Equipment:

8-inch square metal brownie pan

parchment paper

offset spatula (or spoon)

skewer (or fork)

bench scraper (or knife)

→ When Ham and I had our restaurant, Hail Mary, one of the biggest selling items was the house-made Pop-Tarts. I filled delicate and buttery sablée dough with jam made from seasonal fruit and topped them off with rose-scented sprinkles that I'd hand-piped one at a time. And I absolutely hated everything about them.

They would sell out the second we opened our doors, forcing me to impose a strict one-Pop-Tart-per-guest rule. I couldn't train anyone to make them right. The cooks would roll the dough too thick, make them crooked, not add enough filling, or drench them in icing. And God forbid they sprinkle the sprinkles! You know I carefully placed each sprinkle on one at a time with surgical tweezers. All alone, after the staff went home, I'd build, bake, and frost every single Pop-Tart we sold, all while becoming increasingly filled with resentment and hate. We sold them for 5 dollars each—that didn't even cover the cost of the butter and fruit (we weren't in business long).

As soon as many of you learned I was writing a cookbook, I was inundated with Pop-Tart recipe requests. Sorry, guys, it's not happening. I don't make Pop-Tarts anymore because they are stupid. There, I said it. These jammy bars take a fraction of the effort and fill me with no hate, while tasting exactly the same! It's all about that butter and jam, one of the greatest food combinations of all time. Buttery shortbread gets smothered with jam and topped with crumble. No bitter late nights required. Get creative with this easy-peasy recipe, and if you really want a Pop-Tart, try the strawberry variation on page 293.

1. **Set up:** Position a rack in the center and of the oven and heat to 325°F (163°C). Grease an 8-inch square metal cake pan with butter or cooking spray. Line the pan with one long sheet of parchment cut to cover the bottom and two sides. Smooth the parchment with your hands, creasing it into the corners for a snug fit.

2. **Bake the base:** Using your hands and an offset spatula or the back of a spoon, press the shortbread dough evenly into the pan. Using a skewer or fork, prick all over to help the shortbread bake evenly. Bake until lightly browned and the surface feels set and dry, about 25 minutes. Cool until firm but still slightly warm, about 10 minutes (so it's easier to spread the jam).

3. **Top the shortbread and bake:** Dollop the jam all over the baked shortbread crust and evenly spread with the offset spatula or the back of the spoon. Very lightly sprinkle with kosher salt. Clump and scatter the crumble evenly over the top. Return the pan to the oven and bake until lightly golden, about 25 minutes.

4. **Cut and cool:** Cool for 10 minutes, then use a bench scraper or knife to divide into 16 bars while still warm, wiping the blade clean between cuts. Cool completely in the pan. Stored in an airtight container, the bars will last at room temperature for 1 week and in the freezer for 1 month. (Reheat frozen bars in a toaster oven or under the broiler.) →

Mix & Match Jammy Cookie Bars (cont'd.)

Note: This recipe can be doubled and made in a 9 × 13-inch metal cake pan; no adjustments needed to the bake time. I don't recommend baking these in a 9 × 9-inch pan. The layers will be too thin and won't hold together.

Missing Cookies?

Ever baked a batch of cookies, following the recipe to a T, only to end up with fewer cookies than the stated yield? Of course there's the obvious thing that could have gone awry: Your cookies were rolled thicker or portioned larger than the recipe. Then there's the sneaky way to accidentally decrease your yield: undercreaming! The step of creaming together fat and sugar or fat, sugar, and eggs isn't just about mixing stuff together really well. You're also aerating the mixture, adding volume and lightness to your dough and ultimately, making more cookies. Undercreaming a cake can be disastrous, causing it to collapse, become gummy and dense, or even resulting in pockets of fat that erupt straight out of it. With a cookie, it's less noticeable. You might have cookies that are too dense or spread too much, or you might end up with a bit less dough and fewer cookies. Take note of the times in recipes that call for creaming. Butter and sugar might look creamed after 1 minute, but if the recipe is telling you to cream for 4 to 6, there's a reason for it and you should keep going for the full amount of time.

Scrape!

I know what you're thinking, "You want me to stop and scrape the paddle how many times?!" Yes, it's a real pain and adds so much time to the recipe, but stopping to scrape your paddle and bowl is the difference between an okay cake and one that'll have friends and family gasp, "You made this!?" It's most visibly noticeable when creaming butter and sugar. Let the mixer go for 6 minutes without scraping, then stop to take a peek. Among all that airy butter and sugar are occasional pockets that look dense and thick. That's all it takes to create tunnels, erupting batter, or a gummy bottom layer. The same thing is happening when you're mixing in your eggs, flour, and anything else. Uneven mixing is the root of most cake and cookie issues, and to solve them, all you gotta do is scrape!

Some jammy bar inspiration:

Use these adjustments and the Shortbread variations (page 287) and Basic Crumble variations (page 289) to mix things up.

	Shortbread Base	Filling	Crumble	Extras
Strawberry Pop-Tarts Bars	Basic Shortbread (page 284)	Strawberry jam	Funfetti Crumble (page 289)	Icing: Mix 56 grams (½ cup) sifted powdered sugar, 40 grams (2 tablespoons) strawberry jam, and a pinch of salt. Drizzle over cooled bars.
Chocolate Date Pecan Bars	Chocolate Chip Shortbread (page 287)	Date puree	Brown Butter Cinnamon Pecan Crumble (page 289)	Drizzle cooled bars with melted dark chocolate
Citrus Bars	Creamsicle Shortbread (page 287)	Orange marmalade	Basic Crumble (page 288)	
Matcha Lemon Bars	Basic Shortbread (page 284)	Lemon Curd (page 417)	Matcha Almond Crumble (page 289)	

Add-Anything Drop Cookies

Makes 18 to 26 cookies (depending on quantity of mix-ins)

Active: 20 mins. | Total: 45 mins.

Easy | Vegetarian

Ingredients:

113 grams (1 stick) unsalted butter or vegan butter, melted

150 grams (¾ cup) granulated sugar

107 grams (½ cup packed) light or dark brown sugar

1¼ teaspoons Diamond Crystal kosher salt

½ teaspoon baking powder

½ teaspoon baking soda

1 large egg (about 55 grams), straight from the fridge

1½ teaspoons pure vanilla extract

200 grams (1⅔ cups) all-purpose flour

½ cup to 3 cups mix-ins of your choice (see Mix-In Ideas, page 295), plus more for garnish

Special Equipment:

sheet pans

parchment paper

#40 cookie scoop (or 2 spoons)

fish spatula

wire rack

→ This recipe is for when you want cookies instantly. No planning ahead for softened butter or room-temperature eggs, no creaming butter and sugar until fluffy, and no need to even leave the house for specific ingredients. Have fun and stir in whatever you want—M&M's, crushed pretzels, peanuts, potato chips, mini marshmallows, rolled oats, chocolate, and raisins. Your pantry is the limit! Packing the cookie dough with lots of big mix-ins will give you a hunkier cookie. Or keep it chill and finely chopped, for uniform and flatter cookies. Either way, they will be delicious and ready in a snap. Melted whole butter give these cookies a chewy and dense texture, a great contrast for lots of crunchy additions. If you get *really* crazy with the mix-ins and the dough doesn't seem like it wants to hold together, pop it in the fridge to chill and try forming the cookies after an hour. It's incredible just how much you can pack in!

1. **Set up:** Heat the oven to 375°F (190°C). Line two sheet pans with parchment paper.

2. **Make the dough:** In a medium bowl, using a stiff silicone spatula, stir together the melted butter, granulated sugar, brown sugar, salt, baking powder, and baking soda until the mixture looks like wet sand.

3. Add the egg and vanilla and stir until smooth and evenly combined. (If you have time, let this mixture sit for 30 minutes, stirring twice. This dissolves some of the sugar and results in a chewier cookie.)

4. Add the flour and stir until evenly incorporated and the mixture comes together into a soft dough. Add the mix-ins and stir until evenly distributed. (If there are a lot of mix-ins, you may need to fold and smash the dough with the spatula to evenly mix it.)

5. **Portion and bake:** Using a #40 cookie scoop or 2 spoons, divide the dough into 2-tablespoon portions (30 to 35 grams each, depending on mix-ins). Roll into a ball and flatten each portion slightly into a 1-inch-thick disk. Garnish with extra mix-ins. Do not chill the dough before baking (unless there are so many mix-ins it's not holding together)—these cookies are best baked the same day the dough is mixed.

6. Arrange the cookies on the prepared sheet pan spacing them 1½ inches apart. Bake until golden brown around the edges and just set in the center, 11 to 16 minutes. (Bake time greatly varies with the amount and type of mix-ins. Bake one cookie as a tester if you want to be sure.) Using a fish spatula, immediately transfer to a wire rack to cool. Stored in an airtight container at room temperature, cookies keep for 3 days.

**Frito Marshmallow
Cookies**

 Mix-In Ideas

Lisa Frank Cookies	Frito Marshmallow Cookies	Spiced Oatmeal Pecan Date Cookies
This is the recipe in this book that I make the most. It's what I take to sets before a shoot, the rare in-person meeting, podcast recordings, and every dinner party. I buy mini M&M's in bulk so I'm always prepared. I love how over-the-top sweet and nostalgic they are, but be warned, they are ridiculously sugary.	The marshmallows burst out of the cookie during baking, leaving lacy caramel puddles throughout. This works best with Kraft Jet-Puffed mini marshmallows.	These are Ham's favorite cookie. They are chunky and hearty from all the mix-ins and warm spices.

Lisa Frank Cookies:
- Add 1 teaspoon clear (imitation) vanilla extract and ¼ teaspoon almond extract in addition to the pure vanilla extract.
- Stir in ¼ cup rainbow sprinkles and ½ cup mini M&M's.
- After portioning the dough, roll in more sprinkles and top with extra mini M&M's.

Frito Marshmallow Cookies:
- Stir in 1 cup each chopped dark chocolate, lightly crushed Fritos, and mini marshmallows.
- Sprinkle with flaky salt.

Spiced Oatmeal Pecan Date Cookies:
- Use dark brown sugar. Add 1 teaspoon ground cinnamon, ½ teaspoon ground ginger, and ¼ teaspoon ground nutmeg to the butter and sugar.
- Stir in 1 cup each toasted rolled oats, salted toasted pecans (roughly chopped), and chopped pitted dates.

Fruity-Doodle Cookies

(Makes about 24 cookies)

(Active: 30 mins. | Total: 1 hr.)

(Easy) (Vegetarian)

Ingredients:

200 grams (14 tablespoons) unsalted butter or vegan butter, at room temperature

250 grams (1¼ cups) granulated sugar

1 teaspoon Diamond Crystal kosher salt

1 teaspoon baking powder

½ teaspoon baking soda

1 large egg (about 55 grams), straight from the fridge

2 teaspoons pure vanilla extract

60 grams freeze-dried fruit (except banana), finely ground (scant 1 cup)

250 grams (2 cups plus 4 teaspoons) all-purpose flour

Basic Crumble (page 288) or any of the variations (page 289), at room temperature

Special Equipment:

stand mixer (or hand mixer)

spice grinder (or high-powered blender)

#40 cookie scoop (or 2 spoons)

sheet pans

parchment paper

→ These cookies have the soft, cakey texture of snickerdoodles but taste just like pie, with a crumble coating and concentrated fruity punch thanks to freeze-dried fruit. This recipe will not work with regular dried (dehydrated) fruit, which never gets dry enough to blend fine. Luckily, freeze-dried fruit is pretty easy to find these days and has become a total baking staple. Blend the fruit in a spice grinder or high-powered blender just before using, as the powder will quickly absorb humidity from the air and clump. I like these cookies best with vibrant freeze-dried cherries or raspberries, but any fruit other than banana will work. (Banana contains a lot of starch and will result in a gummy and dense cookie.)

---

1. **Set up:** Position a rack in the center of the oven and heat to 350°F (177°C). Line two sheet pans with parchment paper.

2. **Make the dough:** In a stand mixer fitted with the paddle (or a large bowl and a hand mixer—see Notes), cream the butter, sugar, salt, baking powder, and baking soda on medium-high speed until light and fluffy, 3 to 5 minutes, stopping to scrape down the paddle and bowl twice during mixing.

3. Add the egg, vanilla, and ground freeze-dried fruit and mix on medium speed until well combined, about 1 minute, stopping to scrape the paddle and bowl once during mixing.

4. Add the flour and mix on low until the dough comes together, about 30 seconds.

5. **Form the cookies:** Place the crumble in a medium bowl. Using a #40 cookie scoop (see Notes) or 2 spoons, divide the dough into 2-tablespoon portions (35 grams each) and roll each portion into a ball. Drop each ball into the bowl of crumble. Working over the bowl to catch any falling crumble, cup the dough ball and crumble in your palms, then pack the crumble around the dough like you're making a small snowball (if you portion all the dough first, then try to roll in the crumble, it won't stick as well). Arrange the cookies on one of the lined sheet pans, spacing them 1½ inches apart.

6. **Once you've filled one pan with cookies, bake while you form the remaining dough:** Bake the cookies until puffed, cracked, and the crumble on the outside is set and dry, while the inside of the cookie still looks moist and steamy, 12 to 14 minutes (they will seem very soft out of the oven, but will set as they cool). Allow them to cool on the sheet pan for at least 10 minutes. Repeat with the remaining pan of cookies. Enjoy warm or within 3 days. →

Fruity-Doodle Cookies (cont'd.)

What Is Freeze-Dried Fruit?

Notes

Notes
- If using a hand mixer, you will need to increase the speed by one level and double the mixing times.
- If you're using a cookie scoop to portion the dough, be sure to level the dough in the scoop; otherwise your portions will be too big and the bake time will be off.

Freeze-dried fruit is made by freezing fresh fruit, then placing it in a low-pressure environment that causes sublimation, a process where ice transforms to gas while totally skipping the water phase. This zaps the liquid right out of the fruit while preserving all of its fresh flavor and vibrant color, because it hasn't been exposed to the oxidizing effects of heat. The resulting fruit is crisp, dry, and highly concentrated, perfect for blitzing into a fine powder to easily incorporate into whipped cream, frosting, and these perky cookies.

Crumbly Hazelnut Smooches with Dark Chocolate

(Makes about 30 cookies)

(Active: 30 mins. | Total: 1 hr.)

(Easy) (Gluten-free)

(Vegetarian (can be made vegan))

Ingredients:

140 grams (1 cup) skin-on hazelnuts

100 grams (½ cup) granulated sugar

1½ teaspoons Diamond Crystal kosher salt

140 grams (¾ cup plus 2 tablespoons) stoneground white rice flour

100 grams (7 tablespoons) unsalted butter or vegan butter, cut into pieces, at room temperature

1 fancy milk, dark, or vegan chocolate bar (around 100 grams)

Special Equipment:

food processor

sheet pans

parchment paper

#60 cookie scoop (or 2 spoons)

→ These cookies are based on *baci di dama* (which translates to "lady's kisses"), a traditional cookie from northwest Italy, a region known for its plump and aromatic hazelnuts. They usually consist of two tiny cookies that are sandwiched together with a wee dollop of dark chocolate. Even though the dough is straightforward, rolling all those itty-bitty balls and kissing them together with chocolate is a lot of work. Instead, I take a cue from classic peanut butter blossoms, forming each cookie slightly larger and pressing a chunk of chocolate smack-dab into it. When I was a pastry chef, I'd whip these up for all my gluten-free guests, and they've been a go-to ever since. Similar to shortbread, the butter-rich dough makes these cookies melt-in-your-mouth and taste even better the next day. I think these are best made with high-fat, European-style butter, but any butter will work (even vegan!). Be sure to use stoneground rice flour (I like Bob's Red Mill). Very finely milled rice flour will make the dough super crumbly and unmanageable.

---

1. **Set up:** Arrange oven racks in the upper and lower thirds of the oven and heat to 325°F (163°C). Line two sheet pans with parchment paper.

2. **Toast the hazelnuts:** Spread the hazelnuts onto a sheet pan and roast, tossing every 10 minutes, until deeply browned and toasty, 25 to 30 minutes. While hot, transfer to a clean towel and rub off most of the papery skins (don't worry about removing it all). Reserve the sheet pan and keep the oven on.

3. **Make the dough:** In a food processor, combine the toasted hazelnuts, sugar, and salt and pulse the mixture until very finely ground—about the texture of cornmeal. Add the rice flour and pulse to combine.

4. Add the butter and pulse until the mixture comes together into clumps. Dump the mixture onto a clean surface and gently knead to bring together into a crumbly dough that feels like greasy wet sand, about 1 minute.

5. **Portion and bake:** Using a #60 cookie scoop (see Note) or 2 spoons, portion the dough into 1-tablespoon (about 15-gram) balls and arrange on the prepared sheet pans spacing them 1 inch apart. (The dough will feel very crumbly and like it doesn't want to hold together. If using your hands to roll it into balls, be gentle. If using a scoop, level the scoop, place the flat side onto the sheet pan, and release the portion directly onto the pan.)

6. Transfer both pans to the oven and bake until the edges are darker than the middle and the cookies feel set and dry but still soft, 14 to 16 minutes, switching racks and rotating the sheet pans front to back halfway through. →

Crumbly Hazelnut Smooches with Dark Chocolate (cont'd.)

7. **Chocolate topping:** In the meantime, break the chocolate bar into small pieces (one per cookie—you don't need much chocolate for each cookie). As soon as the cookies come out of the oven, drop a piece of chocolate into the center of each one.

8. Cool completely on the sheet pans (the cookies will crisp as they cool). Stored in an airtight container (with a desiccant if you have one), the cookies will keep for up to 2 weeks.

Note: If you're using a cookie scoop to portion the dough, be sure to level the dough in the scoop; otherwise your portions will be too big and the bake time will be off.

Clarified Butter vs. Ghee vs. Brown Butter: What's the Difference?

Butter is an emulsion of fat, water, and protein, but luckily for us, it's an unstable one. Just like in life, instability equals fun times! Just melt butter and boom, it's broken! Ready for you to play with the individual parts, like disassembling a set of Legos and making something brand-new.

When you first melt butter, it crackles and spits as the water simmers and evaporates out of it. Once the sizzling subsides, the butter separates into three layers: The whey proteins float on top, the casein proteins sink to the bottom, and in the middle is pure butterfat.

If you skim off the whey proteins and strain the butterfat to remove the casein proteins, you're left with **clarified butter.** This has the same delicate flavor of regular butter, but with the solids removed, so it's got a higher smoke point—480°F/248°C versus 300°F/148°C for whole butter—ready for sautéing and pan-frying.

If you don't skim or strain but continue cooking the butter, the whey proteins will sink to the bottom and brown along with the casein proteins. Strain this butterfat and you have **ghee,** which is enriched with nutty aromatics and antioxidant compounds from the browning that delay rancidity, in addition to having the higher smoke point of clarified butter because the solids are still removed.

If you cook it to brown the proteins but then don't strain away the brown butter solids, keeping every last flavorful golden bit speckled throughout the butterfat, you've got **brown butter.** It's toasty, it's nutty, it's butterscotch-y—but it's not suitable for high-heat applications, burning even faster than butter because the solids are already halfway there.

Clarified butter and ghee are both great for high-heat applications, with ghee having a longer shelf life and deeper flavor thanks to the browning, while brown butter is all about flavor. What all three have in common is that they've had all their water cooked out. If a recipe is already using brown butter or clarified butter (like my chocolate chip or sugar cookies), you don't have to worry about a thing. But if you're playing around with a recipe on your own, don't forget about that lost hydration! Swapping in clarified butter, ghee, or brown butter for another pure, saturated fat, like coconut oil or lard, will be an easy one-to-one swap. However, if you're browning the butter for a recipe that calls for whole cold, softened, or melted butter, you might need to add some water to prevent the dough or batter from becoming greasy or broken. If the original recipe creams softened butter, you might struggle to get the same lift and stable emulsion from chilled browned butter. With some tweaks in ratios and adjustments in method, you can make any recipe work, but keep in mind that it's rarely a simple swap.

Fruit & Nut Spelt Breakfast Muffins

(Makes 12 muffins)

(Active: 35 mins.) | (Total: 1 hr. 15 mins.)

(Easy) (Vegetarian)

Ingredients:

softened butter or cooking spray for the pan (if not using muffin liners)

200 grams (about 1½ cups) assorted nuts and seeds (chopped if large), like pecans, walnuts, and pumpkin seeds

90 grams (1 cup) old-fashioned rolled oats

200 grams (about 1½ cups) assorted dried fruit (chopped if large), like dates, raisins, and dried cranberries

170 grams (1½ cups) fine grind whole-grain spelt flour

1½ teaspoons Diamond Crystal kosher salt

1¼ teaspoons baking powder

¼ teaspoon baking soda

3 large eggs (about 165 grams)

340 grams (1½ cups) whole-milk Greek yogurt

255 grams (¾ cup) mild honey, like clover or wildflower

1½ teaspoons pure vanilla extract

113 grams (1 stick) unsalted butter or vegan butter, melted

Special Equipment:

sheet pan

standard 12-cup metal muffin tin

muffin liners (optional)

cookie scoop (or spoon)

→ These hearty muffins are light on sweetness and packed with fiber and protein. They taste like if a granola bar and a muffin had a baby. Bake them on the weekend, wrap each individually, and pop them in the freezer. Now you're totally set for twelve weekday breakfasts. I like them best split, toasted, and topped with strained yogurt, honey, and flaky salt. Spelt is an ancient wheat that brings walnut-y depth and whole-grain goodness. This recipe uses the muffin method of mixing (see page 281), where overmixing is a real issue. Get all your vigorous stirring out of the way before adding the flour. Once added, only mix enough to evenly hydrate it, otherwise, the batter can quickly become overworked, baking up dense, dry, and gummy. Because the batter is so crammed full of fruit and nuts, it doesn't dome, and instead, spills out of the muffin cups. The edges grow mahogany and crunchy and are my favorite part.

---

1. **Set up:** Position a rack in the center of the oven and heat to 325°F (163°C). Grease a standard 12-cup metal muffin pan, both the cups and the top of the pan, with butter or cooking spray. (Or use paper liners for the cups, but still grease the top of the pan.)

2. **Toast the nuts/seeds and oats:** On a sheet pan, toss together the nuts/seeds and oats. Evenly spread out and roast in the oven until lightly toasted, tossing once while baking, 15 to 20 minutes. Measure out ¼ cup of this mixture and set aside for topping the muffins. Add the fruit to the remaining nut/oat mixture and toss to combine.

3. Increase the oven temperature to 375°F (190°C).

4. **Make the batter:** In a medium bowl, whisk together the flour, salt, baking powder, and baking soda.

5. In a large bowl, whisk together the eggs until no streaks remain. Add the yogurt, honey, and vanilla and whisk until well combined. Add the melted butter and whisk until well combined.

6. Add the flour mixture to the egg/yogurt mixture, then stir and fold with a stiff silicone spatula until evenly hydrated and no pockets of dry flour remain. Add the fruit and nut mixture and fold until evenly distributed.

7. Using a cookie scoop or a large spoon, divide the batter among the muffin cups and distribute the reserved nut mixture on top. (They will be filled to the brim.)

8. Bake until browned and a toothpick inserted in the center comes out with moist crumbs, 25 to 30 minutes. Cool for 15 minutes in the pan, then use an offset spatula or butter knife to loosen each muffin and remove from the pan. Transfer to a wire rack to fully cool. (Store tightly wrapped at room temperature for 3 days or up to 1 month in the freezer.)

Future Brownies

(Makes 16 brownies)

(Active: 15 mins.) | (Total: 1 hr. 15 mins.)

(Easy) (Gluten-free)

(Vegetarian (can be made vegan))

Ingredients:

softened butter or cooking spray for
the pan

70 grams (¾ cup plus 1 tablespoon;
see Notes) Dutch process, black,
or natural cocoa powder (or a mix),
plus more for dusting (optional)

1 tablespoon instant coffee (or
1½ teaspoons instant espresso
powder)

313 grams (1⅓ cups plus
1 tablespoon) whole milk

113 grams (1 stick) unsalted butter or
vegan butter, cut into cubes

240 grams (2 cups) powdered sugar

125 grams (1 cup) glutinous sweet
rice flour, preferably Koda Farms
Blue Star Mochiko

1½ teaspoons Diamond Crystal
kosher salt

3 large eggs (about 165 grams)

2 teaspoons pure vanilla extract

Special Equipment:

8-inch or 9-inch square metal
cake pan

parchment paper

stand mixer (or large bowl and
hand mixer)

→ These brownies taste like they're from the future. The glutinous sweet rice flour makes them set up firm and springy. The first bite bounces in your mouth, then nearly melts away into a light but fudgy texture. They cut into clean and tidy squares, leave no crumbs behind, and are gluten-free—that sounds like future food to me. Both cocoa powder and rice flour benefit from being hydrated in hot liquid. Blooming cocoa in hot milk makes the flavor extra chocolaty while preventing it from tasting chalky or harsh. The hot milk prevents the glutinous sweet rice flour from being starchy or having too much chew and is key to this brownie's unique texture. If you want deep, dark chocolate flavor, use Dutch process cocoa; for a brighter, milder flavor, use natural cocoa powder; or use black cocoa powder (my favorite) for an inky square that tastes like something from outer space.

---

1. Heat the oven to 350°F (177°C). Grease an 8-inch or 9-inch square metal cake pan with butter or cooking spray. Line the pan with one long sheet of parchment cut to cover the bottom and two sides.

2. In a medium saucepan, combine the cocoa powder and instant coffee. Add the milk, a splash at a time, while whisking constantly, until the cocoa is evenly dissolved. Add the butter cubes and cook over medium heat, stirring and scraping frequently with a stiff silicone spatula, until the butter is melted and the mixture comes to a simmer, about 5 minutes. Cover and remove from the heat.

3. In a stand mixer fitted with the paddle (or in a larger bowl with a hand mixer), combine the powdered sugar, rice flour, and salt and mix on low until evenly combined, about 1 minute. Add the eggs and vanilla and mix on low speed until moistened, then increase the speed to medium and mix until smooth and creamy, about 1 minute. Stop to scrape the paddle and the bowl.

4. With the mixer running on low, stream in the hot milk mixture. Stop to scrape the paddle and the bowl, then increase the speed to medium and mix for at least 2 minutes (you can't overmix this batter, but you *can* undermix it, so take your time with this step).

5. Pour the mixture into the prepared pan and bake until the brownie bounces back when you press the center, 40 to 50 minutes. Cool for at least 10 minutes in the pan, then use the parchment to lift the brownies out of the pan and cut into 16 portions. Dust with cocoa if you like. (Stored in an airtight container, the brownies keep for 3 days at room temperature or 1 month in the freezer.)

Notes
- Make it vegan by swapping the milk for coconut milk, the butter for plant-based butter, and the eggs for 2 flax eggs. Let cool *completely* before removing it from the pan and slicing.
- You can double this recipe to fit in a 9 × 13-inch metal cake pan. No adjustments to time or temperature needed.

Walnut Brown Butter Chocolate Chip Cookies

(Makes 36 cookies)

(Active: 30 mins. | Total: up to 25 hrs.)

(Intermediate) (Vegetarian)

Ingredients:

227 grams (2 sticks) unsalted butter, cut into pieces

150 grams (1½ cups) walnut halves

1¼ teaspoons Diamond Crystal kosher salt, plus more for sprinkling

240 grams (2 cups) powdered sugar

1 tablespoon unsulfured molasses

1 tablespoon milk (any fat percentage) or water

2 teaspoons pure vanilla extract

¾ teaspoon baking soda

½ teaspoon baking powder

1 large egg (about 55 grams), straight from the fridge

250 grams (2 cups plus 4 teaspoons) all-purpose flour

100 grams dark chocolate, roughly chopped (¾ cup), plus more for garnish

100 grams milk chocolate, roughly chopped (¾ cup)

flaky salt

Special Equipment:

fine-mesh sieve

#40 cookie scoop (or 2 spoons)

sheet pan

parchment paper

fish spatula

→ You probably don't need another chocolate chip cookie recipe, but why the hell not? I don't know if this is the ultimate, but it's *my* perfect CCC. Crisp, chewy, tender, and chock-full of salted walnuts and two kinds of chocolate. Walnuts and butter are simmered together, simultaneously toasting the walnuts and browning the butter while also infusing it full of rich, walnut-y goodness. I opt for powdered sugar in place of the usual granulated, yielding extra-tender middles surrounded by a delicate and crisp shell, with a touch of molasses—be sure to use unsulfured molasses, not blackstrap (read more about molasses on page 441)—to bring that traditional brown sugar depth. I normally only like chocolate chip cookies hot out of the oven, but the powdered sugar/molasses combo keeps these tasting fresh for days. Don't skip the 1 tablespoon of milk (or water) added to the dough; that splash is key to the cookie's chewy-crispy texture.

I understand the urge to want cookies ASAP, but letting the dough chill in the fridge for 24 hours makes them chewier and deepens their flavor. Don't try to rush it in the freezer—there's a lot more going on than dough simply getting cold; think low-temperature Maillard reaction (see Caramelization vs. the Maillard Reaction, page 229), gluten development (see So What the Heck Is Gluten?, page 479), and the uncoiling of egg proteins (see Egg Meets Heat, page 58). Take care not to overbake these cookies; they will crisp as they cool. This recipe will not work well with vegan butter or any other substitutions.

---

1. **Brown the butter and nuts:** Set a fine-mesh sieve over a large heatproof bowl. Have a cutting board handy.

2. In a medium saucepan, combine the butter and walnuts and cook over medium heat, stirring frequently, until the butter melts and foams, about 3 minutes. Continue cooking, stirring and scraping frequently with a heatproof spatula, until the sputtering has subsided, the butter solids look deeply browned, and everything smells toasty, 3 to 5 minutes. (The butter will get very foamy and it may be hard to see the color of the solids, so use smell and sound to guide you.)

3. Scrape the butter and nuts into the sieve, allowing the brown butter to collect in the bowl. Shake the sieve to drain off all the butter, then spread the nuts onto a cutting board and sprinkle liberally with kosher salt. Set aside to cool. Scrape any brown butter solids still clinging to the sieve into the bowl of butter.

4. **Make the dough:** Add the powdered sugar to the browned butter and whisk until smooth and creamy. Add the 1¼ teaspoons kosher salt, the molasses, milk, vanilla, baking soda, and baking powder and whisk to combine. (The mixture will look broken; don't worry, the cold egg will bring it back together.)

5. Add the egg and whisk until smooth and well combined. Add the flour and stir with a spatula until the mixture comes together into a soft dough. →

306

Walnut Brown Butter Chocolate Chip Cookies (cont'd.)

6. Roughly chop the walnuts and mix into the cookie dough along with the chopped chocolate, smashing and folding the dough to evenly combine all the mix-ins.

7. Portion and chill the dough: Line a sheet pan (or a large plate if you don't have room in the fridge) with parchment paper. Using a #40 cookie scoop (see Note) or 2 spoons, divide the dough into 2-tablespoon portions (30 grams each). Use your hands to roll into a ball, then flatten into a disk 1½ inches across and 1 inch thick. Top with a piece of extra chocolate and snugly arrange the portions onto the prepared sheet pan (or plate), tightly wrap, and chill in the fridge for 24 hours. (After the initial chilling, you can freeze the dough balls. Once frozen solid, pop them into a zip-top bag and keep frozen until ready to bake—no need to thaw, they will just need 1 extra minute of bake time.)

8. Position a rack in the center of the oven and heat to 375°F (190°C). Line a sheet pan with parchment paper.

9. Arrange as many chilled cookie dough balls as will fit on the lined sheet pan, spacing them 1½ inches apart. Sprinkle with flaky salt.

10. Bake until puffed, lightly browned around the edges, just set, but still soft, about 10 minutes. Immediately after removing the sheet pan from the oven, firmly smack it against the counter 3 or 4 times. This flattens the cookies and crinkles their edges. Use a fish spatula to immediately transfer the cookies to a wire rack to cool. (They will crisp as they cool.)

11. Repeat to bake the remaining cookies. Stored in an airtight container at room temperature (with a desiccant if you have one), the cookies will keep for 1 week.

Note: If you're using a cookie scoop to portion the dough, be sure to level the dough in the scoop; otherwise your portions will be too big and the bake time will be off.

A Very Banana-y Banana Bread

(Makes one loaf)

(Active: 30 mins. | Total: 3 hrs.)

(Intermediate) (Vegetarian)

(Can be made gluten-free)

Ingredients:

375 grams peeled bananas (about 4 medium)

2 large eggs (about 110 grams)

1 large egg yolk (about 20 grams)

2 teaspoons pure vanilla extract

1 teaspoon Diamond Crystal kosher salt

170 grams (12 tablespoons) unsalted butter, cut into pieces

softened butter and granulated sugar for coating the pan

225 grams (1 cup plus 2 tablespoons) granulated sugar

1½ teaspoons baking powder

¼ teaspoon baking soda

225 grams (1¾ cups plus 2 tablespoons) all-purpose flour (or any cup-for-cup gluten-free all-purpose blend)

Special Equipment:

stand mixer and paddle attachment (or large heatproof bowl and hand mixer)

9 × 5-inch metal loaf pan

small offset spatula (or butter knife)

wire rack

→ Bananas are starchy, so in pursuit of the most banana-y banana bread, it's easy to end up with a dense and gummy loaf. This banana bread is light and plush on the outside with a deeply browned crust, courtesy of the creaming method (page 282) and a layer of butter and sugar that caramelizes as the bread bakes. Don't try to rush the creaming step, which is vital to the texture; whipping the cooled brown butter and sugar together creates teeny air pockets that expand when baked.

The bananas become their most flirty and tropical selves by being mashed with the eggs, whose naturally occurring amylase breaks down some of their starches into sugars. The addition of butterscotch-y browned butter enhances the bananas' flavors without getting in their way. Because this batter is so light, mix-ins like chocolate chips or walnuts will sink to the bottom. Instead, this loaf is all about the banana.

1. Mash the bananas: In a medium bowl, mash the banana with a fork until no large lumps remain (if you're not using a scale, this will be about 1½ cups once mashed). Add the whole egg, egg yolk, vanilla, and salt and whisk with the fork until well combined. Set aside.

2. Make the brown butter: In a medium saucepan, melt the butter over medium heat until foamy, about 3 minutes. Cook, constantly stirring and scraping with a spatula, until the sputtering subsides and the solids look deeply browned and toasty, 2 to 4 minutes. Scrape the mixture into the bowl of a stand mixer (or a large bowl if using a hand mixer—see Note). Cool in the fridge until creamy (about 70°F/21°C), about 20 minutes.

3. Set up: Position a rack in the center of the oven and heat to 350°F (177°C). Smear a 9 × 5-inch metal loaf pan with a generous layer of butter and evenly coat with sugar, knocking out any excess.

4. Make the batter: Add the sugar, baking powder, and baking soda to the cooled brown butter. Mix on medium speed, stopping every couple of minutes to scrape the paddle and the bowl, until light and fluffy, 5 to 7 minutes. (It isn't a lot of batter in the bowl, so if you don't scrape often, nothing gets mixed well.)

5. Add half the flour and mix on low until just combined, about 15 seconds. Stop to scrape the paddle and the bowl. Add half the banana mixture and mix on low until just combined, about 15 seconds. Stop to scrape the paddle and the bowl and repeat with the remaining flour and banana mixture. Scrape the paddle and the bowl and give the batter a couple of final stirs by hand with a stiff silicone spatula.

6. Bake: Scrape the batter into the pan and level with the back of a spoon or an offset spatula. Bake until the loaf is deeply golden, springs back when pressed in the center, and a toothpick inserted comes out with moist crumbs, 50 to 55 minutes. →

A Very Banana-y Banana Bread (cont'd.)

7. Transfer the pan to a wire rack to cool for 15 minutes. Run an offset spatula or butter knife along the sides of the loaf to loosen it from the pan, then unmold and cool completely before serving. (Wrapped tightly, the banana bread will keep for 3 days at room temperature and 1 month in the freezer.)

Note: If using a hand mixer, you will need to increase the speed by one level and double the mixing times.

The Ripe Stuff

I like bananas because they grow and change with me, like a Chia Pet you can eat—well, I guess you probably could eat a Chia Pet. Bananas are climacteric fruits, which means they ripen after picking. They start out green and starchy, which is how I like to eat them out of hand, then turn bright yellow and tender, perfect for my morning smoothie, before eventually liquefying into a blackened, sweet treat for my dogs. This is because bananas are real active after picking, releasing ethylene gas, which forms enzymes that work to blacken the peel, soften the fruit, increase the acidity, and convert starches into sugars. And they're not the only fruits who like to keep busy. Avocados, pears, melons, tomatoes, peaches (and more!) all continue the ripening process after picking, so don't worry about a firm peach—with enough time they'll get squishy, as we all do.

Fully blackened bananas may have the most sugar, but they will lead you to dense and gummy banana bread land. Don't follow them there. Instead, look for lots of freckles with a hint of blackening at the ends. There are tons of tricks out there to try and speed up the ripening process. You can put your bananas in a paper bag in an attempt to concentrate the ethylene gas, but this is only marginally faster. Some recipes tell you to freeze or bake your bananas, but the results are all surface, blackening the peel and softening the flesh without converting the starches to sugars.

One hack that actually works makes use of amylase. Amylase is the enzyme produced by the banana's ethylene gas, which is responsible for converting its starches into sugars and just happens to also be kickin' around in egg yolks. This is a trick I learned from the pastry chef and author Stella Parks—and it really works. If you need banana bread immediately (we've all been there) but have only underripe specimens around, mash the bananas along with the eggs from the recipe and let them hang out. After just 30 minutes you'll have accomplished what days in a bag cannot, so go forth and make banana bread NOW!

Light & Crisp Butter Cookies

(Makes fifty 2-inch cookies)

(Active: 1 hr.)

(Total: at least 1 hr. 30 mins.)

(Intermediate) (Vegetarian)

Ingredients:

280 grams (2½ sticks) unsalted butter, cut into pieces

180 grams (¾ cup plus 2½ tablespoons) granulated sugar

1 teaspoon Diamond Crystal kosher salt

½ teaspoon baking powder

2 large egg whites (about 70 grams)

1 tablespoon pure vanilla extract

345 grams (2¾ cups plus 2 tablespoons) all-purpose flour, plus more for rolling

Special Equipment:

stand mixer (or large heatproof bowl and hand mixer)

rolling pin

pastry brush

2 sheet pans

parchment paper

cookie cutters

small offset spatula

→ The key to these snappy butter cookies is clarified butter. We're going to simmer the butter to cook off all the moisture, then strain out the solids, so what we have left is pure, radiant butterfat. Removing the milk solids ensures a crisp and sturdy cookie, perfect for decorating and shipping during the holidays. I prefer not to brown the solids, allowing the delicate flavor of vanilla and butter to shine. If you're making this for people you really love, scrape the seeds of half a vanilla bean into the creaming butter and sugar. Or if you have a spent vanilla pod lying around, add it to the butter as it is being clarified to infuse with flavor.

The yield you get after clarifying butter can vary depending on the initial fat percentage of the butter. For some recipes, a little more or less fat doesn't matter, but for this one it's the difference between a greasy or dry cookie. For that reason, I have you clarify more butter than you will need, then measure out the necessary amount. If you want to skip the clarifying step, use 200 grams (¾ cup plus 2 tablespoons) of store-bought ghee instead. The flavor of the final cookies will be nuttier. Clarified butter has a high smoke point and you can use the extra in your cooking anywhere you'd use oil. Add the solids to rice, pasta, or potatoes for extra richness.

1. **Make the clarified butter:** In a medium saucepan, cook the butter over medium heat, stirring occasionally with a spatula until melted and foamy, about 3 minutes. Reduce the heat to medium-low and continue cooking, stirring frequently, until the sputtering subsides and the milk solids have sunk to the bottom of the pan, about 5 minutes. Pour the clarified butter into a heatproof bowl, leaving the milk solids behind (reserve for another use).

2. Measure out 200 grams (¾ cup plus 2 tablespoons) clarified butter into the bowl of a stand mixer (or a large heatproof bowl if using a hand mixer—see Note). Set aside to cool until room temperature and creamy (70°F/21°C), about 2 hours at room temperature or 30 minutes in the fridge. (Reserve extra clarified butter, if any, for another use.)

3. **Make the dough:** Set the mixer bowl of cooled clarified butter on the stand mixer and fit with the paddle. Add the sugar, salt, and baking powder and cream on medium-high speed until light and fluffy, scraping down the bowl and paddle once during mixing, 4 to 6 minutes.

4. Add the egg whites and vanilla and mix on medium until well combined, scraping down the bowl and paddle once during mixing, about 2 minutes.

5. Add the flour and mix on low until the mixture is well combined and comes together into a ball, about 30 seconds. →

314

Light & Crisp Butter Cookies (cont'd.)

6. Divide the dough in half and pat each portion into a disk. (You can roll the dough right away or wrap it tightly and chill for up to 3 days. Allow the cookie dough to soften enough that if you press the dough you can easily make an indent before rolling out.)

7. Roll out the cookies: Dust a clean surface lightly with flour (a wooden surface is preferred to minimize sticking). Using a lightly floured rolling pin, roll out the dough until it's a scant ¼ inch thick. Use a pastry brush to dust off any excess flour.

8. Line two sheet pans with parchment paper. Using cookie cutters (yield will vary depending on the size of cutter you choose), cut out cookies and transfer them using an offset spatula to the parchment-lined sheet pans, spacing the cookies ½ inch apart. Gather the scraps, reroll, and cut until you've used up all the dough. (For intricate shapes, chill the cut cookies in the fridge or freezer before baking to minimize spreading. Unbaked cookies can be stored frozen and tightly wrapped for 1 month.)

9. Bake: Position the oven racks in the upper and lower thirds of the oven and heat to 350°F (177°C).

10. Transfer both pans to the oven and bake until barely golden around the edges and bottom of the cookie, still pale on top, and dry to the touch, 11 to 13 minutes, switching racks and rotating the sheet pans front to back halfway through. Allow the cookies to cool on the pans. Stored at room temperature (with a desiccant if you have one), they will last for 3 weeks.

Note: If using a hand mixer, you will need to increase the speed by one level and double the mixing times.

Packaging Tips

Because of their long shelf life, these cookies are great for shipping in your next holiday (or any day) cookie box. To make shipping easy:

• Choose cutters that yield cookies that can easily stack in your box.

• For maximum freshness, pack the cookies with a desiccant (read more in Save Your Desiccants!, page 462) or vacuum pack if you can.

• Pack the cookies tightly with shredded paper or tissue to prevent breakage during shipping.

• Include a card describing each cookie and noting any potential allergens.

⇄ Get Loose!

- Add citrus zest (lemon, lime, or grapefruit), finely minced fresh woody herbs (like rosemary, thyme, or sage), or spices (cracked toasted coriander, black peppercorns, cured sumac, or fennel seeds) or instant espresso powder while creaming the butter and sugar.

- Add different extracts in place of or in addition to the vanilla extract.

- Swap the clarified butter for another saturated solid fat, such as virgin coconut oil, ghee, or brown butter (the solids in brown butter will reduce the shelf life to 1 week). Regardless of the fat, make sure it is room temperature and creamy, so it can properly aerate.

- Roll the dough into a log (see the photographs on page 285), freeze, then slice and bake.

- Decorate with royal icing: In a stand mixer fitted with the whisk (or in a large bowl with a hand mixer), combine sifted powdered sugar with enough pasteurized egg whites to reach the consistency you're looking for (thick like toothpaste for intricate piping, thin like buttermilk for glazing). Add a pinch of salt, a splash of vanilla extract, and food color as desired.

- Brush the cookies with egg wash and top with turbinado sugar or sprinkles before baking.

- Pipe out the dough for spritz cookie vibes: When you make the dough, reduce the flour to 330 grams (2¾ cups). Transfer the dough to a piping bag with a large star tip or a cookie press. Pipe or press the cookies onto a sheet pan, leaving ½ inch space between them. Bake at 325°F (163°C) until lightly golden on the edges and bottom, 16 to 18 minutes. Cool completely on the sheet pan.

Light & Crisp Butter
Cookie Variations

Keep Rollin' Rollin'

Tips for rolling tender and buttery things, like cookie and pie dough

- **Surface matters:** Rolling dough on a large wooden cutting board or work surface makes it less likely to stick. The naturally porous and uneven nature of wood offers a bit of traction between the dough and the surface, like when you sprinkle coarse cornmeal or semolina on a pizza peel. Some recommend rolling between parchment paper to minimize sticking. I don't like this method because it restricts how you can move the dough and often leaves wrinkles from the parchment on its surface. Most important, parchment paper is expensive and I'd rather you spend your coin on that good butter instead.

- **Don't be shy with the flour:** I never worry about overflouring my surface before rolling out dough. Any extra flour can easily be brushed off with a pastry brush, while a stuck dough is often unsalvageable.

- **Roll gently and quickly with soft dough, or smash hard for stiff and cold dough:** When a recipe allows it, I prefer to roll out cookie dough just after mixing, while it's still soft and pliable. This is more of a pro move that requires you to work quickly and very carefully. Because the butter is already soft, it can easily melt and cause the dough to stick. If you're starting out, it can be helpful to chill the dough until it's firm but still pliable enough to leave an indent when you press into it. Cold doughs require you to put a little muscle in it when rolling out, but you've got more time to work with.

- **Use outward, not downward pressure:** Use the rolling pin to apply pressure evenly across the dough, from the center to the edges, rotating the dough a quarter-turn after every roll. Tender doughs (like the sugar cookie recipe) can be tough to pick up and turn, so I'll move the pin in various angles across the surface instead. Avoid the urge to apply downward pressure. You're trying to spread the dough out, not smush it down. Take your time and go slow—if you try to roll it too thin too quickly, you'll end up with cracks along the edges and an uneven thickness. For soft doughs, the only downward pressure that should be applied is from the weight of the pin itself.

- **When in doubt, chill it out:** Although not always required, anything with butter or gluten bakes best when you give it a chill after rolling. This firms up the butter, so the dough spreads less and holds intricate shapes better after baking, and it gives the gluten a chance to relax, for a more tender pie crust or cookie. In fact, if at any point you're struggling with a buttery dough, pop it in the fridge for a quick chill.

- **Practice makes perfect:** There are a lot of tools to help you achieve an even thickness, like spacers that slide onto the ends of, or rest under, your rolling pin. I haven't tried one that didn't limit movement and ultimately give me a false sense of control. If those spacers shift a touch or you press a little too hard, they are pretty much useless. But more important, depending on a crutch like that will mean you'll never become a better baker. Yes, rolling out dough is a difficult skill to master. But if you go at it solo, every time you roll you'll get a little bit better.

(Better Than Drake's) Coffee Cake

(Makes 16 pieces)

(Active: 25 mins. | Total: 1½ hrs.)

(Advanced) (Vegetarian)

For the crumb:

softened butter or cooking spray for the pan

180 grams (1½ cups) all-purpose flour

100 grams (scant ½ cup packed) dark brown sugar

1 tablespoon ground cinnamon

½ teaspoon Diamond Crystal kosher salt

¼ teaspoon baking powder

84 grams (6 tablespoons) unsalted butter, melted

For the batter:

1 large egg (about 55 grams), at room temperature

2 large egg yolks (about 40 grams), at room temperature

180 grams (¾ cup plus 1 tablespoon) buttermilk (see Notes), at room temperature

1 tablespoon neutral oil

2 teaspoons clear (imitation) vanilla or pure vanilla extract

1½ teaspoons butter extract (optional)

185 grams (1½ cups plus 2 teaspoons) cake flour

2 tablespoons cornstarch

200 grams (1 cup) granulated sugar

1¼ teaspoons baking powder

½ teaspoon Diamond Crystal kosher salt

⅛ teaspoon baking soda

113 grams (1 stick) unsalted butter, at room temperature, cut into pieces

→ This coffee cake is my ode to Drake's, the best prepackaged cake ever. The interior is lofty and cloud-like, with a tight crumb and rich butter flavor. What makes this cake amazing is also its downfall. It's too light to stack, add mix-ins to, or even top with streusel, so I bake it upside down with the crumb on the bottom. It's a reversed creamed cake, which gives it a fine and tender crumb, much like Drake's. Cake flour and a bit of cornstarch make it ultradelicate and dainty. You *must* use a stand mixer for this recipe—do not attempt with a hand mixer! The mixing times might seem long, but the initial step of mixing the butter puts a jacket on those flour granules, keeping them from developing too much gluten. Just keep mixing and scraping, I promise it'll be okay. No substitutions, like vegan butter or gluten-free flour, will work in this recipe.

1. Set up: Heat the oven to 350°F (177°C). Grease an 8-inch square metal cake pan with butter or cooking spray. Line the pan with one long sheet of parchment cut to cover the bottom and two sides. Smooth the parchment with your hands, creasing it into the corners for a snug fit.

2. Make the crumb: In a medium bowl, use your hands to toss together the flour, brown sugar, cinnamon, salt, and baking powder, breaking up any brown sugar clumps with your fingers. Add the melted butter and rub it into the dry mixture with your fingers until it holds together in large clumps when squeezed in your palms. (Alternatively, you can mix the crumble in a stand mixer fitted with the paddle.) Evenly spread across the prepared cake pan.

3. For the batter: In a medium bowl, whisk the whole egg and egg yolks until no streaks remain. Add the buttermilk, oil, and extracts, and whisk to combine. Transfer to something you can easily pour out of, like a measuring cup with a spout or a 1-quart deli container.

4. In a stand mixer fitted with the paddle, combine the flour, cornstarch, granulated sugar, baking powder, salt, and baking soda on low speed until evenly combined, about 1 minute. Add the butter and mix on medium speed until the butter totally disappears into the dry mixture, leaving very fine crumbs of moist flour, about 5 minutes, stopping once to scrape the paddle and the bowl.

5. With the mixer running on low, stream in one-third of the egg/buttermilk mixture. Increase the speed to medium and mix for 30 seconds. Stop the mixer, scrape the paddle and the bowl.

6. With the mixer on low, stream in another one-third of the egg/buttermilk mixture. Increase the speed to medium and mix for 30 seconds. Stop to scrape the paddle and bowl, then repeat this process with the last one-third of the egg/buttermilk mixture. Stop to scrape the paddle and the bowl and mix on medium speed for 1 minute. It should look smooth, thick, and fluffy. →

320

(Better Than Drake's) Coffee Cake (cont'd.)

Special Equipment:

8-inch square metal cake pan

parchment paper

stand mixer

measuring cup with a spout (or a 1-quart deli container)

serrated knife

7. Scrape the batter over the crumb in the prepared pan. Pick up the pan and firmly tap it against the counter a couple of times. (This distributes the batter and knocks out any large bubbles that could cause tunnels in the cake.)

8. Bake until the top is deeply browned, springs back when lightly pressed, and a toothpick inserted into the middle comes out clean, 45 to 50 minutes.

9. Cool the cake in the pan for 30 minutes, then run an offset spatula or butter knife along the edges to loosen. Use the parchment to lift the cake out of the pan and transfer it to a wire rack to cool completely.

10. Use the parchment to slide the cake onto a cutting board; do not invert (see Notes). Use a serrated knife to cut the cake into 16 even pieces. Invert the cake pieces to serve. Tightly wrapped, this cake will keep at room temperature for 3 days or in the freezer for 1 month.

Notes

- You cannot substitute the buttermilk with either yogurt or homemade "buttermilk" (made with a mixture of milk and lemon juice). It will not react with the leavening the same way. Kefir is an acceptable substitute.
- This cake is so light that it must fully cool and be cut with the crumb on the bottom or the weight of the crumb will compress the delicate cake. It's best to also store the cake crumb-side down.

Rough Puff Pastry

(for Pie Crusts & So Much More!)

> Makes enough for 2 deep-dish pies, 1 double-crust pie, or two 11 × 15-inch sheets

> Active: 20 mins. | Total: 20 mins.

> Advanced | Vegetarian

Ingredients:

300 grams (2½ cups) all-purpose flour

1 tablespoon granulated sugar

1½ teaspoons Diamond Crystal kosher salt

Butter (see Note):
300 grams (2 sticks plus 5½ tablespoons) cold American-style unsalted butter, cut into ½-inch cubes
OR
260 grams (2 sticks plus 2½ tablespoons) cold European-style unsalted butter, cut into 1-inch cubes

130 grams (½ cup plus 1 tablespoon) cold water, plus more as needed

Note: You need to use either the European- or American-style butter measurement, not both.

Special Equipment:

bench scraper

rolling pin

→ Puff pastry is made with a butter block that you envelop in a simple flour and water dough before rolling and folding—a process called lamination. Lamination sounds like a scary technique that belongs at a Kinko's rather than in the kitchen, but it's just about making layers. It refers to any pastry that is composed of sheets of dough streaked with fat. The simplest method is to roll dough into thin sheets before spreading on fat and stacking or layering, as with baklava, strudel, or m'semen.

Another way to laminate is by incorporating cubes, flakes, or one large block of fat into the dough and repeatedly rolling it out and folding it until the fat is layered throughout, like with biscuits or puff pastry. If you over- or underincorporate the butter, you'll lose the layering affect. The goal is for the fat to keep the layers distinct. When the pastry is baked in the oven, the liquid in the dough and in the butter (if butter is utilized) transforms to steam. The steam in turn acts as a physical leavener, pushing apart the layers, while the fat almost fries the dough. That's why laminated pastries are crisp, flaky, and light.

Rough puff pastry is an easy and fast alternative to getting a flaky, buttery, layered dough. Instead of a big butter block (which takes skill and time to form properly), rough puff uses cubes of butter that are worked into layers through several folds. It doesn't puff as high or evenly as a real-deal puff pastry, but it gets you 90 percent of the way there with 10 percent of the effort. This dough is perfect for cheese twists, pigs in a blanket, galettes, and super-flaky pie crusts—something I picked up from chef and author Stella Parks. Rough puff is also a great place to start learning more about lamination as a whole. Master this technique and you'll be ready to jump into all kinds of butter-block action like puff pastry, croissants, kouign-amann, and layered brioche.

Some notes before you get started:

- Working quickly is vital! The butter is the perfect temperature and texture for only a short window of time. If it's a hot day, chill your flour, bowl, spatula, whisk, bench scraper, and rolling pin in the freezer for at least 2 hours before beginning. Roll out the dough on a chilled cutting board, if you've got room to sneak one in your freezer, too. I do not recommend freezing the butter, which, when too cold, can tear through the dough rather than layer within it.

- Don't be tempted to change the batch size. A larger batch needs to be mixed and folded using a different method, while a smaller batch will readily become overworked. If you're making several pies and need lots of dough, it's better to make multiple batches.

- There are two measurements for the butter: one for lower-fat (80 to 82%), American-style butter and another for higher-fat (82 to 86%), European-style butter. For most recipes, they can be used interchangeably, but here the slight difference in fat content and texture drastically affect the dough. American-style butter is stiffer and more difficult to layer into the dough, so it helps to start with smaller cubes, while the softer, European-style butter will melt if cut too small. Be sure to cut into the directed cube size and use the amount given for the type of butter you're using.

1. In a large bowl, whisk together the flour, sugar, and salt. Add the butter cubes and toss them in the flour with your fingers. Working quickly, smash each cube with your thumb and finger **once,** then set aside. (No need to be precise or try to evenly flatten it, just quickly work your way through each cube and don't overwork them. We want big chunks of butter.)

2. Using a stiff silicone spatula, toss the smashed cubes to distribute, then create a well in the center of the flour/butter mixture. Pour all the water into the well at once. Use the spatula to thoroughly stir and smash the mixture along the side of the bowl, until almost all the flour is barely moistened and shaggy, but not wet or fully coming together—some dry bits are okay. (It will take at least 1 minute of mixing before you can accurately assess the hydration of the dough.)

3. Stop and assess the hydration of the dough:
- Are there large pockets of dry flour left? Add more water 1 tablespoon at a time, mixing with a stiff spatula for 1 minute to distribute before adding more.
- Is the butter already melting and smearing into the dough? Pop the whole bowl into the refrigerator to chill before proceeding.
- Do you see large lumps of moistened dough, interrupted with big chunks of butter, and small pockets of dry flour? It's just right! Move forward to the next step.

4. Lightly dust a clean surface with flour and dump out the entire mixture. (It won't look like it's holding together at this point.) Use a bench scraper to roughly gather the mixture into a rectangle and lightly dust the surface with flour.

5. Using a rolling pin, press and roll the dough out roughly into a square until ½ inch thick. (The dough will still look like it's not holding together at this point; that's okay.) Use the bench scraper to fold the top third of the dough and butter bits over the middle. Repeat with the lower third, folding it over so you have a long rectangle of barely together dough. Fold this rectangle of dough bits in half, gathering any pieces that fall off, and press them on top.

6. Lightly dust the work surface and dough once more. Using a rolling pin, once again press and roll out the dough until roughly ½ inch thick. Repeat the process from earlier, using a bench scraper to fold the lower and top third of dough over the middle, and folding the entire rectangle of dough in half. →

Rough Puff Pastry (cont'd.)

What the Hell Happened?

7. Stop and assess the lamination of the dough:
- Are there still large sheets of naked butter and/or the dough isn't holding together? Repeat the earlier process of rolling and folding the dough, then reevaluate.
- Is the dough very soft and the butter melting? Quickly transfer the whole thing to a parchment-lined sheet pan and chill in the refrigerator before proceeding.
- Have the butter cubes mostly vanished (thin streaks of butter are okay) and the dough is looking smooth and holding together? Then you can stop folding here and proceed to the next step!

8. Using a bench scraper, divide the dough in half. If your kitchen is warm, tightly wrap the dough in plastic and chill for 15 minutes before using the dough in a recipe, otherwise, proceed as directed in the recipe. The dough can be made in advance, wrapped, and refrigerated for up to 2 days or frozen for 3 months. The refrigerated dough needs to be brought to room temperature for 20 to 40 minutes before rolling. Frozen dough should be thawed in the refrigerator overnight, then brought to room temperature for 20 to 40 minutes before rolling.

Did the butter melt out of the pastry?
- The butter wasn't worked into the dough enough. Every bit of butter needs to be coated in flour or dough before baking.
- The dough may have needed another fold or the cubes of butter could have been too big or not sufficiently smushed.
- The dough wasn't chilled enough before baking. Working with the dough at all, from rolling it out to building a lattice, quickly warms and softens the butter. It's imperative to make sure the dough is always thoroughly chilled before baking, so the butter can get firm and cold.
- The oven was not at the right temperature. Be sure to always check your oven's accuracy with an oven thermometer before every bake. If the oven temperature is too low, the butter can melt out of the pastry before the proteins and starches in the dough get a chance to set.

Pastry not holding together?
- **Pie slices and pastries easily fall apart in your hand?** The dough didn't develop enough gluten to give it the structure it needed. Your dough needed more water for those gluten-making protein bonds to do their thing. This can also happen if you combine low-protein flour with high-fat butter, and don't give it enough folds or hydration.
- **Soggy bottom on your pie or galette?** Underhydrating your dough left you with pockets of thirsty flour that got their fill from the filling, or your pie filling didn't have enough sugar and/or

What the Hell Happened? (cont'd.)

starch to bind with the water. Next time, add more water to the dough or add more sugar/starch to your pie filling.

Is your pastry dense and hard with no poof?
- There was too much gluten development and the butter was worked too much into the dough. Next time, try to use less water and/or no more than two folds. This can also happen if you combine high-protein flour with low-fat butter, and give it too many folds or excess hydration.
- **Did your pastry shrink after baking?** The dough developed too much gluten, so try less flour and/or no more than two folds next time. This is also more likely to happen with higher protein flour.

Freezing Rough Puff Pastry Dough

This dough is hard to work with once chilled. I prefer to roll it out right away, then store it frozen in sheets for future use, similar to the puff pastry you can buy at the store.

For rectangular sheets:
1. On a lightly floured surface with a rolling pin, roll each half of the dough into a ¼-inch-thick rectangle just smaller than your sheet pan.

2. Line the sheet pan with parchment paper. Fold the dough into quarters and unfold it onto the sheet pan. Top with parchment paper before placing the next sheet of dough on top.

3. Chill in the fridge until firm but still pliable, about 30 minutes.

4. Lightly dust the surface with flour and work with one sheet of dough at a time, keeping the parchment paper underneath it. Have the short end of the pan facing you, fold the top third of the dough over the center, then fold the bottom third over that, to form an envelope. Repeat with remaining dough sheet.

5. Chill in the freezer until firm, then tightly wrap with plastic wrap and store in a zip-top bag in the freezer.

6. When you need the pastry, thaw overnight in the fridge, then bring to room temperature for 10 to 15 minutes before use. →

**Freezing Rough Puff
Pastry Dough
(cont'd.)**

For pie-ready rounds:

1. On a lightly floured surface, using a rolling pin, roll each half of the dough into an ⅛-inch-thick round about 14 inches in diameter.

2. Line a sheet pan with parchment paper. Fold the dough into quarters and unfold it onto the sheet pan. (The ends might extend past the pan, that's okay.) Top with parchment paper before placing the next sheet of dough on top.

3. Chill in the fridge until firm but still pliable, about 30 minutes.

4. Lightly dust the surface with flour and work with one sheet of dough at a time, keeping the parchment paper underneath it. Roll up the dough like a jelly roll, then repeat with remaining sheet of dough.

5. Chill in the freezer until firm, then tightly wrap with plastic and store in a zip-top bag in the freezer.

6. When you need the pastry, thaw overnight in the fridge, then bring to room temperature for 10 to 15 minutes before use.

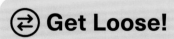 **Get Loose!**

I think it's best to learn how to make rough puff with the forgiving combination of low-protein flour (like Gold Medal) and a slow-melting, stiff, American-style butter. Once you've gotten that down, get creative with other flours and fats. Sometimes that means you'll develop something exciting and new, like the Pumpernickel Rough Puff variation on page 333, while other times you might just waste a whole lotta money, like when I tried to make a foie gras pie crust. Check out the rough puff variations on the following pages to help you get going.

Two Ways to Roll Dough

Cheddar Cheese Rough Puff Pastry

> Makes enough for 2 deep-dish pies, 1 double-crust pie, or two 11 × 15-inch sheets

> Active: 20 mins. | Total: 20 mins.

> Advanced | Vegetarian

Ingredients:

300 grams (2½ cups) all-purpose flour

1 tablespoon granulated sugar

1½ teaspoons Diamond Crystal kosher salt

170 grams (1½ cups) coarsely grated sharp cheddar cheese

200 grams (14 tablespoons) cold, unsalted, American-style butter, cut into ½-inch cubes,
OR
170 grams (12 tablespoons) cold, unsalted, European-style butter, cut into 1-inch cubes

130 grams (½ cup plus 1 tablespoon) cold water, plus more

→ This pastry is an excellent crust for apple pie, Broccoli & Cheese Galette (page 337), and the best-ever pigs in a blanket. Try it with other semihard cheeses, like pepper jack, Manchego, or Comté. If you roll out this dough to a scant ⅛ inch thick, cut into squares, chill, and bake, you've got yourself some killer homemade cheese crackers!

---

1. Whisk together the flour, sugar, and salt. Add the cheese and whisk until evenly incorporated.

2. Add the butter cubes, toss in the flour mixture, and smash each cube just as directed in the Rough Puff Pastry recipe (page 324).

3. Add the water and assess the hydration as directed in the Rough Puff Pastry recipe.

4. Laminate the dough and assess the lamination as directed in the Rough Puff Pastry recipe.

Pumpernickel Rough Puff Pastry

Makes enough for 2 deep-dish pies, 1 double-crust pie, or two 11 × 15-inch sheets

Active: 20 mins. | Total: 20 mins.

Advanced | Vegetarian

Ingredients:

150 grams (1¼ cups) all-purpose flour

130 grams (1 cup plus 1 tablespoon) whole grain rye flour

20 grams (¼ cup) black cocoa powder

1½ teaspoons Diamond Crystal kosher salt

300 grams (2 sticks plus 5½ tablespoons) cold, unsalted, American-style butter, cut into ½-inch cubes,
OR
260 grams (2 sticks plus 2½ tablespoons) cold, unsalted, European-style butter, cut into 1-inch cubes

130 grams (½ cup plus 1 tablespoon) cold water, plus more

40 grams (2 tablespoons) unsulfured or blackstrap molasses

→ Inspired by the flavors and color of pumpernickel bread, this rough puff pastry has a slight bitterness from black cocoa and blackstrap molasses. Try it with sweet or savory applications like Cherry Pumpernickel Pie (page 341) or a cold tart topped with cream cheese and smoked salmon.

1. Whisk together the flour, rye flour, cocoa, and salt.

2. Add the butter cubes, toss in the flour mixture, and smash each cube just as directed in the Rough Puff Pastry recipe (page 324).

3. Stir together the water and molasses, then add to the flour mixture and assess the hydration as directed in the Rough Puff Pastry recipe.

4. Laminate the dough and assess the lamination as directed in the Rough Puff Pastry recipe.

Save Your Scraps!

You made this dough with your own hands, with 100 percent butter, and after reading my very long recipe, you can't let any of it go to waste! As long as you don't let the dough get too warm, you can bake up the ends and trim into these crisp and flaky treats. (Yes, even if they've got a bit of egg wash on them.) Don't try to knead the scraps into a smooth ball, which will overwork the dough. Instead, toss them into a container and pop it in the fridge. When you're ready, loosely gather the dough shreds together and let the rolling pin do most of the heavy lifting.

Cheese Twists

→ Any semifirm or firm cheese will work well here—if it will grate, it'll be great! Think nutty Gruyère, sharp cheddar, or salty parmesan. Avoid very soft or fresh cheeses, like brie or mozzarella, which will make a melty mess.

1. Line a sheet pan with parchment paper.

2. On a lightly floured surface, using a rolling pin, roll out your scraps of leftover dough into a ¼-inch-thick rectangle.

3. With a pastry brush, dust off any excess flour from the surface, then brush lightly with egg wash or water.

4. Cover half the dough with toppings, cheese, and sprinkles of choice (see cheese twist inspirations, below).

5. Fold the undressed dough over the cheese-topped half, brush off any excess flour, and sprinkle with more cheese. Using a rolling pin, gently press and roll until ¼ inch thick.

6. Use a sharp knife or pizza cutter to divide the dough into ½-inch-wide strips.

7. Working with one strip at a time, carefully lift the strip and twist both ends in opposite directions, while gently stretching the dough. Place it on the prepared sheet pan and press the ends onto the pan to keep it twisted.

8. Chill in the freezer for at least 30 minutes. (Once firm, you can store them in a zip-top bag for up to 3 months.)

9. Heat the oven to 375°F (190°C). If desired (but not required), brush with leftover egg wash, milk, or cream. Bake until golden and crisp, 15 to 20 minutes.

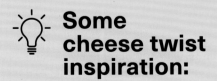

Some cheese twist inspiration:

- **Cheddar with a Kick:** Brush the dough with spicy mustard before sprinkling on sharp cheddar, smoked paprika, and chili flakes.

- **Cacio e Pepe:** Shower on a combo of grated pecorino and coarsely cracked black peppercorns.

- **My Favorite:** Top with shredded white cheddar cheese and nigella seeds (which remind me of the speckled Palestinian cheese called Nabulsi).

Sugar & Spice Spirals

→ Get wild with any sugar, from crunchy turbinado to smoky coconut, and any spice, like ground green cardamom, cinnamon, and even garam masala.

---

1. In a small bowl, mix together the sugar and ground spice.

2. On a lightly floured surface, using a rolling pin, roll out your scraps of leftover dough into a ¼-inch-thick rectangle, dusting with more flour as needed.

3. With a pastry brush, dust off any excess flour from the surface. Fold the top half of the dough over and brush off any excess flour from the dough and board. Fold the bottom half up and brush off excess flour.

4. Brush the dough with egg wash or water. Spread a fine layer of the sugar mixture evenly across the dough.

5. Roll the dough up into a tight log and chill in the freezer until firm, about 30 minutes. (Once firm, you can wrap and store the log in a zip-top bag for up to 3 months.)

6. Line a sheet pan with parchment paper and heat the oven to 375°F (190°C).

7. Using a sharp knife, slice the log crosswise into ¼-inch-thick spirals. Arrange them on the sheet pan 1 inch apart and bake until golden and crisp, 15 to 20 minutes.

Broccoli & Cheese Galette

Serves 4 to 6

Active: 1 hr. | Total: at least 4 hrs.

Advanced | Vegetarian

Ingredients:

Cheddar Cheese Rough Puff Pastry (page 332)

2 tablespoons unsalted butter

2 tablespoons all-purpose flour

225 grams (1 cup) whole milk

170 grams sharp cheddar cheese, coarsely grated (1½ cups)

1 tablespoon Dijon mustard

kosher salt and freshly ground black pepper

1 medium head broccoli (about 12 ounces/340 grams)

1 tablespoon neutral oil

Special Equipment:

rolling pin

pastry brush

→ Covered in cheese is the best way to eat broccoli. Growing up, my favorite after-school snack was a plate of florets zapped in the microwave and topped with a Kraft single. This galette takes me back with its blend of trashy and classy. The cheddar sauce bakes up thick and rich, like a chef-y Velveeta queso. I wrap it up in a cheese-speckled pastry that tastes like an extra flaky Cheez-It. The broccoli grows blackened, crisp, and charred so you feel like an adult even with all that cheese. It will look like an impossible mountain of broccoli, but please pile it all on! I promise it will quickly wilt away to nothing and be just enough. If you want to simplify this recipe, feel free to use store-bought pie dough or puff pastry (thawed if frozen).

---

1. **For the crust:** Make the cheddar cheese rough puff pastry variation. After dividing the dough in half, use one half for the galette and reserve the other half for another use.

2. On a lightly floured surface, using a rolling pin, roll the dough into a 14-inch round ⅛ to ¼ inch thick, frequently rotating the dough and sprinkling with flour as needed. Dust off any excess flour with a pastry brush.

3. Line a sheet pan with parchment paper. Fold the dough into quarters and unfold it onto the sheet pan. (The ends might extend past the pan, that's okay.) Chill in the fridge for at least 2 hours and up to 2 days in advance.

4. **Make the cheese sauce:** In a medium saucepan, melt the butter over medium heat. Add the flour and cook, stirring constantly until the mixture is foamy, light blond, and just beginning to smell toasty, about 2 minutes.

5. Add the milk a splash at a time, whisking constantly. Bring the mixture to a simmer and cook, whisking frequently, until thickened and the sauce coats the back of a spoon, about 5 minutes.

6. Remove from the heat and add the cheddar and mustard, stirring until the cheese is melted (the mixture will be very thick). Season with salt and pepper to taste. Scrape into a small bowl, press plastic wrap directly onto the surface, and refrigerate until fully cooled, at least 2 hours (or make ahead and keep in the fridge for up to 2 days).

7. **Assemble the galette:** Position a rack to the lower third of the oven and heat to 375°F (190°C).

8. Trim and discard the tough end of the broccoli stem. Peel the broccoli stem to remove the tough outer skin. Thinly slice the stem and the florets. (They won't be in even pieces and the florets will crumble, that's fine.) Place in a large bowl and toss with the oil and a big pinch of salt. →

Broccoli & Cheese Galette (cont'd.)

9. Spread the cooled cheese sauce onto the chilled dough round, leaving a 1½-inch border. (Because the sauce is so thick, the crust needs to be fully chilled, or it will tear when you try to spread on the sauce.)

10. Cutting from the edge of dough to the start of the filling, make slits in the border of the galette at 2- to 3-inch intervals (the slits are optional but make for a more beautiful presentation). Fold the flaps up and over the filling, slightly overlapping.

11. Top with the sliced broccoli in an even layer to the edge of the galette (it's okay for it to go over the flaps). (It will look like too much. Don't worry, it will cook down.)

12. Bake until the crust is golden brown and the broccoli has charred, 45 to 50 minutes. Rest for 10 minutes. Using the parchment paper, slide the galette onto a cutting board and cut into wedges. Serve right away.

Cherry Pumpernickel Pie

(Serves 8 to 12)

(Active: 30 mins.)

(Total: at least 6½ hrs.)

(Advanced) (Vegetarian)

Ingredients:

Pumpernickel Rough Puff Pastry
(page 333)

900 grams (about 6 cups) fresh or
frozen sweet or sour cherries,
stemmed and pitted (thawed if
frozen; do not drain)

200 grams (1 cup) granulated sugar

2 tablespoons freshly squeezed
lemon juice

1 teaspoon pure vanilla extract

¼ teaspoon almond extract (optional)

¾ teaspoon Diamond Crystal kosher
salt

1 large egg

1 tablespoon cream, milk, or water

40 grams (5½ tablespoons) tapioca
starch

Special Equipment:

9-inch pie pan (preferably metal)

rolling pin

pastry brush

ruler

foil

parchment paper

→ Sour cherries are only around for a few weeks a year, and I spend those precious days baking and eating as many of these pies as possible. The puckery sour cherries are balanced by the earthy rye crust, and damn, if it's not a looker. But let's be real, most of the time I can't get my hands on sour cherries. Luckily, this pie works just as well with an equal weight of sweet cherries or blueberries without any other adjustments. Do not change the quantity of sugar for sweet fruit. Sugar isn't just adding sweetness, but is vital to the filling setting up into a sliceable consistency. While working with the dough, cutting and weaving the strips for the lattice, make sure everything stays cold. If the butter softens, you'll lose those layers you worked so hard to create. Keep your fridge clear so you can quickly pop the dough in if it feels soft. You can also skip the lattice and top the pie with one batch of any variation of crumble instead (page 289). If you want to simplify this recipe, feel free to use store-bought pie dough (thawed if frozen).

---

1. **For the crust:** Make the pumpernickel rough puff. Divide the dough in half. On a lightly floured surface, using a rolling pin, roll half the dough into a 14-inch round ⅛ inch thick, frequently rotating the dough and sprinkling with flour as needed. Dust off any excess flour with a pastry brush.

2. Fold the dough into quarters and unfold it into a 9-inch pie pan. Gently nestle the dough into the corners of the pie pan and place the pie shell in the fridge to chill for at least 2 and up to 36 hours. (Tightly wrap with plastic if refrigerating for more than 4 hours.)

3. Roll out the second half of the dough into a ⅛-inch-thick rectangle slightly smaller than a sheet pan.

4. Line a sheet pan with parchment paper. Fold the dough into quarters and unfold it onto the sheet pan. (The ends might extend past the pan, that's okay.) Chill in the fridge for at least 2 and up to 36 hours. (Tightly wrap with plastic if chilling for more than 4 hours.)

5. **Make the filling:** In a large bowl, toss together the pitted cherries, sugar, lemon juice, vanilla, almond extract (if using), and salt until combined. Set aside.

6. **Make the egg wash:** In a small bowl, whisk together the egg and cream until no streaks remain. Set aside.

7. **Assemble the pie:** Remove the rectangle of dough from the fridge, and use the parchment paper to slide it onto a cutting board. Use a sharp knife (or pizza cutter) and ruler to cut the sheet crosswise into ½-inch-wide strips. Use the parchment to slide the dough back onto the sheet pan and chill. →

Cherry Pumpernickel Pie (cont'd.)

8. Add the tapioca starch to the cherries and toss to combine. Remove the pie shell from the fridge and scrape the filling into the pie shell. Brush the edges lightly with egg wash.

9. Lay half the strips vertically across the pie at even intervals. Fold back every other strip, then lay one strip horizontally. Fold the vertical strips back over the horizontal strip so it appears woven within them. Repeat the process until all the strips are woven horizontally across the pie. (If at any point the dough feels too soft to handle, put the pie and the dough strips into the fridge to cool.) Reserve the sheet pan and parchment that the rectangle of dough was cooling on.

10. Pinch the edges of the lattice strips and bottom crust together and trim the overhang. Chill in the fridge for 30 minutes to firm up.

11. Heat the oven: Position an oven rack to the lowest position and heat to 500°F (260°C). Place the pie onto the reserved sheet pan lined with parchment paper.

12. Brush the pie with a thin layer of egg wash, avoiding the fruit and sopping up any puddles.

13. Bake the pie: Place in the oven and immediately reduce the heat to 425°F (220°C). Bake until the crust is light golden brown, about 25 minutes.

14. Reduce the oven temperature to 375°F (190°C). Wrap the edges of the pie crust with a strip of foil (to prevent them from burning) and continue to bake until the crust is deeply browned and you can see the filling bubbling through the lattice, 40 to 45 minutes. (If the crust is looking too dark before the filling is bubbling, lightly tent with foil.)

15. Transfer the pie to a rack and cool for at least 3 hours at room temperature before serving. Tightly wrapped, leftovers will keep at room temperature for 3 days. Reheat in a 350°F (177°C) oven.

Whip (& Fold) It Good

Take your desserts to fluff city

Whip (& Fold) It Good

When I was in elementary school, I saw a chef on PBS make a strawberry soufflé. In an instant, watery whites whipped up into a dense foam. Fresh strawberry puree was folded in and the whole thing baked up tall and towering with a pink custardy center. My first attempt didn't have the same finesse. I thought that there had to be some magic, or at least a secret ingredient involved, and I'm not alone. There are many superstitions surrounding whipped desserts. Some chefs insist that loud noises, music, or dancing around while a soufflé is in the oven will make it collapse prematurely. In Lucknow, India, legend states that nimish, a local whipped cream dessert, owes its lift to the dew drops collected on its surface from the cool morning air. But it's not magic, just basic science—protein and fat matrixes. Nimish whips up better after a cold night because the cream and tools have chilled. Soufflés fall in the oven if you've overwhipped the meringue, not because you're cranking Rage Against the Machine. And my first soufflé failure was because I needed a mixer (or at the very least, a sturdy whisk), not a magic wand.

With some agitation, both cream and egg whites balloon up, trapping tons of teeny air bubbles. It's those air pockets that lend semifreddo and ice cream their creamy texture, instead of freezing rock hard. When folded into a cake batter or soufflé base, the air trapped in whipped egg whites expands, lifting the batter so it bakes up tender and light. Egg whites and sugar whipped into a glossy meringue will transform in the oven into a melt-in-your-mouth cookie or become the marshmallowy center of a pavlova. They do this by creating a net that traps air and water. However, cream and eggs build their nets in very different ways. Let's kick things off with whipped cream.

Whipped Cream

Cream is an emulsion of fat, water, and proteins. Phospholipids maintain this mixture of things that don't normally play well together in a happy, emulsified state. They are molecules that go both ways, comfortably hanging out with both fat and water and connecting them, preventing the fat from fully breaking out into droplets. To create billows of pillowy cream, we've got to get some of those phospholipids out of the way through agitation or whipping. Beat cold cream with a whisk for long enough and eventually you can scuff some phospholipids off. This allows the fat to link together and form a net that can trap air and gain volume.

Cold cream is vital when whipping, as it means the milk fat is stiff enough to form a stable net. Warm cream will never whip up, hence the overnight chill that nimish required in a time before refrigeration. As air gets worked into this net, the cream first looks thickened like yogurt, then begins to mound onto itself, before eventually nearly doubling in volume and holding stiff peaks. Keep on beating and you'll rub off all those phospholipids, causing the fat to fully clump together, collapsing the fat matrix, and pushing out all the trapped air and water. This is how you make butter and buttermilk from cream (see What Exactly Is Butter?, page 278).

How to Whip Cream

• **Start with cream that is at least 30% fat:** Fat percentages in cream can range anywhere from 18% for light cream to 60% for clotted cream. Higher fat percentages will make the cream easier to whip (and overwhip) and result in a stiffer whipped cream. I use heavy cream, which clocks in at 36% fat, because it's easy to find and is the standard for most recipes that call for cream in the US.

• **Avoid ultrapasteurized cream:** These creams have been treated at high temperatures that alter the structure of the milk fat, making it harder for them to link up and form a fat matrix.

• **Be extra cautious with unpasteurized or nonhomogenized cream**: On the extreme opposite spectrum from ultrapasteurized, these creams have been minimally processed and quickly go from perfectly whipped to forming grainy bits of butter. I always whip these creams entirely by hand.

• **Keep everything cold:** Make sure you start with cream straight from the fridge. If your kitchen is warm, chill the bowl and whisk by sticking them in the freezer for at least 30 minutes before whipping.

• **If you're whipping by hand:** Use the biggest bowl and whisk you've got. You want to give yourself room to groove. I like to work the cream around the entire bowl.

• **If you're using an appliance:** If using a hand mixer, stand mixer, food processor, or immersion blender, whip the cream until it's the thickness of yogurt, then carefully pulse to your final desired texture. Be aware that mixers can quickly overwhip cream.

• **If you have time:** Chill the whipped cream for 1 hour before using. If will stiffen up further after chilling.

Jazz Up Whipped Cream

• Sweeten cream with granulated sugar, powdered sugar, honey, or maple syrup. Add 1 to 3 tablespoons for every 1 cup at the start of the mixing. This ensures the sugar is evenly incorporated and has a chance to dissolve.

• Whip cream with jam, jelly, or preserves to add flavor, color, sweetness, and a silky body. I recommend no more than ⅓ cup per 1 cup of cream.

• Add fermented dairy for tang and to change the body. Whip cream with cream cheese, crème fraîche, or mascarpone at the start to make it extra thick. Add buttermilk, sour cream, or yogurt *after* whipping to lighten it up.

• Make fruity whipped cream by adding freeze-dried fruit. In a food processor, blitz the fruit into a fine powder with sugar (15 to 40 grams of freeze-dried fruit per 1 cup of cream). Add the cream to the processor, roughly moisten the powdered fruit with the cream by scraping it together with a fork, then pulse until thick and spreadable. (Be careful! Cream can quickly overwhip in the food processor.) Note: Powdered freeze-dried seedy fruits should be sifted first for a smooth texture, while too much freeze-dried banana can result in a gummy texture due to the high starch content.

Whipped Eggs

When eggs whip up, they form a similar net to cream, but this time it's protein (not fat) at play. In its raw and undisturbed state, egg white contains tightly coiled bundles of protein floating around in water minding their own business. Beat them with a whisk and those little bundles start bumping into one another. After enough crashes, they start to uncoil and reconnect with one another to create a big protein net. If this sounds familiar, it should, because this is very similar to what happens when you heat up an egg (read more in Egg Meets Heat on page 58).

A whole egg will get frothy and thick when whipped. Add some sugar and heat gently to coax those protein bundles loose, and whole eggs can double in volume. However, the fat from the yolk prevents major increases in volume. But if you separate the eggs and whip up the whites alone, they swell up to three to four times their original volume, eventually holding stiff peaks. Continue beyond that and, just like when you overcook scrambled eggs, those protein strands will tighten up, pushing out all the air and water that was once trapped within the net, becoming dry and broken. On their own, without salt, acid, or sugar, egg whites are particularly fussy, and easily become overwhipped and broken. Salt and acid, often in the form of cream of tartar, change the electrical charge of the proteins so they're less likely to overwhip, while sugar physically gets in the way of the proteins squeezing too tightly together. If you add enough sugar to egg whites, it can become nearly impossible to overwhip.

Egg whites whipped with sugar is called a meringue. It's how you'll usually whip egg whites for pastry (and every time in this chapter) because it is more stable than whipping them alone. French meringue is the simplest, made by whipping raw egg whites with granulated sugar. Both Italian and Swiss meringues are more stable because they heat up the whites by either pouring in a hot syrup or heating the whites and sugar over a water bath, respectively. Traditionally, meringues are made with granulated sugar, but you can make meringue with any sugar, like brown sugar, honey, maple syrup, or maple sugar. Heavier sweeteners, like molasses, take significantly longer to whip up, but with the help of a

mixer they will get there. I especially like meringues made with powdered sugar. They're very stable and bake up dense, like a Swiss meringue but without the trouble of needing to be warmed up over a water bath, because the ultrafine sugar instantly dissolves.

Since egg foams are made of protein rather than fat, they can handle some heat. Whipped cream has to stay very cold. Even a touch of warmth will make the fat soften and deflate. That's why whipped cream is used mostly in situations where it can remain chilled: as a topping, for layering cakes, lightening mousse, and in semifreddo. On the other hand, as the air trapped within an egg foam heats up, it expands, stretching the protein network and making cakes and soufflés puff. If you've overbeaten your eggs, when the air trapped inside expands it's got nowhere to go, causing all those bubbles to burst and your batter to fall. When you've whipped up whites just right, it'll puff and set into a rigid structure.

How to Whip Egg Whites

• **Start with cold and fresh eggs:** They are easier to separate without cracking the yolk. Some say that old or room-temperature eggs are easier to whip up, but with a hand or stand mixer, the difference is negligible.

• **If you're separating only a few eggs:** After cracking the egg, slide the yolk back and forth between the two shell halves until all the white slides off.

• **If you are separating a lot of eggs:** Crack them all into a bowl and use your hands to scoop out the yolks, passing the yolks from hand to hand until all the white slides off between your fingers. Be especially careful when you crack the first egg into the bowl. After that, the first egg offers a buffer for the next, preventing the yolk from cracking when it hits the bowl. Any rogue yolk spills can be scooped out with a piece of eggshell. (In an airtight container, save yolks in the fridge for 7 days or in the freezer for 1 month.)

• **Make sure your bowl and whisk are clean:** A drop of yolk won't be the end of the world, but a significant amount of fat from a greasy bowl can prevent your whites from gaining maximum volume.

Styles of Meringue

LOW-MEDIUM

salt

MEDIUM-HIGH

sugar

For a French meringue:
- Whip the whites on medium-low with salt or an acid (if using) until they reach soft peaks, before adding sugar. Some egg proteins will not unfurl in the presence of sugar, and we want to give those guys a head start, so the whites whip to their full potential.
- Add the sugar, then whip on medium to medium-high speed until they reach medium or stiff peaks (depending on what the recipe needs).

For an Italian meringue:
- Start whipping the whites on medium with salt or an acid (if using) when your sugar syrup is at 210°F (99°C).
- The egg whites should reach soft peaks when the syrup hits 240°F (115°C). Slowly stream in hot sugar syrup while whipping on medium speed until they reach medium or stiff peaks.

For a Swiss meringue:
- Whisk together the egg whites, salt or an acid (if using), and sugar until well combined. Set over a water bath and cook, while stirring and scraping constantly, until the sugar dissolves or you reach the temperature the specific recipe requires.
- Whip on medium to medium-high speed until they reach medium or stiff peaks.

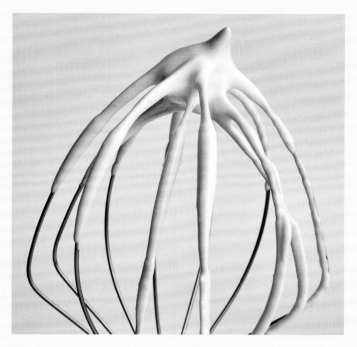

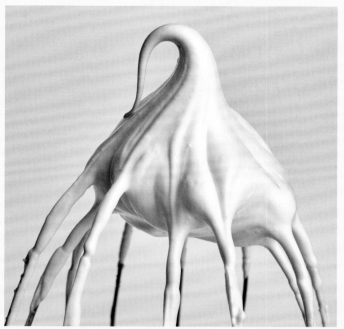

Soft peaks: The whites should easily mound onto themselves, leaving a peak in the bowl when you lift out the whisk, but then quickly fall over. Good for adding some lightness when you're not looking for maximum fluffiness, like in pancakes or waffles.

Medium peaks: Swirl the whisk in the whites and flip over. The meringue should be glossy and thick with a peak that flops over. Best for folding into cakes and soufflés when you want maximum lift and stability. Here the meringue is full of air bubbles, but still leaves room for the network to expand in the oven.

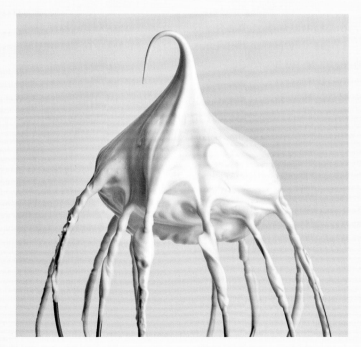

Stiff peaks: Swirl the whisk in the whites and flip over. The meringue should hold straight up with a tip that curls back onto itself. Best used for applications that aren't further heated, like in buttercream and mousse, or when baked on its own, like with meringues, cookies, or pavlova. Here the meringue is maxed out with air and would collapse if folded into a cake or soufflé.

Overwhipped: The meringue in the bowl and on the whisk stands straight up, with no curl or flop. When you try to stir, it doesn't feel flexible or smooth, and instead breaks and cracks. There's no coming back from overwhipped and you should start over.

Whip (& Fold) It Good

Raspberry & Chocolate Icebox Cake

Serves 8

Active: 20 mins.

Total: at least 6 hrs. 20 mins.

Easy   Vegetarian

Can be made gluten-free

Ingredients:

450 grams (2 cups) heavy cream

200 grams (⅔ cup) raspberry preserves

1½ teaspoons pure vanilla extract

½ teaspoon Diamond Crystal kosher salt

227 grams (1 cup) sour cream

one 9-ounce (250 gram) package classic or gluten-free chocolate wafers

fresh raspberries

Special Equipment:

stand mixer (or large bowl and hand mixer)

9 × 5-inch loaf pan

plastic wrap

→ Icebox cakes, along with wiggly Jell-O molds, were an early-twentieth-century way of announcing to the neighbors that you owned an icebox, or what the cool cats back then called fridges. Unlike the Jell-O mold, the icebox cake is one retro trend that's stuck around because it's truly delicious. If you close your eyes, you'll swear you're eating cake. The cookies absorb moisture from the whipped cream, becoming soft and cakelike, while thickening the whip, so you end up with a sliceable cake. The classic icebox cake has cookies and cream vibes, layering whipped cream with chocolate wafers. Instead of plain whipped cream, here I'm flavoring it up with raspberry preserves, which adds a fruity kick against the bitter cocoa wafers.

---

1. **Whip the cream:** In a stand mixer fitted with the whisk (or a large bowl if using a hand mixer—see Note), combine the cream, preserves, vanilla, and salt. Whip on low until slightly thickened, then increase the speed to medium and whip until the mixture holds soft peaks, 4 to 5 minutes. (To check, stop the mixer and lift the whisk from the cream. The cream should mound onto itself. If it's not there yet, continue to mix in 10-second intervals, stopping to check in between.)

2. Add the sour cream and continue whipping until you have medium peaks, about 2 minutes. (When you remove the whisk and flip it over, the cream should be thick and hold a peak that flops over.) Refrigerate while you prep the pan.

3. **Prep the pan:** Lightly moisten a 9 × 5-inch loaf pan with water (this will help the plastic wrap stick). Line with plastic wrap, leaving a few inches of overhang all around.

4. **Assemble:** Using two spoons, plop small dollops of the cream across the bottom and up the sides of the lined pan. Using a small offset spatula, smooth it into a ¼-inch-thick layer.

5. Make a cookie stack by sandwiching together 9 to 11 cookies (depending on how wide your pan is) with a thin layer of cream in between them. Stand them up in the loaf pan. Make two more stacks to fill the pan. Pour on the remaining cream, tap gently to settle the cream into the crevasses, and spread flat with an offset spatula.

6. Top with 3 cookies and wrap with the plastic overhang. Refrigerate for at least 6 and up to 24 hours.

7. **Serve:** Freeze for 30 minutes just before serving (this will help the cake unmold cleanly). Unwrap the top of the cake, invert onto a platter, remove the pan and plastic. Garnish with fresh raspberries, slice, and serve.

Note: If using a hand mixer, you will need to increase the speed by one level and double the mixing times.

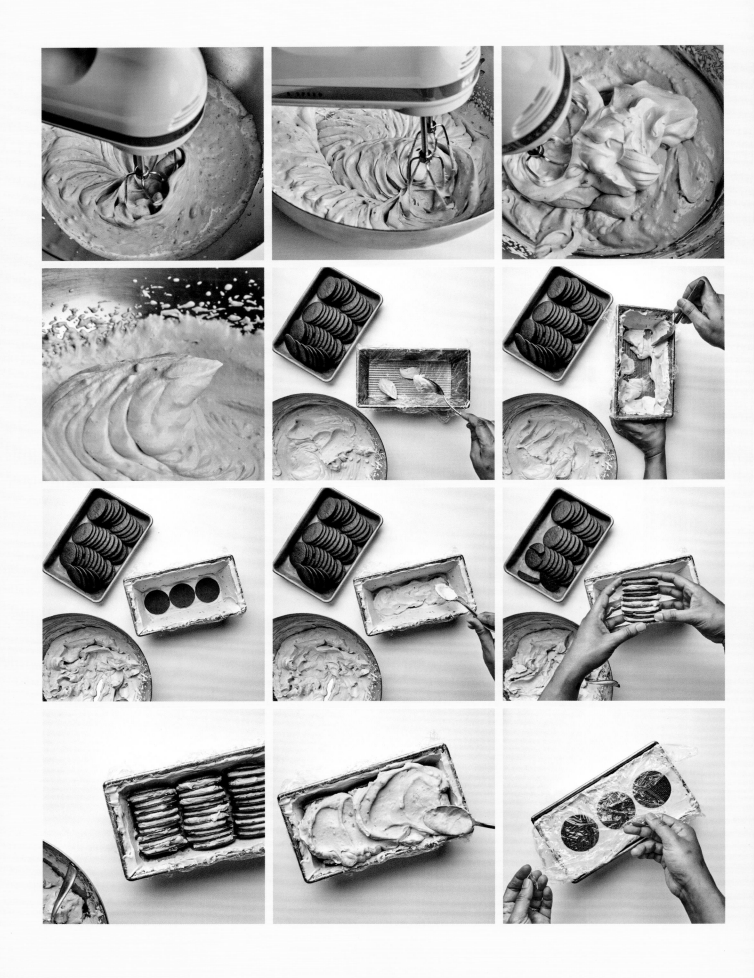

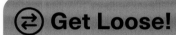 **Get Loose!**

Get creative and make your icebox cake with any combo of cookies or crackers (like vanilla wafers, Ritz crackers, or graham crackers) and any jazzed-up whipped cream (page 349). You can easily make this cake gluten-free by using gluten-free cookies or crackers.

Banoffee Icebox Cake
- Increase the amount of heavy cream to 675 grams (3 cups).
- Omit the raspberry preserves and whip the cream with 50 grams powdered freeze-dried bananas and 50 grams (¼ cup) granulated sugar (along with the vanilla extract and salt).
- Omit the sour cream.
- Layer with vanilla wafers and 2 finely chopped Heath or Skor bars.
- Omit the raspberries and garnish the top with 1 roughly chopped Heath or Skor bar.

Black Forest Icebox Cake
- Omit the raspberry preserves and whip the cream with cherry preserves and 2 tablespoons kirsch.
- Layer with chocolate wafers as directed.
- Omit the raspberries and top with shaved chocolate and fresh cherries.

Strawberry Cheesecake Icebox Cake
- Beat the cream with 170 grams (6 ounces) cream cheese and omit the sour cream.
- Omit the preserves and add 67 grams (⅓ cup) granulated sugar instead.
- Layer with graham crackers.
- Omit the raspberries and top with quartered strawberries tossed with granulated sugar.

Pecan Praline
Meringue Cookies

Pecan Praline Meringue Cookies

(Makes 24 cookies)

(Active: 30 mins. | Total: 3½ hrs.)

(Easy) (Vegetarian)

(Gluten-free)

Ingredients:

4 large egg whites (about 140 grams)

1 teaspoon Diamond Crystal kosher salt

213 grams (1 cup packed) light brown sugar

120 grams (1 cup) pecans, toasted and chopped

Special Equipment:

sheet pans

stand mixer (or large bowl and hand mixer)

parchment paper

→ These meringues are whipped with brown sugar with toasted pecans running throughout, so they have the flavor of the Southern original, but with a light crunch that instantly melts away. You can make a meringue with any sugar, from weightless powdered sugar to thick honey, but the characteristics of the sugar heavily influence how the meringue whips up and bakes. Meringues made with heavier sugars, like brown sugar, maple, and honey, take longer to whip to stiff peaks and may require the aid of a stand mixer. Darker sugars, like molasses or gur, will bake into darker meringues, sometimes with a soft and chewy center, so they'll also need to be baked at a lower temperature or even in a dehydrator if you have one. Start here, then have fun making your own meringue recipes with different sugars, mix-ins, and flavors.

1. **Set up:** Position oven racks in the upper and lower thirds of the oven and heat to 250°F (120°C). Line two sheet pans with parchment paper.

2. **Whip the meringue:** In a stand mixer fitted with the whisk (or a large bowl with a hand mixer—see Note), whip the egg whites and salt on medium speed until they are opaque, thickened, and just hold a soft peak, 4 to 6 minutes. While whipping on medium speed, add the brown sugar 1 heaping spoonful at a time, using your fingers to break up any large clumps.

3. Increase the speed to medium-high and whip until the meringue is glossy and holds stiff peaks, stopping to scrape the bowl if there is any unincorporated sugar on the sides, 8 to 10 minutes. (To check, stop the mixer and remove the whisk from the mixer. Swirl the whisk in the meringue, lift it out, and flip it over. The meringue should hold straight with a tip that curls back onto itself. If it's not there yet, continue to mix in 30-second intervals, stopping to check after each.)

4. Tap a small dollop of meringue onto each corner of the parchment sheets to seal them down to the pans.

5. **Fold in the pecans:** Sprinkle the pecans over the meringue, then, using the head of a stiff silicone spatula, cut down the center of the meringue, then turn the bowl while scooping the bottom of the meringue up and over the top. Repeat until the pecans are evenly distributed.

6. Use two big spoons to plop generous 2-inch dollops of meringue onto the sheet pans, spacing them at least 1½ inches apart.

7. Bake the meringues: Transfer both pans to the oven and bake until the meringues are lightly browned, set but still slightly soft, and easily peel off the parchment (they will crisp as they cool), 1½ to 2 hours, switching racks and rotating the pans front to back halfway through. (To test for doneness, remove one meringue, allow to cool at room temperature, then break open to check its texture. They should be crisp and dry on the outside and slightly moist in the center.)

8. Prop open the oven with a wooden spoon and turn the oven off. Let the meringues cool in the warm oven for 1 hour.

9. Store in an airtight container at room temperature (with a desiccant if you have one) for up to 1 week if the weather is dry, or 2 days if it's humid.

Note: If using a hand mixer, you will need to increase the speed by one level and double the mixing times.

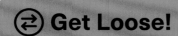 **Get Loose!**

Lemon Meringue Meringues
All the flavor of lemon meringue pie.

- Reduce the salt to ½ teaspoon. Omit the brown sugar and pecans.
- Whip the egg whites with 200 grams (1 cup) granulated sugar and plop the dollops onto clusters of roughly crumbled graham crackers. Bake as directed above.
- Fit a piping bag with a medium plain tip and fill with cooled Lemon Curd (page 417).
- After the meringues are baked and cooled (just before serving), insert the tip of the piping bag into the base of each meringue and fill with curd. Serve right away.

Make a Mess
Put your whipping skills to work by making an Eton Mess, a traditional English dessert of broken meringues, whipped cream, and fruit.

- Toss fresh fruit, like hulled strawberries, chopped mango, or pitted and halved cherries, with sugar to taste. Let sit for 15 minutes to get saucy.
- Bake the cookies as directed above. Make whipped cream. Mix the fruit with whipped cream and broken meringue cookies and divide among serving dishes. Serve right away. (If you want to make it fancy, layer the fruit, cream, and meringues in glasses.)

Vanilla Pavlova with Cocoa & Citrus

(Serves 6 to 8)

(Active: 30 mins.) | (Total: 2 hrs.)

(Easy) (Vegetarian)

(Gluten-free)

For the cocoa whipped cream:

340 grams (1½ cups) heavy cream

2 tablespoons granulated sugar

20 grams (¼ cup) Dutch process cocoa powder

pinch of Diamond Crystal kosher salt

For the vanilla pavlova:

1 vanilla bean (optional)

5 large egg whites (about 175 grams)

1 teaspoon apple cider vinegar or red wine vinegar

1 teaspoon pure vanilla extract

¼ teaspoon Diamond Crystal kosher salt

240 grams (2 cups) powdered sugar

For the topping:

4 or 5 assorted sweet citrus fruit (like Cara Cara or blood oranges, mandarins, and grapefruits)

1 fancy dark chocolate bar

Special Equipment:

stand mixer (or large bowl and hand mixer)

parchment paper

sheet pan

→ Unlike a meringue cookie, a pavlova has varying light and dense textures—crisp on the outside, marshmallowy and soft on the inside, and topped with luxurious whipped cream. Pavlova's unique texture is due to the traditional addition of starch after whipping up the egg whites with sugar and a touch of vinegar for stability. Here, I'm whipping the whites with powdered sugar, which already includes starch, and as a bonus, instantly dissolves. This results in a pillowy center and minimal risk of weeping in the oven. The slightly bitter cocoa whipped cream and tart citrus balance the sweetness of the meringue, but you don't have to stop at this cocoa and citrus combo. Get creative with any flavored whipped cream and pile it high with any ripe fruit. Try flavoring the whipped cream with powdered freeze-dried fruit (following the method for the mango whipped cream in the Cardamom Pistachio Cake, page 388), whip in fruit preserves, or fold in zingy Lemon Curd (page 417). Think of the meringue base as a canvas for you to have fun with.

1. **Make the cocoa whipped cream:** In a stand mixer fitted with the whisk (or a large bowl if using a hand mixer—see Note), combine the cream, granulated sugar, cocoa, and salt and stir to moisten the cocoa. Whip on low until slightly thickened, then increase the speed to medium and whip until the mixture holds soft peaks, 4 to 5 minutes. (To check, stop the mixer and lift the whisk from the cream. The cream should mound onto itself. If it's not there yet, continue to mix in 10-second intervals, stopping to check after each.) The cream gets thick and mousse-y as it sits. Chill in the fridge for up to 2 days before assembly.

2. **Set up:** Position a rack in the center of the oven and heat to 300°F (150°C).

3. Use a 9-inch cake pan or plate to trace a circle on a sheet of parchment paper. Line a sheet pan with the parchment, tracing side down. Make sure your bowl and whisk are thoroughly cleaned before proceeding. Traces of fat will prevent the meringue from whipping properly.

4. **Make the pavlova:** If using the vanilla bean, use a sharp knife to spilt the vanilla bean in half lengthwise. Use the back of the knife to scrape out the seeds. Reserved the pod for another use.

5. In a stand mixer fitted with the whisk (or a large bowl if using a hand mixer—see Note), combine the egg whites, vinegar, vanilla extract, salt, and vanilla seeds (if using). Whip on medium speed until just beginning to look opaque and foamy, 2 to 3 minutes. Add the powdered sugar and whip on medium-high until glossy and the meringue holds stiff peaks, 12 to 14 minutes. (To check, stop the mixer and remove the whisk from the mixer. Swirl the whisk in the meringue, lift it out, and flip it over. The meringue should hold straight with a tip that curls back onto itself. If it's not there yet, continue to mix in 30-second intervals, stopping to check after each.) →

362

Vanilla Pavlova with Cocoa & Citrus (cont'd.)

6. Use a big spoon to mound the meringue onto the parchment within the traced circle. Use an offset spatula or the back of the spoon to shape into a thick disk of even height across (the center will collapse after baking and cooling, forming a nest).

7. Bake until the outside feels crisp, dry, and is slightly cracked. The inside of the meringue will look very moist and pillowy and the pavlova will easily peel off the parchment, about 1 hour (don't overbake, or the inside will become dry and smell eggy). Turn off the oven, prop open the door with a wooden spoon, and allow the meringue to cool in the oven, about 30 minutes. Stored in an airtight container (with a desiccant if you have one), the meringue will keep for 2 days at dry room temperature.

8. Suprême the citrus (see photos on page 27): Using a sharp knife, trim off the top and bottom of the fruit. Stand the fruit upright on your cutting board and slice off the rind, moving the blade along the curve of the fruit, taking care to remove all of the white pith and outer membrane. Working over a bowl, slide the knife in between the membranes to remove each segment, letting them drop into the bowl as you work and collecting any juices that drip out. Squeeze the remaining fruit skeleton to add every last bit of juice to the bowl. (Store cut fruit and any accumulated juice in the fridge for up to 1 day before serving.)

9. Assemble: Just before serving, place the pavlova onto a serving platter. Top with cocoa whipped cream and pile the citrus on top. Use a vegetable peeler to shave curls of chocolate to garnish. Serve right away, spooning the extra juice over each portion.

Note: If using a hand mixer, you will need to increase the speed by one level and double the mixing times.

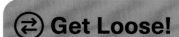 **Get Loose!**

Strawberries & Cream Pavlova
- **For the whipped cream:** Add the spent pod of a vanilla bean to 340 grams (1½ cups) heavy cream, bring to a simmer, and steep in the fridge overnight. Remove the pod, scraping off any cream still clinging to it. Whip the cream with 30 grams (¼ cup) powdered sugar and a pinch of kosher salt.
- Make the pavlova as directed.
- **For the fruit:** Quarter fresh strawberries, toss with granulated sugar to taste, and set aside until they get saucy.
- Top the pavlova with the vanilla whipped cream and macerated strawberries.

Saffron & Mango Pavlova
- **For the whipped cream:** Make the mango whipped cream from the Cardamom Pistachio Cake (page 388).
- **For the pavlova:** Omit the vanilla bean from the pavlova. With a small mortar and pestle, grind a large pinch of saffron with 1 teaspoon granulated sugar and add to the meringue instead.
- **For the fruit:** Cut up fresh mangoes.
- Top the pavlova with the mangoes and mango whipped cream.

Lemon & Blueberry Pavlova
- **For the whipped cream:** Omit the cocoa and whip the cream with grated lemon zest. Fold ½ batch Lemon Curd (page 417) into the whipped cream.
- Make the pavlova as directed.
- Top the pavlova with the lemon whipped cream and fresh blueberries.

Whip (& Fold) It Good

S'mores Ice Cream Pie

(Serves 8 to 12)

(Active: 30 mins.) (Total: at least 4 hrs.)

(Easy) (Vegetarian)

(Can be made gluten-free)

For the pie:

135 grams (9 sheets) classic or gluten-free graham crackers

50 grams (¼ cup) granulated sugar

1 teaspoon Diamond Crystal kosher salt

84 grams (6 tablespoons) unsalted butter, melted

2 pints high-quality chocolate ice cream

For the meringue:

4 large egg whites (about 140 grams); see Notes

200 grams (1 cup) granulated sugar

scraped seeds of 1 vanilla bean (optional)

1½ teaspoons pure vanilla extract

¼ teaspoon Diamond Crystal kosher salt

¼ teaspoon cream of tartar

Special Equipment:

food processor (or zip-top bag and rolling pin)

9-inch metal pie pan (see Notes)

stand mixer (or large metal bowl and hand mixer)

instant-read thermometer

kitchen blowtorch (optional)

→ My family followed halal dietary practices, so as a kid I couldn't eat anything with gelatin, including every kid's favorite soft and squishy treat, marshmallows. So of course I became obsessed with them, especially when burnished and molten in s'mores form. When Ham and I got married, we made our own wedding cake and all seven tiers were s'mores flavored. What I learned eventually is that a marshmallow doesn't even need the gelatin. Toasted Swiss meringue has the same dense, sticky interior and caramelized vanilla flavor. If you don't have a kitchen blowtorch, you can toast the meringue under a broiler, so long as your ice cream is frozen solid. Don't be tempted to cut back on the sugar in the crust. It keeps it crisp beneath the wet ice cream.

---

1. Set up: Position a rack in the center of the oven and heat to 325°F (163°C).

2. Make the crust: In a food processor, combine the graham crackers, sugar, and salt and process until very finely ground. Drizzle in the melted butter and pulse to combine. (Alternatively, place the crackers in a zip-top bag and use a rolling pin to finely smash. Transfer the crumbs to a bowl, add the sugar, salt, and melted butter. Mix with a stiff silicone spatula until thoroughly combined.)

3. Dump the graham mixture into a standard 9-inch pie pan and use your fingers to evenly press it up the sides and along the bottom of the dish. Use the flat bottom and sides of a measuring cup to further pack it into the pan.

4. Place the pan in the oven to bake until the crust is lightly browned, set, and dry, 16 to 20 minutes. Transfer to a rack to cool completely, at least 30 minutes, then freeze for at least 1 hour. (Tightly wrapped, the crust will keep at room temperature for 1 week or in the freezer for 1 month.)

5. Temper the ice cream: Place the ice cream pints in the refrigerator and let them soften until spreadable but not melted, like the consistency of thick cake batter, 30 to 40 minutes.

6. Spread the ice cream into the cooled crust using an offset spatula or the back of a spoon. Cover and transfer to the freezer to chill until fully firm, at least 2 hours and preferably overnight.

7. Make the meringue: Fill a medium saucepan with at least 1½ inches of water and bring to a simmer. In a stand mixer fitted with the whisk (or a large metal bowl if using a hand mixer—see Notes), whip together the egg whites, sugar, and vanilla seeds (if using) until no streaks remain. Place the mixer bowl over the pot of simmering water. Stirring and scraping constantly with a stiff silicone spatula, heat the egg mixture until it registers between 155° and 165°F (68° and 74°C) on an instant-read thermometer, 5 to 7 minutes. →

S'mores Ice Cream Pie (cont'd.)

(When you take the temperature of the mixture, remove the bowl from the pan so the eggs don't curdle when you stop stirring.)

8. Move the mixer bowl to the stand and add the vanilla extract, salt, and cream of tartar. Whip on medium-high speed until the meringue is glossy and holds stiff peaks, 9 to 12 minutes. (To check, stop the mixer and remove the whisk from the mixer. Swirl the whisk in the meringue, lift it out, and flip it over. The meringue should hold straight with a tip that curls back onto itself. If it's not there yet, continue to mix in 30-second intervals, stopping to check after each.)

9. Torch the meringue: Pile the meringue onto the chilled pie. Use the back of a spoon to create swoops and swirls. Lightly brown the meringue using a blowtorch (or under a broiler), then refreeze for up to 4 hours or serve right away.

10. Slice and serve: Cut the pie into 8 to 12 slices using a hot knife (see Notes). Store leftover pie tightly wrapped in the freezer for 1 week.

Notes

- Be sure to use egg whites that have not been pasteurized. Pasteurized eggs have already been treated with heat, and the additional warming over a water bath in this recipe denatures the proteins in the whites too much and they can't whip up. However, if you don't heat them up, the meringue won't have a dense and marshmallowy texture. If you are concerned about eating raw egg whites, know that by warming them above 155°F (68°C), the eggs are fully cooked.
- Do not use a glass pie plate. The extreme temperature swing from freezer to broiler can make the glass break. If you do not have a metal pie pan, use a medium skillet instead.
- If using a hand mixer, you will need to increase the speed by one level and double the mixing times.
- For clean slices, have a tall container of hot water and a clean kitchen towel handy. Dip the knife in the water and wipe clean between slices.

What the Hell Happened?

Did you whip and whip only to never reach a peak, ending up with a syrupy mess instead? If your water bath isn't hot enough when you are heating up the eggs, too much moisture will evaporate from the egg whites before they reach temperature. Make sure the water below the bowl is actively steaming and use a metal rather than glass bowl, which will quickly transfer the heat to the egg whites.

Get Loose!

Try this with any combo of cookies and ice cream. Swap out the meringue for other toppings like The Best Fudge Ever (page 450), Coconut Caramel (page 451), or whipped cream. Want to take things to the next level? Fill the crust with any of the semifreddo variations (page 380). My parents have a Baskin-Robbins, and ice cream cakes and clown cakes are all right, but growing up I was all about their ice cream pies. I begged for one for every special occasion. (Any of you remember those killer cappuccino ice cream bars they sold for a hot minute?) Here's how I like to make those BR classics at home:

Grasshopper Pie
- **For the crust:** Make the Oreo crust from the Chocolate Pudding Pie (page 421). Cool and freeze as directed above.

- **For the ice cream:** Fill with Mint Chocolate Chip Semifreddo (page 380) or use 2 pints high-quality mint chip ice cream; freeze as directed.

- **For the topping:** Skip the meringue. Pipe crisscrossed stripes of The Best Fudge Ever (page 450) on top, then decorate with whipped cream rosettes.

Turtle Pie
- **For the crust:** Make the Oreo crust from the Chocolate Pudding Pie (page 421). Cool and freeze as directed above.

- **For the ice cream:** Fill with Honey Vanilla Semifreddo (page 380) or use 2 pints high-quality butter pecan ice cream. Freeze as directed.

- **For the topping:** Skip the meringue. Once the pie is totally frozen, gently warm the Coconut Caramel (page 451) and spread on top. Return to the freezer.

- Pipe a border with The Best Fudge Ever (page 450) and decorate with whipped cream, pecans, and more caramel.

Mud Pie
- **For the crust:** Make the graham crust as directed on page 366.

- **For the ice cream:** Fill with Coffee Semifreddo (page 380) or use 2 pints high-quality coffee ice cream. Freeze as directed.

- **For the topping:** Skip the meringue. Once the pie is totally frozen, gently warm The Best Fudge Ever (page 450) and spread on top. Return to the freezer.

- Decorate with whipped cream and chopped salted toasted almonds.

Fallen Chocolate Soufflé Cake

(Serves 8 to 12)

(Active: 30 mins.) | (Total: 2 hrs.)

(Easy) (Vegetarian)

(Gluten-free)

Ingredients:

softened butter or cooking spray for the pan

315 grams high-quality dark chocolate, roughly chopped (about 2 cups)

140 grams (10 tablespoons) unsalted butter, cut into pieces

53 grams (¼ cup packed) dark brown sugar

20 grams (¼ cup) Dutch process cocoa powder (see Notes)

2 tablespoons water

2 teaspoons pure vanilla extract

2 teaspoons Diamond Crystal kosher salt

5 large eggs (about 275 grams), separated

100 grams (½ cup) granulated sugar

To Serve:

vanilla ice cream or cold milk

Special Equipment:

9-inch springform pan

parchment paper

stand mixer (or large bowl and stand mixer)

→ Soufflés are super fussy. Not only do you have to whip and fold perfectly, but also your guests better be ready when it is. This soufflé cake is the complete opposite. You want it to fall, so the top buckles and cracks while the inside grows mousse-y and rich. It's really more like the lovechild of a brownie and a chocolate soufflé, sophisticated but simultaneously a rebel. Get the best quality dark chocolate you can get your hands on, but no more than 72% cacao, otherwise the cake can become dry and chalky. I like to use Valrhona Guanaja 70%. The chocolate here isn't simply adding flavor, it's important to the structure and texture of the cake. Low-quality, waxy baking chocolate or chips will make a low-quality cake. I like to have a slice of this alongside an ice-cold glass of milk or a White Russian.

1. **Set up:** Position a rack in the lower third of the oven and heat to 375°F (190°C). Grease a 9-inch springform pan with butter or cooking spray and line the bottom with a round of parchment paper.

2. **Make the batter:** In a large microwave-safe bowl, combine the chocolate and butter and heat in 30-second increments, stirring after each, until melted. (Alternatively, combine the chocolate and butter in a heatproof bowl set over a saucepan of barely simmering water. Heat, stirring often, until melted and smooth.)

3. Add the brown sugar, cocoa, water, vanilla, and salt to the chocolate mixture and whisk to combine. Whisk in the egg yolks until evenly combined.

4. **Whip the egg whites:** In a stand mixer fitted with the whisk (or a large bowl if using a hand mixer—see Notes), whip the egg whites on medium speed until just beginning to look opaque and foamy, 2 to 3 minutes. Add the granulated sugar and whip on medium-high until glossy and the meringue holds stiff peaks, 12 to 14 minutes. (To check, stop the mixer and remove the whisk from the mixer. Swirl the whisk in the meringue, lift it out, and flip it over. The meringue should hold straight with a tip that curls back onto itself. If it's not there yet, continue to mix in 30-second intervals, stopping to check after each.)

5. **Fold the meringue into the batter:** Thoroughly stir half of the meringue into the chocolate base until smooth and evenly combined. Gently fold in the remaining meringue in two batches: Using the head of a stiff silicone spatula, cut down the center of the meringue, then turn the bowl while scooping the bottom of the meringue up and over the top. Repeat until the meringue is evenly distributed.

6. Scrape the batter into the prepared pan. Firmly tap against the counter to distribute the batter and to burst any big bubbles.

7. **Bake:** Transfer to the oven and bake until the cake is puffed, cracked, and feels set, but when you insert a toothpick in the center it's still moist, with an internal temperature →

Whip (& Fold) It Good

Fallen Chocolate Soufflé Cake (cont'd.)

between 180° and 185°F (82° and 85°C), 25 to 30 minutes. (Do not overbake or the cake will be crumbly and dry.) Transfer to a wire rack to cool, for at least 1 hour. (The cake will fall as it cools.) Unclip and remove the springform sides. Slide the cake off the springform bottom and onto a serving plate.

8. Serve with a scoop of vanilla ice cream or a glass of cold milk. (Tightly wrapped, leftovers can be stored at room temperature for 2 days, in the fridge for 1 week, or in the freezer for 1 month.)

Notes
- If using a hand mixer, you will need to increase the speed by one level and double the mixing times.
- If measuring the ingredients by volume, be sure to sift the cocoa first before measuring.

What Is Chocolate?

Chocolate comes from a tree that grows near the equator called *Theobroma cacao*. Jutting out of its branches and trunks are ridged, football-shaped fruits called cacao pods. The pods start out green, then turn vivid orange and red once ripe and ready for harvesting by hand. The ripe pods are filled with large seeds that look like lychees, each covered in sweet white pulp.

These fleshy seeds are fermented, dried, roasted, and husked to become cocoa nibs. Fermentation and roasting is what gives chocolate it's distinct earthy and savory flavor. These nibs are then processed in stone grinders for hours until they become a warm and fluid mass called cocoa liquor (not to be confused with chocolate liqueur, which is the syrupy booze you add to choco-tinis). If you leave this to cool, you'll end up with unsweetened chocolate.

Cocoa liquor is further processed by divvying it up into its two core components: cocoa solids and cocoa butter. Cocoa solids and cocoa butter are then recombined along with various ratios of sugar, vanilla, and other additions (like milk solids or lecithin) to become the chocolate bars, disks, and chips we use for baking and snacking. Once we're talking about chocolate forms, like nibs and powder, some producers label stuff as cocoa while others say cacao. There's no difference between them, it's just a marketing choice. Here's a rundown of the common cocoa/cacao products you'll come across:

Cocoa Nibs
These are to chocolate what peanuts are to peanut butter. It's chocolate before it's ground until smooth and sweetened with sugar. Bitter and crunchy, like munching on a roasted coffee bean, they are best added to cookies, brownies, and granola for texture. Depending on the brand, where the cacao was harvested, and how much the nibs are roasted, they can vary greatly in flavor and texture.

Cocoa Butter
This is the fat portion of cocoa liquor. Cocoa butter's unique texture makes it solid at room temperature while easily melting in your mouth, but without feeling greasy or waxy the way many other saturated fats do. It's relatively neutral in flavor with a faint floral aroma. It's often used in professional pastry kitchens to create thin and snappy chocolate coatings on truffles and bonbons.

Cocoa Powder

Cocoa powder is the finely ground cocoa solids extracted from cocoa liquor. There are three main types of cocoa powder with very different flavors and, most important, pH levels. (pH is a measure of how acidic or alkaline something is: Vinegar is acidic and has a low pH, while egg whites are alkaline and have a high pH.) It's rarely okay to swap one for another in recipes with chemical leaveners, like baking soda and baking powder, which require a specific pH to bake up just right. Here's a breakdown of the various cocoa powders:

- **Natural cocoa powder** is ground cocoa solids without further processing. It's slightly acidic, sharp, and fruity. Its naturally reddish hue was key to the original red velvet cakes.

- **Dutch process cocoa powder** is treated with an alkaline solution. It's darker in color, less bitter, and has a neutral pH. With less acidity in the way, more of the cocoa's mellow, woodsy flavor comes to the forefront, key to chocolaty classics like devil's food cake and fudgy brownies.

- **Black cocoa powder** is an ultra-Dutched cocoa powder that tips the pH from neutral to alkaline. It's significantly darker in color with a fiercely chocolaty flavor. Because the processing intensifies the taste so much, a little goes a long way. I like to swap a spoonful of regular Dutch process cocoa for black cocoa in puddings, ice cream, and brownies when I'm seeking super-dark flavor and color.

Semisweet, Bittersweet & Dark Chocolate

There aren't any legal distinctions between semisweet, bittersweet, and dark chocolate, but typically, semisweet is the sweetest of the three. They all need to contain at least 35% cacao and no more than 12% milk solids (aka milk powder). That cacao part can have any ratio of cocoa solids and cocoa butter. That means one brand of 70% cacao chocolate can have 40% cocoa solids and 30% cocoa butter with a smoother mouthfeel and milder flavor, while another could contain 60% cocoa solids and 10% cocoa butter and taste extra bitter. It's confusing, I know. That's why chocolate percentage isn't a great indicator of how it will taste. One brand's 62% can taste darker than another brand's 72%. Fortunately, it doesn't matter in most recipes. Taste different chocolates to find your favorites.

Milk Chocolate

Milk chocolate must contain at least 10% cacao and 12% milk solids. Many brands just barely meet the legal minimums, making candy that's nearly 78% sugar and cloyingly sweet. But there are some amazing producers out there making milk chocolate with as much as 42% cacao. These milk chocolates are complex, flavorful, and rival many dark chocolates in intensity while having a velvety mouthfeel. Try to find milk chocolate bars with the cacao percentage listed on the label—they're bragging for a reason.

White Chocolate

White chocolate must contain at least 20% cocoa butter and 14% milk solids, but no cocoa solids, so some don't consider it chocolate. High-quality white chocolate should have a short list of ingredients: sugar, cocoa butter, milk solids, lecithin, and vanilla. It will melt into a lush and floral vanilla cream. Avoid any white chocolate that contains palm oil, which will leave a waxy coating on your tongue. Just like milk chocolate, there are a lot of fantastic white chocolates being produced these days with as much as 35% cocoa butter.

**Masa & Buttermilk
Tres Leches**

Masa & Buttermilk Tres Leches

(Serves 8 to 10)

(Active: 45 mins.)

(Total: at least 3½ hrs.)

(Easy) (Vegetarian)

(Gluten-free)

For the cake:

90 grams (¾ cup) masa harina

softened butter (or cooking spray) and all-purpose flour (or gluten-free all-purpose flour blend) for the pan

3 large eggs (about 165 grams), separated

1 teaspoon pure vanilla extract

1 teaspoon Diamond Crystal kosher salt

150 grams (¾ cup) granulated sugar

90 grams (¾ cup) all-purpose flour (or gluten-free all-purpose flour blend)

1 teaspoon baking powder

170 grams (¾ cup) buttermilk

For the soak:

one 14-ounce (397 gram) can sweetened condensed milk

337 grams (1½ cups) buttermilk

225 grams (1 cup) heavy cream

1 teaspoon pure vanilla extract

¼ teaspoon almond extract (optional)

¼ teaspoon Diamond Crystal kosher salt

To Serve:

225 grams (1 cup) heavy cream

2 tablespoons granulated sugar

½ teaspoon pure vanilla extract

→ One of the many fun things about tres leches (besides being absolutely lush with dairy) is that most of the structure comes from whipped eggs. This means gluten doesn't matter so much. Couple that with the high hydration from both the eggs and buttermilk, and you can play around, swapping some of the all-purpose flour with other flours. In this case, I'm adding masa harina, which is made from nixtamalized corn. (If you can't find any, use 90 grams/⅔ cup fine stoneground cornmeal in its place. The flavor and texture will be different, but delicious in its own way.) Masa harina is what you use to make Corn Tortillas (page 491) and tamales. It has a unique earthy flavor that adds depth to this cake. To shake things up even more, buttermilk steps in as one of the three milks, cutting the sweetness with its sharp tang.

1. Toast the masa harina: In a medium skillet, toast the masa harina over medium heat, stirring frequently, until it smells nutty and looks browned, 4 to 5 minutes. Scrape into a medium bowl and set aside to cool.

2. Set up: Position a rack in the center of the oven and heat to 350°F (177°C). Grease an 11 × 7-inch baking pan (or 9-inch round cake pan) with butter or cooking spray and lightly dust with flour, tapping out any excess.

3. Whip the egg whites: In a stand mixer fitted with the whisk (or a large bowl with a hand mixer—see Note), combine the egg whites, vanilla, and salt and whip on medium speed until it holds soft peaks, about 4 minutes. Add the sugar and whip until the whites are glossy and hold medium peaks, 8 to 12 minutes. (To check, stop the mixer and remove the whisk from the mixer. Swirl the whisk in the meringue, lift it out, and flip it over. The meringue should be thick and glossy with a peak that flops over. If it's not there yet, continue to mix in 30-second intervals, stopping to check after each.) Add the egg yolks one at a time, whisking on medium until it disappears into the meringue, before adding the next.

4. Assemble the dry team: Whisk the flour and baking powder into the cooled masa harina.

5. Fold everything together: Sprinkle half the dry mixture over the meringue and fold until mostly incorporated: Using the head of a stiff silicone spatula, cut down the center of the mixture, then turn the bowl while scooping the bottom of the mixture up and over the top. Repeat until everything is evenly distributed.

6. Fold in half of the buttermilk until just absorbed and no more streaks remain. Fold in the remaining dry mixture, then fold in the remaining buttermilk.

7. Bake the cake: Pour the batter into the prepared pan. Bake until the top is set, deeply browned, and a toothpick inserted into the center comes out dry, 40 to 45 minutes (do not underbake).

376

pinch of Diamond Crystal kosher salt

2 pints blueberries

Corny Crumble (page 289), baked (optional)

Special Equipment:

11 × 7-inch baking pan (or 9-inch round cake pan)

stand mixer (or large bowl and hand mixer or whisk)

8. **Meanwhile, make the soak:** In a medium bowl, whisk together the condensed milk, buttermilk, cream, vanilla, almond extract (if using), and salt until combined.

9. **Soak the cake:** As soon as it comes out of the oven, use a skewer to poke lots of holes all over the hot cake. Poke all the way to the bottom of the pan and wiggle the skewer to make sure you have wide holes. Evenly pour the soak over the cake a spoonful at a time, letting it absorb before adding the next. Continue until it's stopped soaking in and you have a layer floating on top of the cake. (Save the extra soak to serve alongside.) Transfer to a wire rack to cool completely, about 2 hours. (Once cool, you can cover and refrigerate for up to 12 hours before serving.)

10. **To serve:** In a stand mixer fitted with the whisk (or in a bowl with a hand mixer or whisk), whip the cream, sugar, vanilla, and salt until you have soft peaks. (To check, stop and lift the whisk from the cream. The cream should mound onto itself.)

11. Spread the whipped cream evenly across the cooled cake and top with blueberries. Serve right away with extra soak and the corny crumble (if using) alongside. (Store leftovers tightly wrapped in the fridge for up to 2 days.)

Note: If using a hand mixer, you will need to increase the speed by one level and double the mixing times.

What Is Masa Harina?

Masa harina belongs in your pantry, and not just for quick tortillas and tamales. To make masa harina, corn is first nixtamalized, meaning simmered in an alkaline solution, before being ground into a paste called masa. Masa is then dried and sold as masa harina. The process of nixtamalization removes the tough seed coat, boosts nutrition, transforms flavors, and allows the corn to come together into a dough. Try making a dough with cornmeal alone and it will never stick together, but masa harina is born for it. In the past there was only one readily available producer of masa harina, but nowadays there are many high-quality brands to choose from. I prefer the flavor and texture of masa harina by Masienda, which is made with stoneground heirloom corn and is easy to purchase online.

Olive Oil Semifreddo with Dark Chocolate Chips

(Makes 1½ quarts)

(Active: 30 mins.)(Total: at least 6½ hrs.)

(Intermediate)(Vegetarian)

(Gluten-free)

For the chips:

85 grams dark chocolate, roughly chopped (heaping ½ cup)

2 tablespoons refined coconut oil (see Notes)

For the semifreddo:

4 large eggs (about 220 grams)

150 grams (¾ cup) granulated sugar

1 teaspoon Diamond Crystal kosher salt

65 grams (⅓ cup) high-quality extra-virgin olive oil

300 grams (1⅓ cups) heavy cream

Special Equipment:

sheet pan

parchment paper

instant-read thermometer

stand mixer (or large heatproof bowl and hand mixer)

freezer-safe container

→ Want to make ice cream but don't have a machine? Semifreddo to the rescue! In ice cream, the churning process introduces air bubbles into a custard base as it freezes, giving it a soft and creamy texture that quickly melts on the tongue. With semifreddo, the introduction of air bubbles happens before freezing, by whipping. We're essentially making a mousse, starting with a whipped egg base, then folding in whipped cream, and freezing. The addition of olive oil gives this semifreddo a slightly savory flavor and chewy texture, excellent against the bitter snap of the dark chocolate chips. This is the place to spring for the best extra-virgin olive oil you can get your hands on.

1. **Make the chips:** In a microwave-safe bowl, combine the chocolate and coconut oil and heat in 30-second increments, stirring after each, until melted. (Alternatively, combine the chocolate and oil in a heatproof bowl set over a saucepan of barely simmering water. Heat, stirring often, until melted and smooth.)

2. Line a sheet pan with parchment paper. Use a small offset spatula or the back of a spoon to spread the chocolate across it in a thin layer (if the layer is too thick, your chips will sink to the bottom of the semifreddo). Place in the fridge or freezer to chill until set, 15 to 30 minutes. Scrunch the parchment to break the chocolate into small pieces no bigger than ½ inch; no need to be precise. (Stored in an airtight container, the chips will keep in the fridge or freezer for 1 month.)

3. **Cook the eggs:** Fill a medium saucepan with at least 1½ inches water and bring to a simmer. In a stand mixer fitted with the whisk (or a large heatproof bowl if using a hand mixer—see Notes), whisk together the eggs, sugar, and salt until no streaks remain. Place the bowl over the pan of simmering water. Stirring and scraping constantly with a stiff silicone rubber spatula, heat the egg mixture until it reaches between 155° and 165°F (68° and 74°C) on an instant-read thermometer, 5 to 7 minutes. (When you take the temperature of the mixture, remove the bowl from the heat so the eggs don't curdle when you stop stirring.)

4. **Whip the eggs:** Set the bowl back in the mixer (or use the hand mixer) and whip the egg mixture on high until pale yellow, doubled in volume, and it falls off the whisk in a thick ribbon, about 5 minutes.

5. With the mixer running on medium-high, very slowly stream in the olive oil. Scrape the egg mixture into a large bowl to free up the mixer bowl for whipping the cream (or leave it and grab another bowl if using a hand mixer).

6. **Whip the cream:** In the same mixer bowl (no need to wash it), whip the cream on medium until it reaches soft peaks. (To check, stop and lift the whisk from the cream. The cream should mound onto itself.) →

Whip (& Fold) It Good

379

7. **Fold:** Stir half the whipped cream into the egg mixture to lighten it. Then fold the remaining cream in two additions: Using the head of a stiff silicone spatula, cut down the center of the mixture, then turn the bowl while scooping the bottom of the mixture up and over the top. Repeat until the cream is evenly distributed.

8. Add the chips and gently stir to roughly distribute.

9. **Freeze:** Scrape into a freezer-safe container and tightly cover. Freeze until set, at least 6 hours and preferably overnight. (Tightly wrapped in the freezer, the semifreddo will keep for 1 month.) Scoop the semifreddo into cones or bowls to serve.

Notes
- You can make the chips with olive oil instead of coconut oil, but they won't be as snappy.
- If using a hand mixer, you will need to increase the speed by one level and double the mixing times.

⇄ Get Loose!

As with ice cream, you can flavor this up any way you like. Swap the granulated sugar for brown sugar, maple syrup, or honey. Heat up the cream before steeping with herbs, tea, spices, or coffee, then chill and whip away. Try adding different extracts, food coloring, or lightweight mix-ins. After partially freezing you can even swirl in fudge, caramel, or preserves.

Mint Chocolate Chip Semifreddo
- **For the chips:** Make the chips with milk chocolate instead of dark.
- **For the eggs:** Reduce the salt to ½ teaspoon. While whipping the eggs, add ¼ to ½ teaspoon peppermint extract, 1 teaspoon vanilla extract, and 1 to 3 drops green food coloring.
- Omit the olive oil. Increase the cream to 340 grams (1½ cups).

Honey Vanilla Semifreddo
- **Infuse the cream with vanilla:** Increase the cream to 340 grams (1½ cups) and place it in a saucepan. Add the scraped seeds and pod of a vanilla bean to the cream. Bring to a simmer, cover, and steep overnight. Remove the pod, scraping off any cream still clinging to it. Whip as directed.
- Omit the chips.
- **For the eggs:** Swap the granulated sugar for an equal *weight* of honey.
- Omit the olive oil.

Coffee Semifreddo
- **Infuse the cream with coffee:** Increase the cream to 340 grams (1½ cups) and place in a saucepan with ⅓ cup ground coffee. Bring the cream to a simmer, then remove from the heat, cover, and steep for 1 hour. Strain and remeasure, topping off with cream as needed to return to the original amount (340 grams/1½ cups). Whip as directed.
- Omit the chips.
- **For the eggs:** Reduce the salt to ½ teaspoon and swap the granulated sugar for an equal *weight* of light brown sugar.
- **While whipping the eggs:** Add 1 teaspoon vanilla extract. Omit the olive oil.

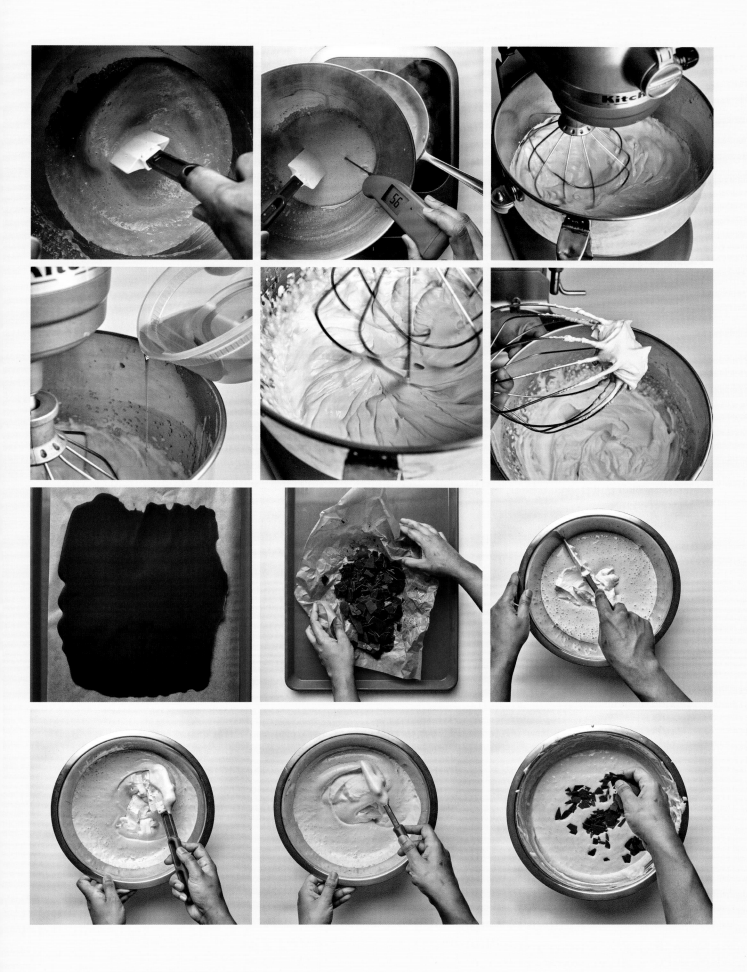

White Chocolate Macadamia Mousse

Serves 8

Active: 30 mins.

Total: at least 6½ hrs.

Advanced   Vegetarian

Gluten-free

Ingredients:

200 grams high-quality white chocolate, roughly chopped (1½ cups)

2 tablespoons unsalted butter

3 large eggs (about 165 grams)

50 grams (¼ cup) granulated sugar

½ teaspoon Diamond Crystal kosher salt

225 grams (1 cup) heavy cream

290 grams (2 cups) salted, roasted macadamia nuts, roughly chopped

Special Equipment:

stand mixer (or large heatproof bowl and hand mixer)

instant-read thermometer (optional)

eight 6- to 8-ounce (180 to 225 gram) serving dishes

→ I know people love to hate on white chocolate, and that's fine because it leaves more for me. High-quality white chocolate is milky, buttery, and heady with vanilla. Pair that with salty macadamia nuts and bam, I'm right back in the '90s at the mall getting a cookie from Mrs. Fields. But fine, if you want, go ahead and swap out the white chocolate for milk or dark, and top with any nut, fruit, or crumble (pages 288–89) that gets you feeling warm and fuzzy.

Be super careful while melting white chocolate, which can easily burn and seize. Remove it from the heat while it's still got some unmelted chunks, then let it finish melting from the residual heat. The whipped eggs and cream are folded into the dense melted chocolate in phases. This keeps as much volume intact as possible and prevents the chocolate from seizing due to the cold cream. Be sure to use high-quality chocolate bars rather than chips, which are often coated in waxes that prevent even melting. If you can find Valrhona Ivoire—a salty, butterscotch-y, caramelized white chocolate—give it a try in this recipe. It makes my absolute favorite mousse.

---

1. **Melt the chocolate:** In a large microwave-safe bowl, combine the chocolate and butter and heat in 30-second increments, stirring after each, until almost fully melted. Remove from the heat and stir with a stiff silicone spatula until fully melted and smooth from the residual heat. (Alternatively, combine the chocolate and butter in a large heatproof bowl set over a saucepan of barely simmering water. Heat, stirring often, until almost fully melted. Remove from the heat and stir with a stiff silicone spatula until fully melted and smooth from the residual heat.) Set aside to slightly cool. (Even after fully melting, white chocolate looks thicker than dark. Be careful not to overheat and burn the chocolate.)

2. **Heat the eggs:** Fill a medium saucepan with at least 1½ inches water and bring to a simmer. In a stand mixer fitted with the whisk (or a large heatproof bowl if using a hand mixer—see Note), whisk together the eggs, sugar, and salt until no streaks remain. Place the bowl over the pot of simmering water. Stirring and scraping constantly with a flexible silicone spatula, heat the egg mixture until warm and most of the sugar has dissolved, 2 to 3 minutes. (To check, remove the bowl from the heat and feel the mixture between your fingers; it should feel only slightly gritty. On an instant-read thermometer it will be between 135° and 145°F/63° and 57°C.)

3. **Whip the eggs:** Set the mixer on the stand (or use the hand mixer) and whip the egg mixture on high speed until it is pale yellow, doubled in volume, and falls off the whisk in a thick ribbon, about 3 minutes. Scrape the mixture into a medium bowl to free up the mixer bowl for whipping the cream (or leave it and grab another bowl if using a hand mixer).→

382

White Chocolate Macadamia Mousse (cont'd.)

4. **Whip the cream:** In the same mixer bowl (no need to wash it), whip the cream on medium speed until it reaches medium peaks. (To check, stop the mixer and lift the whisk from the cream. The cream should be thick with a peak that flops over.)

5. **Fold everything together:** Thoroughly stir half of the whipped egg mixture into the melted chocolate. (You will lose a lot of volume, that's okay.) Gently fold the rest of the egg mixture into the chocolate: Using the head of a stiff silicone spatula, cut down the center of the mixture and turn the bowl while scooping the bottom of the mixture up and over the top and repeating until mostly homogeneous. Fold in the whipped cream in two batches until mostly homogeneous. (The mixture will look loose and deflated; don't worry, it will set up once chilled.)

6. **Serve:** Divide among 8 serving dishes and chill for at least 6 hours and preferably overnight. Sprinkle with the macadamia nuts and serve.

Note
- If using a hand mixer, you will need to increase the speed by one level and double the mixing times.

When 2 Become 1
How to combine the heavy and light stuff without losing all the fluff

After whipping up your eggs or cream, when you incorporate it with other ingredients, you want to keep as many of those air bubbles intact as possible. It's time to fold! This is a move that requires a bit of practice to get right, but with the correct tools and a few tries, you'll be ready for these light-as-air desserts.

- First, make a bubble sacrifice to the batter gods. When combining something light into something dense, thoroughly stir one-quarter to one-half of the light mixture into the dense. You will lose much of the volume from this first mixing, but it makes it easier to evenly fold in the rest.

- Use a stiff spatula with a wide head and the biggest bowl you've got. If you don't have a large spatula, you can also become the spatula: Grip a flexible bowl scraper and be prepared to go arm deep into the mixture.

- Grip the spatula near the head, to give you maximum control. You might get a little messy, but it will be worth it.

- Use the spatula to cut down the center of the mixture, then to scrape under the mixture, while turning the bowl in the opposite direction. Then fold the bottom up and over the top.

- Repeat this motion, cutting down the middle, turning the bowl, and folding the bottom over the top, until everything is evenly incorporated.

**Cardamom
Pistachio Cake
with Mango
Whipped Cream**

Cardamom Pistachio Cake

with Mango Whipped Cream

(Serves 8 to 12)

(Active: 45 mins.) | (Total: at least 3 hrs.)

(Advanced) (Vegetarian)

(Gluten-free)

For the cake:

softened butter or cooking spray

120 grams (1 cup) pistachios, toasted

200 grams (1 cup) granulated sugar

¾ teaspoon kosher salt

½ teaspoon baking powder

½ teaspoon ground cardamom

100 grams (¾ cup plus 4 teaspoons) cake flour or gluten-free all-purpose flour blend

4 large eggs (about 220 grams)

1 large egg yolk (about 20 grams)

70 grams (5 tablespoons) unsalted butter, melted and cooled

For the topping:

30 grams (heaping ½ cup) freeze-dried mango

3 tablespoons granulated sugar

pinch of kosher salt

340 grams (1½ cups) heavy cream

½ teaspoon pure vanilla extract

sliced fresh mango

toasted pistachios

Special Equipment:

9-inch round metal cake pan

parchment paper

food processor

stand mixer (or large heatproof bowl and hand mixer)

instant-read thermometer

388

→ A genoise is a sponge cake enriched with fat, giving it more richness and flexibility than the lean sponge used in a tres leches cake, but with a similar structure from whipped eggs. It's incredibly versatile, ready to roll up, layer, stack, and soak with syrups. Here we're warming the eggs over a water bath to denature their proteins, so we can gain plenty of volume during whipping without having to separate the eggs. Once you get the hang of it, swap the pistachios for an equal weight of any other nut or flour, and swap the butter for an equal weight of any other fat—try hazelnuts with hazelnut oil, coconut flour with melted virgin coconut oil, or cornmeal with extra-virgin olive oil.

---

1. **Set up:** Position a rack in the center of the oven and heat to 350°F (177°C). Grease a 9-inch round metal cake pan with softened butter or cooking spray and line the bottom with a round of parchment paper and grease it as well.

2. **Blend the nuts:** In a food processor, pulse together the pistachios, 67 grams (⅓ cup) of the sugar, the salt, baking powder, and cardamom until very fine. Add the flour and pulse to combine. Transfer to a medium bowl and whisk to make sure everything is evenly incorporated.

3. **Heat the eggs:** Fill a medium saucepan with at least 1½ inches water and bring to a simmer. In a stand mixer fitted with the whisk (or a large heatproof bowl if using a hand mixer—see Note), whisk together the whole eggs, egg yolk, and remaining 133 grams (⅔ cup) sugar until no streaks remain. Place the bowl over the pan of simmering water. Stirring and scraping constantly with a stiff silicone spatula, heat the egg mixture until it is warm and most of the sugar has dissolved, 3 to 4 minutes. (To check, remove the bowl from the heat and feel the mixture between your fingers; it should feel only slightly gritty. On an instant-read thermometer it will be between 135° and 145°F/57°and 63°C.)

4. **Whip the eggs:** Set the bowl back on the mixer (or use the hand mixer) and whip the egg mixture on high speed until it is pale yellow, doubled in volume, and falls off the whisk in a thick ribbon, 2 to 3 minutes. Reduce the speed to medium and, with the mixer running, very slowly stream in the melted butter.

5. **Fold in the dry ingredients:** Remove the bowl from the stand mixer. Sprinkle the dry ingredients over the whipped eggs. Using the head of a stiff silicone spatula, cut down the center of the mixture, then turn the bowl while scooping the bottom of the mixture up and over the top. Repeat until the dry ingredients are evenly distributed.

6. **Bake:** Pour the batter into the prepared pan and firmly tap the pan against the counter to distribute and to pop any large bubbles. Bake until puffed, lightly browned along the edges, and set but the cake →

Cardamom Pistachio Cake (cont'd.)

retains an impression when gently poked, 25 to 30 minutes. Transfer to a rack to cool completely in the pan.

7. **Unmold:** Run a small offset spatula along the edges to loosen. Flip the cake onto a plate, peel off the parchment, and flip once more onto a serving plate.

8. **Make the topping:** In a food processor, combine the freeze-dried mango, sugar, and salt and blitz until finely ground. Add the cream and vanilla, and use a fork to roughly mix, moistening all the mango powder. Pulse until thickened, spreadable, and doubled in volume, taking care not to overwhip. It comes together quickly.

9. **To serve:** Spread the cream onto the cooled cake, using the back of a spoon to create swoops and swirls. Top with fresh mango and pistachios and serve. (Store leftovers tightly wrapped in the fridge for up to 2 days.)

Note: If using a hand mixer, you will need to increase the speed by one level and double the mixing times.

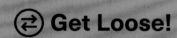 **Get Loose!**

Chocolate Hazelnut Roll Cake
- Swap the pistachios for skin-on hazelnuts. Toast at 325°F (163°C) until deeply browned, 20 to 25 minutes. Place in a clean kitchen towel to rub off the skins.
- Omit the cardamom. Swap the melted butter for hazelnut oil.
- Pour the cake batter into a sheet pan that's been greased and lined with parchment paper. Spread the batter evenly onto the sheet pan and bake at 350°F (177°C) until just set, 12 to 14 minutes.
- Immediately after removing from the oven, invert another sheet pan on top or cover with foil and set aside to steam, soften, and cool.
- Run an offset spatula along the edges of the cake to loosen, then slide the cooled cake onto a clean surface.
- Omit all the topping ingredients. Instead, spread the cake with a thin layer of chocolate hazelnut spread and roll up, peeling off the parchment as you go. Trim off the ends, transfer to a platter, dust with cocoa, and serve.

Coconut Rum Layer Cake
- Swap the pistachios for equal *weight* of coconut flour.
- Omit the cardamom. Swap the melted butter for virgin coconut oil (melted and cooled).
- After baking and cooling, use a sharp serrated knife to split the cake horizontally into 2 layers.
- Omit all the topping ingredients. Instead, make a syrup by combining ¼ cup dark rum, ¼ cup sugar, and 2 tablespoons water. Brush lighlty onto the layers.
- Spread a thin layer of the Coconut Caramel (page 451) between the layers. Frost with whipped cream, pile toasted coconut on top, and drizzle with more caramel.

Smooth Operator

Set the silkiest custards & puddings

Smooth Operator

When I was in middle school, my family took a trip to Vegas with relatives visiting from Georgia. We lived in Southern California, so when any family was in town they'd want to hit up the big three—Disneyland, Universal Studios, and the equally family-friendly Vegas strip. While the parents got rowdy up at the nickel slots, my cousins and I went to an Emeril Lagasse restaurant we couldn't afford. The three of us had the complementary bread, shared a sushi roll appetizer, and finished it off with a slice of banana cream pie. The pie was as classic as could be, graham cracker crust filled with vanilla pastry cream, thick slices of ripe banana, heaped with whipped cream, and showered in chocolate shavings, with sticky caramel swirled to the rim of the plate. As soon as we got back to the valley from Vegas, my cousins and I tried to re-create that pie. Our attempt was not so great. The pudding was lumpy and floury, not rich and smooth like Emeril's. The whipped cream came from a can and we used a frozen pie crust from my parents' Baskin-Robbins. In our defense, the Internet wasn't flush with recipes back then (I actually don't even think we had the Internet yet), so it was a stab in the dark.

Custards and puddings have few ingredients and don't require the same level of precision as a lot of other pastries. An extra splash of milk or swapping the granulated sugar for honey won't be a game changer—whereas with a cake, either of those swaps would lead to disaster. That's because these desserts are more about technique than exact amounts. The custard my cousins and I made was lumpy and floury because it wasn't cooked out enough. Even if we had the right ratio of milk to egg to flour, without the right technique, we couldn't get anywhere near that Emeril-level of smooth-but-still-sliceable custard. However, once you learn the process and techniques for each type of pudding and custard, you can make a recipe your own. Since there's no leavening or caramelization involved, you can play around with different sugars. You can customize the custards to your taste, increasing the ratio of cream and egg yolks if you want it richer, and experiment with nondairy milks, like coconut, soy, or cashew.

Puddings, custards, and curds are all thickened liquids, most often dairy or juice. Whether something is called a pudding, custard, or anglaise depends on what part of the world you are in. Traditionally in the US, most recipes followed the French definitions, but with increasing global influence the terms have become free-flowing and subjective. My French training taught me that a crème anglaise is cream thickened with yolks, pudding is milk thickened with starch, pastry cream is

Hey! Years Later, I Figured It Out. Want to Make Emeril's Banana Cream Pie?

- Make the Vanilla Bean Pastry Cream (page 427) with 28 grams (¼ cup) cornstarch so it's sliceable.

- Make the graham cracker crust from the S'mores Ice Cream Pie (page 366) in a 9-inch deep-dish pie pan.

- Spread ⅓ cup Coconut Caramel (page 451) onto the base.

- Slice 3 ripe bananas and arrange on top of the caramel.

- Whisk the cooled pastry cream until smooth and pour over the bananas. Spread with an offset spatula until flat and refrigerate for at least 2 and up to 12 hours.

- Top with whipped cream. Use a vegetable peeler to shave chocolate on top and drizzle Coconut Caramel all over. BAM!

All the Ways to Pudding

milk thickened with starch and eggs, and curd is citrus thickened with eggs and starch. But we're not in France, so I think we should do whatever the hell we want. For my chocolate pudding, I thicken it with starch and eggs because I want it richer. Instead of just using cream, I add milk to my crème anglaise because I want it lighter. And I like to make curd with buttermilk and citrus juice because I like Creamsicles. I believe if it tastes good, you don't need to follow strict definitions. Instead, let's talk about what different thickening agents do to dairy and other liquids.

Thickening with Acid

One simple way to make a set pudding is by curdling cream with acid to make a posset. The acid causes the tightly coiled bundles of protein already present in dairy to unfurl into long strands. They then hook up together into one mass, setting the dairy into a thick curd. This is also what happens with fermented dairy products, like yogurt and sour cream. In those instances, lactic acid bacteria consume the sugars in milk and transform them into lactic acid, which then curdles the milk. With a posset, the inherent flavor of the dairy doesn't change, but it thickens similarly to yogurt. You can make a posset with anything acidic, from freshly squeezed citrus to vinegar and even wine. The more acid and sugar you add to the dairy, and the longer you give it time to chill, the more firmly set your pudding will be.

Thickening with Gelatin

Have high-quality bone broth on your hands? The kind made with collagen-rich bones and simmered a long time, that's firm and bouncy when cold? That's essentially gelatin. As animal bones and skin simmer, all the connective tissues, collagen, and various peptides attached to them dissolve into the water. Once cooled, these dissolved proteins set into a gel by forming a network that traps the liquid. The flavorless gelatin we use today in the form of sheets or powder is a refined and dried version of this, ready to melt and disperse into liquids, setting juice into jewel-like jigglers, turning sugar syrup into bouncy gummy bears and marshmallows, stabilizing fluffy mousse and pie fillings, and setting cream into quivering panna cotta. There

**All the Ways to Pudding
(cont'd.)**

are vegetarian alternatives, like agar and iota, but they require different methods for dispersal and dissolving, and work with their own unique ratios.

Every brand of gelatin sets differently, some are firmer, more elastic or brittle, clearer or more opaque. Gelatin can be sourced from anything with collagen, most typically pork, but also beef or fish. All this makes it incredibly difficult to make a standardized recipe with gelatin. Gelatin makers need to have a summit and settle things for us consumers once and for all.

For my recipes I use Knox powdered gelatin, which is the most readily available brand in the US. If you're using another brand, it will take some trial and error to figure out exactly how much to use. Anyone who offers a simple conversion from sheets to powder without calling out specific brands should not be trusted. The best way to get to know the strength of your gelatin is by blooming, dissolving, and setting some into water. My panna cotta recipe sets 1 quart of liquid, so by gelling 1 quart of water with your particular brand of gelatin you can get a rough idea of what the texture will end up like, knowing that the cream will result in a softer set.

How to Use Gelatin

• Hydrate the gelatin: For powdered gelatin, sprinkle the gelatin over a small bowl of cold liquid, then use a fork to disperse it. For gelatin sheets, submerge the sheets in ice water.
  › The reason for using ice cold liquid is that warm or hot liquid will cause the outside to hydrate before the inside, leaving grainy bits of gelatin that never fully dissolve, and ultimately throwing off the final set of your dessert.

• Let the gelatin sit in liquid for 10 minutes to fully hydrate. Blooming for longer can make the gelatin set stronger.

• For powdered gelatin, all the liquid you hydrate it in will end up in the recipe. For gelatin sheets, wring out the sheets before using.

• Melt the gelatin in hot liquid no higher than 212°F (100°C). Anything above that temperature can weaken the gelatin and affect how it sets.

• After dissolving the gelatin into the hot liquid, you should strain it just in case there are any undissolved granules left behind.

398

Thickening with Eggs

ACID, EGGS & GELATIN RELY ON PROTEIN NETWORKS TO THICKEN LIQUIDS

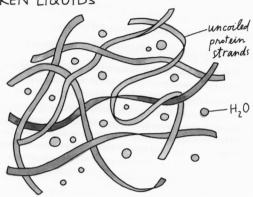

uncoiled protein strands

—H$_2$O

Possets rely on the protein already present in a liquid to thicken it, but eggs bring their own protein bundles to the party. Once dispersed into a liquid and gently heated—either on the stovetop while stirring or baked in the oven—the protein strands in the eggs uncoil. The strands then reconnect to form a protein matrix that traps liquid, sugar, and anything else that's floating around in a net. This gives egg-thickened liquids body. But just like when you're whipping egg whites or making scrambled eggs, the proteins can overcoagulate. Too much heat will cause the protein net to tighten up and fold onto itself, squeezing out all the liquid, resulting in a grainy custard that tastes overly eggy. You must be very careful with how you apply heat to custards that are thickened with eggs alone. Stovetop custards must be stirred constantly, over no more than medium-low heat, and baked custards should be cooked in a water bath if a tender curd without cracks is what you're after.

The same ratio of eggs to liquid can yield wildly different final textures, depending on whether the mixture is baked or stirred. Baked custards set into one big mass, like a panna cotta or posset, but the constant stirring of stovetop custards keeps the protein chains short for a pourable sauce. More eggs and sugar result in a firmer-set curd or thicker pudding.

Eggs alone begin to coagulate at 144°F (62°C), but when they are dispersed into liquid or sugar, the temperature necessary for coagulation increases. That's why when adding eggs to a hot liquid you must go through a step called tempering. If you try to add raw eggs to a hot liquid, the eggs will immediately cook before you can whisk them in, leaving strands and scrambles just like egg drop soup (see Stracciatella alla Romana, page 77). Instead, slowly stream some of the hot liquid into the eggs while whisking vigorously. Once the eggs are sufficiently diluted (one-third to one-half of the hot liquid has been added), you can safely add all the egg mixture to the hot liquid. Some say that tempering works because the eggs are being gently warmed up, when in fact it's all about dilution. If whisking hot liquid into eggs feels like risky business, you can get the same scramble-protection by diluting eggs in a cold liquid and slowly heating it up (like I do for Chocolate Pudding Pie, page 421). Tempering is only needed if the base liquid needs to be heated to steep it with vanilla or another aromatic addition, or to reduce the total cook time when you're making a big batch (anything more than 2 quarts).

It's always a good move to strain egg-thickened custards to remove the chalazae, the tough, stringy bit of protein that keeps the yolk in place. No amount of heat or blending will break it down, and the last thing you want in a smooth pudding is an unexpected lump. Stirred custards should be strained after cooking while baked custards should be strained before.

Thickening with Starch

STARCHES SWELL WITH WATER AND *BURST*, RELEASING CHAINS OF CARBOHYDRATES THAT THICKEN LIQUIDS

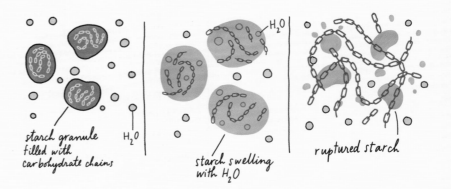

starch granule filled with carbohydrate chains

H₂O

starch swelling with H₂O

ruptured starch

Starches, like cornstarch, tapioca, and the starch in wheat flour, can thicken liquids in a process called starch gelatinization. Don't let the term confuse you, this has nothing to do with gelatin. When starch granules are dispersed in a liquid and heated, they swell with water. The water eventually breaks down the starch molecules inside the granule and forces them to burst into the liquid. This process thickens the liquid with all the now-free-floating starch molecules. The temperature at which starch gelatinizes depends on the type of starch and the amount of liquid, sugar, fat, and protein present.

Cornstarch and flour are the starches you'll most frequently see used in custard and pudding recipes. I prefer cornstarch because it cooks quickly and has a cleaner taste and texture than flour. Flour-thickened custards take a lot of simmering to lose their raw flavor and ultimately taste, well, floury. Cornstarch needs only 1 minute of active simmering to fully gelatinize. However, it does quickly break down. If you simmer a cornstarch-thickened liquid for more than 5 minutes, it will completely lose all its viscosity. That's why for long-cooked stews, gravy, and savory dishes, flour is the go-to thickener.

Thickening with Eggs & Starch

WHEN YOU COMBINE EGGS AND STARCH TO THICKEN LIQUIDS, THE BIG STARCH CHAINS PREVENT EGG PROTEINS FROM OVERCOAGULATING

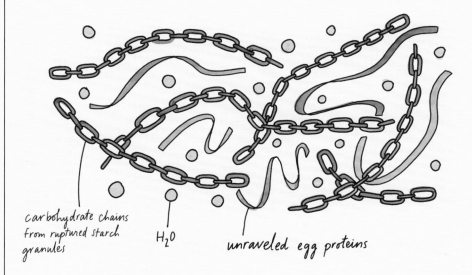

carbohydrate chains from ruptured starch granules

H_2O

unraveled egg proteins

When egg and starch combine, you can cook a custard that's stiff enough to pipe and slice, but still has a creamy and rich mouthfeel—exactly what you want for filling pies, cakes, donuts, and cream puffs.

All the Ways to Pudding (cont'd.)

Remember a few paragraphs ago when I was hammering the importance of not overcooking egg-thickened puddings, lest they curdle, clump, and get all kinds of gross? That is only true when eggs are flying solo, but when combined with starch it's a whole other ball game. Those starch granules, and the molecules that eventually erupt out of them, are so big they physically get in the way of egg proteins, preventing them from overcoagulating.

This is great news, because raw eggs contain a starch-dissolving enzyme called amylase, which needs to be brought to a boil to deactivate. Ever made a pie that looked thick when you poured it into the crust, only to liquefy the next day? That's because you left some amylase alive to eat away at the starch while your custard cooled. To ensure it's been deactivated, make sure to cook all custards, puddings, and curds that contain both eggs and starch for 1 full minute *after* you see the first sign of bubbling. For custards that contain a high quantity of starch, like a pastry cream, it can look scary when you approach that moment because the

Notes Before You Dive In

- Take note of burner temperatures and time cues. If you cook the custards at a lower temperature than suggested, they will take longer to cook, causing excess evaporation. This will result in your final custard or pudding having the wrong texture. The chocolate pudding pie will taste grainy, and the pastry cream will be lumpy. I've noticed that folks who are new to the custard and pudding world get nervous and want to turn down the heat. Don't! Just keep stirring and follow the cues in the recipe. If your milk burns or leaves a film on the bottom of the pan, you might need a pot with a heavier bottom.

- No nonstick pots allowed! Many of these recipes require you to whisk in a pot. Silicone whisks are too flimsy to properly stir a custard. Instead, stick with a stainless steel saucepan that can handle all that metal whisking action. I prefer a pan called a saucier, which has sloped sides, making it easy for you to get into the corners of the pot and evenly mix everything.

- If you've got one, now is the time to bust out your French whisk, whose tapered shape is built for getting into the corners of a pot. If you don't have one, any sturdy metal whisk will do.

mixture will look like it's growing lumps and bumps. Those blobs are from uneven heating, causing the starch in the mixture to gelatinize at varying rates, and not because the egg is curdling. Keep whisking and cooking and it will eventually get smooth and glossy.

Nondairy Dairys

Every nondairy milk, whether we're talking almond milk, soy milk, pistachio milk, or oat milk, is completely different. They have unique levels of protein, starch, and sugar. Even the same variety of faux milk can be different across brands: Some have sweeteners, some curdle with heat, while some are mostly water and get their body primarily from stabilizers like guar and xanthan gums. Except for the posset, which relies heavily on the specific nature of milk proteins to set, all the recipes in this book will work with most heat-stable nondairy milks and creams. Nope, they are not all heat stable! To test out your "milk," bring some to a simmer in a small saucepan before you go wasting eggs and sugar. If it doesn't curdle and break, it's good to go.

But even if the milk doesn't break, you'll have to experiment to get the recipes to work just right with your favorite faux milk. Some thicken significantly once cooked.

That said, there is no substitute for eggs in any of these recipes. Eggs offer structure, body, and flavor with their unique liquid proteins and there is currently no alternative out there that even comes close. (Read more about egg proteins in Egg Meets Heat, page 58.) My preferred nondairy swap for cream is to combine equal volumes of well-shaken full-fat coconut milk with coconut cream (not cream of coconut, which is sweetened and only good for piña coladas). My preferred nondairy swap for whole milk is unsweetened soy milk or homemade cashew milk. Here's how I make it:

- Combine 1 cup raw cashews with 2 cups filtered water. Cover and soak for at least 8 hours at room temperature and up to 24 hours in the fridge.
- Blend the soaked cashews and the soaking liquid in a stand blender until totally smooth.
- Add an additional 3 cups filtered water and blend to combine. (It will look thin but thickens once cooked.)
- Strain through a fine-mesh sieve and use within 3 days.

Lemon Thyme Posset with Honey & Strawberries

(Serves 6)

(Active: 15 mins.)

(Total: at least 7 hrs.)

(Easy) (Vegetarian)

(Gluten-free)

Ingredients:

450 grams (2 cups) heavy cream

4 to 6 sprigs fresh thyme

170 grams (½ cup) mild honey, like clover or wildflower

¼ teaspoon Diamond Crystal kosher salt

75 grams (⅓ cup) freshly squeezed lemon juice (2 to 3 lemons)

454 grams (1 pound) strawberries, hulled (quartered or halved if large)

granulated sugar

Special Equipment:

six 6- to 8-ounce (170 to 225 gram) serving dishes (see Note)

fine-mesh sieve

→ Posset is an old English dessert in which sweetened cream is heated and spiked with an acid, like vinegar or citrus. Here, tart lemon juice thickens heavy cream into a barely set curd, like an incredibly decadent yogurt. It's lightly sweetened with honey and perfumed with woody thyme into the perfect aromatic foil for fresh berries. If you can find lemon thyme to double down on that citrus flavor, go for it. I like to make this in the summer with juicy Tristar strawberries and local heavy cream—a recipe this simple requires the best-quality ingredients possible. To make it your own, try steeping the cream with other herbs or spices (like saffron, vanilla bean, or bay leaf).

1. In a medium saucepan, combine the cream and thyme. Bring to a simmer, cover, and remove from the heat. Steep at room temperature for 1 hour, and preferably overnight, in the fridge.

2. Add the honey and salt and heat the cream over medium heat until steamy and starting to simmer, stirring to dissolve the honey. Remove from the heat.

3. Thoroughly whisk in the lemon juice. Strain through a fine-mesh sieve into something you can pour out of, like a 1-quart deli container or a spouted measuring cup. Dividing evenly, pour about 110 grams (½ cup) into each of six serving dishes. Chill in the fridge until firm and set, at least 6 hours and preferably overnight.

4. Toss the strawberries with sugar to taste. Let sit until juicy, about 15 minutes, and divide over the posset. Serve right away. (Store leftovers tightly wrapped in the fridge for up to 3 days.)

Note: If you don't have six identical dishes, don't fret—me neither. I usually set my custards in a mix of glasses, jars, and shallow bowls. As long as you portion the same amount into each dish, it's pretty cute and lets guests pick the posset (or panna cotta or mahalabia) that calls to them.

Fruit on the Bottom Coconut Mahalabia

(Serves 6)

(Active: 20 mins.)

(Total: at least 4 hrs. 20 mins.)

(Easy) (Vegan) (Gluten-free)

Ingredients:

240 grams (¾ cup) high-quality fruit preserves (any variety)

35 grams (5 tablespoons) cornstarch

two 13.5-ounce cans full-fat coconut milk, shaken

75 grams (6 tablespoons) granulated sugar

¼ teaspoon Diamond Crystal kosher salt

2 tablespoons orange blossom or rose water (or 1½ teaspoons pure vanilla extract)

toasted coconut chips

Special Equipment:

six 6- to 8-ounce (170 to 225 gram) serving dishes

fine-mesh sieve

→ Mahalabia is a starch-thickened pudding found throughout the Middle East. It's traditionally made with whole milk, scented with rose or cardamom, and topped with nuts. It quickly comes together without any eggs, butter, or tempering. Here I make it vegan by using creamy coconut milk for the base. Coconut milk struggles to stay emulsified, with its fat readily breaking into a stiff layer on top, making it tricky to set into a panna cotta or posset all on its own. I solve that problem by simmering it here with cornstarch. A surprise layer of bright jam on the bottom adds pop and extra sweetness. Any jam will work, but bitter orange marmalade helps to cut the rich coconut milk and balance the floral orange blossom water.

---

1. Dividing evenly, spoon about 40 grams (2 tablespoons) preserves into each of six serving dishes, glasses, or jars.

2. In a small bowl, whisk together the cornstarch and 120 grams (½ cup) of the coconut milk until smooth. (Alternatively, shake the cornstarch and coconut milk together in a jar.)

3. In a heavy-bottomed medium saucepan (preferably one with sloped sides, like a saucier), combine the remaining coconut milk, the sugar, and salt. Bring to a simmer over medium heat, whisking occasionally. Meanwhile, set up a large bowl of ice and water.

4. Once at a simmer, whisk or shake the cornstarch mixture again to ensure it's well combined, then pour it into the simmering coconut milk while whisking constantly. Set a timer and simmer for 1 minute to fully cook the cornstarch, whisking constantly. (It will look thick immediately, but if you don't cook it for 1 full minute the pudding will be grainy.)

5. Remove the coconut custard from the heat and whisk in the orange blossom water. Plunge the saucepan into the ice bath and cool the coconut mixture, stirring and scraping the sides and bottom of the bowl, until cold but not set, 4 to 5 minutes. (This will prevent the fat from rising to the surface and forming a skin on the mahalabia.)

6. Strain the custard through a fine-mesh sieve into something you can pour out of, like a 1-quart deli container or a spouted measuring cup. Dividing evenly, pour about 120 grams (½ cup) custard over the preserves in each of the prepared dishes. Chill in the fridge until firm and set, at least 4 hours and preferably overnight.

7. Garnish with toasted coconut chips and serve. (Tightly wrapped, mahalabia will keep in the fridge for 3 days. Garnish with the coconut chips just before serving.)

Vanilla Bean Panna Cotta with Balsamic Vinegar

(Serves 8)

(Active: 15 mins.) | (Total: at least 5½ hrs.)

(Easy) (Gluten-free)

For the infused cream:

565 grams (2½ cups) heavy cream

340 grams (1½ cups) whole milk

1 vanilla bean

For the balsamic syrup:

60 grams (¼ cup) balsamic vinegar

75 grams (6 tablespoons) granulated sugar

For the panna cotta:

60 grams (¼ cup) cold whole milk

1 envelope Knox gelatin (2⅛ teaspoons)

100 grams (½ cup) granulated sugar

¼ teaspoon Diamond Crystal kosher salt

Special Equipment:

fine-mesh sieve

eight 6- to 8-ounce (170 to 225 gram) serving dishes

→ New York is full of killer Italian restaurants, and one of our go-to's is Il Buco Alimentari. They make the glossiest cacio e pepe, somehow have artichokes all year-round, and are responsible for one of my favorite desserts of all time, panna cotta with balsamic vinegar. Whoa, wild I know, but stick with me. The wiggly mass of barely set cream has so-aged-that-it's-syrupy balsamic vinegar dripped on top tableside until you say when. (I always insist on an unholy amount.) After each spoonful of panna cotta melts and coats your tongue, that sharp balsamic kicks in. They use really good stuff, balsamic that's had so much time to age it's thick and sticky like honey. If you don't have a hundred-dollar bottle of vinegar around, then make this syrup instead.

1. **Infuse the cream:** In a medium saucepan, combine the cream and milk. Use a sharp paring knife to split the vanilla bean in half lengthwise. Use the back of the knife to scrape the seeds into the saucepan and also add the pod. Bring to a simmer over medium heat, stirring occasionally, then remove from the heat. (Don't simmer for too long, or you will reduce the dairy mixture and throw off the recipe's ratio.) Cover and steep for at least 1 hour at room temperature and preferably overnight in the refrigerator.

2. **Meanwhile, make the balsamic syrup:** In a small saucepan, combine the vinegar and sugar and heat over medium heat, stirring frequently, until steamy and the sugar is dissolved. Transfer to a heatproof bowl and refrigerate for at least 1 hour to chill. (It will keep indefinitely at room temperature.)

3. **Make the panna cotta:** Pour the cold milk into a small bowl. Evenly sprinkle with the gelatin and use a fork to mix. Set aside to bloom for 10 minutes. (Do not bloom for longer than 10 minutes, which can make the gelatin stronger and result in a stiffer panna cotta.)

4. Remove the vanilla pod, using your fingers to scrape off any cream still clinging to it. Rinse, dry, and reserve for another use.

5. Set up a large bowl of ice and water. Add the sugar and salt to the infused cream mixture and heat over medium heat until steamy and hot, stirring to dissolve the sugar. Remove from the heat and add the bloomed gelatin. Stir until dissolved.

6. Plunge the saucepan into the ice bath and cool the cream mixture, stirring and scraping the sides and bottom of the bowl, until cold but not set, 4 to 5 minutes. (This will prevent the cream from rising to the surface and forming a skin on the panna cotta.)

**Vanilla Bean Panna
Cotta with Balsamic
Vinegar
(cont'd.)**

7. Strain through a fine-mesh sieve into something you can pour out of, like a 1-quart deli container or a spouted measuring cup. Dividing evenly, pour about 125 grams (a generous ½ cup) into each of eight serving dishes and refrigerate until firm, at least 4 hours and preferably overnight.

8. Drizzle some of the balsamic syrup onto the panna cotta and serve right away.

⇄ **Get Loose!**

Panna cotta is one of the more versatile desserts around:

- Swap out the milk for buttermilk or yogurt for a bit of tang; just be sure to add it at the very end, after melting the gelatin and straining, so the cream doesn't curdle.

- Make it extra rich by using all heavy cream or adding coconut milk in place of the milk.

- Steep the cream with any aromatic addition, like tea, coffee, cinnamon, spices, or herbs.

- Replace the granulated sugar with another sweetener, like maple, honey, or brown sugar; just be sure to not let the cream come to a boil or else it will curdle from the acidity of the sugars.

- Adjust the amount of sweetener to taste, keeping in mind that less sugar will result in a softer set.

- Top it with fruit, crumble, meringue, caramel, or anything else you can think up.

Creamy Lemon Squares with Brown Butter Crust

(Makes 16 squares)

(Active: 20 mins.) (Total: about 5 hrs.)

(Easy) (Vegetarian)

For the crust:

113 grams (1 stick) unsalted butter, cut into pieces

spent vanilla pod (optional)

60 grams (½ cup) powdered sugar

¼ teaspoon Diamond Crystal kosher salt

1 large egg yolk (about 20 grams)

120 grams (1 cup) all-purpose flour

For the filling:

5 large egg yolks (about 100 grams)

one 14-ounce can sweetened condensed milk

2 teaspoons finely grated lemon zest

scant ¼ teaspoon citric acid (optional)

pinch of kosher salt

150 grams (⅔ cup) freshly squeezed lemon juice (4 to 5 lemons)

powdered sugar, for dusting

Special Equipment:

8-inch square metal baking pan

parchment paper

→ These lemon squares borrow some magic from Key lime pie. Instead of cooking a traditional curd on the stovetop, here sweetened condensed milk is thickened with lemon juice and yolks. With the power of a posset and baked custard combined, this simple filling is supple and delicate. There's plenty of lemon juice and zest (I really want to make your mouth pucker), so the nutty brown butter crust keeps things grounded. If you've saved a vanilla pod after scraping the seeds for meringue or steeping in cream, add it to the butter while it browns to extract even more of its floral aroma.

1. **Make the crust:** In a medium saucepan, combine the butter and spent vanilla pod (if using) and heat over medium heat until foamy, about 3 minutes. Continue cooking the butter, stirring and scraping frequently with a stiff silicone spatula, until the sputtering has subsided, and the butter solids look deeply browned, 3 to 5 minutes.

2. Remove from the heat, scrape the butter and any browned bits at the bottom into a large bowl. Set aside until cool, slightly solid, but still creamy, about 20 minutes in the refrigerator or 2 hours at room temperature.

3. Heat the oven to 325°F (163°C). Grease an 8-inch square metal brownie pan and line the bottom and two sides with one long sheet of parchment, leaving 1 inch of overhang.

4. Pluck out the vanilla pod (if you used it), scraping off any butter still clinging to it. (Rinse and reserve the pod for another use.) Using a stiff silicone spatula, stir the powdered sugar and salt into the butter. Add the egg yolk and stir until evenly combined. Add the flour and stir until the mixture comes together into crumbs. Use your hands to press the crumbs together into a dough.

5. Dump the dough into the prepared pan. Use your hands and an offset spatula to spread the dough into an even layer. Prick all over with a fork and bake until dry and lightly golden, about 30 minutes. Cool fully, at least 30 minutes. (Tightly wrapped, the crust will keep at room temperature for 5 days.)

6. Increase the oven temperature to 350°F (177°C).

7. **Make the filling:** In a large bowl, whisk the egg yolks, condensed milk, lemon zest, citric acid (if using), and salt until well combined. Add the lemon juice and whisk until evenly incorporated. Pour over the cooled crust.

8. Bake until the center is just set, 14 to 16 minutes. Transfer to a rack to cool for 1 hour, then place in the fridge to chill fully, at least 2 hours and up to overnight. →

Creamy Lemon Squares with Brown Butter Crust (cont'd.)

9. Run an offset spatula or butter knife along the edges of the pan to loosen the bars. Use the parchment to lift them onto a cutting board. Using a sharp knife and wiping it clean in between slices, cut into 16 squares. Dust with powdered sugar and serve. (Tightly wrapped, leftovers can be stored in the fridge for 5 days.)

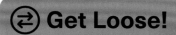 **Get Loose!**

Classic Key Lime Pie
- Assemble and bake the graham cracker crust from the S'mores Ice Cream Pie (page 366) in a 9-inch pie pan.

- Make the lemon square filling, but swap in lime juice (or key lime juice if you can find it) and zest for the lemon zest and juice. Bake as directed for lemon squares.

- After baking and cooling, top the pie with whipped cream.

Creamsicle Bars
- **For the crust:** Don't brown the butter and make the crust with whole softened butter instead.

- **For the filling:** Swap the lemon for orange juice and zest instead. Add 1 teaspoon vanilla extract.

- Bake the squares as directed.

- Make the vanilla meringue from the S'mores Ice Cream Pie (page 366) and decoratively pipe onto the Creamsicle bars. Toast with a kitchen blowtorch or carefully under the broiler.

What Are Vanilla Beans & How to Use Them

Vanilla is my absolute favorite flavor, especially in understated desserts where it can make a big impact, like panna cotta, ice cream, and shortbread. But vanilla beans are freaking expensive and will likely only become pricier over time. They currently grow only in regions threatened by climate change, like the islands of Madagascar and Tahiti, and their production is incredibly labor-intensive. Vanilla beans come from an orchid that blooms only 1 day a year and must be hand-pollinated in that tiny window of time. After harvesting, they're washed and cured, which is when they develop their signature aroma.

Each region's vanilla bean has its own unique aroma, shape, and hue. Typically, Tahitian vanilla is fresh and fruity, Madagascar vanilla is warm and creamy, and Tonga vanilla is rich and earthy. I don't think there's one vanilla bean to rule them all—it's about personal preference.

I always purchase vanilla beans online from reputable retailers. There's no way of knowing how long that one sad vanilla bean on a grocery shelf has sat under fluorescent lights. In my experience they're usually dry, stale, and more expensive than buying in bulk online. A fresh vanilla bean will be plump, pliable, and sticky with aromatic oils. I purchase my vanilla beans from Regalis Foods, Burlap & Barrel, and direct from producers like Nielsen-Massey and Heilala.

Vanilla beans should be tightly wrapped in parchment paper and stored in an airtight container in a cool and dry place. They can grow moldy if wrapped in plastic or stored in the fridge, and they will dry out in the freezer. If you haven't broken into your beans in a while, it's good to air them out for a few minutes every month (it's fun aromatherapy for you, too). If you take care of them, they should last about 6 months.

Because vanilla beans are such a precious thing, I wring every bit of perfume from them that I can:

- Split the vanilla pod in half lengthwise using a sharp paring knife. Use the back of the knife to scrape out all the seeds—they are the most aromatic part.

- Add the seeds to any recipe. The pod can be steeped in liquids. For best results, steep overnight.

- After steeping, rinse and dry the pod and reserve for further uses, such as:
  - Snip into pieces and add to coffee or tea when brewing.
  - If you have a lot of spent pods, puree them in a high-speed blender with sugar until finely ground, then add just enough light corn syrup to bind everything and you've made your own vanilla paste.
  - Add to butter while browning.
  - Place in sugar, maple syrup, honey, liquor, or cocoa powder to saturate with vanilla flavor over time.

- After the pods have had a second infusion, dry them fully, snip into small pieces, and blitz in a spice grinder with salt. This vanilla salt is killer for finishing desserts, candies, and seasoning earthy vegetables, like winter squash, parsnips, and sweet potatoes.

- If I've got a very fresh, high-quality bean, I can get away with using only half the amount called for in a recipe. Cut the bean in half crosswise and wrap just the cut end of the unused half in plastic, then fully wrap the half in parchment and reserve for future use.

Burnt Basque Cheesecake with Ripe Stone Fruit

(Serves 8 to 12)

(Active: 20 mins.) | (Total: 3 hrs.)

(Easy) (Vegetarian)

(Can be made gluten-free)

For the cheesecake:

softened butter and granulated sugar for the pan

680 grams (24 ounces) full-fat cream cheese, preferably Philadelphia brand, at room temperature

200 grams (1 cup) granulated sugar, plus more for sprinkling

¾ teaspoon Diamond Crystal kosher salt

5 large eggs (about 275 grams), at room temperature

1 teaspoon pure vanilla extract

¼ teaspoon almond extract (optional)

340 grams (1½ cups) heavy cream, at room temperature

30 grams (¼ cup) all-purpose flour (or any cup-for-cup gluten-free flour blend)

stone fruit, pitted and halved or quartered (depending on size)

Special Equipment:

9-inch springform pan (see Note)

stand mixer (or hand mixer)

instant-read thermometer

→ The burnt Basque cheesecake popped into our lives overnight and fully took over the world. Of course it was a Spanish chef who broke all the cheesecake rules (this requires no water bath, is baked in a screaming hot oven, and doesn't have a crust) only to make it better than ever before. The high heat makes the cheesecake puff and soufflé in the oven. The outside grows frighteningly caramelized and charred, while miraculously the inside sets into a silky pudding. I don't fully understand it, but I can't stop eating it. Make sure your cream cheese, eggs, and heavy cream are at room temperature. This allows for easy mixing and helps the cheesecake bake through evenly. A dash of almond extract along with vanilla doesn't make it taste like almond, but rather gives it that "Why does this taste so good?" scent.

1. Position a rack in the lower third of the oven and heat the oven to 450°F (230°C). Grease a 9-inch springform pan with softened butter and evenly coat with granulated sugar.

2. In a stand mixer fitted with the paddle (or in a large bowl with a hand mixer), combine the cream cheese, sugar, and salt and mix on medium speed until completely smooth, stopping to scrape the paddle and bowl twice during mixing, 2 to 3 minutes.

3. Add the eggs one at a time while mixing on medium-low, waiting for each one to disappear before adding the next. Stop to scrape the bowl and paddle, add the vanilla and almond extract (if using) and mix for 30 seconds.

4. With the mixer running on medium, slowly pour in the heavy cream. Stop to scrape the paddle and bowl and mix on medium speed for 30 seconds.

5. Remove the bowl from the stand mixer, sift the flour over everything, and stir with a stiff silicone spatula until evenly combined.

6. Scrape the batter into the prepared pan and evenly sprinkle sugar on top. Bake until puffed and the top is deeply caramelized and burnt in places, but still very, very jiggly, 32 to 38 minutes. (An instant-read thermometer will register between 160° and 170°F/71° and 76°C in the center.)

7. Transfer to a wire rack to cool for 1 hour, then unclip the springform sides and slide off the base onto a serving platter. Cool for another hour before serving. Slice into wedges and serve with stone fruit alongside. (Tightly wrapped, the cheesecake will keep in the fridge for 3 days. Serve cold or at room temperature.)

Note: No springform pan? Grease a 9-inch round cake pan with butter and line with 2 overlapping sheets of parchment, making sure it comes 2 inches up the sides so you can lift out the cooked cake. The parchment will crimp and pleat; that's okay.

Lemon Curd

(Makes 1 cup)

(Active: 30 mins. | Total: 2½ hrs.)

(Easy) (Vegetarian) (Gluten-free)

Ingredients:

100 grams (½ cup) granulated sugar

2 teaspoons cornstarch

pinch of kosher salt

4 large egg yolks (about 80 grams)

113 grams (½ cup) freshly squeezed
lemon juice

84 grams (6 tablespoons) cold
unsalted butter, cut into ½-inch
cubes

1 teaspoon finely grated lemon zest

citric acid (optional)

Special Equipment:

blender (optional)

fine-mesh sieve

→ Lemon might be the most popular, but any tart fruit can become a creamy curd. Curd is an egg-thickened, butter-finished custard, but instead of milk or cream we're talkin' tangy fruits like lemon, passionfruit, cranberry, and grapefruit. Less zippy juices and purees, such as pineapple or strawberry, can also come to play but will need to team up with lemon juice or citric acid for balance. The key to a curd's spreadable and almost jammy texture is a high ratio of butter and sugar to eggs and juice, so don't skimp on the acidity.

There are many ways to make curd. Whether you use whole eggs, all yolks, or cornstarch can vary from recipe to recipe. You can add the butter cubes right at the start, while the mixture is cooking, for a more butter-forward flavor, or at the end, as I have here, so the citrus can shine. All curds are good curds to me, but this is the way I like it best. Once you get to know this recipe, get in there and play with the ratios to figure out just how you like it, too. I finish this curd by whipping in the butter using a stand blender for a fluffy finish, perfect for piling high on fruit or between cake layers. If you want a dense, more set final curd, whisk in the butter by hand instead.

This recipe easily scales up, so make as much curd as your heart desires. Just keep in mind that bigger batches will take longer to cook, and take care to follow visual rather than time cues. Here, the lemon juice depends on both starch and egg yolks for thickening, so be sure to cook it for a full minute after the first bubble to deactivate the egg yolks' starch-dissolving enzyme, amylase.

---

1. In a heavy-bottomed medium saucepan (preferably one with sloped sides, like a saucier), whisk together the sugar, cornstarch, and salt. Add the egg yolks and whisk until smooth. Whisk in the juice and cook over medium-high heat, whisking constantly and taking care to get into the corners of the pot, until the mixture just simmers. Once you see the first big burpy bubble, set a timer and cook for 1 minute, stirring constantly.

2. Transfer the mixture to a blender, blend at medium speed, and add the cold butter one cube at a time. (Or you can hand-whisk in the butter for a denser curd.) Pass through a fine-mesh sieve into a small bowl and stir in the zest. Add citric acid (if using) to taste.

3. Press plastic wrap directly onto the surface of the curd and refrigerate until chilled, at least 2 hours and preferably overnight. (Refrigerated in an airtight container, the curd will keep for 2 weeks.)

⇄ Get Loose!

Make any kind of curd following this base recipe. Use it to top grapefruit (page 419) or Vanilla Pavlova (page 362), layer between cakes (page 530), fill Vanilla-Glazed Donuts (page 521), and anything else you can dream up. Just swap the lemon juice and zest for:

Grapefruit Curd: 113 grams (½ cup) freshly squeezed grapefruit juice and 1 teaspoon grated zest

Lime Curd: 113 grams (½ cup) freshly squeezed lime juice and 1 teaspoon grated zest

Pomegranate Curd: 113 grams (½ cup) unsweetened pomegranate juice and 1 teaspoon grated lemon zest

Blueberry Curd: 95 grams (½ cup) blueberries and 56 grams (¼ cup) freshly squeezed lemon juice, blended and strained. Finish with 1 teaspoon grated lemon zest.

Buttermilk Lemon Curd: 56 grams (¼ cup) buttermilk, 56 grams (¼ cup) freshly squeezed lemon juice, and 1 teaspoon grated lemon zest

Grapefruit on Grapefruit

(Makes 8 grapefruit halves)

(Active: 15 mins. | Total: 15 mins.)

(Easy) (Vegetarian) (Gluten-free)

Ingredients:

4 grapefruits

Grapefruit Curd (page 418)

→ I'm someone who wants dessert after every meal, even breakfast, and just broiling a grapefruit with a sprinkle of sugar is not enough. That's where this curd-topped broiled grapefruit comes in. The rich curd adds a touch of decadence to the bitter fruit and any weekday breakfast. Topping fruit with curd and broiling is a classic French move. The curd gets crackly and caramelized while the fruit just warms through. Try it with any seasonal fruit, from juicy peaches to plump figs.

1. Position an oven rack 6 inches below the broiler element and set the broiler to high.

2. Cut the grapefruits in half through their equators. Using a small, sharp serrated knife or steak knife, cut along the grapefruit membranes to loosen each segment. Top each half with 2 tablespoons of curd and broil until caramelized and lightly charred, 2 to 3 minutes. Serve right away.

What Is Citric Acid?

Different kinds of acid are found in all different kinds of food and each has a unique tang. Lactic acid is found wherever lactic acid bacteria has done its thing, like in dill pickles and yogurt. Acetic acid is what makes vinegars sharp and perky. Malic acid is found in many fruits, such as apples, watermelon, and cherries. And citric acid is found in citrus fruits. You can buy refined powdered versions of any of these acids online. I find citric acid to be especially handy for bumping up the flavor of any citrus dessert without having to add more juice, which could alter the final texture.

Chocolate Pudding Pie for Grown-Ups

(Serves 8 to 10)

(Active: 30 mins.) (Total: 3½ hrs.)

(Easy) (Vegetarian)

(Can be made gluten-free)

For the cookie crust:

210 grams (about 18) classic or gluten-free Oreos (or other chocolate sandwich cookies)

¼ teaspoon Diamond Crystal kosher salt

56 grams (4 tablespoons) unsalted butter, melted

For the chocolate pudding:

200 grams (1 cup) granulated sugar

45 grams (½ cup; see Note) high-quality Dutch process cocoa powder

30 grams (¼ cup) cornstarch

½ teaspoon Diamond Crystal kosher salt

3 large eggs (about 165 grams)

450 grams (2 cups) whole milk

255 grams (1 cup plus 2 tablespoons) heavy cream

85 grams dark chocolate, roughly chopped (heaping ½ cup)

1 teaspoon pure vanilla extract

To Serve:

whipped cream

extra-virgin olive oil

flaky salt

→ Jell-O pudding mix might be what drove me into the strong, sweaty arms of the baking and pastry arts. That stuff, the instant kind that thickened right before my impatient six-year-old eyes, is downright magic. When I was old enough for burner privileges, I'd make the stovetop variety and peel off the pudding skin while it was still hot and watch amazed as the skin grew back like a delicious regenerating superhero. This pudding is almost as easy to make, quickly coming together in one pot but with a deep chocolaty flavor that both kid and adult me can get behind. It's essentially a pastry cream—milk thickened with eggs and starch—enriched with cream and chocolate. For the crust, I keep it classic by using Oreo cookies (because they are a perfect cookie). What really levels this pie up from the classic is high-quality Dutch process cocoa powder (my favorite is by Valrhona), dark chocolate, and a final flourish of extra-virgin olive oil and flaky salt. The grassy, bitter olive oil and crunchy salt enhance the earthy flavor of the chocolate. Be sure to use the best EVOO you've got.

---

1. **For the cookie crust:** Preheat the oven to 325°F (163°C).

2. In a food processor, blitz the cookies (with their cream filling) and salt until finely crumbled. Drizzle in the melted butter and pulse to combine. (Alternatively, place the cookies and salt in a large zip-top bag and crush finely with a rolling pin. Transfer the crumbs to a bowl and combine with the melted butter.)

3. Transfer the crumb mixture to a standard 9-inch pie pan. Using the back of your hands, press the crumbs evenly along the walls of the pie pan. then press the crumbs in the middle against the bottom of the pan. Use the straight sides and bottom of a measuring cup to firmly pack the crumbs along the sides and bottom of the pan. Set on a sheet pan and bake until it smells chocolaty and feels dry to the touch, 12 to 15 minutes. Set aside.

4. **For the chocolate pudding:** In a heavy-bottomed medium saucepan (preferably one with sloped sides, like a saucier), whisk together the sugar, cocoa, cornstarch, and salt. Whisk in the eggs until smooth. Gradually add the milk and cream, whisking until smooth.

5. Cook over medium heat, whisking constantly, until the mixture begins to simmer, 5 to 7 minutes. Once you see the first big burpy bubble, set a timer and simmer for 1 full minute, whisking constantly.

6. Remove from the heat and whisk in the chocolate and vanilla until fully melted and incorporated. Using a stiff silicone spatula, scrape the mixture through a fine-mesh sieve and into the prepared pie crust. Use an offset spatula to evenly spread the pudding over the crust. Press plastic wrap directly onto the surface of the pudding (or don't, if you like pudding skin). Cool at room temperature for 1 hour, then transfer to the fridge to fully cool, at least 2 hours and up to overnight.→

Chocolate Pudding Pie for Grown-Ups (cont'd.)

Special Equipment:

food processor (or zip-top bag and rolling pin)

standard 9-inch pie pan

fine-mesh sieve

plastic wrap

7. To slice the pie, fill a tall container with hot tap water and keep a clean kitchen towel handy. Dip a sharp knife into the hot water and wipe dry with the towel after each slice.

8. Top each slice with a dollop of whipped cream, drizzle of olive oil, and sprinkle of flaky salt. Although best served the same day, you can store leftovers tightly wrapped in the refrigerator for up to 3 days.

Note: If measuring the cocoa powder by volume, be sure to sift it before measuring.

What the Hell Happened?

- **Crumbs not holding together into a crust?** They may be too coarsely ground; process them further, then try again.

- **Did your pudding liquefy after cooling instead of setting up firm?** Eggs contain a starch-digesting enzyme called amylase. Puddings, pastry creams, and other custards thickened with both eggs and starch need to be held at a simmer for one full minute in order to deactivate the amylase. If not, your pudding might look thickened in the pot, but become soupy and thin after chilling in the fridge. Don't risk it! Set a timer for 1 minute as soon as you spot the first bubble to make sure you cook it enough every time.

Baking Custards in a Water Bath

Some baked custards need extra love and care, like many traditional cheesecake recipes and my Baked Maple Yogurt (page 424) or Golden Saffron Flan (page 467). These recipes beg for the gentlest heat to prevent the outside from overcooking, becoming dry and curdled, and the top from cracking. It's particularly necessary for custard mixtures that are low in sugar—not a problem for Creamy Lemon Squares (page 411) or chess pies. By resting the pan in a water bath, the area submerged in the bath will never go above the temperature of the water (212°F/100°C), which is significantly lower than the oven temperature. Don't be tempted to simply lower your oven temperature. This will cause the custard to take too long to bake and grow dense due to excess evaporation.

To set up a water bath:
- Bring a lot of water to a boil. A kettle isn't usually enough, so I opt for a large pot instead.

- Get a deep pan that's wide enough for you to fit your pan of custard, like a roasting pan or big skillet.

- To protect the bottom of the custard pan, set a small wire rack or folded towel in the roasting pan or skillet.

- If you're using a springform or removable-bottom pan, wrap the base with plastic wrap and foil to prevent leaking, then fill it with custard. (In the gentle heat of the bath, the plastic won't melt and offers an extra layer of protection against leaks.)

- Place the custard pan on the rack (or towel) in the roasting pan or skillet.

- Pull out an oven rack and set the roasting pan or skillet on the rack, so you're not trying to carry a hot pan filled with water. Add hot water to the roasting pan or skillet (enough to come halfway up the sides of the custard pan) and carefully slide the oven rack in.

Baked Maple Yogurt with Granola & Grapes

Serves 8 to 10

Active: 30 mins. | Total: at least 6 hrs.

Easy | Vegetarian | Gluten-free

For the custard:

one 8-ounce (225 gram) package full-fat cream cheese, preferably Philadelphia brand, at room temperature

200 grams (½ cup plus 2 tablespoons) pure maple syrup

¾ teaspoon Diamond Crystal kosher salt

600 grams (2½ cups) whole-milk Greek yogurt, at room temperature

3 large eggs (about 165 grams), at room temperature

1 large egg yolk (about 20 grams), at room temperature

1 teaspoon pure vanilla extract

To Serve:

halved green or red seedless grapes

maple syrup

granola

Special Equipment:

9-inch deep-dish pie pan (or 2-quart baking dish)

→ My favorite Bangladeshi dessert is misti doi, baked yogurt sweetened with gur, an unrefined sugar. The yogurt is made from milk that's been simmered down for hours until thick and lightly toasted. Although this baked maple yogurt is inspired by misti doi, instead of simmering milk to thicken it, I add richness with cream cheese, and the pure maple syrup offers up earthy flavors similar to gur. If you want to avoid cracks you must be gentle with this custard, not only while it's baking, but also while it's cooling down. Starting with room-temperature ingredients helps everything smoothly combine without overmixing and promotes even cooking. (Overmixing will incorporate air, causing the custard to puff, fall, and crack.) Baking the custard in a water bath prevents the outer edges from overcooking. Lastly, cooling in stages delicately brings us to our final destination: Finish the cooking in a shut-off oven, then cool at room temperature, before chilling fully in the fridge.

---

1. Position a rack in the center of the oven and heat to 325°F (163°C). Bring a large kettle or pot of water to a boil.

2. Make the custard: In a large bowl, combine the cream cheese, maple syrup, and salt and mix with a wooden spoon or stiff spatula until smooth and homogeneous. Add the yogurt, whole eggs, egg yolk, and vanilla and whisk to evenly combine.

3. Pour the custard into a 9-inch deep-dish pie pan (or 2-quart baking dish). Set a small wire rack or folded towel in a roasting pan or skillet large enough to hold the custard pan.

4. Set the custard pan in the prepared roasting pan or a large skillet. Pull out an oven rack and place the roasting pan or skillet on the rack. Pour enough boiling water to come halfway up the sides of the custard pan. Carefully slide the rack into the oven and bake until the filling is mostly set but has a slight jiggle in the middle when you shake the pan, 40 to 45 minutes. Turn off the oven and leave the custard in the cooling oven for 25 minutes. Remove from the oven, lift the pan out of the water bath, and cool at room temperature for 30 minutes. Transfer to the fridge and cool until fully chilled, at least 4 hours and preferably overnight.

5. To serve: Scoop the custard into dishes and top with grapes, maple syrup, and granola.

Vanilla Bean Pastry Cream

(Makes 2½ cups)

(Active: 30 mins.)

(Total: at least 4½ hrs.)

(Intermediate) (Vegetarian)

(Gluten-free)

Ingredients:

450 grams (2 cups) whole milk

1 vanilla bean

4 large egg yolks (about 80 grams)

100 grams (½ cup) granulated sugar

¼ teaspoon Diamond Crystal kosher salt

22 grams (3 tablespoons) cornstarch

1½ teaspoons pure vanilla extract

56 grams (4 tablespoons) cold unsalted butter, cut into ½-inch cubes

Special Equipment:

fine-mesh sieve

→ Pastry cream is a staple in baking, used for filling éclairs, Boston cream pie, napoleons, and so much more. It can be lightened with whipped cream or meringue, enriched with whipped butter, and flavored with spices and herbs. It's thickened with both egg and starch, so it's dense, pipable, and sliceable (making it perfect for filling the Cream Buns with Jam on page 431). The addition of cornstarch prevents the eggs from coagulating, so you can bring the mixture to a simmer without fear of curdling. Once you see the first bubble, be sure to cook the pastry cream for 1 full minute to deactivate the starch-digesting enzyme found in egg yolks. Once you become comfortable with the technique, feel free to play around with ratios, adding more starch if you want it stiff, adding more yolks and butter to make it richer, or swapping out the 4 yolks for 2 whole eggs to lighten it up.

1. **Infuse the milk with vanilla:** Place the milk in a heavy-bottomed medium saucepan (preferably one with sloped sides, like a saucier). Using a sharp paring knife, split the vanilla bean in half lengthwise. Use the back of the paring knife to scrape the seeds into the milk and add the spent pod, too.

2. Bring the milk to a simmer over medium heat, stirring occasionally, and remove from the heat. (Don't simmer for too long, which will reduce the milk and throw off the recipe's ratio.) Cover and steep for at least 1 hour at room temperature and preferably overnight in the refrigerator.

3. Remove the vanilla pod, using your fingers to scrape off any cream still clinging to it. Rinse, dry, and reserve for another use.

4. **Make the pastry cream:** In a medium bowl, whisk together the egg yolks, sugar, and salt until thick and pale, 2 to 3 minutes. Add the cornstarch and whisk until smooth and combined. Coil a wet towel to make a nest for the bowl and rest the bowl on top to secure it.

5. Return the milk to medium heat and bring to a simmer, stirring occasionally. Remove from the heat.

6. Pour half of the hot milk mixture into the egg mixture in a slow and steady steam while whisking constantly. (If pouring from the pot feels too difficult, use a ladle to stream in the hot milk instead.) This dilutes and warms the eggs so they don't curdle.

7. Scrape the diluted egg mixture into the saucepan with the remaining milk and whisk to combine. Cook over medium heat, whisking constantly, until the mixture begins to simmer, 5 to 7 minutes. (It will look lumpy and curdled at first. Keep cooking and whisking and it will get smooth and thick.) Once you see the first big burpy bubble, set a timer and simmer for 1 full minute, whisking constantly. →

**Vanilla Bean
Pastry Cream
(cont'd.)**

8. Remove from the heat and whisk in the vanilla extract and butter cubes until fully melted and incorporated. Using a stiff silicone spatula, scrape the mixture through a fine-mesh sieve into a bowl. Press plastic wrap directly onto the surface and cool at room temperature for 1 hour. Transfer to the fridge and cool completely, at least 2 hours. (Or store in the fridge for up to 3 days.)

9. Once chilled, the pastry cream will look stiff and bouncy. Use a wooden spoon, sturdy whisk, hand mixer, or stand mixer fitted with the paddle to stir the cooled pastry cream until smooth before using. (If it seems too thick for your liking, add milk or cream 1 teaspoon at a time.)

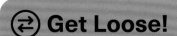 **Get Loose!**

• Want to fill a pie or cake with sliceable pastry cream? Increase the cornstarch to 30 grams (¼ cup).

• Instead of vanilla, infuse the milk with coffee, tea, or spices. After straining, measure the milk and top off if needed. Some ingredients you steep may soak up a significant amount of milk and throw off your ratios.

Cream Buns with Jam

(Makes 6 to 8 buns)

(Active: 30 mins.)

(Total: at least 4½ hrs.)

(Intermediate) (Vegetarian)

For the buns:

6 to 8 brioche buns (depending on size)

high-quality jam, jelly, or preserves

Vanilla Bean Pastry Cream (page 427)

powdered sugar, for dusting

Special Equipment:

fine-mesh sieve

→ Many cultures have a bread-plus-custard type of situation, from squishy Japanese cream pan to cardamom-scented Norwegian skolebrød to buttery French tarte tropézienne. That's because creamy custard with soft bread is universally comforting. I like to invigorate my spirits by spending the morning buying freshly baked brioche, then coming home to make vanilla bean pastry cream to fill it. Think of it like a cream-filled doughnut, but with a lot less work.

Split the buns in half and spread the cut sides with jam. Dollop the pastry cream onto the bottom buns and cover with the top buns. Dust with powdered sugar and serve.

Fruit Custard

Makes about 6 cups

Active: 30 mins.

Total: at least 4 hrs.

Advanced | Vegetarian

Gluten-free

Ingredients:

340 grams (1½ cups) heavy cream

340 grams (1½ cups) whole milk

1 vanilla bean

8 large egg yolks (about 160 grams)

115 grams (½ cup plus 1 tablespoon) granulated sugar

¼ teaspoon Diamond Crystal kosher salt

3 to 5 cups chopped or sliced assorted fruit (like bananas, mangoes, apples, peaches, grapes, and/or pomegranate seeds)

→ Fruit custard is a popular dessert throughout South Asia, likely a throwback from British colonial rule. I like it best with fresh mangoes, bananas, and pomegranate seeds, but any mix of fruit will work. How much fruit you add is up to you; I want mostly custard with the occasional bite of fruit. This custard, or anglaise, is enriched with only egg yolks, so there's no room for error. You know it's done when steamy and slightly thickened, significantly thinner and more delicate than a pastry cream or curd. If it reaches a simmer, the eggs will curdle. If you don't stir thoroughly, egg will scramble in the corners of your pot.

1. **Infuse the cream and milk:** In a heavy-bottomed medium saucepan (preferably one with sloped sides, like a saucier), combine the cream and milk. Using a sharp paring knife, split the vanilla bean in half lengthwise. Use the back of the paring knife to scrape the seeds into the milk/cream mixture and add the pod, too.

2. Bring to a simmer over medium heat, stirring occasionally, and remove from the heat. (Don't simmer for too long, which will reduce the dairy and throw off the recipe's ratio.) Cover and steep for at least 1 hour at room temperature and preferably overnight in the refrigerator.

3. Remove the vanilla pod, using your fingers to scrape off any dairy still clinging to it. Rinse, dry, and reserve for another use.

4. In a medium bowl, whisk together the egg yolks, sugar, and salt until thick and pale, 2 to 3 minutes. Coil a wet towel to make a nest for the bowl and rest the bowl on top to secure it.

5. Return the cream mixture to medium heat and bring to a simmer, stirring occasionally. Remove from the heat.

6. Pour half of the hot cream mixture into the yolk mixture in a slow and steady stream while whisking constantly. (If pouring from the pot feels too difficult, use a ladle to stream in the hot dairy instead.) This dilutes and warms the yolks so they don't curdle.

7. Scrape the diluted egg mixture into the saucepan with the remaining cream mixture and whisk to combine.

8. Cook over medium-low heat, while whisking constantly, until hot, steamy, and the custard thinly coats the back of a spoon, 2 to 5 minutes. (Do not overcook, or the custard will curdle.) Scrape into a bowl, press plastic wrap directly onto the surface, and cool at room temperature for 1 hour. Transfer to the fridge and cool completely, at least 2 hours.

9. Just before serving, stir the fruit into the cooled custard. Or serve the custard without fruit, as a sauce for cake and pie.

Caramelize

Scorching syrups & molten caramels

Caramelize

Everyone knows that sugar is super important in baking and pastry. It makes cakes tender, cookies chewy, and, obviously, all desserts sweet. That's what sugar can do in a team with flour, butter, dairy, and eggs. But sugar can accomplish plenty on its own, too. I'm talking about sauces, candies, and a wide world of chewy, sticky, crunchy treats. Learn a few tricks and sugar can be a goddamned star, developing complex, bitter flavors and a wide range of textures depending on how it is used. In this chapter, I'm gonna teach you some simple and fun techniques to safely play with sugar—but, *safety first!*

Hot Stuff Safety

One of the first treats I made for myself as a kid was caramel. We almost never had desserts around, but you know what they said in *Jurassic Park*, "Life finds a way." On my tippy toes, I could *just* reach the knobs of our microwave. I'd sprinkle sugar onto a Pyrex dish, stud it with raw nuts, and nuke the whole thing until smoky, molten, and void of its cloying sweetness. After it cooled, I'd break up this makeshift praline and munch away. Children, do not try this at home. Actually, this entire chapter requires parental supervision. Hot sugar burns are no joke. I stopped messing around with microwave candy after the dish exploded in my hands, leaving streaks and shards of hot caramel and glass across my arms. Unlike hot oil or water, which you can easily rinse off, caramel holds tight and just keeps searing. Even as a pro, I follow these rules every time:

- **Nothing adorable allowed:** Clear the kitchen of pets, babies, and toddlers, who can easily get in the way and distract you.

- **Alert the household:** Let everyone at home know, so you don't get spooked by a roommate bursting into the kitchen and knock over a pot.

- **Saucepan size matters:** Use the pot the recipe tells you to. A small pot might be necessary to make sure a smaller volume of sugar syrup can be accurately temped with a thermometer, while a larger pot is essential to prevent caramel from bubbling over when cold cream or butter is added. Follow the recipe.

- **Be organized:** Have a landing zone for your spatula, keep kitchen towels handy for grabbing hot pots and sheet pans, and gather all the tools and ingredients for your recipe before you start—you don't want to go looking for anything while the sugar is cooking.

- **Don't multitask:** Stay focused on your bubbling pot, which can quickly go from clear to smoky to blackened to burning through your shoes in a moment.

What Is Sugar?

Granulated sugar, those fine white crystals we reach for most often when baking, is part of a bigger group of molecules called, wait for it . . . sugars. In science talk, granulated sugar is called sucrose. Sucrose has one molecule each of fructose and glucose bonded together. Fructose is a sugar that comes from fruit, tastes very sweet very fast, then quickly fades away. You can also find it in honey, agave nectar, and high-fructose corn syrup. Glucose is on the opposite end of the spectrum, with a lingering sweetness that's milder than sucrose. It's made by plants and algae through photosynthesis, is the building block for all carbohydrates, and the main fuel for all living things. (Oof, talk about pressure.) Single molecules of glucose are typically found in a

438

team with fructose in things like honey, maple syrup, and molasses, while long chains of glucose make up starches. Pure glucose is manufactured by breaking up some of those starch chains. That's how you get corn syrup, a handy-dandy source of pure glucose that no pastry pantry is complete without. There are other sugars (lactose, maltose, galactose), but you rarely encounter them in traditional baking and pastry. Just know they're out there, doing their sweet thing.

Sucrose is the overachieving kid who got all the best qualities of their parents, glucose and fructose. In terms of sweetness, it falls right in the middle— Goldilocks would dig it. Unlike the other two, it doesn't get funky or taste weird in large quantities and it melts and caramelizes at a high temperature (starting around 320°F/160°C), giving you lots of room to groove at various concentrations. Sucrose creates the thickest solution when dissolved in water and is easy to find in its pure form.

What I'm getting at is that sucrose—good old granulated sugar—is the best sugar in the pastry game.

It is made by refining sugarcane stalks or sugar beets (these beets are not the same variety as the beets you eat). First the sugarcane or sugar beets are crushed to squeeze out all their juices, before an initial clarification step to remove proteins, carbohydrates, and other organic compounds. Originally this process involved the use of egg whites or blood, but today most manufacturers use a combination of heat and calcium hydroxide (the same stuff you use to keep pickles crisp). Next, the clarified liquid is boiled to drive off moisture and crystallize the sucrose. After this step, you're left with crystals of sucrose in a syrup of thick and sweet molasses. This first molasses is drained off with the help of a centrifuge and you're left with raw sugar—granules of pure sucrose with a thin coating of molasses. This kind of raw sugar has been around for ages, made first in South Asia around 500 BCE. There it's called gur or jaggery and it's still an important sweetener in South Asian cuisine. The very refined white sugar we use today didn't show up until 1100 AD and only became accessible in the 1800s. To go from sticky gur to free-flowing white sugar, the raw sugar is washed

Granulated Sugar & Friends

and spun again, forcing out a darker and more intense liquid called blackstrap molasses, before being further refined with a material similar to activated charcoal. It's one hell of a journey to go from cane/beet juice to granulated sugar, but it's this level of refinement that lets you cook sugar to high temperatures without it burning and setting into a brittle texture. No other sweetener—honey, gur, maple—can do what sucrose can do.

Granulated Sugar

This is pure sucrose, with a neutral flavor and pH. It's free-flowing and granular, making it easy to measure by volume. You can cook it to high temperatures before it burns or develops off-flavors. When dissolved in water and in higher concentrations, molecules of sucrose want to line up into orderly, tight structures, readily resulting in crystallization. That desire to crystallize is also why sugar can make crispy and crunchy candies.

Light & Dark Brown Sugar

Brown sugar is refined cane sugar with molasses added in specific quantities to mimic true raw sugar but in the form of a consistent product. Both light and dark are just as sweet as granulated sugar, but with a touch of tart and bitter notes from the molasses. Moist and sticky when fresh, they require packing for proper volume measurement, and grow hard and clumpy as they dry out. (If your brown sugar is dried out, freshen it up by placing it in a container with a damp paper towel overnight.) Because of the amino acids and organic compounds in the added molasses, light and dark brown sugars readily burn. Their slight acidity can adversely affect the leavening in recipes designed for granulated sugar, and some recipes are so specific that you cannot even swap between light and dark brown sugar.

Raw Sugars

Raw sugars include gur, jaggery, panela, demerara, and turbinado. They are refined cane sugars that still contain the residual molasses naturally left from the processing. They are essentially the result of reducing clarified cane juice. The texture, flavor, and acidity can vary greatly depending on the brand and region of origin, making them tough to bake consistently with. But they're great in desserts that require less precision, like panna cotta or poached pears. These sugars readily burn, so you cannot make high-temperature sugar syrups or caramels. Be careful when working with hot dairy, as the high acidity in raw sugars can cause hot milk to curdle.

Powdered Sugar (aka Confectioners' Sugar)
This very finely ground refined sugar has had cornstarch or tapioca starch added to prevent clumping. It instantly dissolves in cold liquids, which is why I like it for my Walnut Brown Butter Chocolate Chip Cookies (page 306) and Vanilla Pavlova (page 362). It's used to make fluffy American buttercream, smooth royal icing, and delicate glazes. It can get clumpy over time, so it's best to measure by weight. If you are measuring by volume, however, always sift the powdered sugar first for the most accuracy. Because of the added starch, it's not good for clear syrups or caramels.

Molasses
Unsulfured molasses, the jar with a grandma on the label, is the syrup that's extracted after the first and second centrifuge of unrefined sugar. (That syrup can also then be bleached with sulfur dioxide to become "sulfured" molasses.) It's sweet, dark amber, pleasantly acidic, and key to the flavor of a lot of traditional American desserts, like gingerbread, Cracker Jack, and shoofly pie. Very different from unsulfured molasses is blackstrap molasses, which is the syrup that's extracted from the final centrifuge of sugar, before it's whitened and granulated. It is inky black, has nearly half the sugar of unsulfured molasses, and is very salty. It has become popular recently because it's rich in vitamins and minerals. I like to use it primarily in savory cooking (try glazing some chicken thighs with it!). Both types of molasses are made from sugarcane as a by-product of granulated sugar production. Most recipes that just call for "molasses" are telling you to reach for unsulfured molasses, and you should never assume it can be swapped for another molasses unless a recipe explicitly gives you the go-ahead. This is particularly important when leavenings, like baking soda or baking powder, are

involved, because the significant difference in sugar and acid levels will greatly affect the outcome of the dish.

Honey

The original sweetener. People have been eating honey since, well . . . people. Honey is made through the hard work of bees, who collect nectar, concentrate it through evaporation, then ripen it with enzymes. They even package it up in wax combs. Unlike other sugars, honey is pretty much ready to go straight from the hive. Some honeys are minimally processed, simply drained off the combs and strained. Others are heated and clarified. Depending on the source of the nectar, honey can range from mild and light amber, to intense and deep brown. Stronger flavored honeys, like eucalyptus or buckwheat, are best in desserts where the honey isn't heated and is meant to be the primary flavor. Otherwise, I recommend sticking to mild clover or wildflower honey. Honey is mostly fructose, sweeter than granulated sugar, slightly acidic, and burns at 220°F (104°C). It's not good for high-temperature syrups, caramels, or any candy you want to set crisp and dry.

Maple Syrup

Sugar maple trees are tapped to collect their sap, which is about 3 percent sucrose. The sap is then boiled to concentrate the sucrose; it takes 40 gallons of sap to make 1 gallon of maple syrup. The long simmering makes the syrup taste toasty and caramelized, with notes of vanilla from the wood. It comes in various intensities depending on time of harvest. Early-harvest saps have a higher concentrations of sucrose, require less reduction, and result in a maple syrup with a delicate color and flavor. On the other hand, late-harvest saps have a lower sucrose concentration and need more boiling to become syrupy, giving them a darker flavor and color. Maple syrup from early harvests with lighter color used to be labeled grade A, while later harvest syrups with darker color were called grade B. This was not an indicator of quality but of color and flavor intensity. Because this system was confusing to the average consumer, all maple syrup in the US is now labeled as grade A. They are also labeled with color/taste categories, ranging from golden/delicate to amber/rich to dark/robust to very dark/strong. (I'm partial to the intense flavor of very dark.) Besides sucrose, maple syrup contains glucose, fructose, acids, and amino acids. The additional amino acids cause maple to burn at a lower temperature, so it is not good for high-temperature syrups and caramels. With very little glucose in the mix, maple syrup will readily crystallize into maple sugar and maple cream.

Corn Syrup
Pure glucose. Cornstarch is processed with enzymes to break the long chains of glucose into short chains and individual molecules. These short chains are what give corn syrup its thick, viscous texture and prevent crystallization in sugar syrups and ice creams by getting in the way of sucrose molecules and ice crystal formation. Corn syrup is less sweet than sucrose, thus can temper the sweetness in desserts that require a lot of granulated sugar for texture, like caramels and ice creams. It also retains moisture, helping baked goods last longer and adding chew to brownies and cookies.

High-Fructose Corn Syrup
Here corn syrup is enzymatically processed to convert some of its glucose into fructose. The most commonly used HFCSs have about half their glucose converted to fructose—making them as sweet as sucrose—but there are some that are up to 90 percent fructose. HFCS easily dissolves in water, doesn't crystallize, and is cheaper than granulated sugar. It's mostly used commercially, and you'll probably never even see it in a grocery store. There are concerns over whether HFCS is worse for your health than other refined sugars and syrups, but current scientific research shows that it breaks down in the body just like granulated sugar.

How to Make Sugar Syrups & Caramels

Caramel isn't just delicious, it's downright magical. The way bland granulated sugar can fully transform with nothing but heat still blows my mind. Caramelization is an irreversible process that breaks down sucrose molecules into countless new flavorful compounds, growing less sweet and increasingly complex the darker

How to Make Sugar Syrups & Caramels (cont'd.)

you go. But besides going to brown town, you can simmer sugar and water to specific concentrations to make candies and desserts with different textures and characteristics. Cook a sugar syrup to 230°F (110°C) where it's 20% water and 80% sucrose and it's ready to soak into buttery phyllo for a syrupy baklava (see Twice-Baked Caramelized Cashew Baklava, page 452). Take a sugar syrup to 250°F (121°C) where all but 8% of the water has cooked off, then stir it into sesame paste and watch it cool into flaky sesame halva (see Any Kinda Sesame Halva, page 470). With syrups below 245°F (118°C), it's okay to get funky with brown sugar, honey, or maple. Otherwise, stick to granulated sugar, which won't burn at high temperatures.

There are two methods for making a caramel. You can caramelize sugar by simply pouring it into a dry saucepan and letting it cook all on its own. This is the **dry method** and it allows you to instantly go from granulated to golden. Without any water present, you don't need to worry about crystallization, but it does require a heavy pot, a watchful eye, and constant monitoring. Unless you are experienced with caramel, I wouldn't recommend it for anything but the smallest volumes and only when you need a very simple caramel, like in my Golden Saffron Flan (page 467).

The way I recommend most people make caramel for any amount greater than 1 cup, is using the **wet method,** like in the Coconut Caramel (page 451) and Bitter Mocha Honeycomb (page 460). The wet method uses a splash of water to dissolve the sugar and first create a concentrated sugar syrup, before simmering off all that water, then finally caramelizing the syrup. How much water you add doesn't really matter because the sugar will not brown until all of the water has cooked off. This method takes longer, but works regardless of the quality of your pot or evenness of your heat source.

What Is Crystallization?

On the downside of the wet method of making caramel, once water and sugar join forces, if you're not careful, crystallization can happen. If any sugar syrup splashes onto the side of the pan, the water in it can quickly evaporate, causing the sugar to crystallize. If just one of those rogue crystals makes its way back into the syrup, the whole pot will congeal into a lumpy, white mass. If that happens, don't worry, just add water to dissolve away your sugary sadness and try again. Once browning begins, you are safe from crystallization and can stir or swirl the pot to even out the cooking.

Crystallization is a concern only for caramel recipes that have you cook sugar with water alone. Recipes that add fat, glucose, corn syrup, or acid at the beginning of cooking are unlikely to become grainy. Acid does an amazing thing, breaking down some of the sucrose into its individual glucose and fructose molecules. This is called an invert sugar and it stays fluid forever and never crystallizes. I also often add vinegar to candies and caramel for both texture and flavor.

To prevent crystallization and ensure a smooth sugar syrup or caramel every time, I follow these steps for candy recipes that don't get any help from butter, corn syrup, or acid:

- **Start with the right stuff:** Use a straight-sided heavy-bottomed pot that's the appropriate size for the recipe. A heavy bottom promotes even heating, but even without one, this method is forgiving. Straight sides make it easier to clip on a candy thermometer.

- **Know when to stir:** After adding the sugar and water to the pot, stir the mixture with a fork over medium-high heat just until it begins to dissolve (using a fork allows you to keep your movements small and tight for minimal splashing). Once most of the sugar is moistened and starting to melt, *stop stirring*. Too much stirring before 310°F (154°C), the safe-from-crystallization temp, can make your sugar syrup grainy and clumpy.

What Is Crystallization? (cont'd.)

- **Do less:** Some recipes tell you to wash the sides of your pot with a pastry brush to rinse away any pesky sugar crystals. I prefer a hands-off approach. Cover the pot with a tight-fitting lid and cook until the syrup is actively simmering and all the sugar has dissolved. The water will evaporate, roll down the sides of the pot, and do the work for you.

- **Going for a specific temp?** Uncover the pot and clip on a candy thermometer. Make sure the bulb is submerged in the syrup, but not touching the side or bottom of the pot. Don't stir, don't swirl. Just stand by for syrup extraction when the time is right. Depending on the recipe, you may need to have an ice bath nearby to plunge the pot into and halt the cooking.

- **Going to brown town?** For most caramel recipes, you're not cooking to a specific temperature, you're looking for a shade of brown instead. Once just a teeny bit of browning starts, you're free to stir and swirl. Don't worry about the entire mixture browning evenly; any dark spots will eventually even out. Stop cooking your caramel just before it's reached your desired shade of brown. The caramel will continue to brown after you've removed it from the heat. I like it bitter and dark, so I usually cook it until I see wisps of smoke.

- **Stay back:** If the recipe calls for adding cream at this point, stand back and keep your hand out of the steam. Steam burns rank just below sugar burns in the hierarchy of burns.

Sugar Syrup Temperatures

The boiling point of water at sea level is 212°F (100°C), but sugar can get much hotter. Therefore, you can tell how concentrated a sugar syrup is based on its temperature. Lower temperatures mean there is more water present, higher temperatures mean there is less. By being able to control precisely how much water is in a sugar syrup, you can create countless textures of candy. Here are the common sugar syrup temperatures/stages you'll come across and what kind of candy-making they are best suited for.

Thread Stage
230° to 235°F (110° to 113°C)

20% water

Thick syrup, won't solidify in cool water.

Soft Ball Stage
235° to 240°F (113° to 116°C)

15% water

Syrup forms a soft ball in cold water; good for soft and creamy candies like fudge.

Firm Ball Stage
245° to 250°F (118° to 121°C)

13% water

Syrup forms a firm but still malleable ball when dropped into cold water; perfect for chewy caramel and flaky halva.

Hard Ball Stage
250° to 265°F (121° to 129°C)

8% water

Syrup forms a hard ball in cold water that won't flatten between your fingers; good for candies that need to be whipped, like nougat and marshmallows.

Soft Crack Stage
270° to 290°F (132° to 143°C)

5% water

Syrup solidifies into flexible threads in cold water, ideal for pulled taffy and hard butterscotch.

Hard Crack Stage
300° to 310°F (149° to 154°C)

almost no water

Syrup solidifies into a hard and brittle thread that you can snap in half. Makes crunchy candies like toffee, brittle, and hard candies.

Caramelization Begins
320°F (160°C)

no water remains

This is where browning and complex flavor development begin. With all the moisture gone, there's no risk of crystallization.

Caramelize

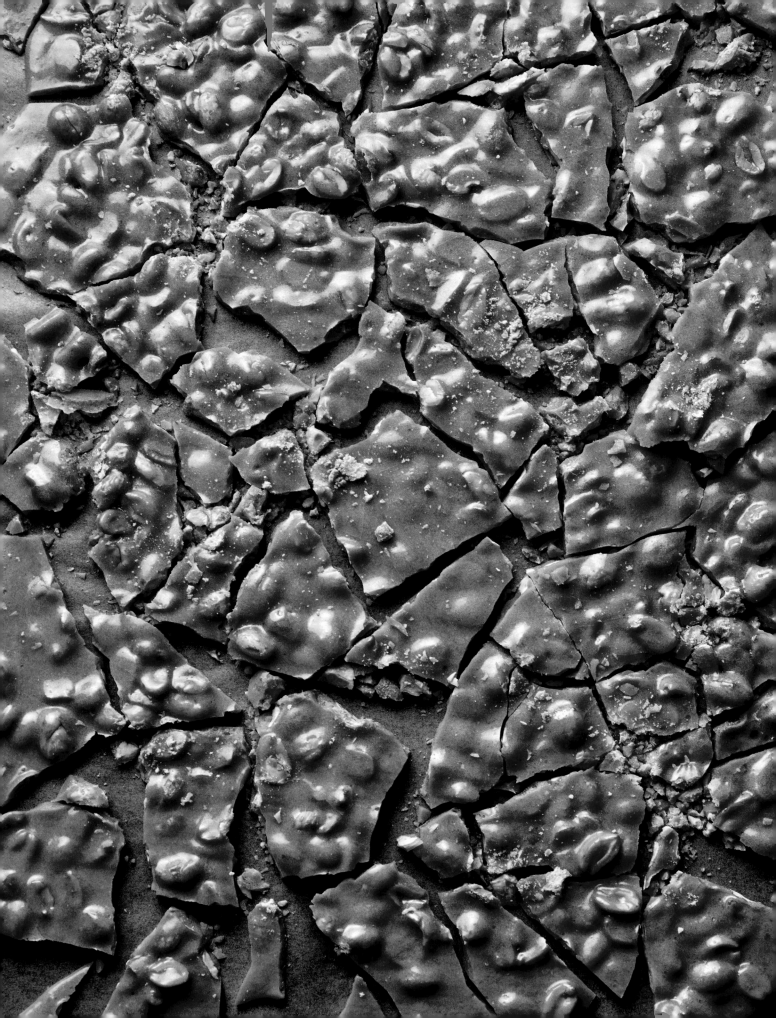

Classic Peanut Brittle

(Makes 1 pound)

(Active: 20 mins. | Total: 50 mins.)

(Easy) (Gluten-free)

(Vegetarian (can be made vegan))

Ingredients:

1 teaspoon Diamond Crystal kosher salt

¾ teaspoon baking soda

300 grams (1½ cups) granulated sugar

75 grams (⅓ cup) water

60 grams (3 tablespoons) light corn syrup

56 grams (4 tablespoons) unsalted butter or vegan butter, cut into pieces

1 tablespoon apple cider vinegar

225 grams (1½ cups) skinless raw peanuts

½ spent vanilla pod (optional)

Special Equipment:

silicone baking mat (or parchment paper)

Cleanup's a Cinch

→ I think classic peanut brittle is the perfect candy, so I'm not adding spices, flaky salt, or swapping in cashews—but you totally can. The only flavor I like to add is a half pod of a used vanilla bean. Even with the seeds removed, the pod gives me a surprisingly rich vanilla flavor. Feel free to skip this if you don't have one around, as I don't think it necessary to crack into a fresh vanilla bean for this humble treat. If you do choose to add other things, you can either add whole spices to steep as the syrup caramelizes or sprinkle the sticky surface of the hot brittle with toasted spices and salt.

Any nut can brittle, just make sure to stick to skinless raw nuts. The hot syrup deeply toasts them and will burn any that are already roasted or still have their skins. If all you have are roasted nuts, add them at the end, after the syrup has caramelized but just before stirring in the salt and baking soda.

This is one candy you can successfully make without a candy thermometer. Cook the syrup until it's an even golden color and you'll know all the moisture has cooked out and your candy will set crisp and snappy.

---

1. In a small bowl, stir together the salt and baking soda. Line a sheet pan with a silicone baking mat or parchment paper.

2. In a medium saucepan (preferably straight-sided), combine the sugar, water, corn syrup, butter, and vinegar. Set over medium heat and stir with a fork—taking care not to splash sugar up onto the sides of the pot—until the butter is melted, the sugar dissolves, and the syrup is actively bubbling, 3 to 5 minutes.

3. Add the peanuts and spent vanilla bean pod (if using) and stir to combine. Cook over medium heat, stirring frequently with a stiff silicone spatula, until the nuts are deeply toasted and the syrup is golden, 7 to 9 minutes.

4. Remove from the heat. Quickly and thoroughly stir in the salt mixture, then scrape the brittle onto the lined sheet pan, pouring it evenly across to distribute the nuts. Use a fork to pull out the vanilla pod (if using). Set aside to fully cool undisturbed, about 30 minutes.

5. Once cool, break into pieces and store in an airtight container (with a desiccant packet if you have one) at room temperature for 2 weeks.

Don't go wasting elbow grease scrubbing sugar-coated pots and tools. Instead, fill whatever pot you cooked the sugar in with water and submerge any candy-coated tools inside. Bring the water to a boil and poof, all the sugar will melt right off. For sugar splatters on the stovetop and counter, let them fully cool before scraping off with a bench scraper or sturdy metal spoon, then scrub off any residue with hot water and a sponge.

Get Loose!

Cashew Cardamom Brittle
• Add 1 teaspoon ground cardamom to the salt and baking soda.

• Swap the raw peanuts for an equal volume of raw cashews, adding them when you would add the peanuts.

Pepita & Chili Brittle
• Swap the raw peanuts for an equal volume of hulled pumpkin seeds and add 5 dried arbol chilies (omit the vanilla pod if using), adding them when you would add the peanuts.

Nut Praline
Spread nut praline between cake layers, top ice cream, stir into pudding, fold into whipped cream, sandwich between cookies, and so much more.

• Smash any cooled nut brittle with the end of a rolling pin into small pieces no larger than 1 inch.

• Transfer the brittle pieces to a food processor (do not attempt in a blender) and pulse, stopping occasionally to scrape the bowl and the blade, until the nuts release their oils and you have a spreadable paste with some crunchy bits of sugar. (This takes a while, stop the processor if it gets too hot.)

The Best Fudge Ever (aka Cocoa Nib Praline)
• Swap the peanuts for an equal volume of cocoa nibs. Stir the cocoa nibs into the syrup after it has become golden (they will burn if added too early). Proceed as directed on page 449.

• Cool, smash into 1-inch pieces, and blitz into a fine powder in the food processor with a big pinch of kosher salt.

• With the processor running, stream in 150 grams (⅔ cup) cold heavy cream, 50 grams (¼ cup) neutral oil, and 40 grams (2 tablespoons) corn syrup. Pour on top of ice cream or layer between cakes.

Coconut Caramel

(Makes 2 cups)

(Active: 25 mins. | Total: 25 mins.)

(Easy) (Vegan) (Gluten-free)

Ingredients:

300 grams (1½ cups) granulated
    sugar

¼ cup water

one 13.5-ounce can full-fat coconut
    milk, well shaken

½ teaspoon Diamond Crystal kosher
    salt

Special Equipment:

candy thermometer

→ This recipe came about when I was trying to make a vegan caramel for all my dairy-free friends. What I ended up with was a sauce that tastes like my childhood. Coconut milk keeps the sauce light and reminds me of the caramel sundaes from McDonald's. Besides for pouring over ice cream, this sauce is ideal for stirring into coffee or lemonade, shaking into a cocktail, and even brushing onto some chicken thighs. Be sure to use a candy thermometer to ensure that the mixture has cooked enough for a thick and pourable consistency. Dunking the pot into an ice bath after hitting the right temperature halts the caramelization and prevents the sauce from scorching from the residual heat.

---

1. In a medium saucepan, combine the sugar and water. Cook over medium-high heat, stirring with a fork, until the sugar is mostly dissolved, about 3 minutes. Cover and continue to cook until just beginning to brown (it's okay to peek), about 5 minutes. Uncover and cook, swirling the pan if needed, until the caramel is just golden brown, 2 to 3 minutes. Remove from the heat, keep your arm and hand away from the steam, and carefully pour in the coconut milk.

2. Clip on a candy thermometer and set the pan back over medium-high heat. Simmer the mixture until it looks thickened and is 225° to 230°F (107° to 110°C), 8 to 10 minutes.

3. Meanwhile, prepare an ice bath in a bowl large enough to submerge the bottom of the pan.

4. Once the sugar has reached temperature, submerge the pan in the ice bath to stop the cooking. Pour the caramel into a heatproof bowl, stir in the kosher salt, and set aside to cool. (The caramel sauce will keep in the fridge for 3 months.)

Twice-Baked Caramelized Cashew Baklava

(Makes about 50 pieces)

(Active: 30 mins. | Total: 1½ hrs.)

(Intermediate)

(Vegetarian (can be made vegan))

For the baklava:

186 grams (1⅓ cups) cashews

50 grams (¼ cup) granulated sugar

2 teaspoons finely grated orange zest

¾ teaspoon ground cardamom

½ teaspoon Diamond Crystal Kosher salt

170 grams (12 tablespoons) unsalted butter or vegan butter, melted

227 grams (8 ounces) frozen 14 × 18-inch phyllo sheets (see Note), thawed

For the syrup:

300 grams (1½ cups) granulated sugar

½ cup water

¼ cup freshly squeezed orange juice

1 tablespoon orange blossom water or 1 teaspoon pure vanilla extract

Special Equipment:

food processor (optional)

pastry brush

wooden skewer

9-inch round metal cake pan

→ Baklava comes in many forms: layered flat and cut into diamonds, scrunched into rolls or nests, and filled with various nuts. The main thing that ties them all together is the flaky and sticky texture you get from stacking super-thin sheets of phyllo dough or gathering up shreds of kataifi, then pouring a thick sugar syrup over them. This style of rolled baklava is my favorite. The tight coils of crisp dough don't shatter or make a mess, while the filling stays put when you take a bite. The addition of acid, here in the form of orange juice, prevents crystallization and ensures a smooth sugar syrup every time. If you want a traditional-tasting baklava, stop after pouring on the syrup. If you're feeling adventurous, pop it in the oven for a second bake. This caramelizes the syrup slightly for deeper flavor and reduces it into a chewy glaze, giving this classic a totally new texture.

1. **Make the filling:** In a food processor, pulse together the cashews, sugar, orange zest, cardamom, and salt until finely ground. (Alternatively, finely chop the nuts in batches. Transfer to a bowl and toss with the sugar, zest, cardamom, and salt.)

2. **Set yourself up:** Have a pastry brush, the melted butter, and a wooden skewer close by. Brush a 9-inch round metal cake pan with melted butter, line the bottom with a round of parchment, and butter the parchment paper. Unfold the thawed phyllo sheets onto a sheet pan and cover with a barely damp kitchen towel.

3. Position a rack in the center of the oven and heat to 375°F (190°C).

4. **Assemble the baklava:** Working quickly so the phyllo doesn't dry out, uncover the phyllo and place one sheet on a clean surface with a short side facing you. (Re-cover the remaining phyllo.) Lightly brush with melted butter. Lay the skewer crosswise across the center and fold the top half of the phyllo sheet over it. Lightly brush with melted butter.

5. Over the phyllo, just below the skewer, spread about 2 tablespoons of the ground cashew mixture evenly across in a strip roughly 1 inch wide. Use the skewer to loosely roll the phyllo from top to bottom.

6. Scrunch up the roll, pushing the ends gently toward the center until ruffled. Slide the roll off the skewer into the cake pan and brush with melted butter. Repeat until the pan is snugly filled with spirals of phyllo rolls. Transfer to the oven and bake until golden brown and crisp, 22 to 25 minutes. →

**Twice-Baked
Caramelized Cashew
Baklava
(cont'd.)**

7. **Meanwhile, make the syrup:** In a medium saucepan, combine the sugar, water, and orange juice. Cook over medium heat, stirring with a fork to dissolve the sugar, until the mixture is syrupy and flows like warm honey, 5 to 7 minutes. Remove from the heat and stir in the orange blossom water.

8. **Add the syrup:** Pour the syrup over the hot baklava. (If you want a traditional, sticky and crunchy baklava, stop here. Cool fully, invert onto a plate, and serve.)

9. **Bake again:** For chewy and extra toasty action, return the cake pan to the oven. Bake until the phyllo is deeply browned and the syrup is bubbling and lightly caramelized, 18 to 20 minutes.

10. Rest for 5 minutes, then run an offset spatula or butter knife along the edge and invert a plate over the pan. Quickly flip the pan to invert the baklava onto the plate. (If the baklava is sticking, gently warm it over a low burner or in the oven and try flipping again.) Cool fully, then use a small, serrated knife to cut into 1- to 2-inch pieces. The flavor and texture significantly improve the next day. (Tightly wrapped at room temperature, baklava will keep for 1 month.)

Note: Phyllo sheets come in various dimensions. If you can't find the size I'm using, don't fret. Each of your baklava rolls may be larger or smaller, but they will ultimately bake up the same.

Spread the Baklava Love!

This baklava has a long shelf life and is very sturdy, making it ideal for mailing to friends and family. Instead of a round cake pan, arrange the baklava rolls in straight rows in an 8-inch square brownie pan, so they are easier to snugly pack into whatever container you are shipping them in. You can double this recipe and bake in a 9 × 13-inch pan; no adjustment to bake time or temperature needed, but the syrup will take longer to cook down.

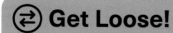 **Get Loose!**

- Swap out the cashews for any other nut. Try pecans, walnuts, pistachios, almonds, or even a combo.

- Swap out the orange zest and cardamom in the filling for another ground spice, dried herbs, or lemon zest.

- Flavor the syrup with whole spices, whiskey, dried herbs, or vanilla beans.

454

Pretzel & Molasses Butterscotch Bars

(Makes 25 squares)

(Active: 45 mins. | Total: 3½ hrs.)

(Intermediate)

(Vegetarian (can be made vegan))

For the pretzel shortbread:

softened butter, vegan butter, or cooking spray for the pan

75 grams pretzels, lightly crushed (about 1 cup)

75 grams (6 tablespoons) granulated sugar

¾ teaspoon Diamond Crystal kosher salt

128 grams (9 tablespoons) unsalted butter or vegan butter, cut into pieces, at room temperature

120 grams (1 cup) all-purpose flour

For the molasses butterscotch:

213 grams (1 cup packed) light or dark brown sugar

180 grams (¾ cup plus 2 teaspoons) heavy cream

170 grams (12 tablespoons) cold unsalted butter or vegan butter, cut into pieces

110 grams (⅓ cup) unsulfured or blackstrap molasses

2 tablespoons vinegar (distilled white, red wine, white wine, or apple cider)

1¼ teaspoons Diamond Crystal kosher salt

→ This malty take on millionaire's shortbread features a salty pretzel short-bread base with molasses butterscotch and dark chocolate topping. Nowadays, butterscotch refers to any caramel-like confection that uses brown sugar instead of white. (Nope, there's no scotch required.) Brown sugar has trace amounts of molasses in it, which gives it that signature tart and smoky flavor. Here I'm bumping up that brown sugar flavor with the addition of molasses and vinegar for an extra perky punch to balance the salty pretzel shortbread base. You can decide how intensely flavored you want these bars to be. Use light brown sugar, unsulfured molasses, and apple cider vinegar to keep things mellow, or amp it up with dark brown sugar, blackstrap molasses, and distilled white vinegar. I used Rold Gold Tiny Twist pretzels here because they fit perfectly in a 9-inch square pan, but you can use whatever crunchy pretzel you've got.

1. **Make the pretzel shortbread:** Heat the oven to 325°F (163°C). Grease a 9-inch square baking pan with butter or cooking spray. Line the bottom and two sides with one long strip of parchment paper, using your hands to smooth it flush to the pan.

2. In a food processor, pulse the pretzels, granulated sugar, and salt until mostly powdery with some gravel-like pieces. (If the pretzels are too chunky, the crust will crumble when sliced.) Add the butter and flour and pulse until clumps form. (Alternatively, place the pretzels in a zip-top bag and crush into fine crumbs with a rolling pin. Combine in a bowl with the flour, granulated sugar, and salt. Add the butter and rub with your fingers until the mixture comes together in clumps.)

3. Tip the crumble into the prepared pan and use your hands and an offset spatula to spread it into an even layer. Bake until the top is dry and lightly golden, 20 to 25 minutes. Set aside to cool, about 30 minutes. The shortbread can be made up to 1 week in advance and stored tightly wrapped at room temperature.

4. **Make the molasses butterscotch:** When the shortbread is cool, in a medium saucepan, combine the brown sugar, cream, butter, molasses, and vinegar. Place over medium heat and cook, stirring occasionally, until everything is dissolved and bubbling, about 5 minutes.

5. Clip on a candy thermometer and continue cooking, without stirring, until the mixture reaches 245° to 250°F (118° to 121°C), about 10 minutes. Meanwhile, measure the salt, so you can quickly stir it in once the sugar reaches temperature. →

Pretzel & Molasses Butterscotch Bars (cont'd.)

For the topping:

150 grams dark chocolate, chopped (about 1 cup)

1 tablespoon refined coconut oil

pretzel twists for garnish

Special Equipment:

9-inch square baking pan (see Notes)

parchment paper

food processor (or zip-top bag and rolling pin)

candy thermometer

6. Remove the saucepan from the heat, unclip the thermometer, quickly and thoroughly stir in the salt, and pour over the cooled shortbread. If needed, tilt the pan to spread evenly. Cool at room temperature until set, about 30 minutes. (If you chill it in the fridge, the chocolate topping won't adhere.)

7. Make the topping: Combine the chocolate and coconut oil in a microwave-safe bowl and heat in 30-seconds increments, stirring after each, until melted. (Alternatively, combine the chocolate and oil in a heatproof bowl set over a saucepan of barely simmering water. Heat, stirring often, until melted and smooth.)

8. Pour the chocolate mixture over the butterscotch and spread evenly to the edges of the pan with an offset spatula. Arrange whole pretzels on top. Refrigerate until completely chilled, at least 2 hours and up to 3 days in advance.

9. Run an offset spatula along the edges to loosen the shortbread from the pan. Use the parchment to lift it out and peel off the parchment paper. With a sharp serrated knife, cut into 25 squares. (Store refrigerated for 3 days or tightly wrapped in the freezer for 1 month. The cookies are best if brought to room temperature before eating.)

Notes:
- You can also make this in an 8-inch square pan or a 9-inch round cake pan, but the layers will be thicker.
- To make this recipe vegan, use vegan butter and swap out the heavy cream for equal parts coconut milk and coconut cream.

Bitter Mocha Honeycomb over Buttery SkyFlakes

(Makes 1 pound)

(Active: 30 mins.) (Total: 2 hrs.)

(Intermediate) (Vegan)

Ingredients:

neutral oil or cooking spray for the pan

about 16 SkyFlakes crackers (enough to cover the baking pan)

2 teaspoons baking soda

½ teaspoon Diamond Crystal kosher salt

350 grams (1¾ cups) granulated sugar

150 grams (⅔ cup) brewed coffee or water

100 grams dark chocolate, chopped (about ⅔ cup)

1 teaspoon refined coconut oil

flaky salt

Special Equipment:

9 × 13-inch metal baking pan

parchment paper

candy thermometer

→ I first had honeycomb while interning at a Fancy Italian Restaurant. I worked on the savory side of things, but I couldn't keep my eyes off the pastry station—at the time run by Chef Brooks Headley—where they were making olive oil ice cream pops, chocolate truffle trees, fresh tangerine Starbursts, and crisp chocolate-coated honeycomb. The honeycomb was made every day for maximum airy crispness, so I ate a lot of yesterday's honeycomb. I also ate the mistakes. When the sugar is cooked too hot, the honeycomb collapses on itself into a dense brittle. Not hot enough and it sticks to your teeth. And don't make this in July if you live in Georgia. Humidity is honeycomb's number one enemy, making the candy dense and sticky no matter what you do. Because texture is what I'm after, I actually leave the honey out of my honeycomb, which can make it tacky and stick to your teeth.

With a candy thermometer and a dry day, honeycomb is a simple candy to make. Once the syrup reaches just above hard crack stage—anywhere between 310° and 315°F (154° and 157°C)—most of the moisture has simmered away but the sugar hasn't caramelized significantly. If you let this sugar syrup cool, you would be left with a hard candy—but if you add baking soda, the hot sugar foams and puffs with bubbles of carbon dioxide, setting airy and light instead. Be sure to use a big enough pot to allow for all that bubblage. Traditionally, honeycomb is made with water. Its flavor comes from caramelized sugar. It can be very sweet, so I make this honeycomb with coffee instead. It makes the treat bitter and intense, which I mellow out by pouring the molten candy over buttery SkyFlakes and topping it all with melted dark chocolate and flaky salt. SkyFlakes are a classic Filipino cracker that were always present in my mom's pantry and purse, but feel free to use any cracker you have on hand. If you're not a fan of bitter flavors, swap the coffee out for an equal amount of water.

1. Grease a 9 × 13-inch metal baking pan with oil or cooking spray. Line the bottom and two sides with one long strip of parchment paper, using your hands to smooth it flush to the pan.

2. Arrange the crackers snugly into the pan, covering the entire base and cutting the crackers with a serrated knife to fit if needed.

3. In a small bowl, stir together the baking soda and salt to have at the ready.

4. In a medium saucepan, combine the sugar and coffee and cook over medium-high heat, stirring with a fork until the sugar is mostly dissolved, 2 to 4 minutes. Cover with a lid and cook until the sugar is totally dissolved and actively simmering, 2 to 4 minutes.

5. Uncover and clip on a candy thermometer. Cook, without stirring, until the thermometer registers between 310° and 315°F (154° and 157°C), 5 to 7 minutes. (The coffee will make the candy foam and smell burnt, that's okay.) Immediately remove the syrup from the heat and remove the thermometer. →

**Bitter Mocha
Honeycomb over
Buttery SkyFlakes
(cont'd.)**

6. Quickly and thoroughly whisk in the baking soda/salt mixture, about 5 seconds. (Be careful, the sugar will bubble and foam.) Immediately pour it across the crackers, tilting the pan to cover them. (Don't spread the honeycomb with a spatula, which will burst the bubbles, making the candy hard and dense.) Set aside to cool completely, about 30 minutes but no longer than 1 hour (if left out for too long, the candy will become sticky).

7. Combine the chocolate and coconut oil in a microwave-safe bowl and heat in 30-second increments, stirring after each, until melted. (Alternatively, combine the chocolate and oil in a heatproof bowl set over a saucepan of barely simmering water. Heat, stirring often, until melted and smooth.)

8. Run an offset spatula or butter knife around the edges to loosen the candy from the pan, lift onto a cutting board, and peel off the parchment paper. Using your hands, break the honeycomb bark into rough pieces. Drizzle chocolate all over and sprinkle with flaky salt. Let the chocolate set at room temperature, about 30 minutes. This is best eaten the same day. Store in an airtight container at room temperature for 3 days.

Note: Wait for the honeycomb to fully set before adding the chocolate; otherwise the candy will deflate and become dense.

**Save Your
Desiccants!**

Sugar is hygroscopic, which means it loves water and will suck moisture right out of the air. That's why it's so great at keeping cakes moist and brownies chewy. On the flip side, all that affinity for water is why brown sugar easily grows clumpy and hard, crisp candies lose their snap, and it is impossible to prepare dry high-sugar treats like pavlova or honeycomb on a humid day. That's why I store candies (or anything crunchy) with a desiccant. You'll often find these little paper packets filled with silica gel in snack foods, like crackers, chips, and cheese puffs. Save them! Wipe them clean, toss onto a sheet pan, and suck the moisture out of them in a dehydrator or low oven (around 200°F/90°C) for 15 minutes. Then store them in an airtight container to toss into anything you want to stay crisp. The desiccants will pull the moisture out of the air before the sugar can get to it.

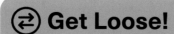 **Get Loose!**

- Line the pan with any cookie or cracker: Teddy Grahams, saltines, Carr's crackers, graham crackers, Milano Mints, Oreo Thins, Ritz crackers.

- Sprinkle crunchies over the melted chocolate: toasted and salted nuts or seeds, crushed cereal, pretzels, granola, dried rose petals.

462

Almond Toffee Popcorn

(Makes 10 cups)

(Active: 35 mins. | Total: 1 hr. 20 mins.)

(Intermediate) (Gluten-free)

(Vegetarian (can be made vegan))

Ingredients:

8 cups freshly popped popcorn (see page 466)

softened butter, vegan butter, or cooking spray for the roasting pan

1½ teaspoons Diamond Crystal kosher salt

1 teaspoon baking soda

250 grams (1¼ cups) granulated sugar

125 grams (9 tablespoons) cold unsalted butter or vegan butter, cut into ½-inch pieces

85 grams (¼ cup) light corn syrup

⅓ cup water

160 grams (1⅓ cups) slivered almonds

1 teaspoon pure vanilla extract

flaky salt

Special Equipment:

parchment paper (or silicone baking mat)

roasting pan (or large metal bowl)

candy thermometer

→ Crunch 'n Munch and Almond Roca were two of my favorite candies growing up, and this recipe smashes them both together, coating freshly popped corn in buttery almond toffee, which is made by cooking sugar and butter together until molten and brown. I start with cold cubed butter and cook the toffee over moderate heat, so the mixture stays smooth and emulsified. If you heat the toffee too quickly, the butter can break out, leaving you with a lump of caramel floating in butter or a slick of grease across your cooled toffee. If you've bought any snacks with desiccant packets in them, save them to toss into the container you store this toffee popcorn in, so it stays crisp and fresh for longer. If you don't like almonds, swap in any skinless nut or seed (or leave them out), just make sure they are raw. The nuts will toast as the sugar browns, and infuse the toffee with its aroma (but if they aren't blanched the skin may burn).

---

1. **Set up:** Line a sheet pan with parchment paper or a silicone baking mat. Spread the popcorn out on the pan. Examine the popcorn, picking out and discarding any unpopped kernels.

2. Heat the oven to 170°F (80°C). Grease a roasting pan (or the biggest metal bowl you have) with butter or cooking spray.

3. Add the popcorn to the greased pan or bowl and place in the oven to stay warm (this will help you get a thin and even layer of toffee on the popcorn). Set the lined sheet pan aside.

4. **Make the toffee:** In a small bowl, stir together the salt and baking soda to have at the ready.

5. In a medium saucepan, combine the sugar, butter, corn syrup, and water. Cook over medium heat, stirring occasionally, until everything is melted and bubbling, about 5 minutes.

6. Add the almonds, clip on a candy thermometer, and cook, stirring frequently as the mixture begins to brown, until it reaches 300°F (149°C), 10 to 12 minutes. (When the sugar is close, remove the popcorn from the oven.) Remove from the heat, unclip the thermometer, quickly and thoroughly stir in the salt/baking soda mixture and the vanilla, and pour the toffee over the popcorn.

7. Quickly fold the mixture until the popcorn is evenly coated in toffee, then scrape onto the reserved lined sheet pan. Sprinkle lightly with flaky salt and use the spatula to break up any large clumps. Set aside until cool and crisp, about 45 minutes. Transfer to an airtight container (with a desiccant packet if you have one) and store at room temperature for 2 weeks.

How to Pop Popcorn

Depending on the brand, variety, and freshness of your popcorn kernels, the final volume of your popped popcorn can greatly vary. When I developed this recipe, I got 8 cups of popcorn from ⅓ cup of kernels. When this recipe was tested, ⅓ cup of kernels yielded only 4 cups of popped popcorn. (Wild!) In this recipe, volume matters more than weight. With only 4 cups of popcorn, you end up with almond toffee with some popcorn in it instead of almond toffee popcorn. Here's how I pop 8 cups of popcorn. However, your kernels may be different from mine. Use this recipe as a starting point, knowing that you might need more kernels to yield 8 cups of popped popcorn.

3 tablespoons refined coconut oil, ghee, clarified butter, or neutral oil (such as sunflower or grapeseed)

⅓ cup popcorn kernels

1. Lay out a clean kitchen towel and place the lid of a large pot on top. Gather the towel around the handle of the lid and secure it with a rubber band or twine. (This will help collect any moisture that condenses on the lid, preventing the popcorn from getting soggy.)

2. In the large pot, heat the fat over medium-high heat along with 2 popcorn kernels. Cover with the wrapped lid and cook, shaking occasionally, until the kernels pop, about 3 minutes.

3. Remove the popped kernels, add the remaining popcorn, and cook, shaking constantly, until you hear the popping die down, 2 to 3 minutes.

4. Immediately remove from the heat and pour the popcorn into a large bowl or onto a sheet pan.

Golden Saffron Flan

(Serves 6)

(Active: 30 mins.) | (Total: 4 hrs.)

(Advanced) (Vegetarian)

(Gluten-free)

For the caramel:

150 grams (¾ cup) granulated sugar

For the custard:

¼ teaspoon Diamond Crystal kosher salt

large pinch of saffron threads

450 grams (2 cups) whole milk

250 grams (1 cup plus 2 tablespoons) heavy cream

100 grams (½ cup) granulated sugar

3 large eggs (about 165 grams)

3 large egg yolks (about 60 grams)

Special Equipment:

8- or 9-inch round metal cake pan

roasting pan (or other large baking dish big enough to hold the cake pan)

small mortar and pestle (or a medium bowl and small dowel rolling pin)

→ Virtually every country that has eggs and milk has flan. Flan belongs to the world, perhaps with different names here or there, like leche flan in the Philippines or crème caramel in France, but it's the people's dessert. I'm not going to make any claims about who did it first, because I think what really matters is that our universal love for this gently set, smooth custard is something that unites us all. This is my (current) preferred ratio for flan, but you really have a lot of room to groove here. I used to like it super rich, with mostly cream and yolks, but the flan my amu made was delicate and light, made with milk and whole eggs. I've quit rebelling and found balance with this not-too-rich, but still oh-so-satisfying version.

Once you understand the technique, feel free to play around with more or less cream, yolks, or sugar. Try swapping in coconut milk or condensed milk, and get nutty with pistachio or cashew milk. You can even ditch the saffron for the more traditional vanilla, or go wild steeping whole spices or coffee in the dairy overnight to infuse it. As long as you have about 1 large egg per 1 cup of liquid, your flan will set. The trickiest part is making the caramel. Because the quantity of sugar for the caramel is relatively low, I use the dry method, caramelizing the sugar all on its own without the addition of water. For the best results, use a heavy-bottomed pot and keep a vigilant eye over the melting sugar. To ensure the flan cooks gently without curdling, it's baked in a water bath. Read more about it in Baking Custards in a Water Bath (page 423).

---

1. **Make the caramel:** Heat a heavy-bottomed medium saucepan over medium heat. Sprinkle in just enough sugar to evenly cover the bottom of the pan and cook, stirring with a fork as needed, until mostly melted, 2 to 3 minutes. Evenly sprinkle in the rest of the sugar 2 tablespoons at a time, stirring with a fork and waiting for each addition to mostly melt before adding the next, until all the sugar has melted into a dark brown syrup, about 5 minutes. (There will be some sugar clumps on the fork in the beginning, but they will eventually melt. Because there is no water, there is no risk of crystallization. Don't worry if some spots are darker than others; they will all even out in the end.)

2. Use a stiff silicone spatula to immediately scrape the hot caramel into an 8- or 9-inch round metal cake pan. Very carefully pick up the pan by the top edges. Tilt the pan to evenly line the bottom and halfway up the sides with the hot caramel. Set aside.

3. **Set up:** Position a rack in the center of the oven and heat to 325°F (160°C). Bring a large kettle or pot of water to a boil. Prepare a roasting pan (or other baking dish large enough to accommodate the pan holding the custard) by placing a ring of foil or a wire rack inside it to act as a booster seat (you want a layer of water between the custard pan and the bottom of the roasting pan). →

Caramelize

Golden Saffron Flan (cont'd.)

4. **Make the custard:** With a mortar and pestle, grind the salt and saffron into a fine powder. (Alternatively, put the saffron and salt in a medium bowl and use the end of a small dowel rolling pin to crush into a powder.)

5. In the same pot you made the caramel (no need to wash it out), combine the milk, cream, saffron/salt mixture, and 50 grams (¼ cup) of the sugar. Bring the mixture to a simmer over medium heat, stirring occasionally.

6. Meanwhile, coil a wet towel into a nest and set a medium bowl on top. Add the whole eggs, egg yolks, and remaining 50 grams (¼ cup) sugar and whisk until no streaks of white remain.

7. Once the milk mixture comes to a simmer, remove from the heat. Gradually add the hot milk mixture to the eggs in a steady stream while whisking constantly. (If pouring the milk directly from the pot feels difficult, pour in a ladleful at a time instead. For photos of this technique go to page 429.)

8. Place the caramel-lined cake pan into the prepared roasting pan and pour in the custard. Pull out an oven rack and set the roasting pan on the rack, so you're not trying to carry a hot pan filled with water. Pour boiling water into the roasting pan to reach about halfway up the side of the custard pan.

9. Bake until the custard is set around the edges with a slight jiggle in the center (an instant-read thermometer will read 175°F/79°C), 35 to 40 minutes.

10. Cool at room temperature for 30 minutes, then cover and transfer to the fridge to cool for at least 2 hours. (The flan can be made and refrigerated up to 5 days ahead.) When ready to serve, run a paring knife or offset spatula along the edge to loosen the flan from the dish and flip over onto a rimmed plate to catch the caramel sauce.

Any Kinda Sesame Halva

(Makes about 1 pound)

(Active: 30 mins. | Total: 4 hrs.)

(Advanced) (Vegan)

(Gluten-free)

Ingredients:

neutral oil or cooking spray for
the pan

350 grams (1½ cups) high-quality,
well-stirred tahini, at room
temperature

1 teaspoon Diamond Crystal kosher
salt

300 grams (1½ cups) granulated
sugar

½ cup water

Special Equipment:

8-inch or 9-inch square baking pan (or
a 9 × 5-inch loaf pan)

parchment paper

candy thermometer

→ In the US, we've come to know halva as crumbly tahini candy. But throughout many parts of the world, the word halva (or halwa, halvah, or halua) refers to a huge variety of dense or flaky sweets made with anything from semolina to chickpeas. Some historians believe the term has Arabic or Persian roots and simply means "sweet," hence the wide array of treats under the moniker.

Sesame halva has few ingredients and is all about technique, but once you master it, you can shake things up with different mix-ins, flavorings, and toppings. Get to know your candy thermometer and how to read it. If the temperature is too low, you'll end up with a spreadable fudge; too high, and you'll have a crunchy crumble. The quantity of sugar syrup in this recipe is small, so use a narrow enough pot to allow the bulb of the thermometer to be submerged in it. Be sure to stir the syrup into the tahini until it is just combined—some hair-thin streaks of syrup remaining is A-OK. All the flavor comes from the tahini, so look for a high-quality brand, like Soom or Seed + Mill. Regardless of whether your halva is perfect, crumbly, or a little saucy, every version is equally tasty, so there's no way to lose.

---

1. Grease an 8-inch or 9-inch square baking pan (or a 9 × 5-inch loaf pan) with oil or cooking spray. Line the bottom and two sides with one long strip of parchment paper, using your hands to smooth it flush to the pan.

2. In a heatproof medium bowl with a stiff silicone spatula or wooden spoon, stir together the tahini and salt. Secure the bowl with a wet towel curled into a nest shape (or get a friend to help you hold the bowl when you add the syrup).

3. In a small saucepan (preferably one with straight sides and a tight-fitting lid), combine the sugar and water (be sure to choose a narrow enough saucepan to allow the bulb of the thermometer to be submerged in syrup). Cook over medium-high heat, stirring with a fork until the sugar is mostly dissolved, about 2 minutes. Cover with a lid and cook until the sugar is totally dissolved and actively simmering, about 2 minutes.

4. Uncover and clip on a candy thermometer. Cook, without stirring, until the thermometer registers 250° to 255°F (121° to 123°C), about 2 minutes. Immediately remove the syrup from the heat and remove the thermometer.

5. Pour the syrup into the tahini in a steady stream, while quickly stirring. Stir until just mixed (some hair-thin streaks of syrup remaining are okay), less than 1 minute. Be careful not to overmix or the halva will become crumbly.

6. Working quickly, scrape the halva into the prepared pan and smooth it into an even layer with an offset spatula. Let cool to room temperature, about 30 minutes. Cover and refrigerate for at least 2 hours. →

7. Run an offset spatula or butter knife along the edges to loosen from the pan, invert onto a cutting board, and peel off the parchment. The halva keeps better if left whole, so cut into pieces as you need them. (Store tightly wrapped in the fridge for up to 3 weeks.)

⇄ Get Loose!

> Stir dry, oil-based, or alcohol-based additions into the tahini when you add the salt: ground spices, extracts, miso paste, peppermint oil, toasted nuts/seeds, and/or chopped dried fruit.

> Finish the syrup with water-based flavorings (they'll make the tahini seize if added directly to it): soy sauce, orange blossom water, or rose water.

> Quickly fold chopped chocolate in just after adding the syrup, so it melts and swirls.

> After spreading the halva into the pan, top the still-warm halva with chocolate, so it melts and forms a chocolate topping.

> Scatter toppings onto the halva before it sets: flaky salt, toasted nuts/seeds, dried rose petals, or candied ginger or citrus.

Better Than a Peanut Butter Cup Halva

• Stir 1 teaspoon vanilla extract and ¾ cup (120 grams) finely chopped roasted peanuts into the tahini along with the salt.

• After spreading the halva into the pan, top the still-warm halva with ⅔ cup (100 grams) chopped milk chocolate. Let sit for 15 minutes to melt, then spread with an offset spatula or the back of a spoon.

• Sprinkle with flaky salt.

Classic Halva with Pistachio, Cardamom & Rose

• Stir ½ teaspoon ground cardamom and ½ cup (80 grams) toasted whole pistachios into the tahini along with the salt.

• Pour 2 tablespoons rose water into the syrup once it comes off the heat.

• After spreading the halva into the pan, top the still-warm halva with ⅓ cup (55 grams) finely chopped toasted pistachios. Gently press to adhere.

Almond Joy Halva

• Stir 1 teaspoon almond extract, 1 teaspoon vanilla extract, and ¾ cup (120 grams) toasted whole almonds into the tahini along with the salt.

• Just after adding the hot syrup to the tahini, quickly fold in ½ cup (75 grams) chopped dark chocolate, so it melts and swirls.

• After spreading the halva into the pan, top the still-warm halva with ⅔ cup (70 grams) toasted unsweetened coconut. Gently press to adhere.

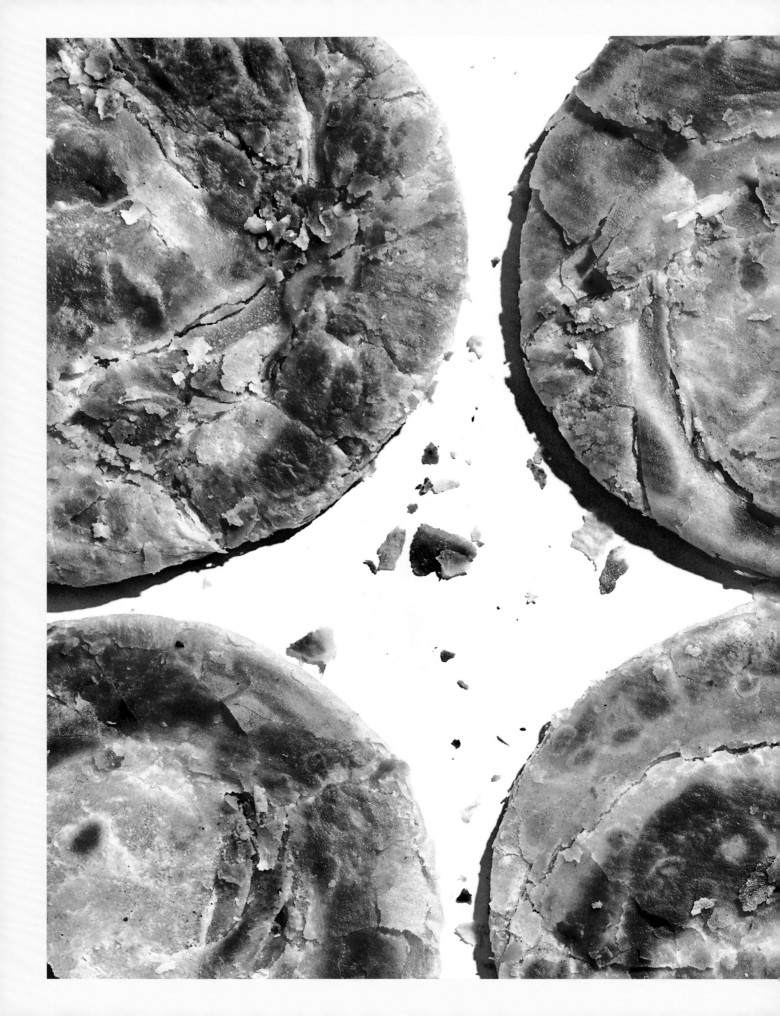

Getting to Know Dough

Easy breads for everyone

Getting to Know Dough

I know everyone got into making naturally leavened bread during the pandemic—making stuff with a starter is fun when you're bored and need a long-term distraction (houseplants don't grow very fast)—but you have to be baking all the time for it to be worth it. Starters are fussy. They're always begging to be fed, you've got to dedicate fridge or counter space to them, and you're constantly trying to figure out what to do with all that sourdough discard.

I don't make bread that often, so when I do, I prefer to bake with commercial yeast or stick to unleavened styles—breads that don't have any yeast at all, like Thin & Chewy Roti (page 488) or Corn Tortillas (page 491). These are breads for people with commitment issues. For the weekend warriors who want to dip their toes into bread making. And best of all, there isn't a single recipe in this chapter that needs a mixer—just a bowl, clean hands, a one-dollar plastic bowl scraper, and a willingness to apply some elbow grease.

As I mentioned in the Just Add Water chapter (page 99), all grains are seeds, packed with everything needed to create life (so yeah, they're pretty freaking nutritious). Humans figured this out early on and have been cultivating grains across the globe for at least twelve thousand years. Now, for that good stuff to become edible, grains need to be cooked. The most portable and shelf-stable way to prepare a grain is by grinding it into flour, mixing it with water, and baking it into bread. The first breads were most likely flatbreads—flour and water pastes cooked on hot stones. But if you let that flour paste hang out for a few days, the naturally occurring yeasts in the air and that were on the surface of the grain will cause the paste to ferment.

Say hello to the original cave-person leavened breads! Fast-forward a few thousand years and you can find bread across myriad cultures in infinite forms: chewy tapioca breads in South America, spongy teff injera in Ethiopia, dense rye breads in Europe, fluffy naan in South Asia, crusty baguettes in France, and squishy Wonder bread right here in the US of A.

Bread can be made from any grain, but the most popular and prevalent are made with common wheat. That's because common wheat combined with water readily transforms into a dough that's both elastic and plastic—meaning it has strength while also being flexible. It's this tension that allows you to form doughs that hold their shape but are still capable of expanding due to the reactions of yeast, chemical leavening, and heat. It bakes into breads that are easy to tear into, while having chew when you eat them. And it allows the dough to expand with countless air bubbles, much like a mousse, then set into a bouncy structure.

All this is possible because of gluten. Breads made with the flour of grains that have no gluten—such as rice, nixtamalized corn, or buckwheat—tend to be dense, heavy, and lack chew. Because more people are avoiding gluten these days, whether for dietary reasons or personal choice, you can easily find doppelgangers of your favorite gluten-full goodies, but they are usually made up of a blend of gluten-free flours, starches, and other additions, like psyllium husk and xanthan gum. Only gluten-full flour can pull off fluffy, crusty, tender, bouncy, and chewy all with water alone.

So What the Heck Is Gluten?

1. DRY FLOUR

GLIADIN

GLUTENIN

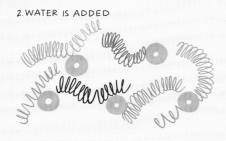

2. WATER IS ADDED

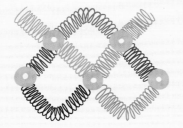

3. ONCE IT'S KNEADED

Gluten is a protein network that forms when glutenin and gliadin, two proteins present in the endosperm of wheat, barley, and rye, hook up with the help of water. Not all gluten is created equal, and it's not about the quantity of the proteins but the amounts of each type. The ratios of glutenin and gliadin present in common wheat create especially strong gluten networks that offer the push-pull necessary for bread. That's why common wheat is also known as "bread wheat"!

Those protein ratios differ by grain. The gluten formed in durum wheat flour, used to make pasta, is more plastic than elastic, making it better for dough that's stretched into thin sheets. Rye flour is full of big carbohydrate structures, called pentosans, that swell with water and interrupt gluten nets, resulting in doughs that can't support as many air bubbles and that bake up dense. Spelt flour has a higher ratio of gliadin to glutenin than "bread wheat," so spelt doughs form weak bonds that bake into mealy breads. But "bread wheat" is just right, which must be why we can't get enough of it.

In the dry flour made from "bread wheat," glutenin and gliadin are inert bundles of proteins. But like sea monkeys, just add water and watch them come alive. The addition of water untangles those bundles and makes it possible for them to form bonds with one another. Too little water and it's tough to maximize those interactions, while too much water disperses and weakens the network. The initial gluten network might be messy, but mixing, kneading, and folding make it orderly and strong, creating more bonds and more organization. That's why a sticky and shaggy dough becomes smooth and taut as you knead it.

What about no-knead doughs? They're really more like self-knead doughs, as the gluten develops through the slow action of yeasty burps that stretch the dough with big bubbles of carbon dioxide.

Bread Basics

Technically, all you need to make bread is flour, water, and agitation. With those three ingredients you can create countess variations simply by tweaking the amount of water and how much the ingredients are agitated. Add a few other things, like yeast, salt, fat, and sugar—and bam! You essentially have everything you need to make almost any bread. Because bread has so few ingredients, it's all about the details.

I was once a pastry chef managing the bread program at two Brooklyn restaurants. (In fine-dining restaurants, when technical things are made in-house, it's always called a "program." I worked at a place that had an "ice program" where bartenders would carefully filter water, freeze, and hand-carve elaborate cubes for cocktails.) A meal at both restaurants started with a complimentary freshly baked loaf: At one, it was a crusty round of focaccia with whipped ricotta and at the other, a mini-baguette-like loaf with herbed crackers. Both breads were made from the same base dough of flour, water, sugar, salt, and yeast. How hard could that be? The first few weeks were an utter disaster. I mixed the dough at the end of every shift to proof overnight. Proofing is a simple word for a complex step, during which yeast gets busy fermenting the dough—eating carbohydrates, burping carbon dioxide, filling the dough with big bubbles, and helping gluten development move along. If it was too chilly, the dough wouldn't fully proof, leaving me with dense and mealy loaves. If it was a warm night, I'd arrive to find the dough invading the pastry kitchen like The Blob, proofing out of control and spilling out of the container onto the counter and floors. Sometimes the chef would accidentally order a different brand of flour or type of yeast, changing the amount of water needed and time required to proof.

It took months of making those two breads every day, and countless hours spent elbow deep in dough, before I began to understand their nuances. I'd check the weather and use warmer water on colder nights or proof the bread in the fridge in the summer months. I came to understand how the dough should feel, so I could add more or less water depending on the brand of flour. With bread there is a lot of licking your finger and holding it up to feel the breeze. It's not magic, it's intuition, and no recipe can give you that. I've developed the recipes in this chapter to be as accurate as I can make them. But even if you use the same brand of flour (King Arthur), salt (Diamond Crystal kosher), and yeast (SAF instant), and measure everything with a digital scale, your kitchen is different from mine. It will take practice to hone your skills and develop your intuition. That's what's fun about bread—you need the precision of pastry combined with the figure-it-out-as-you-go vibe of savory cooking. Here are the things to think about as you start your home bread program.

All-Purpose vs. Bread Flour
There are various "bread wheats"—hard red winter wheat, hard red spring wheat, soft white wheat—each categorized based on the color and quality of the kernels and the season in which the wheat was planted. Their protein content can range anywhere from 8% to 18%. There was a time when flour was sold in bags simply labeled "flour" and bakers had to figure everything out on their own. Now we have more consistency, and flours are blended to give us roughly standardized protein contents.

In the US, flours labeled as "all-purpose" will have a lower protein content than those labeled as "bread flour" by the same brand. However, not all brands are the same. The amount of protein in one brand's all-purpose can be the same as in another brand's bread flour. It's confusing. And it matters, because higher protein content means that you need to increase the hydration (because protein is thirsty) and that there will be more gluten development (bad news if you want a tender cake). It gets even more confusing when you go international, as every country labels flour differently. In France all-purpose flour is significantly higher in protein than all-purpose in the US and is used for making baguettes. Try to bake a baguette with low-protein Gold Medal all-purpose flour and you'll hear the French snicker at you from all the way across the Atlantic.

Unfortunately, at the time of this book's publication, most bags of flour do not list protein content, and the ones that do don't offer an indication of how much of that protein comes from glutenin and gliadin, the proteins that matter most with baking. Whole wheat flours have higher protein content than white flours (of the same brand) due to the inclusion of the germ and endosperm, but those proteins hinder rather than promote gluten development. (Wheat kernels contain a fatty germ, starchy endosperm, and tough outer bran. For white flour, only the endosperm is used.)

So, what's a baker to do? If you're working from a recipe and you know the exact brand of flour used by the author (and have access to it), start there. For this book, I use King Arthur unbleached bread flour (12.7% protein) and Gold Medal unbleached all-purpose flour (10.5% protein); I use two different brands as I have found King Arthur's all-purpose flour to have too high a protein content for tender cakes and cookies. The main reason I use these brands is that I can consistently access both where I live, but if those brands aren't available, go online and look up the protein content of the brands you have access to and use those with percentages comparable to the brands I prefer—just know they might not be labeled as "bread flour" or "all-purpose flour." Use the recipe amounts as a starting point, but be sure to follow the visual cues noted in each recipe, adding more flour or water to the dough until it looks as described. That said, if the recipe states that a dough will be sticky, like in the Perfectly Puffy Pitas (page 502), don't add more flour simply to make the dough easier to work with. Each recipe has a certain hydration level for a reason. Pita dough that's too dry won't puff, and roti dough that's too wet will be impossible to roll out. If you want to take your baking to the next level, take notes on the brand of flour you used and how much you had to alter a recipe to make it work. This is how you can begin to tweak a recipe to work with what you have.

Yeast

Wheat was born to be inoculated, readily fermenting from the naturally occurring yeasts in the air, on the grain, and even transferred from your hands while mixing. But nature takes its own sweet time, so relying on wild yeasts to proof bread requires patience. In the ye olde days of bread making, bakers would save a lump of fermented dough from their last batch of bread to add to the next to kick-start fermentation. Later, people would scoop off scum that accumulated on vats of grains that were fermenting for beer to incorporate into bread dough—the original instant yeast.

Today, we have three types of readily available commercial yeast: fresh yeast, active dry yeast, and instant yeast. Fresh yeast is a moist, compressed cake of yeast that is alive and kickin'. You can add it straight to dough, but for the best results, it should be dissolved into the liquid going into the dough, so that it evenly disperses throughout. There's no need to bloom it. But the problem with working with something that's alive is that it dies, so fresh yeast must be stored refrigerated and has a shelf life of only 2 weeks.

Active dry yeast is composed of inert granules. In the center of each granule are live yeasts in suspended animation, surrounded by a protective coating of dead yeast cells. Active dry yeast is typically first "bloomed," meaning dissolved in water to slough off those dead cells and wake up the yeasty sleepyheads. With instant yeast, on the other hand, every granule is made of

Unfermented vs. Fermented Doughs

Unfermented breads are made from a mixture of flour and water, sometimes with salt, sugar, or fat, and no yeast at all. These simple doughs make unleavened breads that require minimal time and planning, because you're not waiting for the time-consuming action of fermentation to happen. Even without the yeasty burps, properly made unfermented breads will puff and bubble due to the steam created when the dough is cooked. That's why Thin & Chewy Roti (page 488) will balloon while cooked in a hot pan and the surface of crisp matzoh is covered in teeny bubbles. Fermented doughs are ones that contain yeast, either commercial yeast or naturally leavened with yeasts found on the surface of the grain, your hands, and the air. They can be flat, like Perfectly Puffy Pitas (page 502) or lavash, or formed into loaves or buns.

entirely living cells that readily dissolve to start burping and farting right away, so you can add it directly into the dough without dissolving it first.

All the recipes in this book are made with instant yeast. I prefer it because it's easy to use and you get the most bang for your buck. You can use a smaller volume than with active dry yeast because all the cells are alive (why pay for dead yeast?), and there's no water adding bulk as there is with cake yeast. Some fans of cake yeast claim it has better flavor, but I haven't found a noticeable difference, particularly with breads that are fermented overnight, like the focaccia and no-knead white bread in this chapter.

If all you've got on hand is active dry or cake yeast, you can swap them for the instant yeast by using the conversions below and adjusting how the yeast is incorporated. Note, proofing times may vary from those listed in the recipe, so be sure to follow visual cues. And prep the different yeasts as follows:

- Cake yeast: Be sure to fully dissolve it into the water portion of the dough, then proceed with the recipe.

- Active dry yeast: The yeast first needs to be bloomed. To do this, warm up ½ cup of liquid from the recipe to between 100° and 110°F (38° and 43°C) and stir in 1 teaspoon of sugar from the recipe. Sprinkle the yeast over the liquid, stir to dissolve, and set it aside to get foamy before adding to the dough. If the mixture doesn't get foamy after 10 minutes, the yeast may be old and dead. If the liquid isn't warm enough, the yeast will release substances that interfere with proper gluten development. If the liquid is too hot, the yeast dies. For best results, use a thermometer.

	Active Dry	Cake (Fresh) Yeast
For every 1 tablespoon instant yeast, use:	1 tablespoon plus 1 teaspoon	3 tablespoons

Even though these are the "best practices" for using each of these yeasts, the fact is, you can *kind of* do whatever you want. Some folks always predissolve instant yeast even though you don't have to, and I have accidentally added active dry yeast straight into dough without blooming it first. I've even made bread with half the amount of yeast a recipe called for because it was all I had. No matter what you do, it will ferment, and it will become bread. However, when you play fast and loose with yeast, your dough will ferment faster or slower than the recipe indicates. This isn't a big deal, as long as you keep an eye on the fermentation and know what you're looking for.

Is It Proofed?
From the moment you mix flour, water, and yeast to the time you cook your bread, the dough is alive. Water combines with the starches that have ruptured during the milling process, activating enzymatic activity that works to break long chains of carbohydrates into smaller ones. These broken-down carbohydrates are food for the yeast cells. Yeasts chomp down on those sugars, transforming them into carbon dioxide and alcohol. If you've developed your gluten network sufficiently, it can trap those gasses and expand, rather than let those bubbles of carbon dioxide burst. That's why a dough that is properly kneaded and fermented will be filled with air bubbles and smell delightfully funky. Once in the heat of the oven (or fryer or griddle), the yeasts give off one final burst of carbon dioxide as they die. This last puff is called oven spring. It's why correctly proofed donuts have a ring around their perimeter and rustic loaves split across the center.

The key to making yeasted doughs is to know when you've given the yeasts the right amount of time to do their thing. Underproofed doughs will bake up into dense, pale, and misshapen loaves. They have a tight and wet crumb that tastes doughy even after baking. Overproofed doughs will have a weakened gluten structure, baking into pale loaves with a very open or deflated crumb. They will be dry, brittle, and have very little if any oven spring. If you take things really far, overproofed doughs can even have a strong alcohol aroma and off-taste. That's because the yeasts ran out of food and pushed the gluten network to the limit.

Bread recipes offer fermentation times, but in reality, how long dough takes to proof can vary dramatically with temperature and humidity. In a hot and humid kitchen, especially if you're handling the dough with warm hands (like when forming rolls or buns), bread can proof in a fraction of the time stated in a recipe. On the other hand, if it's very cold, your dough may take an alarming amount of time to proof. Regardless of what a recipe says, you've got keep an eye on the dough—or better yet, a finger.

You may have seen some recipes tell you to proof dough until it's doubled in size, but unless you're working with a very wet dough, like focaccia, it can be difficult to judge volume visually. The Poke Test is the best way to tell if your dough has proofed. Give your dough a gentle poke and see how it reacts:

- **Did the dough spring back immediately?** If so, it's underproofed and needs to continue fermenting.

- **Did the dough hold the impression of your finger, without springing back at all?** If so, it's overproofed. Some say you can press the gas out of overproofed doughs, re-form them, and proof again, but this isn't always successful. If you want bread with a perfect crumb, texture, and flavor, you may need to start again. But I recommend that you still bake off that dough for other things. As long as the loaf doesn't bake up tasting too boozy, you can turn it into bread pudding, croutons, or crumbs.

- **Did the dough very slowly bounce back?** Like when you press your hand into a high-quality memory foam mattress? Congratulations, it's perfectly proofed! Cook immediately, pat yourself on the back, and memorize that properly proofed feeling.

Just Keep Poking, Baking & Tasting

The Poke Test seems easy enough, but it takes practice to understand what proofed dough should look and feel like. Pay attention to your dough at all stages. If you think it's properly proofed, bake it, taste it, and judge it. If it does, in fact, taste perfectly proofed, try to remember how the dough felt so you can re-create it. I recommend taking plenty of notes, photos, and videos until you know the dough in your bones.

486

Thin & Chewy Roti

(Makes 12 roti)

(Active: 45 mins. | Total: 1 hr. 15 mins.)

(Easy)

(Vegetarian (can be made vegan))

Ingredients:

240 grams (2 cups) all-purpose flour, plus more for dusting

120 grams (1 cup) whole wheat flour

1 teaspoon Diamond Crystal kosher salt

225 grams (1 cup) warm water

1 tablespoon olive oil or neutral oil, plus more as needed

butter, vegan butter, or ghee

Special Equipment:

rolling pin

→ Unlike pita, which requires an elastic dough with well-developed gluten to hold onto a pocket of air and puff up, overdeveloping the gluten will make roti difficult to roll, so you start with all-purpose rather than bread flour and mix it just enough to come together into a smooth dough. Warm water is also vital because it give the starches in the flour first dibs, swelling with water before the proteins have a drink, minimizing gluten development. Traditionally, roti or chapati are made with atta, a whole wheat flour found in South Asia. It's milled differently and made with a distinct variety of wheat different from the all-purpose and bread flours found in the US. My amu's trick to approximate the texture and flavor of atta was to add some whole wheat flour to the dough. This adds a nutty flavor and hinders gluten development, so you have an easy-to-roll dough.

---

1. **Mix wet and dry, then rest:** In a large bowl, whisk together the all-purpose flour, whole wheat flour, and salt. Make a well in the flour, pour in the water and oil, and use a stiff silicone spatula to mix until all the flour is moistened. Cover and rest for 15 minutes.

2. **Knead and rest:** Using your hands, knead the mixture in the bowl until it comes together into a smooth dough, 3 to 4 minutes. (It won't be elastic and taut; that's okay.) Coat with a thin layer of oil. Cover with a damp towel and rest for 15 minutes at room temperature, or tightly wrap with plastic wrap for up to 2 days in the fridge.

3. **Portion:** Divide the dough into 12 portions (about 50 grams each). Roughly form each portion into a ball and keep covered with a damp towel.

4. **Roll:** Working with one portion at a time, keeping the rest covered, lightly dust the dough and the counter with flour (I've found it easiest to roll them out on a wooden surface). Using a rolling pin, roll out each portion of dough into a 9-inch round about 1/16 inch thick, frequently rotating it to get a nice round shape.

5. **Cook:** Heat a large cast-iron skillet or griddle pan over high heat. Place one roti in the heated pan and cook until bubbles begin to form on the top, 15 to 20 seconds. Flip and continue to cook until the bottom is fully set and developing browned and charred spots, 45 seconds to 1 minute. Flip once more and cook until the second side has also developed browned and charred spots, about 30 seconds.

6. Use a folded clean kitchen towel to press down onto the edges of the roti, encouraging it to puff. Transfer to a kitchen towel, spread on a thin layer of butter, vegan butter, or ghee, and wrap to keep warm. Continue cooking the remaining roti, stacking and buttering as you go. Serve warm. (Roti are best eaten the same day they are made.)

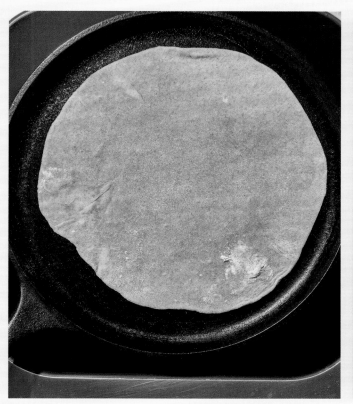

Corn Tortillas

(Makes 12 tortillas)

(Active: 10 mins. | Total: 50 mins.)

(Easy) (Vegan) (Gluten-free)

Ingredients:

200 grams (1½ cups plus
    2 tablespoons) masa harina

1 teaspoon Diamond Crystal kosher
    salt

hot tap water

neutral oil for the pan

Special Equipment:

#40 scoop (optional)

tortilla press (or skillet or glass pie
    plate)

parchment paper (or large
    zip-top bag)

→ All the other breads in this chapter are made with wheat flour and involve kneading, gluten, and sometimes proofing. So why is there a corn tortilla recipe here? Tortillas are the bread that I make the most at home. And since this is my guide to becoming a better cook, I couldn't possibly write a whole book and not include them. They are fast, easy, and if you start with high-quality masa harina, better than anything store-bought. Nothing in this world beats eating a hot tortilla right off the griddle. When we're making tacos at home there's an *eat immediately* rule. We are not waiting for everyone to get their taco at our table.

Masa harina is an instant masa product. Masa is corn that been processed in an alkaline solution through a process called nixtamalization, then ground into a soft dough. If that dough is dried and ground into a flour, it becomes masa harina, ready to become tortillas, tamales, or sopes just by adding water. Because the brands of masa harina vary greatly, I recommend adding the water by feel, starting with a scant cup and adding more by the teaspoon until you get the texture described in the recipe. Making tortillas is all about practice. Your first batch will be far from perfect, but if you keep making them, you'll eventually learn exactly how the dough should feel, how much pressure to use when flattening them, and how hot the griddle should be. These details are the difference between good tortillas and great tortillas.

For the best flavor and texture start with high-quality masa harina; I recommend Masienda or Bob's Red Mill.

---

1. Mix wet and dry: In a medium bowl, use your fingers to whisk together the masa harina and salt. Add hot tap water a little at a time, whisking with stiff fingers, until all the masa is fully moistened but not soggy or wet.

2. Knead then rest: Knead the dough until it forms a ball. It should not be crumbly but also not be so moist that it leaves a sticky residue on your hands. When you poke your finger into the dough it should form an indentation without cracking. If the dough is too crumbly, add water a teaspoon at a time until sufficiently hydrated. If the dough leaves too much sticky residue on your hands, add a teaspoon of masa harina at a time until hydrated properly. Cover with a damp towel and rest at room temperature for at least 40 minutes, or tightly wrap with plastic wrap and chill in the fridge overnight.

3. Heat a cast-iron pan over high heat.

4. Portion, press, and cook: Using a #40 scoop, portion the masa and roll into balls. (Or use your hands to portion and roll the masa into balls about 1½ inches across.) As you are making the balls, cover the masa and portioned balls with a damp towel. The dough can very quickly dry out.

5. Using a paper towel, grease the heated cast-iron pan with a thin layer of oil. →

Corn Tortillas (cont'd.)

6. Line a tortilla press with a sheet of parchment paper folded in half (or a zip-top bag with the top and two sides cut). Have the crease pointing toward the hinge. Place the ball of masa in the center of the tortilla press and press down firmly. (Alternatively, if you don't have a tortilla press, place the portioned masa in the middle of the unfolded parchment paper or the zip-top bag, fold the other half over, creating a masa/parchment sandwich, and press down firmly with a skillet or glass pie plate, which allows you to see the tortilla as you press it.)

7. Gently unfold the parchment paper (or zip-top bag), place the tortilla in your palm, and peel off the parchment paper. In one fluid motion, like waving smoke away from you, gently lay the tortilla down on the cast-iron pan. Cook until lightly speckled underneath, about 1 minute. Flip over and cook until speckled on the other side, about 1 minute. Wrap in a clean kitchen towel and repeat until all the tortillas are cooked. Tortillas are best eaten immediately.

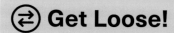 **Get Loose!**

For the Best Taco Ever
Top a hot tortilla with a slice of cold cultured butter long enough to run across the entire center (make it thick). Add a couple of slices of avocado and a generous pinch of smoked flaky salt. No lime. Eat before the butter melts.

For the Best Quesadilla Ever
Lay one pressed but uncooked tortilla on the counter. Fill the center with coarsely grated queso Chihuahua or part-skim mozzarella cheese, mounding it in the center while keeping a scant 1-inch border clear. Top with another uncooked tortilla and use the tines of a fork to crimp the edges closed. Heat a cast-iron skillet with ¼ inch of neutral oil until hot and shimmering. Slide the quesadilla into the oil and cook until crisp and golden, about 1 minute per side. Try to let them rest for 2 minutes before eating.

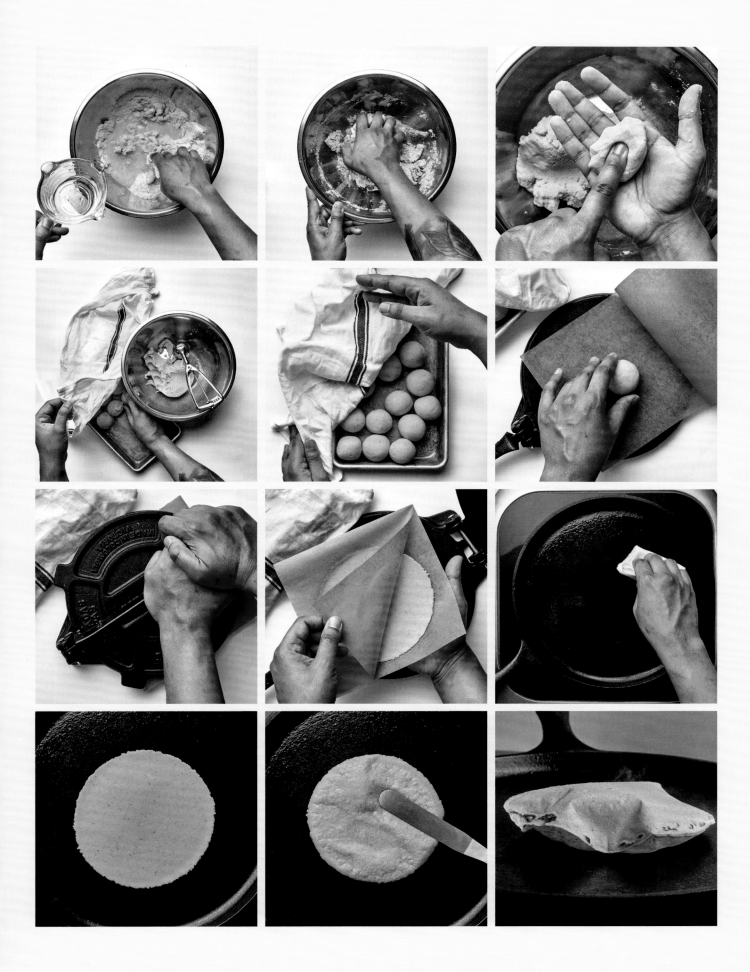

Crusty No-Knead Focaccia

(& How to Make It Pizza)

(One sheet tray)

(Active: 30 mins. | Total: at least 13 hrs.)

(Easy) (Vegan)

Ingredients:

700 grams (5¾ cups plus 1½ tablespoons) bread flour

2¼ teaspoons Diamond Crystal kosher salt

1 tablespoon granulated sugar

¾ teaspoon instant yeast, preferably SAF brand

700 grams (3 cups plus 2 tablespoons) warm water (between 100° and 110°F/38° and 43°C)

170 grams (¾ cup) extra-virgin olive oil, plus more as needed

flaky salt

Special Equipment:

plastic bowl scraper

airtight silicone bowl cover (or plastic wrap)

18 × 13-inch sheet pan (or 9 × 13-inch metal baking pan for a thicker bread)

→ Focaccia is a high-hydration dough, which means there's plenty of water to help the glutenin and gliadin proteins present in the flour hook up and create stretchy gluten strands. All the dough needs is time, so this is not a quick bread. As the yeasts slowly chow down, they burp big bubbles of gas that pull and strengthen the gluten network. Then you come in and give the dough a few folds, which arranges the gluten strands into interlocking nets and gives the bread structure and chew.

This recipe yields a relatively thin and crispy focaccia, perfect for adding toppings to and transforming into sheet pan pizza. If you prefer thick and pillowy focaccia, you have two options: bake this batch size in a 9 × 13-inch metal baking pan or scale the recipe up by one and a half and still bake in the sheet pan. Proofing, bake times, and bake temperature will remain the same.

---

1. Mix wet and dry, then rest: In a large bowl (be sure it is big enough for the dough to double in size in), whisk together the flour, salt, sugar, and yeast. Create a well and pour in the water. Use a stiff silicone spatula to stir together until all the flour is hydrated. Scrape down the sides so there are no rogue bits of dough that can dry out. Cover the bowl with an airtight silicone cover (or tightly wrap with plastic wrap) and rest for 30 minutes.

2. Fold and bulk ferment: Uncover and, working in the bowl, flatten the dough slightly and use a plastic bowl scraper to fold the left side over to the opposite side (like a closing an open book), then flatten the dough. Fold over the top to the bottom and flatten slightly. Flip over and repeat. Cover the bowl with an airtight silicone cover (or tightly wrap with plastic wrap) and set aside to bulk ferment overnight at cool room temperature until the dough is at least doubled in size, has large bubbles, and is very jiggly, anywhere from 8 to 16 hours.

3. Form and proof: The next day, line a sheet pan with parchment paper and use your fingers to evenly spread half the oil (85 grams/ 6 tablespoons) onto the paper. Scrape the dough onto the sheet pan, flattening it out as much as you can. Fold the dough just like before, left to right, then top to bottom. Stretch the dough the best you can to fill the sheet pan. Cover with plastic wrap or invert another sheet pan on top, and proof at room temperature until the dough has doubled in size, fills the pan, and is very jiggly, anywhere from 2 to 5 hours.

4. Bake: Position a rack in the center of the oven and heat to 450°F (230°C).

5. Grease up your hands with oil, then press your fingers into the dough, creating dimples all over. Drizzle with the remaining 85 grams (6 tablespoons) oil and season generously with flaky salt.

6. Bake until both top and bottom are crisp and golden brown, about 30 minutes. Immediately after baking, slide a spatula under the dough and transfer to a rack so it stays crisp. Serve warm. (Focaccia is best eaten the same day it is baked.) →

How to Make It Pizza

Sauce-Topped

→ If topping with sauce, cheese, and/or cooked or quick-cooking ingredients, like pepperoni, olives, rosemary, or spinach:

1. Form and proof the focaccia as directed on page 495.

2. Position a rack in the center of the oven and preheat the oven to 400°F (204°C).

3. Dimple the dough, drizzle with olive oil, and season with flaky salt as directed. Bake until cooked through and lightly golden, about 30 minutes. (You can do this up to 2 days in advance.)

4. Remove from the oven and increase the oven temperature to 475°F (246°C).

5. Top the focaccia with sauce, cheese, and toppings, then bake until the cheese and sauce are bubbling, about 20 minutes. Restraint is key—don't add too much sauce or cheese or the base will become soggy.

6. Transfer to a rack and finish with tender herbs or zest (like basil, parsley, or lemon zest), grated hard cheese (like pecorino or parmesan), and more olive oil.

No Sauce

→ If making a sauceless pizza, topped with dense ingredients that need more time to cook, such as potato, winter squash, or cauliflower:

1. Form and proof the focaccia as directed on page 495.

2. Meanwhile, thinly slice or cut each topping into small pieces. Toss in a large bowl with 85 grams (6 tablespoons) oil and season generously with salt.

3. Position a rack in the center of the oven and preheat the oven to 450°F (230°C).

4. Evenly distribute the topping(s) across the dough. Try not to stack the ingredients too high, keeping them in one layer so they cook evenly and all the way through.

5. Bake until the bottom of the pizza is crisp and the toppings are cooked and browned, about 30 minutes.

6. Transfer to a rack and finish with tender herbs or zest (like basil, parsley, or lemon zest), grated hard cheese (like pecorino or parmesan), and more olive oil.

⇄ Get Loose!

Lemon, Pecorino & Potato Pizza

1. Form and proof the dough as directed on page 495.
2. Meanwhile, thinly slice 5 cloves garlic and chop 2 teaspoons fresh thyme leaves.
3. Peel 680 grams (1½ pounds) Yukon Gold potatoes and cut into ⅛-inch-thick slices. Toss with 85 grams (6 tablespoons) oil and 1 teaspoon Diamond Crystal kosher salt.
4. Position a rack in the center of the oven and preheat the oven to 450°F (230°C).
5. Dimple the dough as directed, then evenly distribute the garlic and thyme across the dough. Then evenly arrange the potatoes over the dough, covering the garlic and thyme, and sprinkle with flaky salt.
6. Bake until the bottom is crisp and the potatoes are cooked through and golden, about 30 minutes. Transfer the pizza to a wire rack.
7. Drizzle with more olive oil. Finely grate over the zest of 2 lemons and shower with grated pecorino cheese. Top with freshly ground black pepper and serve.

Charred Greens & Vegan Queso Pizza

1. Form and proof the focaccia as directed on page 495.
2. Position a rack in the center of the oven and preheat the oven to 400°F (204°C).
3. Dimple the dough, drizzle with olive oil, and season with salt as directed. Bake until cooked through and lightly golden, about 30 minutes. (You can parbake the pizza base up to 2 days in advance.)
4. Remove from the oven and increase the oven temperature to 475°F (246°C).
5. Spread 1½ cups Vegan Queso (page 223) over the pizza base. Pile on 680 grams (1½ pounds) tender greens, such as arugula, spinach, or Swiss chard. (It will look like too much, but don't worry, it'll all cook down.)
6. Drizzle with olive oil and sprinkle with salt to taste. Bake until the greens are wilted and charred in spots, about 20 minutes.
7. Transfer to a rack, finish with pickled jalapeño slices and torn cilantro sprigs, and serve.

Classic Red Sauce Pizza

1. Form and proof the focaccia as directed on page 495.
2. Position a rack in the center of the oven and preheat the oven to 400°F (204°C).
3. Dimple the dough, drizzle with olive oil, and season with salt as directed. Bake until cooked through and lightly golden, about 30 minutes. (You can parbake the pizza base up to 2 days in advance.)
4. Remove from the oven and increase the oven temperature to 475°F (246°C).
5. Spread 1½ cups marinara sauce over the baked pizza base. Sprinkle over 224 grams (8 ounces) grated part-skim mozzarella cheese.
6. Top with your favorite cooked or quick-cooking pizza toppings, such as pepperoni, crumbled sausage, green peppers, or olives. (My favorite combo is soppressata and pineapple.) Bake until the sauce is bubbling and the cheese is melted and browning in places, about 20 minutes.
7. Transfer to a rack and finish with torn basil, grated parmesan cheese, and more olive oil. Serve with chili flakes, dried oregano, and garlic powder alongside.

Za'atar Manakeesh

Za'atar Manakeesh

(Makes 8 manakeesh)

(Active: 30 mins.) | (Total: 2½ hrs.)

(Easy) (Vegan)

For the bread:

360 grams (3 cups) bread flour

1 tablespoon granulated sugar

2¼ teaspoons instant yeast, preferably SAF brand

1½ teaspoons Diamond Crystal kosher salt

225 grams (1 cup) warm water (between 100° and 110°F/38° and 43°C)

75 grams (⅓ cup) extra-virgin olive oil, plus more as needed

For the topping:

113 grams (½ cup) extra-virgin olive oil

100 grams (½ cup) za'atar blend

Special Equipment:

rolling pin

plastic bowl scraper

parchment paper

→ One of my go-to after-school snacks as a kid was (what I now know is called) za'atar manakeesh warmed up in the toaster oven with a side of last night's raitha for dipping. Back then, though, I didn't know what it was called and named the herby rounds "green pizza." My mother picked up stacks of green pizza from a local Middle Eastern grocery/bakery/butcher where she'd also buy halal meat, extra tart desi yogurt, and phone cards for making calls back home. Manakeesh is found throughout the Middle East with various toppings like spiced ground meat or melty Akkawi cheese. The dough is made with olive oil, so it bakes up golden brown and crusty. This is the place to bust out the good extra-virgin olive oil because its flavor will be front and center. Za'atar is a blend of spices, herbs, and sesame seeds that's become pretty popular over the past few years, but be careful because a lot of what's out there is crap. It should be coarsely ground with distinct ingredients rather than blended into fine power. I buy my za'atar from Burlap & Barrel or a Middle Eastern grocery store.

1. **Mix wet and dry, then rest:** In a large bowl, whisk together the flour, sugar, yeast, and salt. Make a well and pour in the water and oil. Using a stiff silicone spatula, stir together until all the flour is moistened. Cover with a slightly damp towel and rest for 15 minutes.

2. **Knead and rest:** Using your hands and with the help of a plastic bowl scraper, knead the mixture in the bowl until it comes together into a dough, about 2 minutes. (It will be sticky and wet, try not to add flour. If it's very difficult to work with, lightly grease your hands and the bowl scraper with oil.) Cover with a slightly damp towel and rest for 10 minutes.

3. **Knead and bulk ferment:** Scrape the dough onto a clean counter and knead (with your hands and the help of the bowl scraper) until it is smooth, taut, and springs back when lightly poked, 6 to 8 minutes. (It will become less sticky as you knead, try not to add flour. If the dough feels too wet to handle, lightly grease your hands, the bowl scraper, and the counter with oil.) Cover with a slightly damp towel and set aside until the dough is barely puffed and slowly bounces back when gently pressed, about 1 hour.

4. **Portion and rest:** Divide the dough into 8 even pieces (about 80 grams each). Cup your palms over each portion of dough and roll them against the counter to form a smooth ball. (If the dough is sticky, lightly grease the counter and your hands. Do not add flour!) Cover with a slightly damp towel and rest for 10 minutes.

5. **Roll and proof:** Line three sheet pans with parchment paper (see Note). Using a rolling pin on a lightly floured surface (I've found it easiest to roll out on a wooden surface), roll out each portion of dough into a 5- to 6-inch round a scant ¼ inch thick, frequently rotating it to get a nice round shape. Arrange the rounds on the sheet pans. Cover with a slightly damp towel or an inverted sheet pan, and proof until the dough is barely puffy and slowly bounces back when gently pressed, about 30 minutes.

6. **Set up:** Position a rack in the lowest position in the oven and heat to 450°F (230°C).

7. **Prepare the topping:** In a small bowl, stir together the oil and za'atar. Divide the za'atar mixture among the dough rounds and evenly spread all over the surface.

8. **Bake:** Bake one pan at a time until the edges are golden brown, 8 to 12 minutes. (Give the oven time to reheat in between batches.) Serve warm or at room temperature. (Tightly wrapped, the manakeesh will keep at room temperature for 1 week.)

Note: Because we're baking one pan at a time, if you don't have enough sheet pans or want to save parchment, proof the dough rounds on the counter instead. Then gently transfer 3 proofed rounds to a lined sheet pan, top, bake, and repeat.

Perfectly Puffy Pitas

(Makes 8 pitas)

(Active: 30 mins.) (Total: 2½ hrs.)

(Intermediate) (Vegan)

Ingredients:

360 grams (3 cups) bread flour

1 tablespoon granulated sugar

2¼ teaspoons instant yeast, preferably SAF brand

1½ teaspoons kosher salt

250 grams (1 cup plus 2 tablespoons) warm water (between 100° and 110°F/38° and 43°C)

1 tablespoon olive oil or neutral oil, plus more as needed

Special Equipment:

plastic bowl scraper

rolling pin

baking stone (or baking steel, cast-iron griddle pan, or large cast-iron skillet)

→ A moist dough is the key to a pita that will puff in the oven—baking up feathery on the inside, crusty on the outside, with just the right amount of chew. Wet doughs can be difficult to work with, but don't be tempted to add flour. Lightly grease the counter and your hands to make it easier to work with. As you knead, the dough will become less sticky, growing smooth and taut. Once you improve your kneading form, you'll find it easier to handle; it just takes a bit of practice to get down.

---

1. **Mix wet and dry, then rest:** In a large bowl, whisk together the flour, sugar, yeast, and salt. Make a well and pour in the water and oil. Using a stiff silicone spatula, stir together until all the flour is moistened. Cover with a slightly damp towel and rest for 15 minutes.

2. **Knead and rest:** Using your hands and with the help of a plastic bowl scraper, knead the mixture in the bowl until it comes together into a dough, about 2 minutes. (It will be sticky and wet; try not to add flour. If it's very difficult to work with, lightly grease your hands and the bowl scraper with oil.) Cover with a slightly damp towel and rest for 10 minutes.

3. **Knead and bulk ferment:** Lightly grease the counter, the bowl scraper, and your hands. Scrape the dough onto the counter and knead until it is smooth, taut, and springs back when lightly poked, 6 to 8 minutes. (It will be very difficult to work with initially. Use a greased bowl scraper to help you pry the dough off the counter.) Cover with a slightly damp towel and set the dough aside to proof until it is barely puffed and slowly bounces back when gently pressed, 40 minutes to 1 hour.

4. **Portion and rest:** Divide the dough into 8 even pieces (about 75 grams each). Cup your palms over each portion and roll each against the counter to form a smooth ball. Lightly grease the counter and your hands if needed. **Do not add flour!** Cover with a slightly damp towel and rest for 10 minutes.

5. **Roll and proof:** Using a rolling pin on a lightly floured surface (I've found it easiest to roll out on a wooden surface), roll out each portion of dough into a 6-inch round that's ¼ inch thick, frequently rotating it to get a nice round shape. (If the dough is too thin or thick, it won't develop a pocket.) Cover and proof until the dough is barely puffy and slowly bounces back when gently pressed, about 30 minutes.

6. **Bake:** Position a rack in the lower third of the oven. Place a baking stone, baking steel, cast-iron griddle pan, or a large cast-iron skillet on the rack and heat the oven to 500°F (260°C). →

Perfectly Puffy Pitas
(cont'd.)

7. Working with as many rounds of dough as will fit on your heated baking surface, gently pick up each pita and lay it onto the baking surface. (For best puffing, keep the side that was up during proofing up during baking.) Be sure to quickly open and close the oven to minimize losing heat. Bake until puffed and barely blond along the edges—do not overbake! Give the oven a couple of minutes to recover any lost heat before baking the next round. (Unless you've got a wood-fired oven, the pitas will not be very browned at this point. If you bake them so long that they brown, the pitas will dry out.)

8. Wrap the baked pitas in a clean kitchen towel to keep warm. If you want extra browning, lightly char a pita directly over a gas flame or in a dry skillet on the stovetop over high heat. Serve warm. (Tightly wrap leftover pitas in plastic and store at room temperature for 3 days or in the freezer for 1 month.)

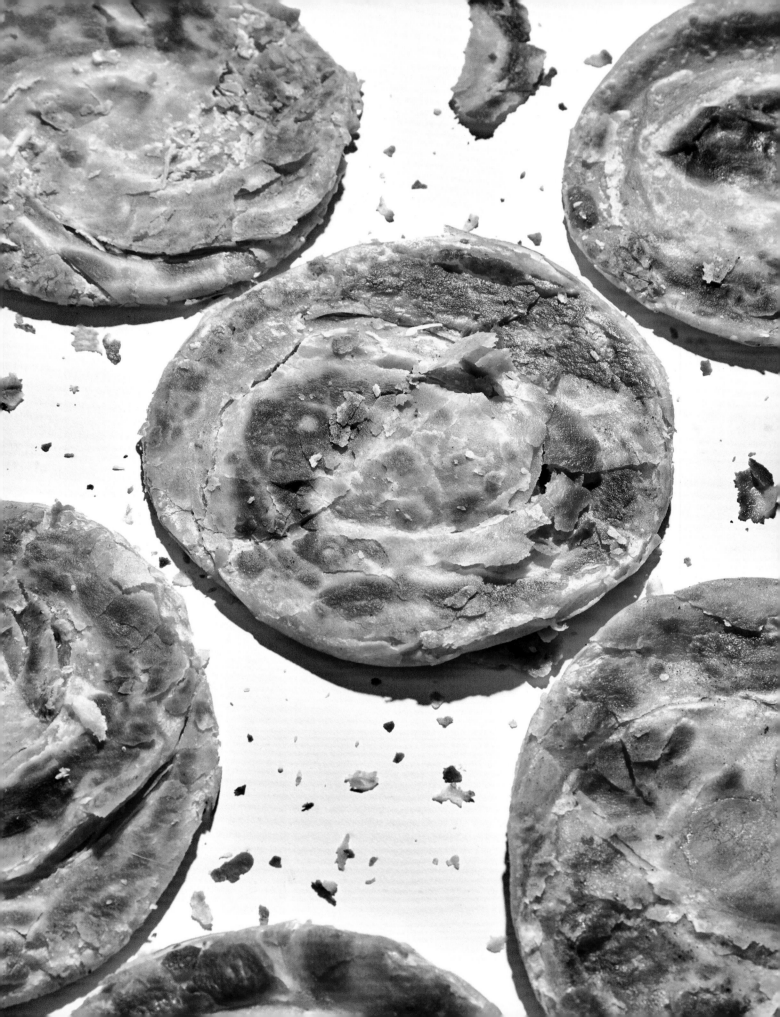

Flaky Brown Butter Lachha Paratha

(Makes 8 parathas)

(Active: 2 hrs. | Total: at least 6 hrs.)

(Intermediate) (Vegetarian)

Ingredients:

227 grams (2 sticks) unsalted butter, cut into pieces

375 grams (3 cups plus 2 tablespoons) all-purpose flour, plus more for dusting

1 tablespoon granulated sugar

2 teaspoons Diamond Crystal kosher salt

225 grams (1 cup) warm water

Special Equipment:

bench scraper

rolling pin

pastry brush

→ Lachha paratha is a laminated bread, which means the bread is made up of countless layers separated by fat, cooking up flaky, crisp, and chewy all at once. Similar laminated, unleavened flatbreads are found throughout North Africa and West, South, and Central Asia with slight variations and different names. This is my version, inspired by the one I grew up eating, but with tweaks I've made over the years. This recipe takes time and is even better if you break it up over a few days. Chilling the coiled dough overnight after forming gives it ample time to rest and stiffens the butter, making it easier to roll out. After the parcooking step, I prefer to cool the parathas fully (preferably overnight) before browning in butter. This allows the starches to reset into a stronger structure through a process called retrogradation, resulting in a flakier bread after the final cook.

---

1. **Make brown butter & ghee:** In a medium saucepan, melt the butter over medium heat until foamy, about 6 minutes. Continue to cook, stirring constantly, until the sputtering subsides and the milk solids are deeply browned, 6 to 9 minutes.

2. Pour the browned butter into a heatproof measuring cup, scraping in all the milk solids. Let it sit undisturbed until the milk solids fall to the bottom, about 2 minutes.

3. Carefully pour all but ¼ cup of the browned butterfat into a small bowl, leaving the milk solids behind in the measuring cup. This browned butterfat is the ghee and the remaining milk solids are the brown butter. Set the ghee aside to use in the dough and to cook the parathas (you may not need all of it). Refrigerate the measuring cup with the brown butter until thickened and creamy but still soft for layering within the parathas. (See Note.)

4. **Mix wet and dry, then rest:** In a large bowl, whisk together the flour, sugar, and salt. Add the warm water and 2 tablespoons of ghee and mix with a wooden spoon until no dry spots of flour remain and the dough comes together in a shaggy mass. Cover with a plate and let rest at room temperature for 15 minutes.

5. **Knead and rest:** Knead the dough in the bowl until it forms a smooth mass, about 2 minutes. Scrape onto a clean, unfloured surface and continue to knead until smooth and elastic, about 8 minutes. (The dough will feel very sticky at first but will grow smooth and soft as you go. Try to avoid adding more flour.)

6. Roll the dough against the surface to form it into a ball. Wash and dry the bowl, grease with ghee, then add the dough, turning to coat it in the ghee. Cover the bowl tightly with plastic wrap. Let rest at room temperature for at least 1 hour and up to 4 hours (if you poke the dough with your finger, it shouldn't spring back). →

Flaky Brown Butter Lachha Paratha (cont'd.)

7. Portion and rest: Using a bench scraper or chef's knife, divide the dough into 8 pieces (about 75 grams each). Working with 1 piece at a time, cup the dough in your palm and roll it against the counter to form into a smooth ball. Use your hands to coat each ball lightly with ghee. Place the dough balls on a plate or just leave on the counter. Cover with a damp towel, plastic wrap, or an overturned bowl and rest for 20 minutes.

8. Form and rest: Stir the reserved chilled brown butter to evenly distribute the milk solids into the fat and make sure it's creamy and spreadable. Roll out 1 piece of dough on a lightly floured surface until as thin as possible. (Don't worry about size or shape at this point—you just want it to be super thin. You should be able to see through it.)

9. Using your fingers or an offset spatula, spread a heaping teaspoonful of chilled brown butter across the dough (it doesn't have to be even, just get it on there) and dust lightly with flour.

10. Starting from the top, roll the dough into a long snake. Coil the ends until they meet at the center, then flip one coil on top of the other and press together firmly. Lightly dust with flour and place on a plate. Repeat with the remaining balls of dough. Once all the balls have been coiled, tightly wrap with plastic and rest in the fridge for at least 2 hours or (preferably) overnight.

11. Parcook: Heat a medium cast-iron skillet over medium-low heat. On a lightly floured surface, working with one piece at a time, roll the dough coils out into scant ⅛-inch-thick rounds, rotating after each roll to keep them evenly round. Brush off any excess flour with a pastry brush. Parcook the parathas in the dry skillet until set and dry, but without taking on any color, 2 to 3 minutes per side. Transfer to a baking sheet or plate as you work (it's okay to stack them). (Tightly wrapped, parcooked parathas will keep in the fridge for 5 days or in the freezer for 1 month.)

12. Pan-fry: Brush the skillet with some of the ghee and set over medium heat. Place a parcooked paratha in the pan and brush with more ghee. Cook, turning every 30 seconds and adding more ghee as needed, until golden brown and crisp on both sides, about 3 minutes. Quickly scrunch to release any steam (this will keep them from getting soggy) and wrap in a kitchen towel to keep warm. Repeat with the remaining parathas, scrunching and stacking as you go. Serve hot.

Note: By divvying up the butter this way, you end up with brown butter for layering within the bread and ghee for cooking the bread. See Clarified Butter vs. Ghee vs. Brown Butter (page 300) to learn more.

Squishy No-Knead White Bread

(Makes one loaf)

(Active: 1 hr. | Total: 31 hrs.)

(Advanced) (Vegetarian)

Ingredients:

585 grams bread flour

1 teaspoon instant yeast, preferably SAF brand

1½ tablespoons Diamond Crystal kosher salt

1 large egg (about 55 grams)

400 grams whole milk, warmed to between 100° and 110°F (38° and 43°C)

80 grams granulated sugar

60 grams neutral oil

cooking spray

Special Equipment:

scale

plastic bowl scraper

9 × 5-inch metal loaf pan

→ This bread is pillowy yet rich, like an extra-soft brioche. It's great for sandwiches, French toast, bread pudding; but even more exciting is that this base dough can be formed into rolls, steamed into soft buns, or fried into feathery donuts. The combination of slow fermentation, high moisture, and folding develops gluten without any kneading. This dough takes some time, but once you get it down, a loaf is just the starting point. I'm giving you the measurements only in grams because this bread requires precision, and it looks and feels different from any of the other doughs in this chapter. This wet and sticky dough bakes up fluffy and tender thanks to the high hydration, sugar, and neutral oil. (Butter would make it dense and less suitable for frying or steaming.) Don't be tempted to add flour if things get awkward—grease yourself, the counter, and your tools with cooking spray instead.

1. **Mix the wet and dry:** In a large bowl, whisk together the flour, yeast, and salt.

2. In a medium bowl, whisk the egg until no streaks remain. Add the milk, sugar, and oil, and whisk until combined.

3. Make a well in the dry ingredients and pour in the wet ingredients. Use a stiff silicone spatula to mix until all the flour is hydrated. Scrape off any dough clinging to the spatula with a plastic bowl scraper.

4. **Fold and rest:** Using the plastic bowl scraper, scootch under the dough and pull it up and over itself. Continue folding the dough, rotating the bowl a quarter-turn after every fold, until it is evenly mixed and beginning to look smooth. Tightly wrap the bowl with plastic wrap and rest the dough for 20 to 30 minutes.

5. **Fold and rest:** Lightly grease the counter and your hands with cooking spray. Use the bowl scraper to scrape the dough onto the counter. Press the dough into a rough 8-inch square. Using the bowl scraper, fold the dough in half from left to right, then bottom to top, leaving you with a 4-inch square of dough. Rotate the dough 90 degrees, flatten into an 8-inch square again, and repeat the folding process two more times (for a total of three).

6. Wash, dry, and grease the bowl. Return the dough to the bowl, tightly wrap with plastic wrap, and let it rest for 20 to 30 minutes.

7. **Repeat step 5:** Lightly grease the counter and your hands with cooking spray. Use the bowl scraper to scrape the dough onto the counter. Press the dough into a rough 8-inch square. Using the bowl scraper, fold the dough in half from left to right, then bottom to top, leaving you with a 4-inch square of dough. Rotate the dough 90 degrees, flatten into an 8-inch square again, and repeat the folding process two more times (for a total of three).

8. Bulk ferment overnight: Roll the dough against the counter to roughly form it into a ball. Then return the dough to the bowl, tightly wrap with plastic wrap, and transfer it to the fridge to ferment for 24 to 36 hours. (Make sure the bowl is very tightly wrapped with plastic so the dough doesn't develop a skin.)

9. Form and proof: Lightly grease the counter and your hands with cooking spray. Use the bowl scraper to scrape the dough onto the counter. Use your hands and a rolling pin to flatten it into a 12-inch square, positioned like a diamond with one corner pointing toward you. Bring the left and right corners to the center, then roll the dough, starting with the corner closest to you, into a tight cylinder. Pinch the seam closed and place the dough into a 9 × 5-inch loaf pan, seam-side down.

10. Loosely cover with a slightly damp towel and proof until the dough reaches the top of the loaf pan and slowly bounces back when gently pressed, 3 to 4 hours.

11. Bake: Position a rack in the lower third of the oven and heat to 350°F (177°C). Mist the top of the bread with cooking spray and bake until it is deeply browned, crisp, and sounds hollow when tapped, 50 minutes to 1 hour. (The internal temperature should be at least 195°F/91°C on an instant-read thermometer.)

12. Tip the loaf out of the pan and set it on a wire rack to cool. Do not slice it until fully cooled. (Store tightly wrapped at room temperature for 3 days or slice and freeze for 1 month.)

Getting to Know Dough

Bacon Fat Rolls with L & T

(Makes 16 rolls)

(Active: 2 hrs. | Total: 32 hrs.)

(Advanced)

For the rolls:

Squishy No-Knead White Bread dough
(page 510)

113 grams (½ cup) rendered bacon
fat, melted

For the sandwiches:

sliced ripe tomatoes

kosher salt and freshly ground black
pepper

mayonnaise

torn crunchy lettuce

Special Equipment:

pastry brush

→ Sheena Otto, the former head baker at Atera in Tribeca, where I used to work, first dreamed up the idea of a crusty, chewy, pork fat–basted sourdough roll. Brushing the buns while cooking makes the exterior almost fry, while soaking in all that porky flavor. She tested them with every fat under the sun, from beef tallow to duck fat, but none got as crackly and crispy as those basted with pork fat. These are inspired by her rolls, made with the no-knead white bread dough and basted with smoky, salty bacon fat. Reserve the fat rendered after cooking bacon in a jar or heatproof container until you have enough for this recipe. These rolls end up tasting like bacon in bread form, so why not fill them with lettuce, tomato, and mayo?

1. Make the dough: Prepare the no-knead white bread dough through the overnight bulk ferment step. Line two sheet pans with parchment paper.

2. Form: On a clean work surface, form the dough into a rough log and cut into 16 portions (about 75 grams each). Cup your palms over each portion of dough and roll it against the counter to form a smooth ball. (If the dough is sticky, lightly grease the counter and your hands. Do not add flour!)

3. Proof: Evenly space 8 rolls per sheet pan, cover with a slightly damp kitchen towel, and set aside to proof until the dough is puffy and it slowly bounces back when you gently press it, about 1 hour.

4. Set up: Position the oven racks in the lower third and upper third of the oven and heat to 350°F (177°C).

5. Bake and baste: Brush the buns with bacon fat, place the pans on the two oven racks, and bake for 10 minutes. Remove from the oven, brush with more bacon fat, and return to the oven, switching racks and rotating the pans front to back.

6. After 10 minutes, remove the pans from the oven and brush the buns with the remaining bacon fat. Return the pans to the oven, again switching racks and rotating the pans front to back. Bake for a final 10 minutes until deeply browned. (The buns will bake for a total of 30 minutes, with 3 coats of bacon fat.) Rest for at least 15 minutes. (Stored tightly wrapped, they will keep at room temperature for 3 days, or wrap them individually and freeze for 1 month.)

7. Make the sandwiches: Using a sharp serrated knife, spilt the buns horizontally in half. Season the tomato slices with salt and pepper and assemble the sandwiches as desired. This is all about your personal preference: I like a generous swipe of Hellmann's mayo, lots of torn Little Gem lettuce, and a thick slice of heirloom tomato. →

Parker House Rolls

Use the Bacon Fat Rolls recipe as a guide for this variation. The dough will be proofed and divided the same way, then formed into an oval shape before stuffing and smothering in butter.

1. Make the dough through the overnight bulk ferment as directed.

2. Shortly before the dough is ready, cut 1 stick (113 grams) of butter in half lengthwise and divide each portion into 8 pats (for a total of 16). Melt an additional 113 grams (8 tablespoons) butter. Have both at the ready.

3. Divide the dough and roll into balls as directed, then use a rolling pin to stretch and roll each ball into an oblong shape, about 2 inches wide and 5 inches long. Place a pat of butter in the center of the dough and fold the dough in half, pressing the edges together.

4. Line a sheet pan with parchment paper. Arrange the pieces next to one another (you want them to be barely touching) on the lined pan, brush with the melted butter, and proof, uncovered, until the dough is puffy and it slowly bounces back when you gently press it, about 1 hour.

5. Meanwhile, heat the oven to 350°F (177°C).

6. Bake until golden, about 30 minutes. Brush with more melted butter while hot and sprinkle with flaky salt. Serve immediately.

Spiced Potato-Filled Steamed Buns

(Makes 16 buns)

(Active: 2 hrs. | Total: 32 hrs.)

(Advanced) (Vegetarian)

Ingredients:

Squishy No-Knead White Bread dough (page 510)

1½ pounds (675 grams) Yukon Gold potatoes (about 10 small potatoes), scrubbed

2 tablespoons Diamond Crystal kosher salt, plus more as needed

4 tablespoons (56 grams) unsalted butter, ghee, or neutral oil

2 tablespoons urad dal (optional)

½ cup cashews, roughly chopped

1 teaspoon black mustard seeds

1 teaspoon cumin seeds

1 medium yellow onion, finely chopped

2-inch piece fresh ginger, peeled and finely chopped

1 to 2 Thai green or serrano chilies, finely chopped

½ teaspoon ground turmeric

½ cup lightly packed fresh cilantro leaves and tender stems, roughly chopped

freshly squeezed lemon juice

cooking spray or oil

Special Equipment:

parchment paper

tiered steamer (preferably 4-tiered)

→ These buns get me warm and fuzzy, reminding me of all the leftover bhaji sandwiches my mom would pack in my lunchbox, with potato masala smooshed between slices of Wonder bread with the crusts cut off. Here, the dough is steamed to replicate that texture, cooking up squishy, tender, and pale as can be. The filling inside these soft buns is inspired by the potato masala you'll find in a masala dosa, but with extra crunch from lots of chopped cashews and made drier so it's easier to stuff. Season the filling aggressively with lemon juice, salt, and chilies, for contrast against the sweet dough. If you're not in the mood for steamed buns, don't sleep on the potato masala! Add a few splashes of water to make it saucier and have it with roti or steamed rice and raitha (or make a Wonder bread sandwich like my mom).

---

1. **Make the dough:** Prepare the no-knead white bread dough through the overnight bulk ferment step.

2. **Meanwhile, make the potato filling:** Place the potatoes in a medium saucepan and add enough water to cover by 1 inch. Add the kosher salt and bring to a simmer over high heat, then reduce the heat to maintain a gentle simmer and cook the potatoes until totally tender and easily pierced with a cake tester, 25 to 35 minutes. Drain and cut them into rough ½-inch pieces.

3. In a medium skillet, melt the butter over medium heat until foamy. Add the dal (if using) and cashews and cook, stirring frequently, until beginning to toast, 1 to 2 minutes. Add the mustard seeds and cumin seeds and cook until everything is toasted, about 1 minute.

4. Add the onion, ginger, chilies, and a big pinch of kosher salt and cook, stirring frequently, until wilted and translucent, 2 to 4 minutes. Add the turmeric and cook until fragrant, about 1 minute. Remove from the heat.

5. Add the potatoes and cilantro to the skillet, mixing and smashing with a stiff silicone spatula, until everything is well combined and looks like a chunky mash. Taste and add lemon juice and more salt to taste. Set aside to cool completely. (The filling can be made up to 2 days in advance.)

6. **Set up:** Cut 4 rounds of parchment paper that will fit inside the baskets of your steamer. Use a skewer or scissors to poke at least 8 holes in each sheet (this will allow the steam to easily move through the basket). Line each basket of the steamer with a parchment round. If you've got a 4-tiered steamer, then way to go! You can steam all the buns at once. Otherwise, lay any remaining parchment rounds on a sheet pan in readiness for a second round of steaming. Grease each parchment sheet with cooking spray or oil. →

Spiced Potato-Filled Steamed Buns (cont'd.)

7. For the buns: On a clean counter, roll the dough into a long log and cut into 16 portions (about 75 grams each). Cup your palms over each portion of dough and roll it against the counter to form a smooth ball. (If the dough is sticky, lightly grease the counter and your hands. **Do not add flour!**)

8. Flatten and stretch each dough ball into a disk with the edges thinner than the center. Place a disk in the palm of your nondominant hand. Spoon ¼ cup potato filling in the center. Pinch the dough up and around the filling and place the filled dough on the counter seam-side down. Cup your palms over the filled dough ball and gently roll it against the counter to close the seam. Transfer to the prepped parchment sheets and loosely cover with a slightly damp towel. Continue filling and rolling buns, arranging 4 buns per parchment round.

9. Set the rolls aside (still covered by the slightly damp towel) to proof until the dough is puffy and it slowly bounces back when gently pressed, 20 minutes to 1 hour. (How long it will take to proof can vary greatly depending on how quickly you can form and fill the dough. If you work slowly, you may need to steam a batch of buns before you've finished forming them all.)

10. Set up a steamer: You can steam the buns in either a medium saucepan or a wok.
- If using a saucepan, fill it halfway up with water and bring to a boil over high heat. Reduce the heat to maintain a simmer. Place the steamer on top, making sure that the bottom basket just fits over the edges of the pot. (If there's a gap, your buns will take longer to steam.)
- If using a wok, add enough water to reach 1 inch (2½ cm) below the bottom of where the steamer will rest. Bring to a boil over high heat, reduce the heat to maintain a simmer, and place the steamer on top.
- Throughout the cooking, keep an eye on the water level and add more hot water as needed.

11. Steam the buns until they quickly bounce back when firmly pressed and the outsides feel slightly tacky, 16 to 20 minutes. Let them rest for 5 minutes and serve them warm or at room temperature. (The buns will keep for 3 days in the refrigerator or 1 month in the freezer. Eat cold, reheat in the steamer, or wrap in a damp towel and microwave.)

How to Make It Uncrustables*-ish

Make the rolls up to the point of stuffing them. Instead of the potato masala, stuff each flattened round of dough with 2 tablespoons Jif or Skippy peanut butter and 2 tablespoons Smucker's strawberry or grape jam. Form, proof, and steam as directed opposite. Eat warm, at room temperature, cold, or even straight from the freezer.

* For the uninitiated, Uncrustables are premade, crustless peanut butter and jelly sandwiches that are sold individually wrapped and are the best airport preflight snack.

518

Vanilla-Glazed Donuts

(Makes 16 donuts and holes)

(Active: 3 hrs. | Total: 33 hrs.)

(Advanced) (Vegetarian)

Ingredients:

Squishy No-Knead White Bread dough
(page 510)

cooking spray

refined coconut oil for frying (about
60 fluid ounces/1.8 liters)

300 grams (2½ cups) powdered sugar

70 grams (5 tablespoons) buttermilk,
whole milk, or heavy cream

1½ teaspoons vanilla paste or
1 tablespoon pure vanilla extract

Special Equipment:

donut cutters (or a 3-inch and a 1-inch
round cutter)

parchment paper

rolling pin

candy thermometer

→ Yes, donuts are a bread! As a kid we'd have donuts exactly twice a year, after each early-morning Eid prayer (yes, there are two Eids!). It's the promise of donuts that got me out of bed and into my scratchy salwar kameez. My favorite has always been a fresh vanilla-glazed donut. I'd leave the chocolate icing, cream filling, and sprinkles for my sister.

Frying can seem intimidating, but it's all about having the right stuff. A heavy Dutch oven retains heat better than stainless steel, for fewer temperature swings. I never fry without an analog candy thermometer, which lets me monitor the heat better than a digital probe. Refined coconut oil makes for a crisp exterior that's never greasy. It's also more stable than fluid neutral oil, allowing you to strain and fry with it over and over again. As long as the oil never goes above 450°F (230°C), it will not break down or develop off-flavors. For the best deal, buy it in bulk online.

1. **Make the dough:** Prepare the no-knead white bread dough through the overnight bulk ferment step.

2. **Form:** Cut parchment paper into sixteen 5-inch squares and arrange on two sheet pans. Add any extra strips alongside for the donut holes. Lightly mist the counter with cooking spray, scrape the dough onto the counter, and mist the dough. Using a rolling pin, roll until ½ inch thick. Using a greased donut cutter (or a 3-inch and 1-inch round cutter) stamp out the donuts. Transfer the donuts to the squares of parchment and set the donut holes on the extra strips alongside. Gently knead together the scraps, let rest for a few minutes, then reroll and cut out more donuts.

3. **Proof:** Cover the sheet pans loosely with a kitchen towel and set aside to proof until the dough is puffy and slowly bounces back when pressed, about 1 hour. (Depending on how fast you are at rolling them out, some donuts may be proofed before others. Have the oil ready to go so you can fry as they are proofed.)

4. **Fry:** Add enough coconut oil to a medium Dutch oven to come 2 inches up the sides. Clip a candy thermometer to the side of the pan. When the dough is nearly proofed, heat over medium to 350°F (177°C). Adjust the heat throughout cooking to stay near that temperature. Set a wire rack in a sheet pan.

5. Working with one at a time, use the square of parchment to lift a donut and carefully place the whole thing into the hot oil, then use tongs to peel off the parchment paper. Use a spoon to lift the donut holes off the paper and into the oil. Fry no more than 2 donuts or 6 holes at a time, so the oil temperature doesn't drop. Cook until golden brown on one side, then flip and repeat on the other side, 1 to 2 minutes per side. (They should be fluffy, golden, and not greasy; for more on this, see What the Hell Happened? on the next page.) Use a slotted spoon or spider to transfer the donuts to the wire rack to cool slightly. →

Vanilla-Glazed Donuts (cont'd.)

6. **Make the glaze:** Once the donuts are cool enough to handle, in a medium bowl, whisk together the powdered sugar, buttermilk, and vanilla until smooth. It should be thick enough to coat a spoon. Add more sugar or liquid as needed to achieve the right texture.

7. Working with one donut at a time, drop it into the glaze and flip it over with a fork to fully coat. Lift out the donut with the fork and hold above the bowl for a few seconds to let any excess glaze drip off. Return to the rack to dry. (Donuts are best eaten the day they are made.)

8. Once the oil is cool enough to handle, but still fluid, pass it through a fine-mesh sieve into a heatproof container and reserve for future frying.

What the Hell Happened?

If you're iffy about how to judge the doneness of your donuts, fry a tester donut hole first. Then taste and evaluate using the following notes as your guide. If they are overproofed, there's not much you can do. However, underproofed donuts can be given more time to rise and oil temperature can be adjusted.

- **Greasy and spongy?** The dough was overproofed.

- **Dense and dry?** The dough was underproofed.

- **Greasy and pale?** The oil temperature was too low.

- **Dark and dense?** The oil temperature was too high.

⇄ Get Loose!

Maple Bars

1. Prepare the Squishy No-Knead White Bread (page 510) dough through the overnight bulk ferment step.

2. Cut parchment paper into twelve 3 × 7-inch rectangles. Roll out the dough into a 10 × 12-inch rectangle about ½ inch thick (with a short side facing you). Use cooking spray to lightly grease the blade of a pizza cutter or sharp knife. Halve the rectangle of dough crosswise (this creates rectangles that are 10 × 6 inches), then slice lengthwise into 6 rows. Each bar will be about 1½ inches wide and 6 inches long.

3. Transfer the bars to the cut pieces of parchment paper and proof as directed.

4. Fry as directed. Dip the tops in maple glaze (recipe follows) and lightly sprinkle with smoked flaky salt.

Maple Glaze

56 grams (4 tablespoons) unsalted butter, cut into pieces

85 grams (¼ cup) maple syrup

106 grams (½ cup packed) dark brown sugar

2 tablespoons whole milk

180 grams (1½ cups) powdered sugar

½ teaspoon pure vanilla extract

1. In a medium saucepan (preferably one with sloped sides, like a saucier), combine the butter, maple syrup, brown sugar, and milk over medium heat. Cook, whisking constantly, until dissolved and smooth but not yet bubbling, about 5 minutes.

2. Remove from the heat and sift the powdered sugar on top. Add the vanilla and whisk until smooth. You want the glaze to coat a spoon. Add more milk or sugar if needed to achieve the right texture.

3. Dip the donuts while the glaze is still slightly warm.

After Party!

Layer cakes for days

After Party!

Apparently there was a stretch of months, when I was barely counter height, that I'd bake and frost a Betty Crocker box mix cake every single day. I have no memory of this, but uncles and aunts like to tell me the story of a wee me singing Happy Birthday to myself and blowing out a wildfire of candles on repeat. I don't know why my parents would allow this, other than the fact that it was probably adorable. However, knowing what unreliable narrators brown elders tend to be, part of me doubts the legitimacy of this tale. Some of it is likely true: I have been cake-obsessed from day one. And what a freaking origin story! Throughout grade school, while other girls had diaries (and friends), I had notebooks filled with sketches of towering layer cakes. Doodles with squiggles and swirls represented the various layers, fillings, flavors, and toppings. Sometimes I brought those sketches to life with cake mixes decorated with icing, sprinkles, and plastic Pocahontas figurines from my parents' Baskin-Robbins.

My husband, Ham, and I made our own wedding cake. It was s'mores flavored and comprised five 8-inch-tall cakes. I really liked the idea of it looking classy on the outside but being trashy on the inside, which is kinda how I feel about myself. Each cake had six alternating layers of devil's food and yellow cake, stacked with graham cracker buttercream, milk chocolate ganache, and marshmallow creme. All homemade, of course. We decorated it with dark chocolate branches with pink meringues fashioned to look like cherry blossoms. It was all connected with a trail of flexible ganache, a technique Ham picked up at one of the fine-dining restaurants he had just trained at. No matter who you are and how many years of training you have, I do not recommend making your own wedding cake. I was adding the finishing touches while being chased around by the hair and makeup team. Then a tropical storm hit, and the cake was damaged on the way to the venue. Ham had to redecorate the whole thing with nothing but an offset spatula. It ended up a little trashy inside *and* out.

I've been daydreaming about cake for as long as I can remember. Even though I may get to bake a tiered and towering marvel only a few times a year, I still like to spend my free time letting my mind wander and fantasize about the layers, the filling, and the frosting. I don't even like to *eat* cake. For my birthday every year, I bake myself a blueberry pie (and that's the whole party). But I love the entire process: the planning, the baking, the assembling, the decorating, and finally, the drama that comes with serving a multilevel masterpiece. What better way to show someone you care than by presenting them with something that clearly took hours to make? The idea of a massive mountain of cake being shared by many is a literal symbol of food bringing people together. I believe you can heal the world with a big-ass cake.

Here, I'm giving you base recipes for yellow cake, Swiss meringue buttercream, and homemade sprinkles, along with everything you need to know to customize the flavors and make them your own. That, in combination with various filling recipes from throughout the book, like The Best Fudge Ever (page 450), any kind of citrus curd (see Get Loose!, page 418), crumbled halva (see Any Kinda Sesame Halva, page 470), Coconut Caramel (page 451), Vanilla Bean Pastry Cream (page 427), and more, and I hope I've armed you with everything you need to make all your cake dreams come true. Once you've got these techniques down, the only limit is your imagination. These are all very advanced recipes, so don't jump in here if you haven't worked your way through (at least some) of the pastry chapters. You will need a scale and a stand mixer, but what better way to celebrate how far you've come (or pretty much anything) than by baking a cake!

Base Yellow Cake

(Makes three 8- or 9-inch layers)
(Active: 1 hr.)
(Total: 2 hrs. plus cooling time)
(Advanced) (Vegetarian)

Ingredients:

softened butter or cooking spray for the pans

540 grams bleached cake flour

570 grams buttermilk, at room temperature

1 tablespoon pure vanilla extract

600 grams granulated sugar

225 grams unsalted butter, at room temperature

75 grams refined coconut oil, at room temperature

4½ teaspoons baking powder

2 teaspoons Diamond Crystal kosher salt

¾ teaspoon baking soda

3 large eggs (about 165 grams), at room temperature

9 large egg yolks (about 180 grams), at room temperature (see Note)

Special Equipment:

three 8 × 3-inch round metal cake pans (or 9 × 2-inch round pans)

parchment paper

fine-mesh sieve

stand mixer

→ This is a super tender and moist cake, with a fine, plush crumb inspired by the box mixes I grew up baking. Unlike a box mix, this is a difficult recipe with many steps, components, tons of creaming, and stopping to scrape, scrape, scrape! You've gotta get your ingredients *and* equipment right on this one: Do not attempt without allowing your eggs, buttermilk, butter, and coconut oil to come to room temperature. If any of those ingredients is cooler than 60°F (16°C) or warmer than 75°F (24°C), you'll end up with a greasy and broken batter that bakes into a dry and dense cake. I don't recommend warming ingredients in the microwave, which won't heat them evenly. Instead, plan ahead and let everything sit out at cool room temperature at least 2 hours before baking, and up to overnight. Precision is key, so I'm only offering measurements in grams. The cake must be made in a stand mixer; a hand mixer will never achieve the same volume or emulsify this large a batch properly. This cake is mixed using the creaming method. Read about it on page 282 and practice it by making A Very Banana-y Banana Bread (page 310) before jumping into this recipe.

I like to bake these cakes in 8-inch round cake pans that are 3 inches deep, which, once stacked, will be very tall and dramatic, but if all you've got are 9 × 2-inch rounds, that will work, too. (Don't use an 8 × 2-inch pan, though; the batter will not have enough room to rise.) Only have one cake pan? You can bake one layer at a time and keep the remaining batter covered at cool room temperature. (Keep it away from the hot oven, but don't put it in the fridge.) This will result in a slightly less fluffy cake, but will still be tender and delicious all the same. After inverting and removing the first cake, be sure to cool the pan under cold running water before adding more batter and baking the next one.

I know I'm asking for a lot here, but in return, I'm not giving you one recipe, I'm giving you a guide to make any cake you can dream up. Customize the cake batter with different extracts, herbs, zests, instant coffee, or small mix-ins like poppy seeds or sprinkles (big chunks can weigh the batter down). As long as you don't change the core components of the cake, like the flour, butter, eggs, leavening, and buttermilk, you've got room to safely flavor it however you want.

---

1. **Set up:** Position oven racks in the upper and lower thirds of the oven and heat to 350°F (177°C). Grease three 8 × 3-inch round (or 9 × 2-inch round) metal cake pans with butter or cooking spray and line the bottoms with rounds of parchment paper. (If you have only one or two cake pans, position the rack in the center of the oven and grease and line the pan/s as directed.)

2. **Prepare the wet and dry teams:** Pull out a sheet of parchment paper the size of a sheet pan. With a fine-mesh sieve, sift the cake flour onto the parchment and set aside. Combine the buttermilk and vanilla in something you can easily pour out of, like a spouted measuring cup or a 1-quart deli container.

3. **Cream until fluffy:** In a stand mixer fitted with the paddle, combine the sugar, butter, coconut oil, baking powder, salt, and baking soda. Mix on medium speed until fluffy and light, stopping twice to scrape the paddle and the bowl, 6 to 8 minutes in total. (Be careful not to undermix at this stage.) →

530

Base Yellow Cake (cont'd.)

4. **Add the eggs:** With the mixer on medium, add the whole eggs and egg yolks one at a time, waiting for them to disappear into the batter before adding the next, 10 to 15 seconds each. After adding the last egg, stop to scrape the paddle and the bowl and mix for 1 minute on medium-low speed. (Don't overmix at this stage.)

5. **Alternate adding the dry and wet:** Turn off the mixer. Pick up the ends of the parchment paper with the flour and use it to funnel one-third of the flour into the butter mixture. Mix on low until almost incorporated, about 10 seconds. With the mixer on low, slowly stream in one-third of the buttermilk and mix until incorporated, about 15 seconds. Stop to scrape the paddle and the bowl. Repeat in two more rounds with the remaining flour and buttermilk, alternating between them. Stop the mixer. Scrape the paddle and the bowl and give the batter a few final stirs by hand with a stiff silicone spatula, making sure to reach the bottom of bowl where pockets of flour usually hide.

6. Divide the batter (about 760 grams per pan) into the prepared cake pans. (If you have only one or two pans, hold the rest of the batter at cool room temperature—so, not near the oven—until ready to bake the remaining cake/s.) Tap each pan firmly against the counter a few times to burst any large bubbles. Quickly spin each pan, which will evenly distribute the batter and push it up the sides to minimize doming.

7. **Bake:** Place two pans on the lower rack and one on the top rack of the oven (if baking only one or two pans, set them side by side on the center rack). Bake until the tops are browned and the center of the cake springs back when gently pressed, 40 to 50 minutes. (I prefer not to rotate the delicate cakes, which can collapse if moved around before the crumb sets. The color on the top will be uneven, but you're not going to see it once stacked.)

8. **Unmold:** Place the cake pans on a wire rack to cool for 15 minutes. Run an offset spatula or thin butter knife along the edges to loosen, then flip the cakes out onto a plate. Peel off the parchment paper and flip once more onto a rack to cool completely, at least 1½ hours. (Once fully cooled and tightly wrapped, the cakes can be stored at room temperature for up to 3 days or in the freezer for 1 month.)

Note: It's easier to separate the eggs straight out of the fridge while they are still cold, then let the whole eggs and yolks sit out (covered) for at least 2 hours to evenly come to room temperature.

No Shame in My Imitation Vanilla Game

Pure vanilla, the kind harvested from hand-pollinated orchids with a sultry aroma and hefty price tag, is my favorite flavor. (Read more about vanilla beans on page 413.) That doesn't mean there isn't room in my heart (and pantry) for imitation vanilla. The aromatic compound leading the way in real vanilla's sexy scent is vanillin. Imitation vanilla is made from synthetic vanillin derived primarily from wood pulp left over from the paper-making process. Its aroma smacks you in the face with floral pungency, while the authentic stuff is more delicate and nuanced. I think of the two as completely different products, appreciating each for its unique bouquet. Imitation vanilla is used in boxed cake mix, pancake mix, and brownie mix. It's essential to the flavor of packaged cookies and cake. Everything from Pepperidge Farm to Betty Crocker and Duncan Hines have a hit of it. I grew up on all those classics, so imitation vanilla is an essential flavor for me. It's what makes the Lisa Frank Cookies (page 295), (Better Than Drake's) Coffee Cake (page 320), and Funfetti Cake (page 544) taste nostalgic.

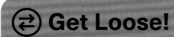 **Get Loose!**

- Add citrus zest, instant coffee or espresso powder, seeds from a vanilla bean, or finely chopped woody herbs (like rosemary, thyme, or sage) when creaming the butter and sugar.

- Add different extracts (like peppermint, almond, coffee, or coconut) to the buttermilk. Want that authentic box-mix vibe? Add clear (imitation) vanilla along with the pure stuff.

- Add small mix-ins (like sprinkles, poppy seeds, sesame seeds, or finely chopped chocolate) by hand during the final stirs of the batter.

How to
Make Swiss
Meringue
Buttercream

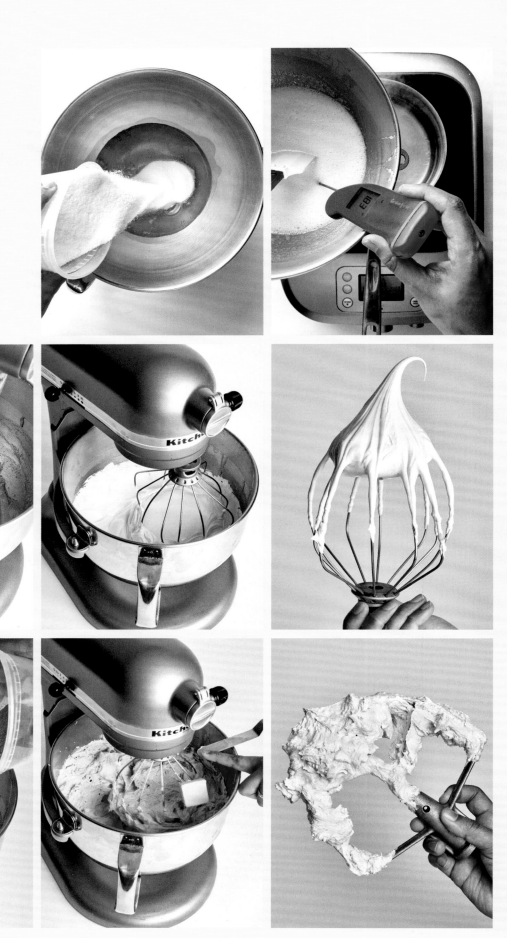

Start Here

Base Swiss Meringue Buttercream

(Makes 8 cups)

(Active: 45 mins.) | (Total: 45 mins.)

(Advanced) (Vegetarian)

(Gluten-free)

Ingredients:

7 large egg whites (about 245 grams)

360 grams (1¾ cups plus 1 tablespoon) granulated sugar

1 tablespoon pure vanilla extract

1¼ teaspoons Diamond Crystal kosher salt

¾ teaspoon cream of tartar

678 grams (6 sticks) unsalted butter, cut into 1-tablespoon pieces, at room temperature (60° to 70°F/ 16° to 21°C)

Special Equipment:

stand mixer

instant-read thermometer

→ There are lots of buttercreams out there. American buttercream is dense and sweet, easily made by whipping together powdered sugar and butter. French buttercream is extra rich and custardy, starting out with a base of whipped egg yolks. But Swiss meringue buttercream is my favorite, whipping butter into a feathery meringue, so it's light in texture, flavor, and bright white. This makes it the most versatile buttercream, ready to let other additions, like chocolate or jam, really pop without ever tasting too sickly sweet. Temperature and equipment are key to making this buttercream properly. You will need an instant-read thermometer to ensure that the egg whites have cooked enough so your buttercream is stable and ready to take on other additions. The butter needs to be room temperature, so it's flexible and primed to whip full of air bubbles. The buttercream must be made in a stand mixer, as a hand mixer will never achieve the same volume or emulsify this large a batch properly.

If you've never made a Swiss meringue before, read more about it on page 352 and try the S'mores Ice Cream Pie (page 366) before diving into this one. But once you get this base buttercream down, the possibilities for riffing are endless: Flavor it with various extracts, herbs, and zest. You can whip up to 300 grams of any high-fat or high-sugar fluid—like caramel, cool melted chocolate, or fruit preserves—into the buttercream. Add vibrant color and flavor by whipping finely ground freeze-dried fruit into the meringue base before adding the butter.

---

1. **Make the meringue:** Fill a medium saucepan with at least 1½ inches water and bring to a simmer. In the bowl of a stand mixer fitted with the whisk, whip together the egg whites and sugar until no streaks remain. Place the mixer bowl over the pan of simmering water. Stirring and scraping constantly with a stiff silicone spatula, heat the egg mixture until it registers between 175° and 185°F (79° and 85°C) on an instant-read thermometer, 10 to 12 minutes. (When you take the temperature of the mixture, remove the bowl from the pan so the eggs don't curdle when you stop stirring.)

2. Move the mixer bowl to the stand and add the vanilla, salt, and cream of tartar. Whip on medium-high speed until the meringue is glossy, holds stiff peaks, and is cool to the touch, 9 to 12 minutes. (To check, stop the mixer and remove the whisk from the mixer. Swirl the whisk in the meringue, lift it out, and flip it over. The meringue should hold straight with a tip that curls back onto itself. If it's not there yet, continue to mix in 30-second intervals, stopping to check after each.)

3. Once the meringue is at or below 90°F (32°C), on medium speed, whip in the butter 1 tablespoon at a time until all of it has been incorporated. It will look deflated, broken, and curdled initially, but once you've added all the butter, it will become fluffy and smooth.

4. Stop the mixer and scrape the bowl and whisk with a spatula. Switch to the paddle attachment and mix on medium-low speed for 1 minute; this will knock out any big air bubbles and make the buttercream smooth and creamy. →

Base Swiss Meringue Buttercream (cont'd.)

5. Use right away or store at room temperature in an airtight container for 24 hours or in the fridge for 1 month. If refrigerated, temper before using (see Note).

Note: To temper cold buttercream, melt ⅓ cup of the buttercream in the microwave or on the stovetop. Transfer the cold buttercream to a stand mixer fitted with the paddle and beat on medium speed while pouring in the melted buttercream. Mix until creamy and fluffy. (I think tempering buttercream is a real pain, so I always make it just before assembling my cake.)

⇄ Get Loose!

- **Use a different sugar:** Swap some or all of the granulated sugar for an equal weight of brown sugar (light or dark), honey, maple syrup, piloncillo, gur, or molasses. (Do not try to use any sugar substitutes, like stevia or xylitol.)

- **Add different extracts:** Add rose water or orange blossom water, or liqueurs when you add the vanilla extract.

- **Add ground freeze-dried fruit:** After the meringue has reached full volume and cooled to 90°F (32°C) or below, and before adding the butter, whip in up to 50 grams of finely ground freeze-dried fruit. Once evenly incorporated, add the butter 1 tablespoon at a time and proceed as directed.

- **Add chocolate, caramel, nut butter, or fruit preserves:** During the final 1 minute of mixing, after you've switched to the paddle attachment, add up to 300 grams of any high-fat or high-sugar fluid addition, like melted chocolate (no warmer than 82°F), fruit preserves, caramel, dulce de leche, or nut butter.

Buttercream Troubleshooting

- After you add about half the butter, the buttercream will look curdled and broken. Don't worry, it will come together after you add all the butter.

- For the buttercream to properly whip, the butter and meringue need to be around the same temperature—an instant-read thermometer is your best friend. You want the butter to be between 60° and 70°F (16° and 21°C) and the meringue below 90°F (32°C).

- If after whipping the buttercream looks soupy and greasy, chill the entire bowl in the fridge for 15 minutes, then try mixing again. If the buttercream looks dense and not fluffy, gently warm the bowl over simmering water and try mixing again.

Base Sprinkles

(Makes 4 cups)

(Active: 2 hrs.) (Total: 14 hrs.)

(Intermediate) (Vegetarian)

(Gluten-free)

Ingredients:

454 grams (3¾ cups) powdered sugar

¼ teaspoon cream of tartar

pinch of Diamond Crystal kosher salt

2 large egg whites (about 70 grams)

food coloring (whatever color/s you'd
   like)

Special Equipment:

stand mixer

pastry bags

sheet pans

parchment paper

→ Sprinkles require just royal icing and lots of time. At its most basic, royal icing is a simple mixture of powdered sugar and egg whites that sets up crisp and dry. The key is mixing the icing until it's the texture of toothpaste, so it's not too thick to squeeze, but can still hold the shapes you pipe out. You can keep it simple, piping long lines that you can break up into sprinkles of different lengths, but I prefer to pipe one at a time, so they are uniform with rounded ends. You can even get wild, by piping zigzags, tiny hearts, squiggles, and dots. Flavor them up with various extracts, cocoa powder, and powdered freeze-dried fruit or coffee.

---

1. **Make the royal icing:** In a stand mixer fitted with the whisk, combine the powdered sugar, cream of tartar, salt, and egg whites. Whip until everything is moistened and you have a thick paste. Stop the mixer and scrape the bowl and whisk as needed to ensure everything is evenly combined.

2. Add water, 1 teaspoon at a time, until the mixture is thick and smooth like toothpaste. Divide the mixture into small bowls (as many bowls as you want colors of sprinkles). Add food coloring to each bowl and stir to evenly distribute the color.

3. **Set up:** Scrape each portion of icing into a piping bag and tie the ends closed. Line three sheet pans with parchment paper. With sharp scissors, cut a small opening at the end of a piping bag. Pipe a small dap of icing under the corners of the parchment to secure it to the sheet pan.

4. **Pipe the sprinkles:** Pipe short lines (or squiggles, zigzags, or any small shape) of icing onto the lined pans until you've used up all the icing. Set aside to fully dry overnight. (If you don't want to pipe all the icing at once, tape the opening of the pastry bag closed and place the bag in an airtight container. Store in the fridge for up to 2 weeks and bring to room temperature before piping. The mixture might look broken. If so, just knead the bag to bring it back together.)

5. Once dry, use a large spatula to lift the sprinkles off the parchment and transfer them to an airtight container. (The sprinkles will keep at room temperature indefinitely.)

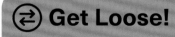 **Get Loose!**

• **Add flavorings:** Use extracts or liqueurs, rose or orange blossom water, cocoa powder, finely ground freeze-dried fruit, or matcha.

• **Make them different colors:** Use food coloring or natural dyes like beet juice and butterfly pea flower powder.

• **Change the shape:** Pipe them into different sizes, shapes, letters, or numbers.

Dream in Cake

Now that you're armed with base recipes, plan your own creative combo of cake, buttercream, and sprinkle, customizing each with the "Get Loose!" options that follow the recipe for each element.

Then level it up with some extras:

- **Add a boozy soak:** In a small saucepan, heat up ½ cup each alcohol, water, and sweetener until dissolved. Lightly brush the cooled syrup onto the layers of cake for extra flavor and moisture. For example, try bourbon and brown sugar, gin and honey, rum and coconut sugar.

- **Add crunchy mix-ins for surprise texture:** Stir mix-ins into the buttercream that is layered between the cakes. Try chocolate pearls, toasted and chopped nuts, chocolate-covered espresso beans, broken meringues (page 360), or any of the crumbles (pages 288–89).

- **Fill the layers with more than just buttercream:** Pipe a retaining wall of buttercream around the edge of each cake layer, so you can fill it with curd (see Get Loose!, page 418), Vanilla Bean Pastry Cream (page 427), fudge (see The Best Fudge Ever, page 450), Nut Praline (page 450), or Coconut Caramel (page 451).

- **Add fresh fruit:** Spread a thin layer of buttercream onto a layer of cake, pipe a retaining wall of buttercream, then fill with sliced fresh fruit before topping with another thin layer of buttercream.

Have fun and let your inner kid run wild on sugar-fueled, sprinkle-coated rage!

540

How to Build Your Multilayered Masterpiece

1. Level the cake layers: If you have a cake turntable or cake stand, place one layer on it. Otherwise, invert a cake pan onto a smooth surface and place the layer on top. Working with one layer at a time, use a sharp serrated knife to slice off the top of the cake so it's flat. (If your cake didn't dome much, you can skip this step.) To get an even slice, place one hand on top of the cake and rotate the cake while holding the knife steady and slowly moving it across the top.

2. Stack and fill the layers: Set one layer on your final serving plate or stand. Add 1 cup of buttercream and use a large offset spatula to spread it into a thick, even layer. (Or, if you want to add a squishy filling, like curd or custard, spread a thin layer of buttercream on the cake, then use a pastry bag to pipe a thick retaining wall of buttercream around the edge, and spread your filling inside.) Top with the second layer and repeat. After topping with the third layer, transfer to the fridge to chill for at least 30 minutes. This firms up the buttercream in between the layers, so it doesn't squish out while you frost the top and sides.

3. Apply a "crumb coat" (if you want): Plop 1 cup of buttercream on top of the cake. Use a large offset spatula to evenly cover the entire cake with a thin layer of buttercream. You will end up with crumbs mixing into this layer, that's okay. We're just trying to lock the crumbs in at this point to they don't end up in your final layer of buttercream. As you cover the cake, make sure you have a separate bowl to wipe the excess buttercream off your spatula, so you don't get crumbs in the remaining buttercream. Chill until just firm, about 20 minutes. If you're just going for casual swoops and swirls, you can skip this step and move ahead to heaping all the buttercream on. →

How to Build Your Multilayered Masterpiece (cont'd.)

4. Frost and decorate: Heap the remaining buttercream on top of the cake. Use a large offset spatula to spread the buttercream into an even layer on top while working the excess onto the sides. Use the spatula to cover the sides and top, using gentle pressure and evenly working it all over the cake, removing excess buttercream as you work. (It's easier to start with a lot of buttercream on the cake, then scrape it off as you smooth it.) Spread it flat and even or use the tip of the spatula to create swoops, swirls, and stripes. Decorate with sprinkles (or other garnish).

5. To store the cake: If you haven't filled the cake with a custard or curd, you can store the cake at room temperature for up to 24 hours. Otherwise, refrigerate for up to 3 days. Let it come to room temperature for at least 2 hours before serving. (To store leftovers, coat any cut sides of the cake with leftover buttercream, press plastic wrap directly onto the surface, and refrigerate for 3 days, or wrap in foil and place in an airtight container and freeze for up to 1 month.)

How to Cut
a Big Cake

1. Have a tall container with very hot water, a clean kitchen towel, and a sharp serrated knife handy.

2. Dip the knife into the hot water and wipe it clean with the towel before and after each cut

3. Score the top of the cake following these images for either 12 or 24 portions before you make your first cut. You may need to remove some garnishes.

4. Use the entire length of the blade to make long strokes.

5. I like to wear gloves, so I can support each slice with my hands as I transfer it to a plate. It's helpful to have a friend hold plates close to the cake so you're not going too far with each towering piece.

Some inspiration to get your cake juices flowing:

Funfetti Cake with Rose Sprinkles

For the cake: In addition to the pure vanilla extract, add 1 tablespoon imitation vanilla and ½ teaspoon almond extract. After the final mixing of the batter, use a stiff silicone spatula to gently fold in 95 grams (½ cup) store-bought sprinkles (homemade sprinkles fade once baked).

For the buttercream: In addition to the pure vanilla extract, add 1 tablespoon imitation vanilla.

For the sprinkles: Swap the water for rose water.

Strawberries & Cream Cake

For the cake: Add the seeds of 2 vanilla beans to the butter and sugar during creaming.

For the buttercream: Add 40 grams finely ground freeze-dried strawberries after the meringue has whipped to stiff peaks, but before adding the butter.

Between the layers: Spread a thin layer of strawberry preserves between the layers. Use a piping bag to pipe a retaining wall of buttercream around the edge, arrange thinly sliced fresh strawberries on top, then fill with Vanilla Bean Pastry Cream (page 427).

For the sprinkles: Add 25 grams finely ground freeze-dried strawberries to the powdered sugar.

Lemon Poppy Seed Cake

For the cake: Add 2 tablespoons finely grated lemon zest to the butter and sugar during creaming. After the final mixing of the batter, use a stiff silicone spatula to gently fold in 95 grams (½ cup) poppy seeds.

For the buttercream: Omit the cream of tartar and instead add 1 tablespoon each lemon juice and lemon zest.

Between the layers: Instead of covering with buttercream, use a piping bag to pipe a retaining wall of buttercream around the edge, then fill with 1 batch Lemon Curd (page 417).

For the garnish: Omit the sprinkles and decorate with lemon rounds instead.

Coconut Caramel Cake

For the cake: Swap refined coconut oil for virgin coconut oil. In addition to the pure vanilla extract add 1 tablespoon coconut extract. After baking and slicing off the top, brush each layer with a soak of dark rum and brown sugar.

For the buttercream: During the final 1 minute paddling of the buttercream, slowly pour in 1 batch of cooled Coconut Caramel (page 451), no warmer than 82°F (28°C).

For the garnish: Omit the sprinkles and decorate the top and sides generously with toasted coconut flakes.

Mocha Cake

For the cake: Add 1½ tablespoons espresso powder (or 3 tablespoons instant coffee) to the butter and sugar during creaming. Add 1 tablespoon coffee extract to the buttermilk in addition to the pure vanilla extract.

For the buttercream: Swap the granulated sugar for light brown sugar. Add 1½ tablespoons espresso powder (or 3 tablespoons instant coffee) to the sugar and egg whites during the initial heating. During the final 1 minute paddling of the buttercream, add 300 grams melted and cooled milk chocolate (no warmer than 82°F/28°C).

Between the layers: Sprinkle chocolate-covered espresso beans on top of the buttercream.

For the sprinkles: Add 40 grams sifted cocoa to the powdered sugar. Instead of water, add chocolate liqueur or coffee liqueur.

Blueberry Pancake Cake

For the cake: Add 1 tablespoon butter extract to the buttermilk in addition to the pure vanilla extract.

For the buttercream: Swap the granulated sugar for an equal *weight* of maple syrup or pancake syrup.

Between the layers: Spread a thin layer of blueberry preserves. Arrange fresh blueberries on top, then spread on a thick layer of buttercream.

For the garnish: Omit the sprinkles and decorate with fresh blueberries instead.

Mint Chocolate Chip Cake

For the cake: Add green food coloring to the butter and sugar during creaming. Add 1 tablespoon mint extract to the buttermilk in addition to the pure vanilla extract. After the final mixing of the batter, use a stiff silicone spatula to gently fold in 100 grams (¾ cup) finely chopped dark chocolate.

For the buttercream: Swap the granulated sugar for dark brown sugar. During the final 1 minute paddling of the buttercream, add 300 grams melted and cooled dark chocolate (no warmer than 82°F/28°C).

For the sprinkles: Add 2 teaspoons mint extract and dye the mixture with green food coloring.

Peanut Butter & Chocolate Cake

For the cake: Add the seeds of 2 vanilla beans to the butter and sugar during creaming.

For the buttercream: During the final 1 minute paddling of the buttercream, add 150 grams melted and cooled dark chocolate (no warmer than 82°F/28°C) and 150 grams well-stirred creamy natural peanut butter.

Between the layers: Make a batch of Classic Peanut Brittle (page 449) and crush it up. Sprinkle half between the cake layers (reserve the rest for garnish). Top with a thick layer of the peanut butter chocolate buttercream.

For the garnish: Omit the sprinkles and decorate with the remaining crushed peanut brittle and shaved chocolate instead.

Putting It All Together

Many of the recipes in this book make a great meal all on their own, while some are best enjoyed teamed up on a table together. Here's a list of menus to try out with game plans to help make the prep efficient and easy.

Comfort food you can cry into

(Serves 1 to 3 (depending on how sad you are))
(Easy)

1. Make the pie and chill in the fridge.

2. Make the salad and chill until ready to eat.

3. Make the pomodoro and eat right away alongside the salad.

4. Whip cream and top pie. Depending on how quickly you made and ate dinner, the pie might not be set yet. That's okay; you're sad so you are allowed to eat it out of the pie pan.

For steamy summer nights

Serves 3 or 4

Intermediate

Watermelon Chaat with Lime, Ginger & Cashew Clumps	37
Chilled Green Tahini Soba	145
Crispy-Skinned Salmon with Radishes & Nuoc Cham	245
Honey Vanilla Semifreddo	380

The day before:

1. Make the semifreddo and freeze.

2. For the soba, make the green tahini sauce, cook and cool the soba noodles, and make the red onion salad.

3. Make the cashew clumps for the watermelon chaat.

The day of:

4. Toss the soba with the tahini sauce and top with onions.

5. Broil the salmon and radishes.

6. While the salmon cooks, make the nuoc cham and watermelon chaat.

7. Serve the salmon, chaat, and soba right away. Follow it up with a scoop of semifreddo, and hopefully you've cooled off.

To eat on the couch while watching a movie

Serves 6

Intermediate

House Salad	18
Classic Red Sauce Pizza	497
Almond Toffee Popcorn	464

Two days before:

1. Make the toffee popcorn; try not to eat it all.

The day before:

2. Make the focaccia dough up through the overnight bulk ferment.

3. Prep the pizza toppings.

4. Wash and dry the lettuce for the salad.

The day of:

5. Form and proof, and prebake the focaccia following the directions for Classic Red Sauce Pizza (page 497).

Just before serving:

6. Top and bake the pizza.

7. While the pizza bakes, dress and plate the salads.

8. Cut the pizza into squares and serve alongside the salad and popcorn.

For cozy winter nights

Serves 6 (with leftovers)

Intermediate

Braised Short Ribs with
Anchovy & So Much Garlic   178

Steamed vegetables, such as baby
potatoes, carrots, & Swiss chard

Vanilla Pavlova with Cocoa
& Citrus   362

Three days before:

1. Dry-brine the short ribs.

Two days before:

2. Make the cocoa whipped cream for the
pavlova and refrigerate.

The day before:

3. Cook the short ribs, cool in the braising
liquid, and refrigerate.

The day of:

4. Bake the pavlova.

5. Cut the citrus for the pavlova and refrigerate
until ready to eat.

6. Wash, strip, and tear Swiss chard leaves. Cut
carrots into 2-inch pieces. Scrub potatoes.

7. Set up a steamer and start steaming the
potatoes and carrots.

8. Reheat the short ribs (I prefer not to skim
off the fat because I like to dunk the steamed
veggies into the beef fat, but you do you).

9. When the potatoes and carrots are tender,
pile in the Swiss chard and steam until the
greens just wilt.

10. Serve the short ribs and the fatty sauce
with the steamed veggies.

11. Just before dessert time, pile the cocoa
whipped cream and citrus fruit onto the pavlova
and serve.

Cocktail party for friends you want to impress

Serves 8 to 12

Intermediate

**Oysters and shrimp are expensive, so fill up
your guests on the other stuff, then serve the
big-money items last.**

Nutty & Salty Gunpowder Spice
for Dunking, with crudités   34

Snappy Shrimp with Punch-You-
in-the-Face Cocktail Sauce   218

Broiler-Popped Oysters with
Tomato Butter   241

Deviled Egg Dip   74

Cheese Twists   334

552

Assorted olives, pickles & cured meats

Up to one month in advance:

1. Make the gunpowder spice.

2. Make the rough puff pastry, form into cheese twists, and store in the freezer.

Two days before:

3. Make the cocktail sauce.

4. Mix a double batch of tomato butter (you might not need it all).

5. Boil and peel eggs for the deviled egg dip.

6. Clean your house and pick out your party outfit.

The day before:

7. Buy shrimp and oysters. Get at least 3 shrimp and 2 oysters per person (plus 4 extra in case there are duds).

8. Clean, poach, and chill the shrimp.

9. Scrub the oysters and store in the fridge on ice.

10. Wash and cut the crudités.

11. Make the deviled egg dip (but don't garnish).

12. Pick out and set up serviceware: platters, plates, glasses, etc.

The morning of:

13. Bake the cheese twists.

14. Remove the cured meats from the fridge so they can come to room temperature.

15. Pull the tomato butter from the fridge so it's easy to spread onto the oysters.

16. Prep big-batch cocktails, like dirty martinis, margaritas, cosmos, and spiked punch (you can find great recipes online—or task your guests to bring them).

One hour before guests arrive:

17. Plate the cheese twists.

18. Plate the olives, pickles, and cured meats (make sure to set out a small dish for the pits).

19. Plate the crudités with the gunpowder spice.

20. Plate the cocktail sauce and shrimp (but keep in the fridge for later).

21. Prep the salt bed for the broiled oysters.

As guests arrive:

22. Let them get started on cocktails, cheese twists, olives, pickles, cured meats, and crudités.

23. After some snacking, garnish and serve the deviled egg dip with lots of crackers.

Once the party gets going:

24. Serve the shrimp cocktail.

25. Preheat the broiler for the oysters.

26. Get a friend to help you broil the oysters and serve (after all that good stuff, no one's gonna see them coming, so even if there are only 2 per person, your guests will be thrilled, I promise!).

Amu's ambitious Sunday-morning spread

Serves 4 to 6

Advanced

2 Frizzled Desi Omelets with Onion & Chilies	70
Flaky Brown Butter Lachha Paratha	507
Citrus Raitha	17
Radishes & cucumbers	
Fruit Custard	432

Two days before:

1. Mix the paratha dough; rest, roll out, and form into coils (up to step 10).

The day before:

2. Roll out and parcook the parathas (step 11).

3. Mix together the citrus raitha, but don't top with pomegranate seeds (steps 1 to 2).

4. Make the custard and refrigerate.

Sunday morning:

5. Cut the fruit and stir into the custard, place in a serving dish, and refrigerate until ready to serve.

6. Cut radishes in half, slice Persian (mini) cucumbers into thick coins, and arrange on a plate.

7. Place the raitha in a serving dish and garnish with the pomegranate seeds.

8. Make 2 frizzled desi omelets, place on a platter, cut into wedges, and hold at room temperature while you cook the parathas (step 12).

9. Get your family to set the table and be ready to receive hot and flaky parathas.

10. Cook the parathas until browned and crisp; serve right away. (We never wait for everyone to get a paratha; instead each person digs in as soon as they get theirs. Parathas are best eaten hot, so just go for it. Oh, and don't forget to dip some paratha into custard for dessert.)

554

Ham's favorite meal (yes, it's a double-starch dinner)

Serves 6

Advanced

Two days before:

1. Make the mahalabia.

2. Make the tahini sauce for the kofta.

The day before:

3. Rinse and parboil the rice for the tahdig and refrigerate (steps 1 to 3).

4. Make the cucumber salad and refrigerate.

5. Make the grated tomato and sumac onions for the kofta and refrigerate.

6. Mix the kofta and refrigerate.

The day of:

7. Remove the rice, tahini sauce, grated tomatoes, and sumac onions from the fridge to come to room temperature.

8. Mix the pita dough and bulk ferment (steps 1 to 3).

9. Mix the tahdig layer and steam the rice. The rice can hold warm on super-low heat, covered, until ready to serve.

10. Portion the pita dough, roll out, and proof until puffy (steps 4 to 5).

11. Meanwhile, preheat the oven and form the kofta.

12. Cook the pitas (steps 6 to 7) and wrap in a towel to keep warm.

13. Switch the oven to broil and cook the kofta.

14. Serve hot pitas, kofta, and rice with cucumber salad, tahini sauce, grated tomatoes, and sumac onions.

15. Serve the mahalabia for dessert.

Thank You

To Ham!
My partner in everything. Thanks for letting me talk at you for hours, for reading every word, for making sure I ate something other than popcorn, for taking care of the dogs, for reminding me to put the phone down, for never judging me when I went unshowered, and for always making sure the fridge was stocked with cucumbers, cheese, and radishes (even though I only ever ate the cheese).

To everyone who helped me make this book:
Photos by Laura Murray—thanks for switching from hard light to soft light and back to hard light over and over again. **Design by Chris Cristiano**—thanks for stepping in at the last second and making this book so freakin' cool. **Illustrations by Aly Miller**—thanks for somehow making protein coagulation and gluten formation cute. **Cross Testing by Ali Slagle**—thanks for calling me out when I was using waaaay too many bowls. **Culinary Assistance by Helena Picone**— thanks for forever changing the way I hear the word "opportunity." **Hair & Makeup by Amanda Wilson**—thanks for having my back on every. single. set. **Wardrobe by Nasrin Jean-Baptisite**— thanks for all the fun sleeves. **Editing by Tom Pold** (and the entire team at Knopf)—I probably shouldn't tell you this, but as soon as I met the Knopf team on Zoom over at Kitty's apartment, I was sold. I met with other publishers because, you know, business, negotiations, *Shark Tank.* But I knew instantly that no other team understood what I wanted this book to be. Thanks for all your guidance, endless patience, knowing when to leave me alone, and then also knowing when I needed lots of support. You made this whole thing a lot less terrifying.

To Core! Team! Sohla!
Kitty, Celena, Ashley, Addie, Madeline, Joe, Grace, Kai. You are a terrifying group. I'm glad you're on my side. Thanks for making it easy for me to focus on the fun stuff because I know you've got me covered.

To all the smart, passionate, hardworking people I'm privileged enough to work with on the reg: The team at NYT Cooking—Emily, Vaughn, Scott, Gabriella, Gina, Shirley. The team at the Big Brunch—Dan, Will, Cassie, Sarina, Andrew. The team at History—Jon, Pete, Ken, Giff. The food media family—Stella, Rick, Priya, Khushbu, Carla, Ryan, Hilary, Aliza, Sho, Sal, Elazar. You all inspire me, push me, and taught me that my voice matters.

To Amu—thanks for being my first chef. You taught me how to cook, eat, and find joy in every meal. To Abu & Apu—thanks for hangin' in there even when things got rough; I know I didn't always make it easy for you. To Papa El-Waylly, Tamara, Zhaleh—thanks for welcoming me into your family like I'd always been a part of it.

To the friends who've been there from the beginning and will be around till the end. The family and childhood friends I only ever see on the holidays but still come to eat at the places I've worked, cheer me on from the sidelines, help my parents with their email when I can't go home, and supported me when everyone told me to quit—you know who you are, and I know I never tell you, but I fucking appreciate it all.

And to all the Internet friends—the viewers, followers, journalists, and editors. My life would not be possible without all of you out there making the recipes, watching the videos, liking my posts, and covering my work.

I really hope you don't think this book sucks.

References

Books

Amendola, Joseph, and Nicole Rees. *The Baker's Manual: 150 Master Formulas for Baking.* 5th ed. Hoboken, NJ: John Wiley & Sons, Inc., 2003.

Amendola, Joseph, and Nicole Rees. *Understanding Baking: The Art and Science of Baking .* 3rd ed. Hoboken, NJ: John Wiley & Sons, Inc., 2003.

America's Test Kitchen. *The How Can It Be Gluten Free Cookbook.* Boston: America's Test Kitchen, 2014.

Berens, Abra. *Grist: A Practical Guide to Cooking Grains, Beans, Seeds, and Legumes.* San Francisco: Chronicle Books, 2021.

Block, Eric. *Garlic and Other Alliums: The Lore and the Science.* Cambridge, UK: Royal Society of Chemistry Publishing, 2010.

Blumenthal, Heston. *Historic Heston.* London: Bloomsbury, 2013.

Culinary Institute of America. *Mastering the Art and Craft: Baking and Pastry.* 2nd ed. Hoboken, NJ: John Wiley & Sons, Inc., 2009.

Culinary Institute of America. *The Professional Chef.* 8th ed. Hoboken, NJ: John Wiley & Sons, Inc., 2006.

Davidson, Alan. *The Oxford Companion to Food.* 3rd ed. Oxford: Oxford University Press, 2014.

Headley, Brooks. *Fancy Desserts.* New York: W. W. Norton & Company, 2014.

Kamozawa, Aki, and H. Alexander Talbot. *Ideas in Food: Great Recipes and Why They Work.* New York: Clarkson Potter, 2010.

Khosrova, Elaine. *Butter: A Rich History.* Chapel Hill, NC: Algonquin Books of Chapel Hill, 2016.

Kurlansky, Mark. *Salt: A World History.* New York: Penguin Books, 2002.

McGee, Harold. *On Food and Cooking: The Science and Lore of the Kitchen.* 2nd ed. New York: Scribner, 2004.

Migoya, Francisco. *The Modern Café.* Hoboken, NJ: John Wiley & Sons, Inc., 2010.

Myhrvold, Nathan, and Francisco Migoya. *Modernist Bread.* Bellevue, WA: The Cooking Lab, 2017.

Myhrvold, Nathan, Chris Young, Maxime Bilet, Ryan Matthew Smith. *Modernist Cuisine: The Art and Science of Cooking*. Bellevue, WA: The Cooking Lab, 2011.

Nosrat, Samin. *Salt Fat Acid Heat: Mastering the Elements of Good Cooking*. New York: Simon & Schuster, 2017.

Page, Karen, and Andrew Dornenburg. *The Flavor Bible: The Essential Guide to Culinary Creativity, Based on the Wisdom of America's Most Imaginative Chefs*. New York: Little, Brown and Company, 2008.

Parks, Stella. *BraveTart: Iconic American Desserts*. New York: W. W. Norton & Company, 2017.

Prueitt, Elisabeth, and Chad Robertson. *Tartine: A Classic Revisited*. San Francisco: Chronicle Books, 2019.

Robertson, Chad. *Bread Book: Ideas and Innovations from the Future of Grain, Flour, and Fermentation*. Berkeley, CA: Lorena Jones Books, 2021.

Sharma, Nik. *The Flavor Equation: The Science of Great Cooking Explained*. San Francisco: Chronicle Books, 2020.

Smith, Andrew F. *The Oxford Companion to American Food and Drink*. Oxford: Oxford University Press, 2007.

This, Hervé. *Molecular Gastronomy: Exploring the Science of Flavor*. Translated by Malcolm DeBevoise. New York: Columbia University Press, 2006.

Internet Resources

- americastestkitchen.com
- cooking.nytimes.com
- kingarthurbaking.com
- seriouseats.com

Index

(Page references in *italics* refer to illustrations.)

564

Index

575

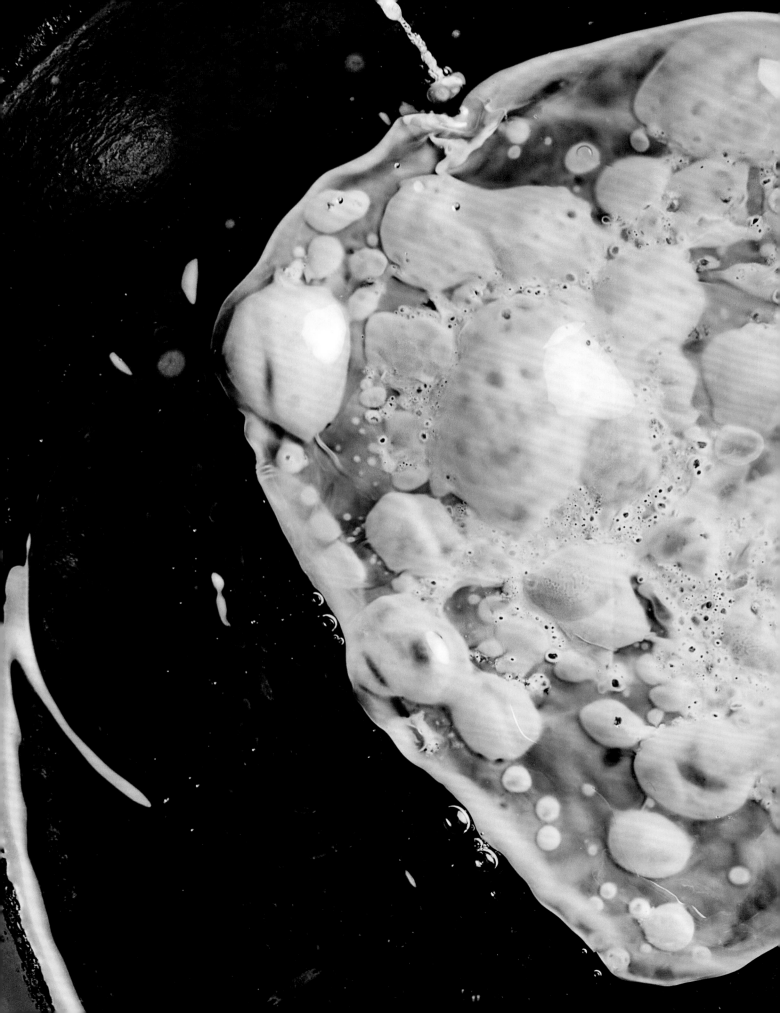

THIS IS A BORZOI BOOK PUBLISHED BY ALFRED A. KNOPF

www.aaknopf.com

Knopf, Borzoi Books, and the colophon are registered
trademarks of Penguin Random House LLC.

Library of Congress Cataloging-in-Publication Data
Names: El-Waylly, Sohla, author. | Murray, Laura, photographer.
Title: Start here : instructions for becoming a better cook /
Sohla El-Waylly ; photographs by Laura Murray.
Description: First edition. | New York: Alfred A. Knopf, 2023. |
Includes index.
Identifiers: LCCN 2022054789 (print) |
LCCN 2022054790 (ebook) | ISBN 9780593320464 (hardcover) |
ISBN 9780593320471 (ebook)
Subjects: LCSH: Cooking. | Baking. | Cooking—Technique. |
LCGFT: Cookbooks.
Classification: LCC TX714 .E426 2023 (print) |
LCC TX714 (ebook) | DDC 641.3—dc23/eng/20221122
LC record available at https://lccn.loc.gov/2022054789
LC ebook record available at https://lccn.loc.gov/2022054790

Some of the recipes in this book may include raw eggs, meat,
or fish. When these foods are consumed raw, there is always
the risk that bacteria, which is killed by proper cooking, may
be present. For this reason, when serving these foods raw,
always buy certified salmonella-free eggs and the freshest
meat and fish available from a reliable grocer, storing them in
the refrigerator until they are served. Because of the health
risks associated with the consumption of bacteria that can be
present in raw eggs, meat, and fish, these foods should not
be consumed by infants, small children, pregnant women, the
elderly, or any persons who may be immunocompromised. The
author and publisher expressly disclaim responsibility for any
adverse effects that may result from the use or application of
the recipes and information contained in this book.

Cover photographs by Laura Murray
Cover design by Ariel Harari
Manufactured in China
First Edition